Controlling Costs in Foodservice

Maureen Leugers, MBA, RD
Director of Segment Marketing, Gordon Food Service
Grand Rapids, Michigan

Publisher
The Goodheart-Willcox Company, Inc.
Tinley Park, Illinois
www.g-w.com

Library of Congress Catalog Card Number 2012041680

ISBN 978-1-61960-166-6

1 2 3 4 5 6 7 8 9 10 — 14 — 19 18 17 16 15 14 13

The Goodheart-Willcox Company, Inc. Brand Disclaimer: Brand names, company names, and illustrations for products and services included in this text are provided for educational purposes only and do not represent or imply endorsement or recommendation by the author or the publisher.

The Goodheart-Willcox Company, Inc. Safety Notice: The reader is expressly advised to carefully read, understand, and apply all safety precautions and warnings described in this book or that might also be indicated in undertaking the activities and exercises described herein to minimize risk of personal injury or injury to others. Common sense and good judgment should also be exercised and applied to help avoid all potential hazards. The reader should always refer to the appropriate manufacturer's technical information, directions, and recommendations; then proceed with care to follow specific equipment operating instructions. The reader should understand these notices and cautions are not exhaustive.

The publisher makes no warranty or representation whatsoever, either expressed or implied, including but not limited to equipment, procedures, and applications described or referred to herein, their quality, performance, merchantability, or fitness for a particular purpose. The publisher assumes no responsibility for any changes, errors, or omissions in this book. The publisher specifically disclaims any liability whatsoever, including any direct, indirect, incidental, consequential, special, or exemplary damages resulting, in whole or in part, from the reader's use or reliance upon the information, instructions, procedures, warnings, cautions, applications, or other matter contained in this book. The publisher assumes no responsibility for the activities of the reader.

The Goodheart-Willcox Company, Inc. Internet Disclaimer: The Internet listings provided in this text link to additional resource information. Every attempt has been made to ensure these sites offer accurate, informative, safe, and appropriate information. However, Goodheart-Willcox Publisher has no control over these websites. The publisher makes no representation whatsoever, either expressed or implied, regarding the content of these websites. Because many websites contain links to other sites (some of which may be inappropriate), the publisher urges teachers to review all websites before students use them. Note that Internet sites may be temporarily or permanently inaccessible by the time readers attempt to use them.

Library of Congress Cataloging-in-Publication Data

Leugers, Maureen.
    Controlling costs in foodservice / Maureen Leugers, MBA, RD, director of segment marketing, Gordon Food Service Grand Rapids, Michigan.
    pages cm

    Includes bibliographical references and index.
    ISBN 978-1-61960-166-6
    1. Food service--Cost control. I. Title. II. Title: Controlling costs in food service.

TX911.3.C65L48 2014
647.95068--dc23   2012041680

Cover Image: Tatuasha, Brian Goodman, erwinova, J van der Wolf/Shutterstock.com

Reviewers

The author and Goodheart-Willcox Publisher would like to thank the following professionals who provided valuable input to this edition of *Controlling Costs in Foodservice*.

Beth Augustyn, MA
Hospitality Management Instructor
Institute for the Culinary Arts
Metropolitan Community College
Omaha, Nebraska

Frank Benowitz, CHE
Professor
Hotel, Restaurant and Institution
 Management & Culinary Programs
Mercer County Community College
West Windsor, New Jersey

Molly J. Dahm, PhD
Program Director
Hospitality Administration/
 Culinary Arts
Lamar University
Beaumont, Texas

Linsley T. DeVeau, EdD, CHA
Professor
Hospitality Administration
Lynn University
Boca Raton, Florida

Joyce Hyunjoo Hwang, PhD
Assistant Professor
School of Travel Industry Management
University of Hawai'i at Mānoa
Honolulu, Hawaii

Richard Ghiselli, PhD
Department Head
School of Hospitality & Tourism
 Management
Purdue University
West Lafayette, Indiana

Ken Jarvis, CCE, CEC, CHE
Professor
Hotel Restaurant Management
Anne Arundel Community College
Arnold, Maryland

Andrew Lawrence, MS, CFE
Assistant Professor
Hospitality Management
Monroe Community College
Rochester, New York

Martha Rardin, MSM, RD, CD
Director
Nutrition and Dietetics
Hendricks Regional Health
Danville, Indiana

Jeffrey A. Sheldon, CCE
Hospitality Programs Chair
Midwest Culinary Institute
Cincinnati State Technical and
 Community College
Cincinnati, Ohio

Belinda de Villa-Lopez, MA, CHE
Lecturer
Collins College of Hospitality
 Management
California State Polytechnic University
Pomona, California

Tianshu Zheng, PhD
Assistant Professor
Department of Apparel, Events, and
 Hospitality Management
Iowa State University
Ames, Iowa

Introduction

To generate a profit, all types of businesses and organizations—large and small, commercial and noncommercial—must have strong cost-control practices. Cost control is the process an operation uses to ensure that its forecasted sales and expenses conform to its plans, goals, and objectives. Controlling costs is a key role of managers and involves keeping firm control of an operation's costs, while continuing to meet customer expectations.

However, many foodservice managers do not have a strong grasp of the many facets of cost control. Some foodservice businesses focus on the culinary or the customer service aspects of a business without much consideration of cost. By not managing their operations in the most cost-effective and efficient way possible, they risk failure.

Controlling Costs in Foodservice provides you and other aspiring foodservice managers with this knowledge in an easy-to-understand, practical format. This comprehensive text covers the principles of control in all major areas of foodservice management—from menu planning and product purchasing to production and waste management. Since labor is one of the largest expenses of any foodservice operation, you are given tools to measure and control labor-related costs. Revenue control and facilities management are covered in chapters of their own. Colorful charts and tables depict budgets, financial reports, and other management instruments that you need to understand and be able to create. The text ends with a chapter that discusses the growing importance and use of technology by foodservice operations to control costs.

In addition, each chapter contains several feature boxes that cover current and emerging trends, technological innovations, and valuable tools and resources. Features address sustainability issues, such as recycling and waste control, energy conservation practices, and the purchase of energy saving equipment. These topics are of growing importance and relevance in the foodservice industry.

Questions and activities at the end of each chapter give you the opportunity to test your comprehension of the chapter content and enhance and extend your learning. You will step into a manager's shoes and solve the types of problems that frequently occur in foodservice operations. You will create and build a foodservice operation of your own as a course project. As you progress through the course, you will devise a menu for the operation, select foodservice equipment, price menu items, schedule labor, and so forth.

After completing this course of study, you will be well on your way to embarking on a successful and fulfilling career in foodservice management. If you are already a manager, the practical applications and real-world examples will assist you in increasing your effectiveness and the profitability of your operation.

Maureen Leugers

About the Author

Maureen Leugers is currently the Director of Segment Marketing with Gordon Food Service (GFS). She sets strategic direction for the company and oversees the development of services that effectively support the long-term profitability of GFS customers—restaurants, and foodservice operations in healthcare and educational institutions.

Leugers is a registered dietitian and worked in healthcare settings for almost 20 years as a director of food and nutrition services. She has operational expertise and experience in human resource management, budgeting, and strategic planning.

She received an MBA from the University of Saint Francis in Indiana, where she also taught a course in operations management in the business department. She was also an adjunct professor in the dietetic internship program at Ball State University's Department of Consumer and Family Sciences. She oversaw a course curriculum for interns that included foodservice operations management, budgeting, and staffing.

Leugers is a sought-after national speaker for healthcare foodservice organizations on all aspects of operations management, but cost control is the most requested topic. She is a member of several professional groups: Association for Healthcare Foodservice (AHF), Association of Nutrition & Foodservice Professionals (ANFP), Dietitians in Business and Communications, Academy of Nutrition and Dietetics, Dietetics in Health Care Communities, and the Indiana Dietetic Association.

The Textbook

A lot of planning went into creating *Controlling Costs in Foodservice*. Components were added to each chapter that reinforce learning and help you develop the skills you need to manage a foodservice operation. To help you get started, each chapter begins with a list of objectives that summarize the chapter's learning goals.

Foodservice Mathematics

Foodservice managers must be able to use mathematics to solve problems related to cost control. *Controlling Costs in Foodservice* contains many of the formulas that are commonly used in foodservice operations. For easy reference, each formula is highlighted in color and centered in the column in which it appears. The text also includes case studies, or realistic examples, that illustrate how the formulas are used in working situations. As presented, the calculations are easy to follow.

For the student who needs a math refresher, the first chapter presents a brief overview of basic math concepts, such as the conversion of decimal numbers into percentages. Following the math review is a section that gives examples of how math is used in foodservice operations to solve everyday problems. These math applications are discussed in more detail in the chapters that follow.

Many of the activities at the end of each chapter must be solved using math skills and the math formulas given in each chapter.

Feature Boxes

Each chapter contains several informative boxed features covering informational resources and current issues and trends in the foodservice industry. There are four types of feature boxes:

Trends describes new or emerging trends that currently impact or are expected to impact cost control in the foodservice industry.

Waste Not focuses on sustainability and how foodservice operations that conserve resources can reduce costs and minimize negative environmental impacts.

Technology describes many new technologies that foodservice operations can use to control costs.

Bookmark This highlights helpful organizations, publications, and resources that are available online.

End-of-Chapter Elements

The end-of-chapter section includes elements that reinforce chapter content and extend learning and comprehension. These include summaries, questions, and activities.

- *Key Terms* lists vocabulary terms that are used and defined in the chapter.
- *Recap* provides a useful summary of the key ideas presented in the chapter.
- *Review Questions* includes questions that test reading comprehension and reinforce learning.
- *Applying Your Knowledge* includes questions and application exercises that require the use of higher-level critical-thinking skills. Information is presented in charts and spreadsheets in many of these activities. Spreadsheets can be completed by either filling in the charts on paper, or by going to the companion website and using spreadsheet software.
- *Course Project* is an application activity that is one component of a project spanning the entire course. It builds as you progress through the text.

Back of the Book

Two appendices at the back of the text provide easy access to frequently referenced information. The first appendix lists all of the formulas used in the text. The other appendix contains tables of commonly used foodservice conversions.

Following the appendices is an alphabetized glossary that lists all of the key terms presented in the text with their definitions. A bibliography, organized by chapter, lists many of the resources the author used during the research and writing of this textbook. The last pages are filled by an alphabetized index of the textbook content.

Textbook Supplements

The textbook is just one part of a carefully designed package of products. Used together, these products help students and instructors achieve maximum benefit from the course. A *Study Guide* and a *Companion Website* reinforce the textbook content and allow students to practice and build their skills. Instructors are provided with an Instructor's Resource CD, the Instructor's Presentations for PowerPoint, and an ExamView® Assessment Suite for creating and managing tests for each chapter. Descriptions of these products follow.

Study Guide

Students will find helpful tools in the *Study Guide*. The guide, which follows the organization of the textbook, can be used to review the text content and test comprehension. Each chapter contains a chapter notes section that outlines key chapter content, including mathematical formulas. A chapter review section contains questions that test comprehension of key terms and concepts. Answers to *Study Guide* questions and activities are also given.

Companion Website

The website is located at www.g-wlearning.com/culinaryarts/ and contains copies of the spreadsheet application activities found in the Applying Your Knowledge section at the end of most chapters. Activities can be completed on the website using spreadsheet software. Students can save their spreadsheet files in a location designated by the instructor, such as on the school's computer network or on students' own flash drives. A standard naming convention should be created for documents. The textbook recommends that files be named as follows: FirstnameLastname_Activity#-##.xlsx (i.e., JohnSmith_Activity4-13.xlsx). The answers to the website problems are provided in the instructor's resource materials.

In addition to the spreadsheet activities, the website includes e-flash cards and matching activities that students can use to quiz themselves on vocabulary terms.

Instructor's Resource CD

The Instructor's Resource CD contains information useful to instructors as they teach the course. It includes answer keys to the end-of-chapter review questions and activities that appear in the textbook. Detailed chapter outlines are available on the CD, as well as blank copies of many of the forms and financial reports referenced in the textbook, such as the operations budget form and the cashier's report.

Instructor's Presentations for PowerPoint and ExamView *Assessment Suite*

Instructors can use the presentation slides to supplement lecture materials and ExamView software to create tests that assess student comprehension.

Table of Contents

Chapter 1
Principles of Control in a Foodservice Operation 1
  Functions of Management 1
    Planning. 2
    Organizing 2
    Leading 2
    Controlling 2
  Cost Control 2
    Calculations as a Cost-Control Function 3
  Basic Math Review. 4
    Fractions 4
    Percentages 4
    Decimals 5
    Ratios 5
  Practical Foodservice Applications 5
    Using Ratios 6
    Determining Selling Price 6
    Comparing Product Prices 6
    Determining Food or Labor Cost per Meal Served. 8
    Variance Calculations 9
    Quality Measures 10

Chapter 2
Menu Planning as a Control Tool 14
  How the Menu Impacts the Operation. 15
    Equipment. 15
    Food 15
    Storage 15
    Kitchen Layout 15
    Labor 15
    Atmosphere. 16
    Brand or Message. 16
  Factors to Consider in Selecting Menu Items. 16
    Taste and Flavor Combinations 16
    Appearance, Color, and Texture 16
    Ethnic Style 16
    Variety of Offerings 17
    Nutritional Content 17
    Price 17
  Menu Formats. 18
    Standard Menu 18
    Cycle Menu 18
    Market Menu 19
    Combination Menu 19

Menu Sections. 19
Menu Presentation. 21
Sources of Menu Ideas. 21
Pricing the Menu 22
Menu-Pricing Methods 22
   Food Cost Percentage Method 22
   Contribution Margin Method. 24
   Prime Cost Method 24
   Texas Restaurant Association (TRA) Markup Method. 26
   Summary of Menu Pricing Methods. 27
Marketing Techniques in Menu Pricing 28
   Odd Pricing. 28
   Even Pricing 28
   Promotional Pricing. 28
   2.5-Times Price Spread 29
   Reference Pricing 29
Menu Descriptions. 29
   Truth-in-Menu Laws 30
Menu Layout Affects Sales 31
   By List 31
   By Page 31
   By Number of Pages 32
   By Page Location 32
Menu Engineering 32
   Stars 32
   Plow Horses 33
   Puzzles. 33
   Dogs 33
   Ranking Menu Items 33

Chapter 3
**Cost Control in Purchasing, Receiving, Storage, and
Inventory Management**. 38
Purchasing. 38
   Purchasing Methods 39
   Noncommercial Foodservice Purchasing. 43
   Purchasing Specifications 43
   Considering the Yield Percentage When Purchasing 45
   Purchasing Quantities 46
   Value Analysis 48
   Distributor Selection 50
   Requisitions and Purchase Orders 51

Receiving 52
  Qualified Staff 52
  Necessary Equipment 52
  Receiving Policies and Procedures 52
Storage 55
  Location 55
  Size 55
  Storage Guidelines 56
Inventory Control 58
  Physical Inventory 58
  Perpetual Inventory 59
  Calculating Cost of Food Sold 59
  Inventory Turnover 60

Chapter 4

Cost Control from Production to Waste Management 64

Production 65
  Production Systems 65
  Food Production Areas 67
  Production Controls 68
Portion Control 72
  Portion Size Determination 73
  Implementing Portion Control 74
Presentation and Service 75
  Presentation 75
  Service 75
Waste Management 77
  Product Maximization 77
  Leftover Management 79
Controlling Costs by Practicing Food Safety and Sanitation 79
Controlling Other Costs 80
  Supplies 80
  Professional Services, Fees, and Other Costs 82

Chapter 5

Labor Cost Control 85

Foodservice Labor Needs 86
Labor Costs 86
  Employee Benefits and Payroll Taxes 87
Selecting and Retaining Staff 88
  The Job Description 88
  Recruiting 89
  The Job Application 89
  Interviewing 90
  Orientation and Training 91

Supervision 94
Performance Appraisal 94
Retention 94
Determining Labor Needs 96
Job Analysis 96
Job Routines 96
Work Simplification Study 98
Organizational Chart 100
Position Control Sheets 100
Calculating Labor Requirement of a Position 101
Scheduling Labor 101
Factors That Affect Scheduling 102
Analyzing Labor Costs 106
Labor Cost Percentage 107
Covers per Labor Hour 108
Labor Cost per Cover 108
Labor Cost per Meal 108
Labor Cost per Labor Hour 109
Meals per Productive Labor Hour 109
Analyzing and Benchmarking Results 110
Limits of Labor Analysis 111

Chapter 6
Beverage Cost Control

Beverage Cost Control 116
Types of Beverage Services 116
Beverage Classification 117
Purchasing 118
Receiving 120
Storage 120
Issuing 121
Inventory 121
Inventory Control Methods 122
Calculating the Cost of Beverages Sold 124
Affect of Sales Mix on Beverage Cost Percentage 125
Pricing 126
Beverage Cost Percentage Method 126
Contribution Margin Method 127
Prime Cost Method 127
Serving 128
Standardized Recipes 128
Point-of-Sale Systems 128
Guest Checks 129
Dispensing Systems 129
Standardized Glassware 129
Serving Responsibly 129

Chapter 7

Facilities Management as a Cost Control Tool 136
  Utility Cost Control 136
    Types of Energy 137
    Controlling Utility Costs. 138
    Utility Cost Control Audit 142
  Preventive Maintenance Programs 143
    Contracting Preventive Maintenance 145
  Risk Management 145
    Steps in Risk Management 145
    Ways to Manage Risk 146

Chapter 8

Operating Budget and Performance Reports. 151
  Budgets 151
  The Operating Budget 152
    Sales 152
    Cost of Sales 152
    Labor 154
    Prime Cost. 155
    Other Controllable Expenses 155
    Controllable Income 156
    Noncontrollable Expenses 156
    Operating Income 157
    Corporate Overhead 157
    Interest Expense 157
    Other Income/Expense. 157
    Income before Income Taxes. 158
  The Budgeting Process 158
    Step 1: Establish a Timeline 158
    Step 2: Consider Goals. 158
    Step 3: Gather Data 158
    Step 4: Determine Level of Costs 159
    Step 5: Submit Budget for Approval 160
  Cash Budgets 160
  Fixed and Flexible Budgets. 162
  Performance Reports 164
  Financial Ratios 166

Chapter 9

The Capital Budget 172
  Capital Assets 172
  Pre-Planning 173
  Determining Need 173
  Capital Investigation 176
    Capital Requirements 176
    Sources of Information 177
    Buying New versus Used 178
    Calculating Depreciation 180
    Soliciting Bids 180
  Justifying the Request 181
    Calculating Payback Period 183
    Completing a Request for Capital Asset Form 184
  Prioritizing Requests 184
  Purchasing or Leasing the Asset 185
    Purchasing Outright 186
    Borrowing Cash to Purchase 186
    Hire Purchase 186
    Leasing 187
    Weighing the Options 187

Chapter 10

Revenue Control 191
  Revenue Loss 191
  Employee Selection and Screening 193
    Employee Bonding 194
  Cash Handling Policies and Procedures 194
    Separation of Duties 194
    Cash-Drawer Practices 195
    Cashier Job Duties 196
    Deposit Practices 199
    Using a Safe 200
  Fraud Using Guest Checks 201
  Monitoring of Cash Handling 202
    Direct Monitoring 202
    Indirect Monitoring 204
  Corrective-Action Process 204
  Patron Theft 204
    Banquets and Catered Events 205

Chapter 11

Financial Management 209
Financial Statements 209
   Statement of Income 209
   Balance Sheet 217
   Equity. 219
   Statement of Cash Flows. 219
Financial Analysis 220
   Comparative Analysis. 220
   Ratio Analysis. 223
Trend Analysis 227

Chapter 12

Controlling Costs through Technology 234
Computerizing Foodservice Operations 234
   Purchasing. 235
   Receiving 237
   Inventory 237
   Menu Planning and Production. 239
   Point of Sale 242
   Labor Management 243
   Office Systems and Financial Management 243
Enterprise Software Systems 245
High-Tech Foodservice Equipment. 246
Advantages and Disadvantages of Information Technology 247
   Advantages. 247
   Disadvantages 249

Appendix A—List of Equations Used 252
Appendix B—Conversion Tables 260
Glossary 264
Bibliography 273
Index 279

Chapter 1

Principles of Control in a Foodservice Operation

Learning Outcomes

After studying this chapter, you will be able to

- summarize the four basic functions of management.
- understand the role of cost control in the success of an operation.
- recall five areas in which basic math skills are used in a foodservice operation.

Growing up, Jade dreamed of owning and operating her own upscale restaurant. From an early age, she begged her mother to let her help prepare various recipes. During high school, she planned and prepared meals for her family and received rave reviews. Following high school, Jade worked as a waitress at a white-tablecloth restaurant and as a breakfast cook at a family restaurant. After a year, she felt ready to pursue her dream of operating a restaurant.

Like other aspiring entrepreneurs, Jade met with a bank loan officer about obtaining a small business loan. In explaining why the bank could not give her a loan, the loan officer said, "It is obvious that you have a passion for the business and a few basic skills, but I strongly encourage you to learn how to run a restaurant like the business that it is." She encouraged Jade to enroll in a hospitality management program with a focus on foodservice management. In this program, Jade would learn the functions of management—including how to manage resources and control costs in a foodservice operation. She will learn how to apply mathematics to solve problems in foodservice management.

This chapter provides a brief overview of the functions of management that are essential to running a successful foodservice operation. One of these functions, and the focus of this text, is the management function of control. Control refers to the effective management of resources. In addition, this chapter reviews some of the basic mathematical calculations that are fundamental to running a small business and some of their applications in foodservice.

Functions of Management

There are four basic functions of management—planning, organizing, leading, and controlling. All four are essential to running any type of business or operation, 1-1. One part cannot work well without the other parts. Planning, organizing, and leading are covered in greater depth in other business courses. Following is a brief overview.

1

Functions of Management

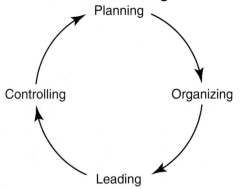

Figure 1-1. The four functions of management are planning, organizing, leading, and controlling. As this illustration shows, the functions are cyclical, meaning that each one follows another.

Planning

Planning, the first step in setting up a business, is the process of determining what an operation will be. It involves defining an operation's goals and objectives and the steps that will be necessary to achieve them. Plans should be routinely reviewed to make sure they continue to be relevant to an operation's overall goals and objectives.

Organizing

Organizing is the second management function. **Organizing** is the process of deciding what tasks need to be completed, who will perform those tasks, and how the tasks will be coordinated. During this step, the staffing is determined. How many people will be needed? Where and when will they work? Who will report to whom?

Leading

Once the staff is hired and the operation's organizational structure is in place, it is time to implement the plan. One or more leaders are needed to provide guidance and to ensure that the staff understands and completes their expected functions.

Leading, the third basic function of management, is the process of directing people to meet the goals and objectives set in the planning phase. Leadership includes motivating people, communicating effectively, providing feedback on employee performance, and listening and responding to employee needs.

Controlling

Controlling is the process of monitoring the performance of the operation against its plans. This is accomplished by setting measurable goals, measuring the results, and comparing those results against the goals. If results are not in line with goals, the reason for falling short needs to be determined and corrective action taken. When an operation is *in control*, expectations are met. In other words, control is an ongoing process of comparing expected results against actual results. In order to do so, the operation must

- define its expected results
- have a plan in place to achieve those results
- provide the resources that enable it to meet its goals
- modify its structure, methods, or tools, as needed, to meet its plan and measure the results

Cost Control

Cost control is one aspect of the control function of management. **Cost control** is the process an operation uses to ensure that its forecasted sales and expenses conform to its plans, goals, and objectives. The successful foodservice manager balances quality with financial control to yield a profit for the business and secure its continued success. Balance does not mean cutting corners, but rather keeping a firm control on costs incurred by the operation. These costs are generated by the menu, the operation's level of service and ambiance, and other efforts to meet customer expectations.

𝔅𝔬𝔬𝔨𝔪𝔞𝔯𝔨 𝔗𝔥𝔦𝔰

U.S. Small Business Administration

Each year, 10 million people consider starting foodservice and other businesses. Yet only 3 million of them get their businesses up and running, according to the U.S. Small Business Administration (SBA). The SBA offers a wealth of information on how to establish and manage a successful operation. They provide
- guidelines for writing business and marketing plans
- information on financing options
- online training and counseling services
- instructions on how to apply for business licenses and permits
- information on how to comply with business laws and regulations
- links to business application forms

To learn more, visit www.sba.gov/

Cost control is a critical function that should be required of every foodservice operator. However, many foodservice operations lack strong cost controls. These operations may be small and run by people who lack the knowledge and skills to set up cost-control systems. For example, the cook may be the manager. While the cook may be great at food preparation, he or she may lack the training and skills necessary to understand and monitor the financial part of the business. Some foodservice businesses fail because they focus entirely on the culinary aspect of the business, or on customer service, without consideration of cost.

Why is cost control so important? Consider the following:

$$Sales - Cost = Profit$$

or

$$Cost = Sales - Profit$$

To control costs and enhance profits, a manager needs to understand the relationship between *cost*, *sales*, and *profit* (or *loss*). **Cost**, or expenses, is the dollar amount spent to create the good or service being sold. **Sales**, or revenue, result from the exchange of goods or services for payment or promise to pay.

Cost is subtracted from sales to determine whether the operation had a profit or a loss. **Profit** is the dollar amount remaining after all expenses have been paid. A **loss** is the amount incurred when the expenses of an operation are greater than its sales.

All operations—both for-profit and not-for-profit—need to make enough money from sales to cover the costs of doing business. An operation can increase its profits in two ways—by increasing sales or by decreasing expenses. The successful manager understands where the numbers come from in the profit equation. He or she knows how to measure and monitor those numbers and how to take steps to improve them to create greater profits.

Calculations as a Cost-Control Function

Many calculations are performed throughout this text. Basic math skills are required in all aspects of foodservice operations. Every manager should have these skills in order to effectively and efficiently run a foodservice operation through a strong cost-control system. Math skills are used in
- standardizing and converting recipes
- purchasing food and supplies
- determining staffing needs
- determining selling prices

- forecasting the amount of food to produce
- controlling inventory
- preparing budgets
- analyzing customer satisfaction and other quality measures
- evaluating sales results

The following section provides a basic math review. The rest of this chapter discusses five areas of a cost-control system that require the use of these math skills.

Basic Math Review

A manager needs basic math skills to effectively and efficiently run a foodservice operation through a strong cost-control system. These skills include the use of fractions, decimals, percentages, and ratios.

Fractions

Fractions, percentages, and decimals can be considered one in the same. They all deal with parts of a whole. A **fraction** is made up of a numerator (the top number) and a denominator (the bottom number). The numerator is the part and the denominator represents the whole. The fraction ¾ is read as *three parts of the whole of four*. For example, if a pie is cut into four equal pieces and Troy eats ¾ of the pie, he has consumed three of the four pieces, or he ate three parts of the total of four that was there.

Percentages

A percentage is another way of expressing a part of the whole. The word **percent** is from the Latin words *per centum* meaning "per hundred." A percentage is another way of expressing a fraction in which the denominator is 100. The percent symbol % is used after a number when writing percentages.

Fractions can be expressed as percentages. For example, if Troy's pie is cut into four pieces, the four pieces represent 100 percent of the whole pie. The three pieces, or parts that Troy ate represent what percentage (n) of the pie? The answer is found by setting up an equation to convert ¾ to an equivalent fraction using 100 as the denominator.

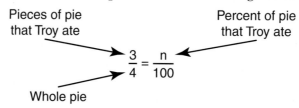

Cross multiply and solve for n to find what percentage of the pie Troy ate.

$$4 \times n = 3 \times 100$$

$$4n = 300$$

$$n = \frac{300}{4}$$

$$n = 75$$

So, ¾ is equivalent to 75%.

A percentage can be greater than the whole, which is 100 percent. For example, 200 percent is greater than 100 percent and is equivalent to two wholes.

Decimals

Decimals are another way of expressing a part of the whole. A **decimal** represents a fraction based on the number 10. A decimal point separates the whole (to the left of the decimal point) from the part (to the right of the decimal point). Therefore, the number *5.67* represents five wholes and 67 parts. When writing decimals, the positions to the right of the decimal point are called *places*. The first number to the right of the decimal is the tenths place. The second number is the hundredths place, and so on. The decimal *0.67* is six tenths and seven hundredths, which is read as "67 hundredths," and means 67 parts of 100.

Decimals and Percentages

How do decimals relate to percentages? A decimal is easily expressed as a percentage by moving the decimal point two places to the right and adding the percent symbol.

$$0.67 = 67\%$$

If a decimal number only has a digit in the tenths place, such as 0.6, a zero is placed in the hundredths spot and the decimal point is moved.

$$0.60 = 60\%$$

As stated above, decimals and percentages show the same relationship. To convert a percentage to a decimal, the decimal point is moved two places to the left.

$$67.0\% = 0.67$$

When converting percentages to decimals, any place created when moving the decimal point should be filled with a "0".

$$04\% = 0.04$$

Both percentages and decimals can also be expressed as fractions.

$$67\% = 0.67 = \frac{67}{100}$$

Or

$$4\% = 0.04 = \frac{4}{100}$$

Ratios

A **ratio** expresses how one number relates, or compares, to another. The ratio, $X{:}Y$, is stated "for X numbers of the first item, there are Y numbers of the second item." Or more simply, "the ratio is X to Y." A ratio can be written in a number of ways.

$$X{:}Y = \frac{X}{Y} = X \text{ to } Y$$

Practical Foodservice Applications

Percentages, ratios, fractions, and decimals are used every day in foodservice operations to control costs. The next sections provide several practical examples of calculations used in foodservice. Other chapters will cover these applications in more detail.

Using Ratios

A baker knows she sells two sugar cookies for every seven chocolate chip cookies she sells. The cookie sales can be expressed as the ratio 2:7. If she bakes 420 chocolate chip cookies, how many sugar cookies will she need to bake? She can use the ratio to answer this. The ratio of sugar cookies to chocolate chip cookies can also be written as a division problem:

$$\frac{2}{7} = 2 \div 7 = 0.286$$

For every chocolate chip cookie, the baker needs 0.286 sugar cookies. For 420 chocolate chip cookies, the baker needs to bake 120 sugar cookies.

$$420 \times 0.286 = 120$$

Determining Selling Price

Many foodservice operations base the selling price of a menu item on the cost of the food used to make it. They want to limit the food cost to a certain percentage of the selling price—a *food cost percentage*. A common food cost percentage used by foodservice operations is 30 percent. For instance, if the ingredients used to prepare a menu item cost $10, the operation wants $10 to account for no more than 30 percent of the selling price. What should the selling price be to achieve this goal? The foodservice operator can determine the selling price by using the following calculation in which X is the selling price.

$$\frac{\$10}{X} = 30\%$$

$$\frac{\$10}{X} = \frac{30}{100}$$

$$30X = \$10 \times 100$$

$$30X = \$1,000$$

$$\frac{30X}{30} = \frac{\$1,000}{30}$$

$$X = \frac{\$1,000}{30}$$

$$X = \$33.33$$

If the food cost is $10, and the food cost percentage is 30 percent, the operator sells the menu item for $33.33.

Comparing Product Prices

When making decisions about which food products to purchase, a manager often compares the prices of two or more products. The comparison can be inaccurate if it is based solely on the purchase prices. Factors such as pack size and product yield must be taken into consideration when comparing product prices. The manager must answer the question, "What is the best price per unit?"

Considering Pack Size

For example, a manager finds that frozen corn can be purchased in two ways:

- in a case that contains 12 two-pound bags and costs $20
- in a bulk case that weighs 30 pounds and costs $23

With all other things being equal, how can the manager determine which product is the least expensive per pound?

The first step in answering this question is to compute the total number of pounds in the case of two-pound bags:

Number of Bags per Case × Weight per Bag = Weight per Case

12 bags per case × 2 lb. per bag = 24 lb. per case

Now, the comparison is between a 24-pound case selling for $20 and a 30-pound case costing $23. For the comparison to be accurate, the price per pound for each option must be calculated.

$$\frac{\textbf{Price per Case}}{\textbf{Weight per Case}} = \textbf{Price per Weight Measure (Pound)}$$

Price per pound of frozen corn in the case containing 12 two-pound bags:

$$\frac{\$20 \text{ per case}}{24 \text{ lb. per case}} = \$0.83 \text{ per lb.}$$

Price per pound of frozen corn in the 30-pound bulk case:

$$\frac{\$23 \text{ per case}}{30 \text{ lb. per case}} = \$0.77 \text{ per lb.}$$

Which frozen-corn product should the manager buy? The best buy is the product that is the least expensive per unit (pound), or the frozen corn in the 30-pound bulk case.

Considering Product Yield

Foodservice managers frequently need to compare the price of a raw or unprocessed product with that of a processed product. Examples of processed products include trimmed and chopped lettuce; eggs that are boiled, shelled, and chopped; and cooked meats. To accurately compare prices between a raw and a processed product, managers must consider the *yield*. **Product yield** is the amount of a product that is usable after trimming, cooking, or other processing.

For example, a foodservice manager may need to determine which of the following is the better deal:

- fresh or uncooked beef roast at $1.77 per pound
- precooked beef roast at $2.30 per pound

At a lower price per pound, the fresh beef roast may appear to be a better deal. However, meat often loses weight during cooking as fats and juices drip away. Also, parts of the fresh beef roast may need to be trimmed away. Suppose that after the fat is trimmed from the fresh roast and it is cooked, the product yield is 75 percent of the purchased weight— 25 percent of the product was lost in trimming and cooking. The amount paid for the meat has not changed, but the weight available to serve has decreased.

On the other hand, although the precooked beef roast costs more—$2.30 per pound—it has a higher product yield of 97 percent. Which is the better price per pound? For each roast, the manager needs to determine the price per pound (X) for the amount of the product that remains.

Uncooked or fresh roast beef (1 pound)
First, 75% is converted to a decimal number.

$$75\% = 0.75$$

Then, the values are plugged into the formula:

$$X = \frac{\text{Purchase Price}}{\text{Product Yield \%}}$$

$$X = \frac{\$1.77 \text{ per lb.}}{0.75}$$

$$X = \$2.36 \text{ per lb.}$$

Precooked roast beef (1 pound)
First, 97% is converted to a decimal number.

$$97\% = 0.97$$

Then, the values are plugged into the formula:

$$X = \frac{\text{Purchase Price}}{\text{Product Yield \%}}$$

$$X = \frac{\$2.30 \text{ per lb.}}{0.97}$$

$$X = \$2.37 \text{ per lb.}$$

Comparing just the product prices, the fresh product is slightly less expensive per pound ($0.01) than the precooked one. However, this does not include the labor cost to trim the product, the utility cost to cook it, and other costs that may be associated with preparing the fresh beef roast not required for the precooked beef roast. After considering these costs, the manager may decide that the precooked roast beef is the better value.

Determining Food or Labor Cost per Meal Served

Another common calculation in foodservice management is determining the cost to produce a meal. These include the costs of food and labor per meal served. Recall that a ratio shows the relationship between two numbers. In this case, the relationship is between the number of meals served and the cost of the food or labor used to prepare those meals. The food cost per meal can be calculated using the following equation:

$$\text{Food Cost per Meal} = \frac{\text{Cost of Food to Prepare Meals}}{\text{Number of Meals Served}}$$

Waste Not

Tough Law Targets Food Waste

A recently enacted Vermont law will ban the disposal of many forms of waste, including food waste, from landfills. The law will require large waste producers, including foodservice operations, to separate food from other solid waste. The waste will have to be composted on site or hauled to a certified compost facility. This is part of a larger effort in Vermont and elsewhere to divert nutrient-rich organic waste from landfills to the soil.

Most Vermont residents will have until 2020 to comply with the new requirements. However, those producing more than 104 tons of food and other organic waste a year will have to comply by 2017. The law applies to businesses located within 50 miles of a certified compost facility.

If an operation serves 100 meals at lunch and the food cost to prepare those meals was $500, what is the food cost per meal served?

$$\text{Food cost per meal} = \frac{\$500 \text{ food cost}}{100 \text{ meals served}}$$

Food cost per meal = $5.00

The labor cost per meal is calculated using a similar equation.

$$\text{Labor Cost per Meal} = \frac{\text{Labor Cost}}{\text{Meals Served}}$$

If the labor cost to prepare the lunch meals is $600, what is the labor cost per meal?

$$\text{Labor cost per meal} = \frac{\$600 \text{ labor cost}}{100 \text{ meals served}}$$

Labor cost per meal = $6.00.

In summary, it costs the operation $5 in food costs and $6 in labor costs to serve each meal.

Variance Calculations

Earlier in this chapter, this formula was introduced:

Sales – Cost = Profit

If sales are greater than costs, the difference is positive and the company makes a profit. If costs, or expenses, are greater than sales, the difference is negative and the company experiences a loss. In other words, the company spent more on expenses than it made in revenue, or sales.

As stated earlier, the goal of cost control is to keep expenses down to maximize profit. Managers receive reports that indicate the amount of revenue received and the amount of dollars spent to cover costs. The manager must calculate—not only the above equation—but also check the individual revenue and expense categories to determine what is driving the profit or the loss. This is covered in more detail in other chapters.

When reviewing reports to assess actual performance compared to budget goals, a manager looks at the variance. The **variance** is the difference between a budgeted amount and an actual amount. Variances are calculated for revenues, expenses, and profit.

Budget – Actual = Variance

Trend

Controlling Costs and Creating Trends

Food industry trends can be driven by the preferences of consumers. For example, consumers tend to be more cost-conscious during hard economic times. However, chefs and foodservice operators also originate trends, often out of economic necessity. For example, to offset higher food costs, many chefs use value-priced cuts of meat—flank, hanger, or flat steak—to create flavorful dishes. Hamburgers have experienced a surge in popularity, with "gourmet" hamburgers replacing steaks and other more expensive center-of-the-plate options. Less-costly substitutes for expensive cuts of pork, lamb, and poultry have become more popular as well. Chicken thighs are appearing on more restaurant menus. They are moist and flavorful and about one-third the cost of chicken breasts. Although these trends are motivated by a need to control costs, they must result in meals that appeal to customers to be successful.

A manager may want to determine the variance as a percentage difference. To do so, the following equation is used:

$$\frac{\text{Variance Amount}}{\text{Budgeted Amount}} \times 100 = \% \text{ Difference}$$

For example, a restaurant is budgeted to spend $1,000 on cleaning chemicals for the month of June. It actually spent $900. What is the variance?

$$\$1,000 - \$900 = \$100 \text{ variance}$$

What is the percentage difference?

$$\frac{\$100}{\$1,000} \times 100 = 10\%$$

The restaurant spent 10 percent less on cleaning chemicals for the month of June than it had planned or budgeted. Stated another way, the account for cleaning chemicals was under budget by 10 percent for June.

Quality Measures

A manager is also responsible for determining how well the operation is performing in regard to quality. A foodservice operation will not survive if it serves poor-quality food or if the service is deemed unacceptable by customers. As a form of control, a manager measures and monitors the quality of the operation. This is accomplished through quality measures. A **quality measure** is a means to rate the level of perceived value placed on the parameter being evaluated.

One quality measure, or parameter, is customer satisfaction. A foodservice operation often surveys its customers to learn their perspectives on its performance. The manager may compare that result with results from previous surveys. The manager may also compare the results with those of similar operations. Customer satisfaction is often expressed as a percentage, as in, "Out of a total number of responses—the whole—what is the percentage of people who rated the restaurant as 'excellent?'"

Technology

Monitoring Food Safety Practices through Video Technology

A suspected incident of foodborne illness can be costly for a foodservice operation. It may have to close down while the local health department investigates. This can result in lost revenue, fines, and legal action by customers. Many cases of foodborne illness in foodservice establishments are caused by improper food handling by employees. This is why food safety training should be a top priority.

Video tracking technology, first developed by the military, is giving managers new tools to train and monitor employees' food safety practices. Cameras set up in work areas feed images to software programs. The programs can detect employee noncompliance—instances when employees are not wearing gloves or hair restraints, for example. The video images of these selected events are uploaded to a website for review by the manager. A manager can also be alerted as the incident occurs, so it can be addressed immediately. Similar programs allow managers to monitor hand washing and cash-handling practices.

For example, suppose a customer survey yields a total of 90 responses, and 65 of them rated the restaurant as "excellent." What is the percentage of "excellent" responses? This question can be answered by using the following calculation:

$$\frac{65}{90} = 0.72$$

The decimal is converted to a percentage by multiplying it by 100.

$$0.72 \times 100 = 72\%$$

The manager now knows that 72 percent of the customers surveyed rated the restaurant as excellent. Next, the manager interprets these results—are they good or bad? There are several ways to answer this question. The current survey results can be compared with previous survey results to determine if the current results are better or worse, and by how much. Suppose that 70 percent of respondents rated the restaurant as "excellent" in the previous survey. How much did the restaurant improve? Since the last survey, 2 percent more of the customers surveyed rated the restaurant as "excellent." A manager records results of quality measures over time to monitor the success of the operation in meeting customers' expectations.

Key Terms

planning	sales	decimal
organizing	profit	ratio
leading	loss	product yield
controlling	fraction	variance
cost control	percent	quality measure
cost		

Recap

- Management has four key functions: planning, organizing, leading, and controlling.
- Many foodservice operations lack strong cost controls.
- The difference between sales and cost is profit; all businesses need to generate enough sales to cover costs.
- Basic math skills are needed in many aspects of a foodservice operation.

Review Questions

1. Define the four basic functions of management: planning, organizing, leading, and controlling.
2. Explain why strong cost controls are often lacking in the foodservice industry.
3. Name five aspects of foodservice in which basic math skills are used.

Applying Your Knowledge

4. If sales equal $100,000 and costs equal $90,000, what is the profit or loss? If the numbers are reversed, what is the profit or loss?
5. Which of the following cleaning products is the better value?

   Soclean: Costs $6.00 per gallon and 0.5 ounces yields 1 gallon of solution. Smellsfresh: Costs $3.50 per gallon and 1 ounce yields 1 gallon of solution.
6. A recipe that yields 48 servings uses 12 tomatoes and 1.5 pounds of mozzarella cheese. The tomatoes cost $0.75 each and the cheese costs $3.00 per lb. What is the raw food cost per serving?
7. Refer to the recipe in question 6. If the restaurant wants to have a 25 percent food cost, what must it charge customers for the tomato-cheese dish?
8. Suppose you manage a restaurant and your current annual food budget is $500,000. You plan to use a new vendor next year to save 3 percent on your food budget. What amount should you budget for food with the new vendor?
9. An operation served 500 meals at a food cost of $3,000. What is the food cost per meal?
10. The budgeted amount for food cost in January was $11,000. The actual cost for January was $10,000. In February, the budgeted amount for food cost was $10,500. The actual cost for February was $10,200. Calculate the variance for both January and February.

Course Project

Like Jade at the beginning of the chapter, you may have dreamed of running a foodservice operation. Each chapter of this text focuses on an area of running a foodservice operation. Most chapters include a component of a course project. Together, the components create a full case study on controlling costs in a foodservice operation.

11. Select one of the following types of food service establishments for your course project:

    Deli/grill

    Bistro café

    Family restaurant

    Senior-living community offering restaurant-style dining

    Upscale, white-tablecloth restaurant

    Based on your selection, write a brief description of the operation. Include its location and ambiance (atmosphere). The description should allow the reader to visualize the establishment.

Chapter 2
Menu Planning as a Control Tool

Learning Outcomes

After studying this chapter, you will be able to

- list aspects of an operation that are impacted by the menu.
- explain factors to consider when selecting food items for a menu.
- describe menu formats and sections.
- cite sources of menu ideas.
- calculate the menu selling price using various menu-pricing methods.
- write a menu-item description.
- appropriately place highly profitable or featured items in the correct location on the menu.
- fill out a menu evaluation form.

Menu planning is one of the most important tasks of a foodservice manager. A **menu** is a list of the food and beverage items offered in an establishment. However, the menu is also the foundation on which everything else is built—it drives the operation and affects every area of it. A menu largely determines whether or not an operation is profitable. It determines what food, equipment, and labor are needed. In an ideal business environment, the menu is planned before the first hole is dug or the first brick is laid in construction of a foodservice establishment.

The main purpose of a menu is to sell the food and beverages offered by an operation. It is a tool used to communicate with the customer. Therefore, significant thought must be given to the menu. It is critical that managers understand the parts, pricing strategies, and marketing capabilities of menus. To ensure that menus generate the greatest possible profit, managers should know how to evaluate menus and the items in them. This chapter focuses on these points and discusses the skills managers need to successfully plan and evaluate menus.

How the Menu Impacts the Operation

In general, the menu should be written to avoid overburdening one area of the kitchen. Consideration should also be given to available equipment and storage, the staff's culinary skills, and the amount of available labor. Finally, an operation's menu should target the type of customer it wishes to attract. It can be used to communicate the identity of a foodservice operation and help create its atmosphere and image. The following sections explain the impact of the menu on various aspects of the operation.

Equipment

The contents of a menu determine what equipment is needed and in what quantities. For example, a menu dominated by fried foods requires an operation to have a fryer with sufficient capacity to meet demand. If a menu offers a wide array of items, a variety of cooking equipment is required. In an existing kitchen, the available equipment must be considered when developing the menu.

A menu writer must also consider the capacity of the kitchen to get menu items to customers within a timeframe. The timeframe is determined by customer traffic in a dining room or at a take-out counter. In an institutional setting, the timeframe is determined by the number of guests receiving meals.

Food

When a menu is varied, a larger food inventory is required. The larger the inventory, the more time must be spent on ordering items, and the more difficult it becomes to control costs. Security also becomes more difficult to maintain. These topics are discussed in another chapter.

Storage

How many items will be on the menu? Will the menu be dominated by items made from fresh or from frozen ingredients? The answers to these questions determine the amount of freezer space, refrigeration, and storage needed. Failure to consider these needs when planning the menu will result in a storage crisis and a frustrated staff.

Kitchen Layout

The menu impacts how the kitchen should be designed. The design depends on the processes required to produce menu items and the types of equipment needed for each process. Menu developers need to know which menu items are prepared in a sequence of steps. They need to determine if equipment is arranged, or can be arranged, to accommodate this sequence. Designing the kitchen to provide efficient use of both labor and equipment is critical.

Labor

The number of employees needed—and the necessary level of skill they must possess—is directly related to the menu. Employees in a burger-and-fries place that uses frozen hamburger patties and French fries do not need the same skill set as the staff of a fine-dining restaurant that features signature sauces and freshly made desserts. Also, a menu with a wide variety of items may require an operation to hire additional staff to prepare everything on the menu.

Atmosphere

A menu should reflect the atmosphere of the dining room, although this is not always the case. White tablecloths, soft music, fresh flowers, and fine china are generally not seen or expected in a "burger joint." Likewise, fresh Maine lobster and signature spinach salads would rarely be served on paper plates to customers seated in hard plastic booths.

Brand or Message

The menu should communicate a brand or message to the customer. It should establish the identity of an operation and help shape how the operation is perceived by customers. Fast food or fine dining? Sports bar or family friendly restaurant? Special occasion or everyday dining? Whatever the message, whatever the brand, the menu should convey this to the customer.

Factors to Consider in Selecting Menu Items

The contents of a menu must work together as a total package. The number of items offered should not be too many or too few. There should be enough variety to satisfy customers, yet not so much as to weaken the establishment's brand. The following sections cover some important factors to consider when selecting food items for the menu.

Taste and Flavor Combinations

Many establishments experiment with various seasonings, spices, and flavor combinations to win over customers. For instance, a mild fish item, married with a flavorful sauce, may be a winning combination. A key to successful menu planning is the inclusion of items with a variety of tastes and flavors that complement each other.

Appearance, Color, and Texture

Picture this meal: baked chicken, mashed potatoes, corn, cottage cheese with pineapple, angel food cake, and white milk. The meal's appearance at a place setting would be uninviting because it lacks color. When determining what to serve together, the menu writer should aim for a variety of colors and textures to provide a pleasing plate combination. Substituting asparagus for the corn and tossed salad for the cottage cheese, can greatly improve the appearance and texture of this meal.

A menu combination should have at least one bold color and one different texture. Varying the shapes and sizes of what is offered is also important. Finally, a variety of preparation methods can add interest to a meal. Menu items can be fried, baked, sautéed, broiled, and so forth.

Ethnic Style

If an establishment focuses on a particular ethnic style, the menu should reflect that. An Italian restaurant's menu will be heavy on pasta and sauces. A casual restaurant catering to a variety of palates may offer a few Italian items, along with a taco salad and a chicken stir-fry. Customers are becoming more knowledgeable about foods from other parts of the world. As a result, menus are changing. For example, a menu focusing on Italian fare may specify which part of Italy the flavors and menu selections come from.

Variety of Offerings

Some restaurants offer a variety of menu items, ethnic choices, children's selections, and the like. Other restaurants—such as steakhouses and seafood restaurants—are very focused in their offerings. Their menus are dominated by items that are the core focus of the establishment. However, even these restaurants need to offer some variety for guests who will not want to order the core foods. For instance, consider a group of friends dining out at a well-known steakhouse. Perhaps one person in the group does not eat beef and another person has cholesterol concerns. They will be pleased to see a few seafood items on the menu, in addition to the signature steaks that made the restaurant famous.

Nutritional Content

Nutritionally balanced menus are essential in the healthcare and educational environments. Operations that serve certain populations—correctional facilities, daycare centers, and places that prepare and serve meals to older adults—must comply with nutrition requirements set by governing bodies. Other establishments should consider nutritional balance as well. Customers who consider dining out to be a treat may disregard the nutritional value of menu items, but others may want the option of making healthy choices.

Defining what is perceived of as "healthy" at a particular moment can be a challenge. Various diet trends come and go. For a restaurant, healthy is whatever the customer defines it to be—vegetarian, low fat, high protein, or low sodium, for example. Therefore, menu planners should consider offering a few items that meet these needs. Better yet, the staff can be trained to prepare and serve menu items to accommodate customer needs.

Price

A menu should include items of varying prices. Some customers may be looking for low-priced items. On the other hand, customers who rarely eat out may want to splurge on higher-priced menu items. The inclusion of items of varied prices offers something for both patrons.

Trend

Menu Labeling Law

Many public health advocates say nutrition labeling on menus help consumers make healthier decisions about what they eat. The Affordable Care Act of 2010 requires chain restaurants with 20 or more locations to provide nutrition labeling on many of the foods they offer. In addition, owners of 20 or more vending machines have to reveal calories for certain items they sell. Restaurant menu boards and drive-through menu boards must display

- the calorie content for items that are sold at least 60 days a calendar year.
- an authorized statement about suggested daily caloric intake.
- a statement regarding the availability of additional nutrition information. Written information about fat, sodium, cholesterol, and other ingredients must be available on request.

The U.S. Food and Drug Administration (FDA) estimates the average cost of compliance for each establishment at $1,100. The costs are incurred for new signage, new menus, nutrient content analysis, and employee training. For many chain restaurants, the corporate office is footing the bill. However, most franchise owners must pay the entire cost themselves. Some say the costs are significant and higher than the FDA estimate. For more information on menu labeling requirements, visit www.fda.gov/

Menu Formats

A foodservice operation can choose from a variety of menu formats, including standard, cycle, market, and combination menus. The next sections discuss each of these menu formats in detail.

Standard Menu

The popular **standard menu** offers the same items every day. Regular customers may not need to look at a standard menu. They already know what they will order because the menu does not change. An advantage of a standard menu for the foodservice operation is that it knows what to prepare every day. Since the purchasing and ordering processes are consistent, money can be saved on storage and inventory costs. Another advantage is that the cooks are familiar with the recipes and the waitstaff know exactly what is on the menu.

A disadvantage of the standard menu is just that—it is standard. A frequent customer may become bored with the same offerings and seek out a new place for a different experience. In addition, it is more difficult to make changes to the menu. A standard menu is generally of a permanent design. The addition or deletion of an item may require the printing of new menus at additional expense.

Cycle Menu

A **cycle menu** repeats itself on a predetermined schedule. For instance, a four-week cycle menu offers the same menu every four weeks. If a dinner of meatloaf and mashed potatoes are served on Monday of week one, it will be offered again for Monday dinner four weeks later. Cycle menus are common in noncommercial or institutional settings.

The advantages of a cycle menu are similar to those of the standard menu. Since the menu repeats itself on a scheduled basis, ordering and purchasing are simplified. Also, the staff is familiar with the menu and recipes. Since this type of menu is usually used in a noncommercial setting, the number of customers changes little from week to week. For example, the number of children in a school's lunch program remains fairly constant throughout the school year. The same can be said for a nursing home—the number of residents remains about the same from week to week. Therefore, the foodservice operator can predict how many meals will be needed well in advance of meal preparation.

A disadvantage of a cycle menu is that it can become routine. In a school or nursing home, a common complaint may be, "It's the first Monday of the month—it must be meatloaf!" There are several ways to make a cycle menu less predictable. The cycle can be lengthened. For example, a four-week cycle can be expanded to five weeks. When the menu extends beyond a month, dinner on the first Monday of the month will not always be meatloaf.

Another strategy is to make the number of days in the cycle less than or greater than seven. For example, a menu can cover an eight-day cycle. What was served on Monday the first week will be served on Tuesday of the second week. However, there are disadvantages to extending the day cycle. Consider a menu that has a traditional Sunday dinner of roast beef, mashed potatoes and gravy, green beans, salad, and apple pie. In an eight-day cycle, this meal will next be served on Monday. Secondly, some menus require more staff time than others. The manager needs to ensure that the number of staff on duty is always sufficient to prepare the menu. A rotating cycle can make staff planning difficult.

Market Menu

Market menus have been around for a long time, but are gaining in popularity. A **market menu** may change routinely—even daily—to take advantage of what is seasonally available. For example, a chef may visit the local farmer's market and purchase fresh produce for the evening meal. Or, the chef may vary the seafood choices based on market availability or conditions.

The market menu is popular for several reasons. It allows the operation to take advantage of specialty offerings, or items that may be less expensive at certain times of the year. Customers may appreciate the freshness and novelty in the menu. They may enjoy being surprised.

The advantages of having a changing menu can also be disadvantageous. This type of menu appeals to the adventurous diner. However, many people select a restaurant to order a favorite item or because they "know what they are getting." Another disadvantage is that it requires a highly trained staff—they must adapt to the constantly changing menu. Meal planning and preparation can be challenging. Producing a meal with items from the farmer's market may require more skill than producing a meal from a standard recipe and items ordered in advance for the menu.

Combination Menu

A **combination menu** incorporates at least two of the other menu types. For example, an establishment may use a standard menu, but offer certain items on a cyclical basis. A combination menu allows an operation to take advantage of the strengths of different menu formats, while minimizing their weaknesses.

A common combination menu combines a fixed menu with a soup-of-the-day offering. The soups are on a weekly cycle, while the rest of the menu stays the same. An establishment may have a menu that combines the standard and market menus. The menu is fixed, but specials are offered to take advantage of seasonal items and bargains from vendors. For instance, Copper River salmon is available only three to four weeks each year. A restaurant may offer it on its fixed menu during this timeframe. Menu specials also give the staff an opportunity to experiment with menu ideas.

Menu Sections

Most menus are divided into sections—appetizers, entrées, sides, desserts, and beverages. Some menus further separate the sides or side dishes. Depending on the focus of the menu, soups and salads may be listed separately, included in the appetizer section, or included in the sides section, **2-1**.

Some operations organize their menus based on dayparts. In the foodservice industry, a **daypart** is defined as a specific meal period. A separate menu may be developed for breakfast, another for lunch, and a third for dinner. Or, different dayparts may be featured on separate pages of the overall menu.

Other operations offer a separate children's menu, as well as separate sections for desserts or beverages. They customize their marketing based on the clientele, or to bring focus to the specific course. Providing a separate menu for alcoholic beverages, for example, results in a more concise and uncluttered core menu. A customer can focus on the menu selections separate from the wine list. A customer who does not want an alcoholic beverage can ignore the wine list.

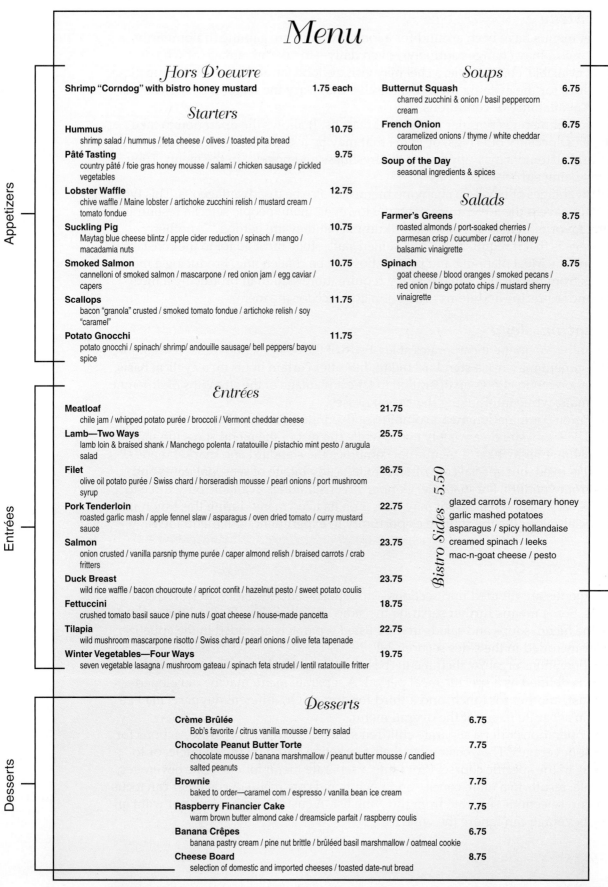

Menu

Appetizers

Hors D'oeuvre

Shrimp "Corndog" with bistro honey mustard	1.75 each

Starters

Hummus	10.75
shrimp salad / hummus / feta cheese / olives / toasted pita bread	
Pâté Tasting	9.75
country pâté / foie gras honey mousse / salami / chicken sausage / pickled vegetables	
Lobster Waffle	12.75
chive waffle / Maine lobster / artichoke zucchini relish / mustard cream / tomato fondue	
Suckling Pig	10.75
Maytag blue cheese blintz / apple cider reduction / spinach / mango / macadamia nuts	
Smoked Salmon	10.75
cannelloni of smoked salmon / mascarpone / red onion jam / egg caviar / capers	
Scallops	11.75
bacon "granola" crusted / smoked tomato fondue / artichoke relish / soy "caramel"	
Potato Gnocchi	11.75
potato gnocchi / spinach/ shrimp/ andouille sausage/ bell peppers/ bayou spice	

Soups

Butternut Squash	6.75
charred zucchini & onion / basil peppercorn cream	
French Onion	6.75
caramelized onions / thyme / white cheddar crouton	
Soup of the Day	6.75
seasonal ingredients & spices	

Salads

Farmer's Greens	8.75
roasted almonds / port-soaked cherries / parmesan crisp / cucumber / carrot / honey balsamic vinaigrette	
Spinach	8.75
goat cheese / blood oranges / smoked pecans / red onion / bingo potato chips / mustard sherry vinaigrette	

Entrées

Entrées

Meatloaf	21.75
chile jam / whipped potato purée / broccoli / Vermont cheddar cheese	
Lamb—Two Ways	25.75
lamb loin & braised shank / Manchego polenta / ratatouille / pistachio mint pesto / arugula salad	
Filet	26.75
olive oil potato purée / Swiss chard / horseradish mousse / pearl onions / port mushroom syrup	
Pork Tenderloin	22.75
roasted garlic mash / apple fennel slaw / asparagus / oven dried tomato / curry mustard sauce	
Salmon	23.75
onion crusted / vanilla parsnip thyme purée / caper almond relish / braised carrots / crab fritters	
Duck Breast	23.75
wild rice waffle / bacon choucroute / apricot confit / hazelnut pesto / sweet potato coulis	
Fettuccini	18.75
crushed tomato basil sauce / pine nuts / goat cheese / house-made pancetta	
Tilapia	22.75
wild mushroom mascarpone risotto / Swiss chard / pearl onions / olive feta tapenade	
Winter Vegetables—Four Ways	19.75
seven vegetable lasagna / mushroom gateau / spinach feta strudel / lentil ratatouille fritter	

Sides

Bistro Sides 5.50

glazed carrots / rosemary honey
garlic mashed potatoes
asparagus / spicy hollandaise
creamed spinach / leeks
mac-n-goat cheese / pesto

Desserts

Desserts

Crème Brûlée	6.75
Bob's favorite / citrus vanilla mousse / berry salad	
Chocolate Peanut Butter Torte	7.75
chocolate mousse / banana marshmallow / peanut butter mousse / candied salted peanuts	
Brownie	7.75
baked to order—caramel com / espresso / vanilla bean ice cream	
Raspberry Financier Cake	7.75
warm brown butter almond cake / dreamsicle parfait / raspberry coulis	
Banana Crêpes	6.75
banana pastry cream / pine nut brittle / brûléed basil marshmallow / oatmeal cookie	
Cheese Board	8.75
selection of domestic and imported cheeses / toasted date-nut bread	

Figure 2-1. This menu is forganized with the sections most foodservice operations use: appetizers, entrées, desserts, and sides.

Menu Presentation

Menus are presented in various ways. Paper menus are common in restaurants that provide table service. Menus are displayed on boards above serving counters in fast food restaurants. At sidewalk cafés or bistros, menus are often communicated on chalkboards.

In a noncommercial setting, such as an employee cafeteria, menus may be communicated via e-mail, a website, or a voicemail system. Some foodservice operations display their menus on plasma screens at the entrances. The screen may also communicate coming events at the facility.

Finally, menus may simply be verbally announced. This can occur in very casual settings, such as summer camps. At an upscale social setting, the maître d' may announce the menu to the guests.

Sources of Menu Ideas

Menu ideas can come from a variety of sources. One of the best sources is the customer. Smart operators take time to talk with customers about what they want and expect. Some operators hold annual consumer focus groups—consumers are asked a variety of questions about their likes, dislikes, and expectations. Customer surveys are another means of finding out what customers want. Employees are another great source of menu ideas. They are consumers themselves and they are on the front lines of a foodservice establishment. They see which items customers choose and often hear feedback about items on the menu.

Menu ideas can come from researching the competitions' offerings. Research can involve visiting other establishments with a few staff members and having them evaluate the similarities and differences between menus. Pointers may be picked up by observing customers in competing establishments.

Industry publications that cover what is popular or trendy in the market can be helpful. Recipes and menu ideas are standard features. Similarly helpful are industry events such as the National Restaurant Association (NRA) show or state restaurant shows. They provide tried-and-true menu options, in addition to the latest ideas. Finally,

Technology

Campus Dining Apps

Campus foodservice managers are using dining apps to connect with student diners who have smart phones and other mobile devices. The free apps allow diners to access

- dining hall hours of operation
- menus and daily specials
- nutritional information
- food allergy information
- dining hall wait times

Some colleges hire outside companies to develop dining apps, while others create their own. The apps are linked to databases of information that must be regularly updated by foodservice managers. Despite the effort involved in keeping information current, the apps provide managers with cost benefits. Students can access information without requesting it from staff. The apps can be used to advertise and promote their services, saving money on print advertising. Dining apps can help an operation improve sales and stay more engaged with their customers.

manufacturers and distributors offer menu ideas for the products they sell. If a sales representative for a distributor or manufacturer shows a manager a new product, the manager can ask for recipe and menu ideas based on the item. Sales representatives can be challenged to provide ideas that promote an operation's brand or message.

Pricing the Menu

Various types of menu pricing are used in the industry. Each item is listed and assigned its own price on an **à la carte** menu. *À la carte* is a French expression meaning "from the menu." It is generally used in one of two ways—each menu item is priced and ordered separately, or the customer receives a side dish at no extra charge with each main-course item.

Table d'hôte is a French phrase that means "host's table." A menu using **table d'hôte** pricing offers complete meals for a fixed price. For instance, for $27, a customer receives a complete meal, including appetizer, salad, entrée, sides, dessert, and a nonalcoholic beverage. Often, the customer is provided a selection from each grouping, but the overall price remains the same. Under entrée, the menu may offer a choice of filet mignon or Chilean sea bass.

In **combination pricing**, some menu items are priced à la carte, while others are priced with a few menu items included. Appetizers, desserts, and beverages are frequently individually priced. Entrée selections may come with preselected side dishes, or offer several choices from a given list of sides. The customer receives the entrée and sides for one set price.

Menu-Pricing Methods

The appropriate pricing of menu items is critical to the financial success of an operation. Selling prices must cover the expenses incurred in producing menu items. Prices must also produce a profit for the operation. For each menu item, the objective is to identify the price that produces the greatest profit without alienating the customer. If customers perceive that prices are too high given the quality of menu items, they will not patronize an establishment. If prices are too low, profitability suffers.

Menu pricing is both an art and a science. Determining what the market will bear is an art. It requires knowledge of like-items on the market offered by the competition and how much they cost. The person pricing a menu speculates about the right price point for his or her establishment. The science of menu pricing involves the various pricing methods used in the industry, including

- food cost percentage (factor system)
- contribution margin
- prime cost
- Texas Restaurant Association markup

Food Cost Percentage Method

In the food cost percentage method, sometimes called the *factor system*, the selling price of a menu item is based on the desired fraction of the price that the food cost represents. For example, if a menu item's selling price is $10 and the cost of the food used to make it is $2, the food cost percentage is 20 percent. The desired food cost percentage is a goal set by the manager.

Some operations establish a standard food cost percentage and use it to price all of their menu items. Others vary the food cost percentage based on the type of menu item. For example, an operation might use a 25 percent food cost to calculate appetizer prices, but 40 percent to price entrées. The food cost percentage can also be taken from the average used in the industry or estimates of the percentage used by competitive operations.

Using the food cost percentage method, the selling price of a menu item can be calculated in two ways. First, it can be found by dividing the food cost by the standard or desired food cost percentage.

$$\frac{\text{Food Cost}}{\text{Desired Food Cost \%}} = \text{Selling Price}$$

For example, suppose a restaurant manager has a goal, or desired food cost percentage, of 40 percent food cost for an entrée. In other words, the cost of the food purchased for the item should represent 40 percent of the item's selling price. If the food cost is $4, it is divided by 40 percent. The selling price of the menu item would be $10.

$$\frac{\$4.00}{40\%} = \text{selling price}$$

The manager would then convert percent to decimal and divide.

$$\frac{\$4.00}{0.40} = \$10 \text{ selling price}$$

There is a second way the food cost percentage method is used to calculate the selling price. It uses a factor to calculate a selling price which yields the desired food cost percentage. The menu item's food cost is multiplied by the pricing factor to determine the selling price.

$$\text{Food Cost} \times \text{Pricing Factor} = \text{Selling Price}$$

The pricing factor is derived from the desired food cost percentage. The pricing factor is determined by dividing 100 percent by the desired food cost percentage.

$$\frac{100\%}{40\%} = 2.5 \text{ pricing factor}$$

If a menu item has a food cost of $4.00, the manager can use the pricing factor 2.5 to calculate a price that yields a 40 percent food cost.

$$\$4.00 \times 2.5 = \$10.00 \text{ selling price}$$

What if the manager then decides to lower the desired food cost percentage from 40 percent to 30 percent? The same process is used.

$$\frac{100\%}{30\%} = 3.33 \text{ pricing factor}$$

$$\$4.00 \times 3.33 = \$13.32 \text{ selling price}$$

To confirm that the food cost does indeed represent 30 percent of the selling price, the manager can perform the following check:

$$\frac{\$4.00}{\$13.32} \times 100 = 30\%$$

The disadvantage to using the food cost percentage method is that it only considers food cost in setting menu prices. Other factors—labor costs, overhead costs, or the market value of menu items—are not considered. *Market value* is the amount a customer is willing to pay for an item based on what other operations are charging.

Contribution Margin Method

When the contribution margin method is used to determine a menu item's selling price, factors in addition to its food cost are considered. The **contribution margin** of a menu item is the dollar amount remaining after the *variable costs* are subtracted from the selling price.

Selling Price – Variable Costs = Contribution Margin

Variable costs are those expenses that increase or decrease as the activity of a business increases or decreases. In the foodservice industry, variable costs include the costs of

- products—including food—that are used to produce a menu item
- labor expenses that increase and decrease with an operation's activity level
- materials and other supplies used in an operation's production and service areas

Fixed costs are expenses that do not change in proportion to the activity of a business. They cost the same amount regardless of the level of sales. Fixed costs include the expenses of

- rent
- insurance premiums
- property taxes
- management salaries

Semi-variable costs have elements of both fixed and variable costs.

When the contribution margin method is used, food cost, as well as everything else that is needed to produce and sell the menu item, is taken into consideration. The price chosen for the menu item must be high enough to make a contribution to the profit of the operation. It must also assist in covering the overhead of the operation. Put another way, the contribution margin is the amount available to pay for fixed costs and provide for any profit after variable costs have been paid. The higher the contribution margin, the more profit the operation will make. The desired contribution margin comes from the manager's assessment of the potential sales for the operation, fixed costs that must be paid, and the costs of items such as china and supplies.

Using the contribution margin method to determine the selling price of a menu item, an operator adds the desired contribution margin to the product cost.

Product Cost + Desired Contribution Margin = Selling Price

For example, the variable cost calculation for a menu item called the "Mexican Hamburger" is shown in **2-2.** The operator selling the Mexican hamburgers would need to price the hamburger at a level that

- recovers the $2.69 in variable costs to produce the hamburger
- contributes an appropriate amount for the operation's fixed costs
- makes a profit

Prime Cost Method

The prime cost method is similar to the food cost percentage method because it uses the cost of food in the calculation. However, it also includes the expenses of wages, employee benefits, and payroll taxes.

Prime Cost = Food Cost + Wages + Employee Benefits and Payroll Taxes

Returning to the example of the Mexican hamburger, the prime cost of the item is the cost of the recipe, plus the cost of the staff's time, and the cost of the benefits and payroll taxes paid. If the payroll cost to prepare, serve, and clean up after this dish

Menu Item: Mexican Hamburger			
	Component Cost		**Total**
Recipe Cost	Hamburger Patty	$0.43	
	Bun	$0.19	
	Fire Roasted Salsa	$0.03	
			$0.65
Payroll Cost	Cook	Time	10 minutes	
		Hourly wage	$10.00	
			$1.67
	Server	Time	3 minutes	
		Hourly wage	$3.50	
			$0.18
	Dishwasher	Time	1 minute	
		Hourly wage	$8.00	
			$0.13
Supply Cost	Wrapper	$0.02	
	Bag	$0.03	
	Napkin	$0.01	
			$0.06
TOTAL VARIABLE COST			**$2.69**

Figure 2-2. Contribution margin is the difference between sales and variable costs. Variable costs include food, labor, and supplies.

is $1.98, and employee benefits and taxes equal 20 percent of wages, or $0.40, then the prime cost would be calculated as follows:

Prime cost = $0.65 + $1.98 + $0.40 = $3.03

The prime cost is divided by the operation's prime cost percentage to arrive at a selling price for the hamburger.

$$\frac{\text{Prime Cost}}{\text{Prime Cost \%}} = \text{Selling Price}$$

In another example, suppose it costs $3.75 in food and $2.00 in wages to produce a salmon fillet. An additional 20 percent, or $0.40, is paid out in payroll taxes and employee benefits. If the operation uses a prime cost percentage of 50 percent for entrées, what is the selling price of the salmon using the prime cost method? First, the prime cost is determined using the formula given earlier:

Prime Cost = $3.75 + $2.00 + $0.40

Prime Cost = $6.15

Next, the prime cost is divided by the prime cost percentage to arrive at the selling price.

$$\text{Selling Price} = \frac{\$6.15}{0.50}$$

The selling price would be $12.30.

Texas Restaurant Association (TRA) Markup Method

Another method used for pricing menu items is the Texas Restaurant Association (TRA) markup method. This process takes into account labor expense, all other expenses excluding labor and food, and profit when assigning selling prices. This process basically takes the sum of the nonfood expenses plus the percent profit, and then subtracts that from the sales to arrive at the food cost percentage. Therefore, the amounts used in the TRA method are found in the operating budget, which is discussed in detail in another chapter. The steps in the process are as follows:

1. Express budgeted labor cost as a percent of budgeted sales.
2. Add up all other budgeted expenses (excluding food and labor) and express the sum as a percent of budgeted sales.
3. Express the budgeted profit as a percent of budgeted sales. Usually, this percent profit will vary based on the menu category. Common targets for percent profit are:
   - *appetizers:* 40%
   - *desserts:* 25%
   - *beverages:* 45%
   - *popular entrées:* 10 to 20%
   - *high-cost menu items:* 15%
   - *slower-moving entrées:* 20 to 25%
4. Add the percentages from steps 1 through 3, and subtract this sum from 100%. This number is the desired food cost percentage to use when calculating the selling price.

To calculate the selling price, the actual cost of ingredients used to produce the menu item is needed. This actual food cost is calculated during recipe development. Then the following formula is used to calculate the menu price:

$$\frac{\textbf{Actual Food Cost}}{\textbf{Desired Food Cost \% (in decimal format)}} = \textbf{Selling Price}$$

For example, suppose a menu item had the following costs:

Budgeted labor cost = 20%

Other budgeted expenses (excluding labor and food) = 45%

As a slower-moving entrée, the percent profit = 25%

45% + 20% + 25 % = 90% total cost without food

100% − 90% = 10% food cost percentage

If the actual food cost to produce the menu item is $1.50:

$$\frac{\$1.50}{0.10} = \$15.00 \text{ selling price}$$

Summary of Menu Pricing Methods

All four methods of determining the sale price are used in foodservice operations. The method used depends on the sophistication of the operation and the skill set of the manager or owner.

Food cost percentage is the most frequently used method. Most operators are taught this method early in their careers and stick to it. Many operators are taught to use 33 percent as the standard food cost percentage. Unfortunately, this does not take into consideration what price the market will bear for an item or the varying labor, supplies, and overhead required for different menu items. This method does not account for things such as food waste, or what an operation may throw away. It only considers raw food costs.

The contribution margin method assists the operator in getting closer to actual cost and profit requirements when considering selling price. As with the food cost percentage method, it does not account for the total cost and profit potential of all the items on the menu. It simply looks at one item at a time to determine its selling price. Also, this method can often result in operators failing to account for market value.

The prime-cost method is most frequently used by large chain restaurants and more sophisticated operators. This method requires adequate technology and processes to track financial data and compute the menu-pricing formula. The prime-cost method is a more complete means of determining prices. However, it does not account for the market value of a menu item.

In the end, an operator needs to look at each menu item separately and determine a price that seems reasonable. Applying a single pricing method or mark up to each item to return the same profit level may result in items being over- or underpriced compared with the competition. For example, if the cost to produce a hamburger is twice as much for Operator A as it is for similar operations, Operator A cannot price the burger at twice that of the competition. Customers would not pay the higher price. In this example, the operator's cost is excessive. An operator can only charge the typical market price for a hamburger.

Waste Not

Storm Water Pollution

When disposed of improperly, oil, grease, detergents, and degreasers can damage an operation's plumbing system and lead to costly repairs. If these materials flow into storm drains, they pollute rivers and groundwater. To properly dispose of these materials, foodservice operators should

- discard used washwater into the sewer system rather than floor drains
- use nontoxic cleaning products
- provide training to employees on proper spill cleanup
- cover dumpsters and waste containers to keep rainwater out
- replace or repair leaky dumpsters
- recycle oil and grease rather than pour it down the sink or floor drain

In some areas, local ordinances prohibit the release of waste into storm drains and health department inspectors monitor storm water pollution. Foodservice operators can contact their local health departments for additional resources and information on area regulations.

Marketing Techniques in Menu Pricing

The prices calculated using the methods discussed in the previous section are rarely the prices printed on the menu. For instance, it would be unusual to see a menu item priced at $12.30. Instead, one of several marketing techniques would likely be used to set the actual price. Marketing techniques focus on the message the price communicates to the customer, or the psychology of the selling price. The price influences the customer's perception of a menu item. The goal is to find the price that provides the operator with the highest profit, while remaining acceptable to the customer. Common marketing techniques include

- odd pricing
- even pricing
- promotional pricing
- 2.5-times price spread
- reference pricing

Odd Pricing

Odd pricing is a psychological marketing technique used in many industries, including the foodservice industry. Odd pricing is thought to create the illusion that an item costs less than it actually does. Using **odd pricing**, an operation assigns prices to its menu items that are just below even-dollar amounts. For example, an item may be priced at $6.95 instead of $7.00. Since people tend to round numbers down rather than up, customers would associate $6.95 with $6.00 rather than $7.00. With this in mind, many operators price menu items with numbers ending in *.25, .75, .95, .29, .59, .79,* and *.99.*

This technique is useful when an operator wants to increase a price. When the price is raised incrementally—from $8.75 to $8.85, for instance—the change is rarely detected by the customer. The customer will still view $8.85 as $8.00, just as the customer views $8.75 as $8.00. The operator gains an additional $0.10 per sale, while the customer views the price as unchanged.

Even Pricing

An operation using the **even-pricing** technique assigns prices ending in zero to menu items—such as $10.00, $9.50, or $22.50. Even pricing is frequently used to price entrée items. Where odd pricing conveys a bargain, even pricing conveys quality. If even pricing is used, it is important that the menu item lives up to customer expectations.

Promotional Pricing

An operation using the **promotional-pricing** technique temporarily offers menu items at discounted prices. This technique is used to entice customers to either purchase something new or to visit the operation during a slow day or time. Some restaurants use coupons or rebates for promotional pricing. Others discount menu items by a certain dollar amount or percentage, such as "$2.00 off" or "10 percent off." Another popular promotional technique is, "Buy one, and get one free."

Many casual-dining restaurants use a promotional-pricing technique that allows the customer to select items from three different menu categories for one set price. For instance, a customer may choose between two appetizers, three entrées, and two desserts for a total price of $15.99. This is often referred to as *bundling.*

Finally, some operations may use time-based promotions. *Early-bird specials* encourage customers to arrive before the busier, traditional mealtime. An early-bird special might be offered to attract customers to a restaurant between 4:00 p.m. and 5:00 p.m. when business is slower. Discount coupons can entice customers to patronize an establishment on a weeknight when volume is typically lower than on weekends. Finally, operations use the "limited time offer" technique to offer a new menu item or to give customers a special price on a current offering. The goal is to introduce an item or to increase sales. These are frequently advertised with table tents or menu inserts.

While promotional pricing is commonly used, a manager needs to ensure that the desired results are achieved. The goal of promotional pricing is to bring more guests into the operation. If sales revenue and profits do not increase, the promotional pricing initiative should be reevaluated or discontinued.

2.5-Times Price Spread

All of the prices on a menu must be within a range that consumers consider acceptable. According to the **2.5-times price spread** technique, the most expensive menu item should never be more than 2.5 times the cost of the least-expensive item. If a $0.79 hamburger is the lowest-priced item on a cafeteria menu, the highest-priced item should not exceed $1.98. If the lowest-priced entrée in an upscale restaurant is $16.00, the most expensive entrée should not exceed $40.00.

Reference Pricing

Most consumers compare prices when they shop for goods and services. They do the same when dining out. If the price for a menu item at Operation A is lower than the price for the same or a similar item at Operation B, the customer will perceive the former as a good value. However, the customer will expect the higher-priced item to be of better quality and the service to be superior. If an operation chooses to charge higher prices than comparable establishments, they should anticipate that customers may be more demanding.

Menu Descriptions

A menu description is a means of marketing an item to the customer. Well-written descriptions are enticing. The trick to writing them is to find the balance between too much and too little description. Menu-item descriptions were less important in the past. Consider two menus—one from the 1950s, **2-3,** and a contemporary menu, **2-4.** The 1950s menu simply states each menu item. The contemporary menu lists each menu item, along with a description of how it is prepared and with what ingredients. The following are a few suggestions for writing effective descriptions:

- *Ingredients.* Include only the primary ingredients, not the entire recipe.

Figure 2-3. This is an example of a typical menu from a foodservice establishment in the 1950s.
©Denise Kappa/Shutterstock

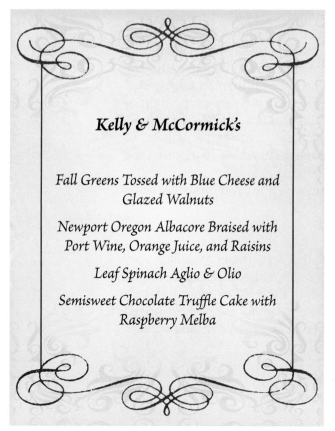

Figure 2-4. This is an example of a contemporary menu. Marketing has become a key component of any sale. A menu item needs a good description to "sell it" to the customer. ©kstudija/Shutterstock

Within the menu image:

Kelly & McCormick's

Fall Greens Tossed with Blue Cheese and Glazed Walnuts

Newport Oregon Albacore Braised with Port Wine, Orange Juice, and Raisins

Leaf Spinach Aglio & Olio

Semisweet Chocolate Truffle Cake with Raspberry Melba

- *Preparation.* State the preparation method used. For instance, a menu item can be listed as "braised tuna."
- *Portion.* Include portion sizes on cuts of meat, noting if the portion size is appropriate for sharing. For example, a menu may state that a filet mignon weighs 8 ounces or that the signature salad serves two.
- *Place of origin or unique story.* The origin of seafood is often important to a discerning customer. The knowledge that the salmon is from Alaska could cause a customer to select it over other menu items. Stating that it is "Copper River salmon," which is available only a few weeks each year, would be key information to provide.
- *Sides.* Including descriptions of side dishes that accompany entrées can enhance the overall menu description. Knowing what side dish accompanies an entrée may be the deciding factor for a customer choosing between menu items.
- *Protein focus.* Since proteins tend to be the highest-priced items, operators should ensure that they are described well to entice guests to purchase them. Besides stating the protein, the description should also give the following information, if applicable:
  - region of origin
  - cooking method used
  - sauces or added ingredients
  - any sides that will be served

For example a salmon entrée can be described as "Grilled Norwegian salmon in a lemon, buttered, dill sauce, served with sautéed spinach and fingerling potatoes." Menu descriptions make the menu come alive for the customer. Adding just the right words enhances the appeal of each item and allows the operator to command a higher price.

Truth-in-Menu Laws

In writing a menu, an operator must be sure the descriptions accurately reflect the items to be served. Truth-in-Menu laws require the menu description to accurately state the type, form, style, amount, method of preparation, and content of the menu item. For example, stating that a New York strip steak weighs 16 ounces, but serving a 12-ounce cut, is a violation of the Truth-in-Menu laws.

In addition, the Food and Drug Administration (FDA) regulates health claims made on and about products. This applies mostly to product labels, but can apply to menus. Stating that eating the "Bunless Burger" will lead to weight loss would be a false health claim and cannot appear on a menu.

Serving Customers with Food Allergies

More than 15 million Americans have food allergies. Eating or drinking something that triggers an allergic reaction can make them seriously ill. Some allergic reactions are fatal. Studies show that about half of food-allergy deaths involve people who consumed something served in a foodservice operation. Even minute amounts of an ingredient can trigger a serious reaction in some people.

Foodservice operations have been held liable by courts when customers became ill after being provided with incomplete or incorrect information about menu items. They have been held liable when allergens were introduced into food due to cross-contact between different foods. The cost of fighting a lawsuit or losing one can force an operation out of business. In some parts of the country, operators can be cited if they do not enact precautions.

"Welcoming Guests with Food Allergies" trains foodservice staff to safely prepare and serve food to guests who have food allergies. It can be downloaded free from the Food Allergy & Anaphylaxis Network (FAAN) website in either English or Spanish. It includes information about the following:

- foods that cause allergic reactions (90 percent of reactions in the United States are caused by peanuts, tree nuts, eggs, soy, fish, shellfish, milk, and wheat)
- what to do if a customer has an allergic reaction
- how to read ingredient labels to identify allergens
- how to create a food-allergy management plan

Other FAAN resources include posters, videos, slide presentations, and special tips for those who work in school cafeterias and hospitals.

Menu Layout Affects Sales

According to market researchers, the placement of items on a menu can significantly impact sales. People do not read menus—they scan them. Knowing which areas of a menu tend to draw a typical customer's eye, and placing key items in those areas, can generate more sales dollars.

By List

The first and last slots in a list of menu items receive the most attention. Placing high-profit or signature items in these locations is a good idea. The middle of a list receives the least attention. This is where labor-intensive or difficult-to-produce items can be placed. However, sometimes a high-profit or signature item must appear in the middle of the list. Attention can be drawn to it by boxing it or by using color or shading.

By Page

The inside menu pages receive the most attention from customers. The most popular items should be placed here. The back page is rarely viewed. Knowing that, many restaurants list beverages, children's menus, or desserts on the back of the menu. Some operations use the back as a separate menu. For example, restaurants that are open for all three meals may put the breakfast menu on the back.

One-Page Menu

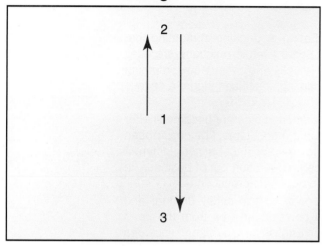

Two-Page Menu

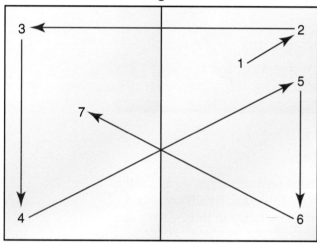

Three-Page Menu

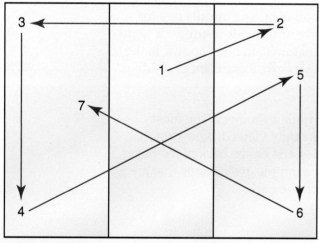

Figure 2-5. The customer's eyes are drawn to certain locations on a menu. Placing profitable items where the customer will look first is a great marketing technique. The numbers indicate the order in which a customer will read a one-page, two-page, or three-page menu.

By Number of Pages

The placement of featured and profitable items is determined by the number of pages in the menu, **2-5**. A Gallop poll found that, on average, people spend 109 seconds reading a menu. If the menu is several pages long, they tend to order from the first few pages, or from the pages they can scan through in 109 seconds. As a result, an operation should place popular items on the first few pages of a menu.

By Page Location

The placement of menu items on a page is important. Researchers have found that the eyes are drawn to certain locations on an open menu. On a two-panel menu, the eyes are drawn to the top right. On a three-panel menu, the eyes are drawn to the center. Therefore, the most profitable items should be placed in these locations. Attention can be drawn to other items by the use of borders, font changes, and the like.

Menu Engineering

In the previous section, you learned that profitable items should occupy the spaces on the menu that tend to draw a customer's eye. How do you know which items to place in these key locations? These decisions are made using *menu engineering*.

Menu engineering is a process that separates menu items into four classes based on their popularity and profitability. Popularity is determined by the number of sales a menu item generates. Profit is determined by subtracting the cost from the revenue generated from the sale of the item. Information about popularity and profitability is then used to grow sales and profit. The four classes used in menu engineering are called *stars*, *plow horses*, *puzzles*, and *dogs*, **2-6**.

Stars

Stars are menu items that are highly popular with customers and generate high profit margins. Stars should be placed in the most prominent areas on the menu. Since these items are popular and profitable, operators want to be sure that customers consistently select them.

Plow Horses

Plow horses are popular items that do not make as much money for the operation as some other items. Since customers like them, their prices can be gradually increased to make them more profitable. The operator should keep an eye on the ongoing popularity of a plow horse as its price is increased to ensure it remains a customer favorite. The item may have been popular due to its lower price.

Puzzles

Unlike a plow horse, a puzzle is a menu item that has a good profit margin, but is infrequently selected by customers. An operation can entice customers to try the item and possibly encourage repeat purchases. This can be done by decreasing the price. The reduced profitability may be offset by an increase in overall sales. A second strategy to increase sales is to offer a temporary discount or a promotion on the item.

Dogs

Dogs are menu items that are not popular or profitable. Dogs can be removed from a menu or tweaked to improve their ranking. The price of a dog can be adjusted to improve its profitability. The recipe or the ingredients can be changed to decrease the cost, effort, and time required to produce the item. Managers need to remember that it is the quality of the items on the menu that matters—not the quantity. They should not be afraid to delete dogs from a menu.

Ranking Menu Items

A menu evaluation form is used to rank menu items based on their popularity and profitability, **2-7**. Some operations also rank menu items according to the time it takes to prepare them and the difficulty of preparation. One menu evaluation form should be completed for each menu section—appetizers, entrées, and so forth. The following steps are used to complete the form.

Menu Planning		
Item Type	**Popularity**	**Profit Margin**
Star	High	High
Plow Horse	High	Low
Puzzle	Low	High
Dog	Low	Low

Figure 2-6. Understanding and evaluating a menu based on whether items are stars, plow horses, puzzles, or dogs, can help an operator make good menu revisions and increase sales.

Menu Evaluation Form							
Desserts							
Menu Item	**Popularity Points**	**Moneymaker Points**	**Total Points**	**Star**	**Puzzle**	**Plow Horse**	**Dog**
Chocolate Mousse Cake	3	2	5	X			
Cheese Cake	2	4	6			X	
Apple Pie	1	5	6			X	
Rice Pudding	4	3	7				X
Fruit Bowl	5	1	6		X		

Figure 2-7. This sample menu evaluation form ranks desserts according to their profitability. The lower an item's total points, the more profitable it is.

Step One. Determine Item Popularity

List all the items in the section being evaluated. Use sales levels to determine the popularity of each. Sales levels can be obtained in several ways—from point-of-sale software, by manual tallies of check request sheets, or by asking the waitstaff to tally items when they are ordered. Regardless of the method used, sales should be tracked over a period of time—as long as one year and not less than three months. The number "1" is placed next to the most-popular item. The number "2" is placed next to the second-most-popular item, and so forth until all items are ranked.

Step Two. Determine Item Profitability

Next, the Moneymaker column is completed based on the contribution each item makes to profit (sales minus expenses). The number "1" goes in the column next to the most-profitable item. This process is continued until all the items are ranked.

Step Three. Total Points

The points across each row are totaled. The manager determines which of the following classes each menu item falls into.

- *Stars:* Items with the lowest scores.
- *Puzzles:* Items that score between dogs and stars. These great moneymakers are easy to prepare, but may not be popular.
- *Plow horses:* Items that score between dogs and stars. They received good popularity points, but are not great moneymakers.
- *Dogs:* Items that rank in the top 10 percent (highest scores).

The goal is to maximize the number of stars on the menu, minimize the dogs, and tweak the puzzles and plow horses until they reach a good balance between popularity and profit. The manager can adjust the price or the recipe of a dog, puzzle, or plow horse to increase the overall profitability of the operation. Or a manager may choose to eliminate the least profitable items from the menu.

Menu engineering is an ongoing process. The menu will never be perfect and items may move between classes. Also, customers and trends may change. Each time the menu is adjusted, the balance of the four classes will change. Therefore, an operator should complete this process at least once a year.

Key Terms

menu	à la carte	odd pricing
standard menu	table d'hôte	even pricing
cycle menu	combination pricing	promotional pricing
market menu	contribution margin	2.5-times price spread
combination menu	variable costs	Truth-in-Menu laws
daypart	fixed costs	menu engineering

Recap

- The menu impacts every aspect of an operation—including food, labor, equipment, layout, ambiance, and profit.
- Different types of menus are used in foodservice operations.
- Menu ideas come from trade shows, manufacturers, distributors, customers, employees, and trade journals.
- Various methods are used to determine the price for a menu item that produces the greatest profitability without alienating customers.
- The contribution margin is the dollar amount left over after variable costs are subtracted from the selling price
- Marketing strategies focus on the message the price communicates to the customer.
- A well-written description of a menu item can entice customers to purchase it.
- Where items are placed on a menu can significantly impact sales.
- Menu engineering is the process used to determine the popularity and profitability of menu items, to rank them, and to use the information to grow sales and profit.

Review Questions

1. Briefly explain why the menu should be written before anything else is planned in a foodservice operation.
2. State how the menu affects the following aspects of the foodservice operation.
    A. equipment
    B. food
    C. storage
    D. brand or message
3. What menu substitutions would you make to this menu to create an attractive plate: baked white fish, white rice, corn, cheesecake?
4. Why is it important to offer some variety on the menu, even if the operation wishes to be known as a particular style of restaurant, such as a steakhouse?
5. What is a market menu?
6. Name five different sections of a menu.
7. Name three ways in which a menu may be communicated to a customer.
8. List three sources of menu ideas.
9. Explain the difference between à la carte and table d'hôte pricing.
10. If a menu item is priced at $7.99, what menu pricing marketing technique is being used? What message is the manager conveying about the item?

11. State where you would place a highly profitable menu item in a menu with the following number of pages:
    A. one page
    B. two pages
    C. three pages

12. Chicken parmesan is a plow-horse item on a restaurant's menu. Explain what that means and what steps a manager can take to improve its overall performance.

Applying Your Knowledge

13. A manager is given the following information about a menu item. Determine its selling price using the food cost percentage method.

    Food cost = $4.00
    Cost of labor to produce the menu item = $2.00
    Employee benefits and payroll taxes as a percentage of labor cost = 20%
    Food cost percentage = 45%
    Prime cost percentage = 55%

14. Using the information given in the previous exercise, determine the selling price of the menu item using the prime-cost method.

15. Given the following menu items, create descriptions to include on the menu:
    A. 14-ounce New York strip steak
    B. mashed potatoes
    C. vegetables

Exercise 2-16

Complete the following exercise on the companion website:
www.g-wlearning.com/culinaryarts/

16. Jaime, the owner of the Riverside Cove Restaurant, uses the Texas Restaurant Association (TRA) system to price menu items.
    A. Use the common targets for percent profit for various menu categories found in the chapter to determine the selling price for the following menu items:

Menu Category	Food Cost
Appetizer	$0.75
Dessert	$1.00
Beverage	$0.50

	Appetizer	Dessert	Beverage
Budgeted labor cost %	18	18	18
Other budgeted expenses % (excluding labor and food)	35	35	35
Profit % desired from menu item			
Food cost percentage desired			
Actual cost of item			
Sell price			

B. The Riverside Cove Restaurant is located in Springfield, a large bustling city. Jaime has plans to open a second location in the smaller suburban town of Middleburg. Jaime's market survey indicates that the citizens of Middleburg are not willing to pay the same prices as the Springfield customers. With this in mind, she realizes that menu prices must be adjusted while still generating a profit. The Springfield location's most popular entrée sells for $11.90 using a 50 percent prime cost. Using the prime cost method, what prime cost percentage must Jaime use if she wishes to lower the selling price by $1.50 at Middleburg?

	Springfield Entrée Price	Middleburg Entrée Price
Prime cost percentage	50%	
Food cost	$1.75	$1.75
Wages	$3.50	$3.50
Benefits percent	20%	20%
Sell price	$11.90	$10.40

C. Jaime determines that she must maintain a 50 percent prime cost, but believes she can reduce her costs due to wages at the Middleburg location. Find the amount that Jaime can spend on wages for this entrée if she wants to maintain a 50 percent prime cost and a $10.40 selling price.

	Springfield Entrée Price	Middleburg Entrée Price
Prime cost percentage	50%	50%
Food cost	$1.75	$1.75
Wages	$3.50	
Benefits percent	20%	20%
Sell price	$11.90	$10.40

Course Project

The Course Project is a full case study on controlling costs in a foodservice operation. Each chapter presents one component of the project. Refer to other completed components to answer the following questions.

17. Write a lunch menu for your foodservice establishment. Assume an average customer count of 200 for lunch. The menu should include the following items:
3 appetizers
4 entrées
5 side dishes
4 beverages
3 desserts
18. Design the menu layout and create a physical menu. Explain how the design reflects financial considerations.
19. Develop a recipe for one appetizer, one entrée, and one dessert. For each recipe, list the ingredients needed and determine the quantity of each ingredient needed to prepare 50 portions. Estimate the cost of each ingredient and cite the source for each estimate.
20. Price the three menu items using one of the pricing methods described. Name the menu pricing method used and provide your calculations.

Chapter 3

Cost Control in Purchasing, Receiving, Storage, and Inventory Management

Learning Outcomes

After studying this chapter, you will be able to

- explain the main purpose of purchasing.
- list the purchasing methods commonly used.
- describe the contents of a product specification.
- evaluate two similar food products using value analysis techniques.
- identify the main goals of receiving.
- describe general storage requirements, including food safety considerations in receiving and storage.
- explain the difference between a physical inventory and a perpetual inventory.
- calculate inventory turnover.

Food, and supplies to some extent, generate a large part of an operation's expenses. Food cost can account for 35 to 50 percent of the total expenses of some foodservice operations. The cost of supplies can make up an additional 10 percent of total expenses. Therefore, understanding and controlling the costs of food and supplies is critical to an operation's financial success. Decisions made to control food and supply costs may inadvertently affect labor costs. This chapter provides the foodservice manager with the skills necessary to control food and supply costs at the stages of purchasing, receiving, storage, and inventory control, **3-1**.

Purchasing

Once the menu is finalized, the foodservice manager purchases the food and supplies necessary to produce and serve the menu items. The manager's goals are to establish an efficient purchasing method and to buy each product at the lowest-possible price. The product must also be bought in the quantity and quality needed. Buying too much creates excess inventory and can result in financial loss. Buying too little can result in customer dissatisfaction and financial loss.

Purchasing Methods

Establishing an effective and efficient purchasing method is critical. All purchasing methods involve the supply chain. A **supply chain** is the coordinated system that moves products or services from the source to the customer. In foodservice, the chain begins with the source of the food or supply, such as a farm, and is followed by the manufacturer, distributor, and finally the foodservice operator.

A **vendor**, or *supplier*, is an entity that supplies goods or services to companies or consumers. A **distributor** is an entity that has agreements with one or more companies that allow it to offer and sell their products. In the past, supply chains were more segmented than they are today. Each type of food and supply category had a separate source or vendor. For example, a foodservice operation would buy from a dairy, a seafood house, a paper distributor, a beef seller, a bakery, and a produce company.

Today, foodservice operators have more options for purchasing. Supply chains have been streamlined and more *broad-line distributors* are used. A **broad-line distributor** is a type of distributor that has many clients which it supplies with a wide variety of goods. Also referred to as *broad-liners*, they offer and deliver most of the food and supply items an operator needs.

What Impacts Food and Supply Costs?

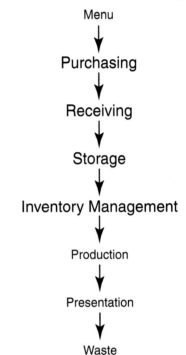

Figure 3-1. Once the menu is developed, food and supply costs can be impacted at each stage—from purchasing through inventory control.

Trend

Locally Sourced Foods

One of the hottest trends in foodservice is the growing popularity of locally sourced foods. Many operations buy some of their menu ingredients—usually seasonal produce such as fruits, vegetables, and herbs—from local farmers. There are also places that market themselves as farm-to-table restaurants. Their chefs and restaurant owners build close relationships with local farmers and learn how the food is grown. They often visit the farms to pick their own ingredients, which may be served to customers just hours later.

Locally grown produce can be picked at peak ripeness because it is not transported long distances. It is often more flavorful and nutritious than produce that must ripen in transit. For this reason, the demand for locally grown items is growing among consumers. Many of them shop at farmers markets themselves. Offering locally grown items on the menu also appeals to people who want to support local farmers, boost local economies, preserve farmland, and reduce pollution.

However, there are drawbacks. Relying on small local growers for menu ingredients can present challenges to foodservice operations, especially larger operations. Costs are often higher. Small growers cannot offer the discounts and lower prices of large food-growing operations and distributors. Chefs may not have time to visit farms and farmers markets as often as they would like. The availability and supply of items may fluctuate more than those of large-volume producers.

Foodservice operations weigh the advantages of buying locally against the disadvantages. More information can be found at the website of the Chefs Collaborative, a network of chefs who support sustainable cuisine. Resources include: "Five Tips for Managing Food Costs When Running a Sustainable Kitchen."

Purchasing methods commonly used in foodservice operations include the following:

- multiple sources of supply
- bid
- prime vendor or one-stop shop
- routine order

Each system offers advantages and disadvantages, **3-2**.

Multiple Sources of Supply

The multiple-sources-of-supply method is a combination of the multivendor method and the weekly bid method. Buyers using the **multivendor method** purchase items from a variety of vendors, usually by product type. There may be advantages to using a supplier that specializes in a product. For example, a company that only sells seafood might offer greater variety and expertise in this product line. Their products may be fresher than what a broad-liner can offer. The price difference varies based on the item.

Buyers using the **weekly bid method** obtain quotes, or bids, from a variety of suppliers for every item to be purchased. A **bid** is a request for prices for supplies, services, or contracts. This method is sometimes called the *spreadsheet method* because the buyer enters the price quotes into a spreadsheet. The vendor with the lowest price for that week wins the bid for the item.

The weekly bid method is demonstrated in **3-3**. In this example, vendor B receives the business for three items—tomatoes, potatoes, and ground beef. Vendor C receives the order for the lettuce and the tilapia, while vendor D receives the order for the green beans. Purchasing in this manner, the total cost for the order is $120.10. If the buyer chose to purchase from a single vendor, vendor B offers the best deal at $127.15

Purchasing Method	Advantages	Disadvantages
Multiple-Sources-of-Supply Method	• Lowest raw-food cost per item	• More time spent on ordering, receiving, and invoicing
Bid Method	• Potentially lower raw-food costs • Less time spent on weekly pricing	• Locked into price during price fluctuations • Limits ability to purchase alternative items from other vendors during contract
Prime-Vendor Method	• Obtain the best bottom-line price • Builds relationship with a single vendor • Minimal time spent on weekly orders • Opportunity to receive additional services from vendor at no or minimal cost • Vendor sales rep can offer more consultative services during sales call versus simply being an order taker and price negotiator	• Individual costs of raw-food items may be higher
Routine-Order Method	• Builds relationships with routine sales representatives	• More time spent on ordering, receiving, and invoicing

Figure 3-2. Foodservice operations use various purchasing systems. Each has advantages and disadvantages.

Item	Vendor A	Vendor B	Vendor C	Vendor D
Green beans, 6 #10 cans	$35.00	$27.00	$33.50	**$23.75**
Head lettuce, 12 count	$15.00	$18.00	**$14.95**	$19.00
Tomatoes, 75 count	$20.00	**$18.75**	$22.00	$20.50
Potatoes, 100 count	$15.00	**$14.90**	$16.50	$15.50
Ground beef, 10 pounds	$22.50	**$21.75**	$22.00	$23.00
Tilapia, 24 four-ounce servings, frozen	$27.00	$26.75	**$26.00**	$27.25
Total bid	$134.50	$127.15	$134.95	$129.00

Figure 3-3. The weekly bid or spreadsheet method is one way to determine from whom to purchase a product. Vendors bid on each item on a weekly basis. The operator places all bids on a spreadsheet and then determines who has the lowest price.

for the items. By using the multiple-sources-of-supply method, and buying items with the lowest prices, the operation saves $7.05. This savings is the main advantage cited by buyers who use this method.

There are some disadvantages to purchasing in this way. Soliciting prices from the various vendors takes more time than using a single vendor. Price quotes must be received, recorded, and analyzed. Then, the manager must decide which products to buy from which vendors and process the order for each one. After an order is received, an invoice is processed for payment. Finally, a check must be cut for payment and mailed to each vendor. All of these steps involve additional labor, not only in the order process, but also in the receiving and invoice payment steps. This cost is estimated at $100 per invoice.

Consider the example given in **3-3**. By purchasing each item from the lowest bidder for that item—instead of buying all the items from vendor B which had the lowest total bid—about 5.5 percent in food costs could be saved. This is calculated as follows:

Total lowest item bids = $23.75 + $14.95 + $18.75 + $14.90 + $21.75 + $26.00 = $120.10

Vendor B's lowest total bid = $127.15

$127.15 − $120.10 = $7.05 savings

$$\frac{\$7.05}{\$127.15} = 0.055, \text{ or } 5.5\%$$

If a buyer spends $1,000 to purchase food and supplies twice a week, at a total of $2,000, the buyer would save $110 per week in raw food costs.

$2,000 × 0.055 = $110 savings per week

However, six invoices would need to be processed each week using this method (two orders per week for three different vendors). At $100 per invoice, the cost to process these orders would be $600. This cost must be added to the food costs to determine the total cost.

Purchases per Week − 5.5% Savings + Cost to Process Orders = Total Cost

$2,000 − $110 + $600 = $2,490 total cost

If the buyer purchased all of the food items from vendor B, the total spent for the food items is greater, but only $200 is spent for invoice processing (two orders per week from one vendor).

$2,000 + $200 = $2,200 total cost

All costs must be evaluated when making purchase decisions. What first appeared to be a savings of $110, ended up being an increase of $290 ($2,490 − $2,200).

Bid

The **bid method** is similar to the multivendor method, but the price quotes are for a set period of time—usually 6 or 12 months. Vendors are asked to submit prices for the items the buyer wishes to purchase. Each vendor submits a bid and the buyer awards the business based on the results. The bid can be by item, by category (for example, canned fruits), or by total order. The buyer agrees to purchase the items from the vendor and the vendor agrees to hold the items at those prices for the length of the bid.

One advantage to using this method is that the process of locating vendors occurs less often. The buyer also has a good idea of how much will be spent on food and supplies during the period covered by the bid. A disadvantage of using the bid method is the cost of processing invoices when multiple vendors are awarded the business. Additionally, if the price of an item is bid as "firm," the price for the item over the course of the bid does not change. If a market price goes up, the buyer will benefit by paying a price lower than the market price. If a market price drops, the buyer will lose by having to pay a price greater than the market price.

Prime Vendor

Sometimes an operation negotiates and contracts with a broad-line supplier for the majority of the items it needs. This purchasing method is called the **prime vendor method**, or the *one-stop-shop method*. This supplier is referred to as a **prime vendor**. At least 80 percent of the operation's foodservice purchases are from the prime vendor.

Generally, a request for proposal (RFP) is submitted by the vendor to the buyer. The buyer may strictly stipulate what is included in the RFP, provide general guidelines to the vendor, or let the vendor determine the format and information submitted. The buyer may solicit RFPs from just one vendor or from multiple vendors. An RFP states the pricing program that will be used. A **pricing program** outlines what a vendor agrees to charge for various items over the course of the agreement.

Generally, prices are submitted as *fixed* or as *cost plus* by product category subgroup. A **fixed price** remains the same for a stated period of time. For example, a case of green beans containing six number 10 cans is priced at $25 per case for a period of six months. A **cost-plus price** is the total of the product's cost to the vendor plus a certain markup. For example, if a vendor pays $20 for a case of green beans and has an agreement with a buyer to charge cost plus 10 percent, the buyer will pay $22.

Vendor's Cost + (Markup % × Vendor's Cost) = Buyer's Cost

$20 + (0.10 × $20) = $22 buyer's cost

If the vendor's cost increases during that six months to $20.50 per case, the buyer then pays $22.55.

$20.50 + (0.10 × $20.50) = $22.55 buyer's cost

If the price of green beans decreases for the vendor, the price the buyer pays also decreases.

In addition to a pricing program, an RFP generally includes information such as services the vendor will provide, delivery days and times, credit terms, and order methods. Frequently, a vendor provides financial incentives in return for the guarantee of a level of business from the buyer. These incentives, which are often in the form of a rebate, are given to the buyer for increases in volume or delivery size, and quick payment. In other words, a vendor may entice a buyer to increase total purchases by offering a percentage rebate for an incremental increase in volume. For example, a vendor may offer a 1 percent rebate for an increase of $1,000 per delivery.

Once the RFP is presented, the operation determines if it wishes to enter into a contract with the vendor. If it does, a contract is signed and the prime vendor relationship begins. The prime vendor relationship allows the operator to spend less time and resources on weekly price negotiations. Instead, the operator can have the vendor assist him or her with business development, or show new products and services. In addition, quarterly or biannual business reviews can be conducted. This is an opportunity for the vendor and the operator to share issues and concerns and set goals and objectives for the next six to 12 months.

Routine Order

Many foodservice operations purchase food and supplies from vendors by calling in their order, providing their sales representatives with the order, or by using the vendor's ordering system (such as an Internet-based model). This purchasing method is called the *routine order method*. In the **routine order method**, the buyer tends to buy the same items week after week from the same vendor(s). A buyer may switch to another vendor if an issue arises with a vendor, an item, or a price. Also, another vendor can entice the buyer to switch by offering an item at a lower price.

The advantage of this method is that the buyer establishes a pattern of purchasing and becomes familiar with the vendor(s). Ordering is efficient if orders are placed using a direct-order-entry system (vendor-supplied software system). Although a vendor-buyer relationship can be established, it is not as strong as the relationship developed by buyers using the prime vendor method. Finally, the use of multiple vendors requires more labor and additional invoice processing.

Noncommercial Foodservice Purchasing

In the noncommercial foodservice industry, buyers use all of the purchasing methods discussed. The most common method used in healthcare foodservice (hospitals and nursing homes) is the prime-vendor method through a *group purchasing organization (GPO)*. A **group purchasing organization (GPO)** is a company that leverages the purchasing power of a group of businesses to obtain discounts from vendors. The GPO negotiates the contract for the facility and the facility receives guaranteed pricing and financial incentives based on its compliance to the contract. Common methods of purchasing for schools (K–12, colleges, and universities) and governmental operations (jails, prisons, senior meal programs) are the GPO and the prime vendor and bid methods.

Purchasing Specifications

The various methods used to purchase were described. Now it is time to explore how foodservice operations determine what food and supply items to buy. Once a menu is written and recipes developed, a shopping list of necessary food and supplies can be generated. One of the keys to successful purchasing is ensuring that the items ordered meet the specifications of the recipe and menu and are obtained at the lowest-possible cost. The foodservice operation needs to determine its expectations regarding product quality and how the product will be used on the menu.

For example, George's Grill offers a blue plate special each day. Thursday's blue plate special is
- grilled chicken breast
- mashed potatoes and gravy
- buttered green beans
- tossed salad with dressing
- banana cream pie
- coffee, tea, or milk

If George set up his operation correctly, each menu item has a *standardized recipe*. A standardized recipe is a set of instructions to produce a consistent food product—including the amounts of ingredients and the preparation method used. Standardized recipes are discussed in more detail in the chapter that covers production.

From the standard recipes, George knows which items are convenience items and which are to be prepared from scratch. A **convenience item** is a food that has been processed to some extent, which decreases preparation time. For example, the banana cream pie could be purchased already made, or George can purchase each ingredient in the recipe for the operation's baker to make the pie.

A standardized recipe includes the *specifications* for each food item, **3-4**. A **specification** is a written description of the requirements a product must have to be considered for purchase. For example, George's chicken recipe states that a six-ounce chicken breast is needed. When purchasing ingredients for this recipe, he needs to look for a six-ounce chicken breast from his vendor. The options for chicken breast offered by a vendor are listed in **3-5**. Of the 20 chicken-breast products available, five meet the six-ounce requirement for the recipe. George would need to review the specifications to determine which products are viable options. For instance, some of the chicken breasts are marinated, others are precooked. Does the recipe specify a certain type of chicken? What are the quality expectations of the operation and, more importantly, the customer? Finally, what is the price difference of the various products offered? All of these questions must be answered to determine which product will meet the needs of the recipe.

A food specification can include
- the name of the product or standard
- Federal grade, brand, or quality designation
- product condition
- product package
- the amount per container

Federal Grade, Brand, or Quality Designation

Not all products are of the same quality, even though they carry the same name. For example, canned green beans can vary significantly in quality. The quality level of an item is called its *grade*. The foodservice industry uses the U.S. grade standards established by the United States Department of Agriculture (USDA) to define the quality of canned green beans. A product carries a grade of A, B, or C, depending on factors such as uniformity, size, color, number of blemishes, and texture.

A can of U.S. Grade A green beans is of high quality, while a can of U.S. Grade C green beans contains beans that have blemishes and may be uneven in size. All grades are safe to consume. The manager needs to determine the level of quality required in the product, and weigh that against the cost of the item. For example, U.S. Grade C green beans may be acceptable for vegetable soup, but not appropriate as a vegetable for a catered banquet.

Product	Specification
Banana	100-125 count. Fruit shall be plump, firm, bright-colored, free from scars and bruises. There shall be no discolored skins (½ cup serving).
Beef patty	Beef U.S. Grade Good or Better, not to exceed 25 percent fat, 2.67 ounce patty, six patties per pound. No soy, meat by-products, binders, or extenders. Meat shall be free of bone, meets Institutional Meat Purchase Specification #1136.

Figure 3-4. Food specifications are used to define the item for purchase. They state such things as the quality, size, drain weight, color, and grade of the product and allow operators to compare equivalent items when purchasing a product.

Product Condition

Product condition states the form in which the product is desired. Canned, frozen, fresh, whole, sliced, and diced are examples of product condition. Green beans may be purchased whole, cut, fresh, frozen, or canned. The product specification needs to be clear so that the right green bean is delivered to the operation.

Product Package

Food comes packaged in a variety of ways. This section specifies a manager's expectations as to how the product will arrive. For example, green beans can come in cans, bags, boxes, or cases.

Amount per Container

This section answers the question of how much product will be contained in each purchase unit. Canned green beans are available in a #10 can. According to the industry standard, a #10 can weighs between 6 lbs. and 7 lbs. 5 oz., depending on the product contained in the can. When sold, the standard pack contains six #10 cans per case.

A specification for canned green beans may read: Canned green beans, Grade A, whole, ABC Food Company, six #10 cans per case.

Considering the Yield Percentage When Purchasing

Controlling food costs requires a manager to look at invoice costs, or prices charged by vendors. However, a product's invoice cost is often not the same as its "cost on the plate," or the cost of serving the product to the customer. To control food costs, a manager must consider cost on the plate, especially when purchasing meats and fresh produce.

The difference between the invoice cost and the plate cost is the result of the product's yield. For example, when ground beef is purchased in the raw state and cooked, the total weight decreases. The invoice cost of the ground beef has not changed even though there is less ground beef after cooking.

When purchasing raw meats and produce, buyers must use the as purchased (AP) quantity to obtain the needed edible portion (EP) quantity. **As purchased (AP)** refers to the amount of a product—expressed in weight or count—that a vendor delivers to a foodservice operation. **Edible portion (EP)** is the actual yield from a particular meat or produce item after losses from cooking and trimming. A **product yield percentage**, also known as a *yield conversion* or a *yield factor*, is used by buyers to calculate the AP quantity that must be purchased to obtain the needed EP quantity.

Item	Description
218540	CHIX BRST FLAT MRNTD 7Z 12#
159190	CHIX BRST FLAT MRNTD 6Z 12#
159200	CHIX BRST FLAT MRNTD 5Z 12#
159210	CHIX BRST FLAT MRNTD 4Z 12#
374780	CHIX BRST FLAT MRNTD 3Z 12#
606499	CHIX BRST FLAT MRNTD BROTH 28-6Z
606529	CHIX BRST FLAT BROTH DBL 28-6Z
850233	CHIX BRST FLAT MRNTD BROTH 32-5Z
509078	CHIX BRST FLAT MRNTD BROTH 40-4Z
708372	CHIX BRST T-PRSD ITAL 40-4Z
485756	CHIX BRST FLAT MRNTD BROTH 54-3Z
268851	CHIX BRST T-PRSD REDC SOD 54-3Z
453100	CHIX BRST T-PRSD DBL 48-8Z
191830	CHIX BRST T-PRSD 28-6Z
453110	CHIX BRST T-PRSD SUPER 28-6Z
268831	CHIX BRST T-PRSD 32-5Z
191840	CHIX BRST T-PRSD 40-4Z
453090	CHIX BRST T-PRSD 36-4.5Z
191820	CHIX BRST T-PRSD 54-3Z
357610	CHIX BRST RTC GRLL MARKS 32-5Z

Figure 3-5. Vendors offer many different items of the same product type. A manager cannot request "chicken breast" from the vendor, but must specify a product based on the quality, price, and customer expectations. This list provides options available from a vendor for chicken breast.
Courtesy of Gordon Food Service

$$\text{Product Yield \%} = \frac{\text{EP Weight}}{\text{AP Weight}} \times 100$$

Standardized yield percentage charts are published that help operations purchase the right AP quantity to produce a needed EP quantity. However, yield percentages can also be calculated by the operation. For instance, to calculate the product yield percentage for head lettuce, the lettuce is weighed before and after it is cleaned and trimmed. Suppose that the lettuce was purchased at $25.96 and weighed 22.25 pounds. After cleaning and trimming, it weighed 16.75 pounds. The product yield percentage would be calculated as follows:

$$\text{Product Yield \%} = \frac{16.75 \text{ lb.}}{22.25 \text{ lb.}}$$

$$\text{Product Yield \%} = 75\%$$

The buyer knows the amount per pound paid for the AP quantity, but must calculate the price per pound for the EP quantity, or the EP cost. The formula to calculate EP cost is

$$\frac{\text{AP Cost}}{\text{Product Yield \%}} = \text{EP Cost}$$

The cost per pound for the cleaned and trimmed lettuce could be calculated as follows:

$$\frac{\$25.96}{22.25 \text{ lb.}} = \$1.17 \text{ AP cost per lb.}$$

$$\frac{\$1.17}{0.75} = \$1.56 \text{ EP cost per lb.}$$

The cost for lettuce as it is served to the customer is actually $1.56 per pound. If the purchase price per pound ($1.17) were used to calculate food cost and price the menu item, the food cost would be inaccurate and the menu price would be too low.

Suppose the buyer could purchase lettuce that is already trimmed and cleaned for $1.59 per pound. If this price were compared to the purchase price per pound for the head lettuce, $1.17, it would seem high. However, it is close to the EP cost per pound of $1.56. By buying the lettuce that is already trimmed and cleaned, the operation would save further. In addition to EP cost, other factors such as quality, and water and labor costs must be considered.

Purchasing Quantities

Once a match is made between the product specification and the availability of the item from the vendor, the buyer must decide how much of the product to order.

Waste Not/Bookmark This

Produce Calculator

Almost 30 percent of the garbage generated by restaurants consists of food waste. Much of it results from inefficient purchasing methods, such as inflated estimates of the amount of produce needed for service. Excess produce often rots and is thrown away.

The Oklahoma Farm to School produce calculator is an online resource that enables foodservice managers to better estimate their produce needs. For instance, if fresh tomatoes are needed, a manager enters the number of meals being served into a spreadsheet. The calculator determines the amount of tomatoes to order. Managers also enter costing data to determine price per pound and price per serving. To learn more about the produce calculator, visit the Oklahoma Farm to School website.

Forecasting

If the product is a featured menu item, the buyer should have some data on which to base an estimate of the quantity needed. The operator can use historical data about the amounts previously produced, sold, and left over. Forecasting refers to the use of historical data to predict future trends, including future sales. Assuming that an operation will sell a similar amount of the item on a given day, the forecast can be used to determine the purchase quantity for the next delivery.

For example, say that George's Grill produced 30 servings of the grilled chicken for the Thursday special. Twenty servings were sold. Since the special runs every Thursday, George's buyer can anticipate that 20 servings will be sold on average each week. The buyer would forecast that at least 20 servings need to be purchased and prepared for the following Thursday's special.

However, if George wants to make sure adequate product is available for the special, his forecast will be slightly higher than the historical data. George may decide to purchase and produce 25 servings for the special the next Thursday. The process is repeated the following Thursday, leading to tighter and tighter control of the amount purchased and prepared.

Routine items, such as coffee, napkins, takeout containers, margarine, and orange juice, must also be ordered. Decisions about how much to order may involve the following considerations:

- How frequent are deliveries? What lead time is needed to order and receive items?
- How much storage space is available?
- What minimum amount of the product must be kept on hand? When an insufficient quantity of a product is kept on hand, it may run out before the next delivery.
- What maximum amount of the product does the operation want to keep on hand? Keeping too much inventory means money is used to purchase items not needed right away. This money could have been used for other things. This is often referred to as "having money tied up in inventory." An operation wants to minimize the money tied up in inventory. In addition, having too much product in inventory can lead to an increased risk of spoilage and theft.

Usage Method

Another approach to determining the amount to order is called the *usage method*. The **usage method** involves the following steps:

Step one: Manager determines the average amount of a product used per day.

Step two: Manager sets a minimum level to keep on hand and a maximum level that should not be exceeded.

Step three: Manager determines the **par level** or *par stock*. This is the level at which more of the product should be ordered.

Take purchasing green beans as an example. After studying the amount of green beans it uses, an operation finds it uses an average of two cans each day. The manager decides to have no less than six cans (one case) and no more than 30 cans in inventory at any given time. How many cans should be on the shelf before another order is made? In this example, assume that orders are placed every Tuesday for Wednesday delivery, and that on average, two cans are used each day. Therefore, from Wednesday of the first week until Tuesday of the following week, the operation will consume 14 cans of green beans.

- A total of 20 cans is required (6 cans minimum on hand + 14 cans used by the operation = 20 cans).

- Each case contains six cans.

$$\frac{20 \text{ cans}}{6 \text{ cans per case}} = 3.3 \text{ cases}$$

- Partial cases cannot be purchased (round 3.3 cases up to 4 cases). Therefore, when it is time to reorder on Tuesday, the order should be for four cases:

Value Analysis

Monitoring and controlling food and supply costs over time are important management functions. Conducting a *value analysis* is an excellent way to accomplish these tasks. A **value analysis** is a process that measures how well an item performs its job relative to its cost, **3-6**. It results in the selection of a product that is cost-effective, a good fit from a labor standpoint, and of a quality appropriate for recipes and expected by customers.

Some key areas that are evaluated for savings in a value analysis are

- the use of a vendor's private label item instead of a national brand
- pack size
- the grade of the product
- the use of value-added (labor-savings) items
- quality

The following is an example of a value analysis for the chicken breast on George's blue plate special. The vendor carries 14 chicken breast items ranging in size from 5 to 6 ounces. Eight of the options are marinated. The per-portion costs range from $0.47 to $0.95. If George offers the chicken blue plate special every Thursday and averages 25 sales per week, his value analysis of the highest and lowest cost options would be as follows:

Per Portion Cost × Sales per Week × Weeks per Year = Annual Cost

Highest-cost option

$0.95 per portion × 25 sales per week × 52 weeks per year = $1,235 annual cost

Lowest-cost option

$0.47 per portion × 25 sales per week × 52 weeks per year = $611 annual cost

$1,235 – $611 = $624 per year in savings

Using value analysis, George could save $624 annually by selecting the lowest-cost option.

Value Analysis Steps

1. Review top 50 purchased items by descending dollar amount with sales representative.
2. Consider list of alternative products provided by sales representative.
3. Compare the cost versus quality for the intended use of each alternative.
4. Sample new product(s) to determine if they meet operation's needs.
5. Determine the product that best meets needs for the price, and order accordingly.
6. Repeat the process, looking at the second 50 items; continue until all products have been reviewed.
7. Repeat this process on a semiannual basis.
8. Track and report savings for inclusion in monthly performance report.

Figure 3-6. Value analysis is an important tool to use in determining which products to purchase. Successful purchasing requires that a manager conduct a value analysis process on a semiannual basis.

Ideally, a value analysis occurs on an ongoing basis. The process is applied to all of the items an operation purchases. However, a value analysis is worthwhile even when conducted only twice per year. The next sections look at each key area in a value analysis using examples from George's blue plate special.

Private Label versus National Brand

The blue plate special uses green beans. Vendors often offer frozen green beans under their own private label. A private label item carried by the vendor may cost less than a national brand item, although it is equal in quality to the national brand product. It may even be the exact same product. In general, private labels give buyers opportunities to save money on food costs. However, buyers need to check the specifications of private label items. These products should meet or exceed what is desired for the intended use. Before buying private label green beans, George should compare its cost and quality with that of a national brand.

Pack Size

Frozen green beans come in a variety of pack sizes depending on the offerings of the manufacturer and the vendor. In this example, suppose frozen green beans come in two pack sizes:
- a bulk case that weighs 30 pounds
- a case of 12 bags, each weighing 2 pounds

In general, the larger an item's pack size, the less expensive it is per unit. Based on price alone, the 30-pound case should be the best deal for George's Grill. However, other things need to be considered. For example, how much freezer space is available and how long will it take to use the 30-pound case of green beans? Whatever George cannot use before it reaches the end of its shelf life will be lost. These questions need to be answered and evaluated as part of a value analysis.

Grade of Product

When ordering, foodservice managers need to consider grade, which is based on an item's intended use and customers' perception of their operation. For example, George's Grill is a mom-and-pop restaurant offering good food at economical prices. George does not need to purchase the highest-grade green beans for his blue plate special. However, the manager of a five-star, white-tablecloth restaurant will probably want the highest-grade green beans. The choices made by each manager are driven by customers' perceptions and expectations, which would be different at each establishment.

If George also uses green beans in his homemade vegetable soup for Friday's special, a lower grade is acceptable. George must decide if the same lower-grade green bean is acceptable to use for the Thursday and Friday specials. If the answer is yes, a larger pack size is a great option for George.

If George decides that only a higher-grade green bean is acceptable for plate presentation, he must make sure there is sufficient storage space for two grades of green beans. Lacking storage space, George's best option may be to buy a higher-grade green bean for both uses. Conducting a value analysis can help George make the best decision.

Value-Added Products

Value-added products are typically convenience items that are used to save labor. In general, the cost of a value-added product is higher than the cost of purchasing the ingredients and making it from scratch. However, this may no longer be the case when other factors are considered.

George should conduct a *make-or-buy analysis* for his operation. In other words, he needs to decide whether he should use value-added products in the blue plate special, or to make them from scratch. Mashed potatoes, gravy, tossed salad, and pie come as value-added products. Does George want to purchase potatoes that must be peeled, cooked, and mashed, or will an instant mashed-potato product be acceptable? In addition to the product cost, he must consider the amount of labor and skill needed, utility costs, and the perception of the customer. In another example, if George's Grill is famous for homemade pies, then purchasing frozen pies will not be an acceptable option.

Quality Review

The next step in a value analysis is to review the quality of the item being purchased to ensure it meets the needs of the operation. Before selecting a marinated chicken breast product from the nine options the vendor carries, George must assess how they differ in quality. Prices vary among the choices. The chicken products may differ in that they may be whole meat, processed, or tenderpressed. They can differ in the amount of marinade injected into the breasts.

Understanding the product specification requirements is critical. At this juncture, it may be helpful to conduct a *product cutting* in order to determine which item best meets the needs of the operation. In a **product cutting**, the vendor brings in the items per the buyer's specifications for evaluation. To be most effective, a cutting should be a blind study, meaning the items are not labeled in any way. In the case of the chicken breast, George would have nine different items to sample; each would be prepared to the recipe. He would rank the items in order of preference. In a blind comparison, the identities of the items are revealed after the ranking. The costs are reviewed and the best purchasing decision can be made. Once again, it is important to answer the question, "What is the best product given the application and the customer perception?"

Distributor Selection

Throughout this discussion on purchasing, several references have been made to a distributor. A final key step in the purchasing process is selecting a distributor. The following factors should be considered when choosing a distributor:

- distribution area
- delivery days and time options
- variety and quality of products
- in-stock ratio (includes accuracy of delivery)
- on-time delivery record
- order requirements (minimum-order size)
- method to place orders, such as Internet-based, direct-order-entry (DOE) system
- technology available and support provided
- extent of value-added services (nutritional information, food safety, in-service training for staff, educational opportunities, and so forth)
- willingness to form a strong working relationship based on commitment
- integrity (reputation) of the distributor
- payment terms
- regulatory compliance

In the end, the decision made should be based on the best interest of the operation—not on emotions, personal needs, or personal relationships.

Requisitions and Purchase Orders

Two forms are commonly used in the purchasing process—the requisition and the purchase order. A requisition form, which is initiated by a department or area of the operation, informs the purchasing department of the products needed and in what quantities. The purchasing department contacts vendors and buys the items requested.

A purchase order (PO) is the form used when the vendor is contacted for the purchase, **3-7**. It is a contract between the buyer and the seller. The PO contains the name and address of the vendor and the name and address of the buyer. It also indicates the item(s) requested, the quantity of each, the negotiated price, and the delivery and payment terms. Most important, the PO form has an assigned number which can be used to track the purchase from order, through delivery, and finally, through the payment process. As a means of control, no item should be received into an operation, or be paid for, without a PO.

George's Grill		**Purchase Order**	
200 State Street		PO Number: 1250	
City, State, Zip		Date: 3/30/20XX	
Phone Number			
E-mail Address			

Vendor:	**Ship To:**
ABC Distributor	George's Grill
100 Main Street	200 State Street
City, State, Zip	City, State, Zip

Purchaser	**Terms**
George Smith	30 days

ITEM #	DESCRIPTION	QTY	UNIT PRICE	TOTAL
123456	Tuna Ahi seared slcd vac-pk 32-3oz	2 cases	150.00	300.00
234567	spaghetti sauce 6-10	1 case	30.00	30.00
			Subtotal	$330.00
			Tax Rate	5%
			Tax	$16.50
			Other	
			Total	$346.50

Authorized Signature _____ Date _____

Figure 3-7. This is an example of a purchase order from George's Grill to ABC Distributor.

Receiving

After food and supplies are purchased, they will arrive in the operation's receiving area. Controls in the receiving area are essential for controlling costs in the operation. In an operation, receiving

- ensures all items ordered are received and that each item is complete
- verifies the items received are not damaged or compromised
- checks that the items received meet the stated specifications
- verifies the price on the invoice matches the price on the order

To properly carry out these functions, the receiving area must have qualified staff, necessary equipment, and receiving policies and procedures.

Qualified Staff

Competent, well-trained staff is essential for an effective and efficient receiving process. Each member of the receiving staff should possess

- an understanding of the ordering process
- basic computer skills
- the ability to understand food and supply specifications and to verify that delivered items meet ordered specifications
- the ability to read and interpret an invoice
- competence using equipment to weigh, measure, and count ordered supplies and measure temperatures
- organizational skills to maintain an efficient receiving dock
- knowledge of food safety and sanitation, **3-8**

In addition, receiving personnel should have the authority to reject items. Rejected items do not meet specifications, are damaged or unsafe, were not ordered, or are incorrectly priced.

Necessary Equipment

To ensure an efficient receiving process, the receiving area must be well-organized and properly equipped. There should be a location for the product-specification binder. The receiving area should include a worktable, scales for weighing items, thermometers to verify product temperatures, and the means of transporting products, such as carts, flatbed trucks, and dollies. Other helpful items include

- a computer
- identification charts showing various types of produce and cuts of meat
- weights and measures conversion charts
- a clipboard holding orders and the delivery schedule for the day
- a marker for labeling and dating items

Receiving Policies and Procedures

As with all areas of a foodservice operation, the manager needs to establish policies and procedures for receiving. These need to address the four main functions of receiving. In addition, the receiving area should have established hours of operation. If hours are not set, deliveries may arrive when the manager or trained receiving personnel are not available. Policies should address access to the receiving area, which should be limited to control the receiving and storage of items. This also helps control theft.

Food Safety and Sanitation Practices in Receiving

Delivery Truck

- Check the cleanliness of the truck.
- Inspect the truck for signs of rodent or insect activity.
- Randomly check entries in the temperature log of the truck.

Receiving Products

- Inspect all foods.
- Ensure that refrigeration and freezer space is available for anticipated deliveries.

Poultry

- Ensure there is no discoloration.
- Check that it is firm to the touch.
- Smell for abnormal odors.
- Should not be sticky.
- Check that the temperature is 41°F or below.

Fresh Meats

- Check that it is firm and elastic.
- Should be moist, not dry.
- Flesh should be red or pink; fat should be white.
- Check that the temperature is 41°F or below.

Fresh Fish

- Gills should be bright red and moist.
- Check that the flesh is firm.
- Check that the eyes are clear and bulging.
- Smell for "fishy" odor; should not be present.
- Check that the temperature is 41°F or below.

Produce

- Inspect for insect damage and excessive dirt.
- Look for rotting and discoloration.
- Ensure packaging is intact.
- Check for cross contamination from other products on the truck.

Milk

- Check that the delivery date is before the sell-by date.

Eggs

- Check that all eggs are clean and not cracked.
- Verify proper refrigeration temperature.

Frozen Foods

- Check for signs of thawing and refreezing (large ice crystals).
- Look for wet boxes.

Canned Goods

- Reject cans that are leaking, bulging, or severely crushed or rusted.
- Damaged cans are acceptable only if no fracture is seen in the seal.

Figure 3-8. All of the time and costs associated with a strong purchasing and receiving program can be undermined by inadequate food safety and sanitation practices. Following these basic tips is essential.

Policies and procedures also need to address
- the frequency with which the weight of delivered items should be verified
- the inspection of fresh produce for quality and quantity
- the verification of items against the order and product specifications
- the comparison of prices when ordering against the invoice
- the dating of items and inventory rotation
- credit procedures (discussed in the next section)

Credits

A credit is issued when a product received does not meet specifications or when an order is missing an item. This credit can be issued by the delivery driver or by the accounting department of the distributor. In either case, a credit memo should contain the name of the supplier, invoice number, date, delivery error, and amount of the credit. One copy of the credit memo should be sent to the supplier. One copy should be attached to the invoice for proper bill processing. A last copy should remain in the receiving area.

If an item or a shipment is rejected, the delivery person needs to be informed. Also, the explanation for rejecting the order should be noted on the invoice in language that is tactful, but firm. A credit memo or adjustment for the error should be received.

Technology has made credit procedures easier. Some vendors use wireless credit processing so the delivery person can immediately issue a live credit memo at delivery. It not only eliminates the possibility of a credit memo being lost, but also credits the operation's account immediately and decreases the dollars tied up in the billing process.

Security in the Receiving Area

Due to the volume of product processed by receiving, there are many opportunities for *theft* and *collusion*. Foodservice operators rely on the integrity of the vendor, the vendor's delivery person, and the receiving staff. What are some ways that theft and collusion can happen? Consider the following scenarios.

An employee opens a case of steaks to weigh them for verification of product specifications. Once the case is opened, he or she removes four steaks, places them in an empty box or a coat pocket, and takes them home. This is theft. **Theft** is defined as taking property, such as food, that does not belong to the person taking them.

Foodservice managers must also be concerned with collusion in the receiving area. **Collusion** is defined as a secret agreement or cooperation between people for purposes that are illegal or deceitful. Some common practices include
- falsely inflating prices and taking the difference in kickbacks
- delivering an ordered product to one location, but falsely indicating it was received at another location
- shorting a delivery at one location and selling the product to another establishment

Consider this scenario. The manager orders three cases of steaks. The driver delivers two cases and keeps one on the truck. The receiving person notes that three cases are received. The driver and the receiving person meet and split the case of steaks at a later time. The driver and the receiving person are in collusion. Another example of collusion occurs when a vendor and a manager agree to a higher cost. The operation is charged the higher cost. The vendor and the manager split the difference between the true cost and the inflated cost. The manager is receiving a kickback from the vendor.

How can collusion and theft be prevented? A foodservice manager should buy from reputable suppliers and hire employees with integrity. Beyond that, security cameras in the receiving area are a good deterrent. Also, the manager should conduct random walk-throughs to check the operation. Finally, a good system of checks and balances often catches illegal activity. For instance, items received should be verified against usage or sales. This is easily accomplished through the use of computerized foodservice management systems.

Storage

The food and supplies in an operation represent money and should be guarded. Proper, secure storage maintains the integrity of the products, discourages theft, and is critical to controlling costs. Types of storage for food and supplies include dry, frozen, and refrigerated. Supplies are generally stored in a dry-storage area. Consideration must be given to location, size, and layout for all types of storage areas.

Location

Storage areas should be located as close to the dock and receiving areas as possible. A location should be chosen that makes theft difficult. Storage should also be located near the production area to limit the number of steps necessary to retrieve products for preparation and service.

Size

Unfortunately, providing storage is often an afterthought in the layout and design of a kitchen. Nothing is more frustrating to a foodservice team than having inadequate space to properly store and rotate products. This makes it difficult for them to locate products when they are needed. To determine the necessary amount of space, a foodservice manager should consider the menu and the variety of items used, the number of meals served, and the desired frequency of deliveries.

The menu impacts the amount of storage space needed. An operation with a varied, frequently changing menu may need more storage space than an operation with a limited, unchanging selection. A menu largely based on convenience items, such as frozen entrées, requires more freezer space than a menu based on scratch cooking.

Several methods are commonly used to estimate storage needs. One method bases the amount of storage on the number of meals served. It gives consideration to whether the item to be stored is a dry good, or a good that needs refrigeration or freezing. For dry goods, this method uses a factor of 0.75 square foot per meal served.

Number of Meals Served × 0.75 Sq. Ft. = Estimated Storage Space Needed

Technology

Foodservice Software

Restaurants have a pre-tax profit margin averaging between four and six percent, according to the National Restaurant Association (NRA). With such a narrow margin, there is little room for inefficiency and waste. Foodservice software programs address key factors that impact the profit margin. They allow owners to

- manage food and beverage inventory
- reduce stock levels and food waste
- process accurate food and beverage orders
- detect vendor price increases
- calculate menu item and recipe costs
- evaluate menu profitability and adjust menu pricing

Many operations find foodservice software programs well worth the cost to purchase them.

For items that must be refrigerated or frozen, the method uses a factor of 1 to 2 cubic feet of refrigerator and freezer space per meal served.

Number of Meals Served × 1 (or 2) Cu. Ft. = Estimated Storage Space Needed

The second method bases storage requirements on the quantities of food and supplies needed to produce the operation's menu items for two weeks. This is determined by the manager. Storage requirements are then based on the space needed to store those quantities. This method may appear to be more accurate since it is based on the menu items needed to serve the average number of patrons. However, the amount of supplies to have on hand and the frequency of deliveries can change the square footage calculations. An operation located in a remote area, or one that wants to limit the number of deliveries per week, may need more storage space to stay adequately supplied between deliveries. An operation that tends to take advantage of lower prices by buying in larger quantities also needs more storage area.

Some foodservice managers believe that having too much storage space can be as costly as having too little. The more space available, the higher the utility costs to heat and cool the area. The greater the space, the more labor hours are required for cleaning. More space facilitates excess inventory which can lead to disorganization. A manager often cannot control the amount of space allocated for storage. Instead, the manager must match the menu needs and purchasing practices to the amount of space available to control food and supply costs.

Storage Guidelines

Storage areas should provide spaces where food and supplies are organized and easily accessible, but protected from contamination and spoilage. Storage guidelines should address labeling and rotation, shelving, spacing, climate control, and pest management.

Labeling and Rotation

To limit food spoilage, items should be labeled with a use-by or expiration date when they are received. They should then be stored using the practice known as *FIFO*. **First in, first out (FIFO)** is a storage method in which inventory is rotated as it is put away to ensure that the oldest products are used first. For example, two cases of green beans are ordered and received. When the green beans are taken to the storeroom, a case of green beans is already on the shelf. The two cases just received should be labeled and placed behind the existing case of green beans to ensure that the next green beans to be issued will be the oldest ones on the shelf.

Shelving

The basic equipment needed for storage is shelving. Adjustable shelving makes the best use of storage space by allowing for various configurations of shelving space and height. This accommodates a variety of box, packaging, and can sizes.

Specialty shelving is available for some products. Can racks hold cans on their sides and are angled to allow the cans to roll to the front. They decrease the amount of space required and allow for easy rotation of the product. If space is limited, an operation may invest in racks or shelving on rolling tracks. These shelves can be rolled together to increase floor space. When an item is needed, the shelves are rolled apart for access. Open shelving is often recommended to enhance air circulation around the food products.

Spacing and Organization

Spacing is key to storage efficiency and safety. Products should be spaced close enough to minimize the square footage used, but far enough apart to allow for proper rotation, ease of ordering, inventory control, and safety.

The best practice is to organize products by category. Items can be more easily located, which increases the efficiency of the order, delivery, and inventory processes. For example, all frozen vegetables can be placed in one area of the freezer, while frozen baked goods occupy another. The dry-storage area can be organized into sections for fruits, starches, vegetables, and condiments. Labeling each area is a great way to assist in product location.

Regulatory agencies require that food and supplies are stored away from walls and at least six inches off the floor. This spacing prevents any pests from accessing the supplies. It reduces the possibility of water damage due to minor drain backups or splashing during mopping. In some states, the height at which food and supply items can be stored is also regulated. Some states specify that products cannot be within 12 to 24 inches of the ceiling to ensure that sprinkler systems work properly in the event of fire.

Safe handling of food is another key consideration in product spacing and location. This is especially true in the refrigerated areas. For example, raw foods should be placed on bottom shelves to prevent them from dripping onto and contaminating ready-to-eat foods and other products.

Climate Control and Ventilation

All three types of storage—frozen, refrigerated, and dry—must have the proper temperature and ventilation controls. Humidity control is also a concern in the dry and refrigerated storage areas. Some operations pay a great deal of attention to refrigerator and freezer temperatures, but give little thought to the storeroom. High temperatures or large temperature fluctuations can reduce food quality and lead to early deterioration of items. This is why the labels on many products state that they should to be stored in a cool, dry place. Humidity is another consideration in the dry storage area, **3-9**.

A variety of issues may contribute to problems with humidity and temperature in a dry storage room. For example, heat from the kitchen can raise the humidity in the storage room. Kitchen equipment produces much heat during peak production times which can build up. If water pipes run through the ceiling, and if the kitchen and storage areas are not separate, the kitchen heat will warm the cold water running through the pipes. This can cause condensation, which raises the humidity level in the storage area. Closing the door to the storeroom can help isolate it from kitchen heat.

There are other reasons why temperatures can rise in storage areas. Condensers for the refrigerator and freezer are often located there. Since they give off heat, they can raise the temperature. Having windows in a storeroom may result in elevated temperatures. Replacing the windows with thermal glass allows for better temperature control.

Storerooms should be examined for temperature, ventilation, and humidity issues, and adjustments should be made when possible. One adjustment would be the installation of dehumidifiers to take moisture out of the air. Second, water pipes can be insulated to minimize direct contact between the pipes and the heat in the room. This prevents

Storage	Temperature	Humidity
Dry	50° to 70°F	50%–60%
Refrigerator	32° to 40°F	75%–85%
Freezer	−10° to 0°F	—

Figure 3-9. Using proper storage temperatures and humidity assists in preserving the quality, freshness, and safety of products. They are also regulated by the government.

condensation on pipes. Finally, there should be adequate ventilation to keep the storage area free of excessive heat, steam, condensation, smoke, and fumes.

Larger operations may have several refrigerators in the storage areas. They may use different refrigerator units for different food types so that each can be set at an ideal temperature for the food it stores. This allows for better temperature control, as well as ease in location and rotation of the products. Produce, meats, and dairy items should be separated and stored under separate refrigeration when possible. Each of these food types has temperature and humidity ranges that are optimal for maintaining quality and safety. However, most operations do not have this luxury. In most cases, food must be stored at temperatures that are within a reasonable range for the products.

Pest Control

Rodents, flies, roaches, and other pests can cause serious problems for a foodservice operation. They are best controlled by preventing their access to the operation; eliminating their sources of food, water, and shelter; and by hiring a pest control professional.

The foodservice staff should walk through the kitchen and storage areas looking for opportunities for pests to enter the operation. They should look for holes or small openings in the walls or floors, and small tears in the window screens. To maintain a pest-free environment, the operation should scrutinize its handling and storage of garbage. Garbage should be kept out of the storage areas. Many operations contract with reputable pest-control companies that offer expertise, preventive treatments, and routine inspections.

Inventory Control

Controlling inventory is a key function of foodservice management. Inventory control includes

- assuring that the fewest dollars necessary are tied up in inventory
- documenting the amount and value of inventory on hand
- monitoring slow-moving items
- monitoring inventory turns
- informing the buyer when inventory is low
- comparing inventory to actual product usage to determine proper control in the frequency of ordering to menu needs

Again, food and supplies sitting in storerooms, refrigerators, and freezers represent dollars. This valuable inventory needs to be closely monitored and managed. Taking an inventory on a routine basis allows foodservice managers to identify items that are not being used. These slow movers tie up dollars that can be better used for other operational needs. The identified slow mover should be removed from the menu going forward.

To operate effectively, managers must know the amount and value of inventory on hand. This information is needed for accurate financial reporting of the company's assets. It also enables food costs to be calculated during a period of time. The first step is to count the inventory currently on hand. This can be done using one of two inventory methods—physical or perpetual. Some operations use a combination of both methods.

Physical Inventory

When conducting a **physical inventory**, employees go into the storage areas and count all items on hand. In other words, they physically enter the storage areas and count box by box. Once this is completed, the value of inventory on hand can be calculated and the true food or supply cost determined.

Perpetual Inventory

Perpetual inventory is a system in which the inventory count is updated on a continuous basis. It is an accurate system. However, since it requires significant time and labor to manage, some foodservice operations do not use it. In perpetual inventory systems, a record is made of each item purchased. Each time the item is issued out of the storage area for use in production or for serving, the amount used is subtracted from the inventory. Some operations use a notecard tracking system. Each item is written on a notecard, and employees log changes on that card. Other operations use computerized systems so they always know the current value of their inventory. Even with a perpetual inventory system in place, random audits are necessary. An audit may involve selecting a number of items and tracking their routes through the receiving, storage, and production areas.

Although this system creates tighter controls, there are still opportunities for collusion and theft. For example, a receiving person can record that three cases of steaks were issued out to the cooks for preparation when two cases were actually sent. Errors can be made when harried employees fail to note items removed from inventory for use in production. Since no system is foolproof, operations must devise ways to monitor the system and to validate the true value of their inventory. Even with a perpetual system, some operations may require a complete physical inventory once a year.

Calculating Cost of Food Sold

Once an inventory is taken, a manager can determine the cost of food sold during a given time period. The cost of food sold is needed to calculate the food cost percentage and assess the operation's performance. The ending inventory amount from the previous time period is used as the beginning inventory amount. The cost of food sold during a time period is then calculated as follows:

(Beginning Inventory + Purchases) – Ending Inventory = Cost of Food Sold

Suppose that an operation has an ending inventory of $8,000 in April. During May, purchases totaling $9,000 were made. The manager performed an ending inventory on May 31 that was valued at $6,000. What was the cost of the food used during the month of May?

$8,000 + $9,000 = $17,000 cost of food available

$17,000 – $6,000 = $11,000 cost of food sold

The foodservice operation can use the cost of food sold information to calculate their food cost percentage for the period. If this operation had sales of $31,452 during May, what was their food cost percentage in May?

$$\frac{\text{Cost of Food Sold}}{\text{Sales}} \times 100 = \text{Food Cost \%}$$

$$\frac{\$11,000}{\$31,452} \times 100 = 35\% \text{ food cost}$$

Generally, a physical inventory should be taken every month to allow for monthly calculations of the cost of food sold. The last inventory of the fiscal year serves as the ending value for the year, a value required in financial statements for all businesses. To make completing a physical inventory easier, foodservice operations should

- conduct the inventory after business hours. This removes distractions and eliminates the chance of items being removed before being counted.
- use inventory teams of two people, one to count and one to verify and record the amounts.

- use an inventory sheet or other document that lists all items purchased.
- arrange the products on the inventory sheet in the same order of the storage areas.
- count each item by its unit of purchase. For example, if ground beef is purchased by the pound, it should be weighed during inventory. Once the inventory is completed, the manager should review the results. Any numbers that appear to be inaccurate should be questioned and double-checked.

Inventory Turnover

Operations use *inventory turnover*, or *inventory turn*, to measure how effectively they are managing inventory. **Inventory turnover** is the number of times an operation's inventory has been sold and replaced in a given period of time. It is important to turn the inventory to ensure that products are fresh. Also, maintaining an ideal number of turns ensures that excess dollars are not tied up in inventory.

The number of times the inventory turns over in a given time period varies depending on the menu and the operation. However, a typical commercial operation aims for 3 to 5 turns per month; sometimes more are desired. Noncommercial operations—such as hospitals and nursing homes—try to have 2½ to 3 turns per month. They are required to keep a sufficient supply of food on hand in case of emergencies. While these requirements vary by state and by operation type, a 3-day supply is typical. Commercial businesses can maintain tighter control (fewer days) because this requirement does not apply to them.

How are inventory turns calculated? First, the average inventory value must be determined.

$$\frac{\text{(Beginning Inventory Value + Ending Inventory Value)}}{2} = \text{Average Inventory Value}$$

Using the May inventory values from the earlier example, the average inventory value is calculated as follows:

$$\frac{(\$8,000 + \$6,000)}{2} = \$7,000 \text{ average inventory value}$$

To calculate inventory turns, the cost of food sold during the period is divided by the average inventory value.

$$\frac{\text{Cost of Food Sold}}{\text{Average Inventory Value}} = \text{Inventory Turns}$$

The cost of food sold was given as $11,000. The average inventory value was calculated to be $7,000. Inventory turns would be calculated as follows:

$$\frac{\$11,000}{\$7,000} = 1.57 \text{ inventory turns}$$

This is low given that a typical commercial operation tries to have three to five turns per month. An operation can turn the inventory faster by ordering less product at one time, or by increasing usage. Both methods cause the amount of food on hand to be used up faster. The amount of a product on hand is balanced against the amount of product the operation expects to use. Managing inventory is a balancing act.

Key Terms

supply chain	fixed price	usage method
vendor	cost-plus price	par level
distributor	routine order method	value analysis
broad-line distributor	group purchasing	value-added products
multivendor method	organization (GPO)	product cutting
weekly bid method	convenience item	theft
bid	specification	collusion
bid method	as purchased (AP)	first in, first out (FIFO)
prime vendor method	edible portion (EP)	physical inventory
prime vendor	product yield percentage	perpetual inventory
pricing program	forecasting	inventory turnover

Recap

- An efficient purchasing method allows an operator to buy products in the price, quality, and quantity necessary to produce menu items, without creating excess inventory.
- Foodservice buyers can use four different purchasing methods: multiple sources of supply, bid, prime vendor, and routine order.
- Value analysis is an eight-step process that should be completed on a biannual basis to determine how an item is performing.
- An efficient receiving system ensures that the items ordered are delivered at the correct price and specification.
- In storage, consideration must be given to location, layout, shelving, space, climate control and ventilation, pest control, and product rotation.
- Food safety begins in the receiving area.
- To operate effectively, managers must know the amount and value of inventory on hand.

Review Questions

1. Name four commonly used purchasing methods and briefly describe each.
2. List the advantages of the prime vendor purchasing method to the foodservice operation.
3. Explain the value of defining product specifications.
4. Why is it important to consider the yield percentage of an item when purchasing?
5. Compare forecasting and usage methods for determining purchase amounts.
6. Describe the steps in value analysis.
7. Name at least six things to consider when selecting a distributor.
8. Name the four functions of receiving.
9. State the types of storage and the temperature and humidity requirements of each.
10. Compare perpetual inventory and physical inventory.

Applying Your Knowledge

11. A 10-pound case of ground beef costs $17.00. It has an 80 percent yield percentage. A 10-pound case of ground sirloin costs $19.50. It has a 91 percent yield percentage. What is the most cost-effective item to purchase?

12. A restaurant serves 500 meals per day. How much footage should it allow for dry storage? Refrigerator/freezer storage?

13. An operation ends the month of January with an inventory value of $7,000. During the month of February, they purchase $12,000 in food. At the end of February, a physical inventory is taken. The result indicates that the inventory is valued at $5,000. What is the cost of the food used in February?

14. Refer to the following table to answer problems A–C:

Item	Vendor A	Vendor B	Vendor C	Vendor D
Green beans, six 10-pound cans	$35.00	$27.00	$33.50	$23.75
Head lettuce, 12 count	$15.00	$18.00	$14.95	$19.00
Tomatoes, 75 count	$20.00	$18.75	$22.00	$20.50
Potatoes, 100 count	$15.00	$14.90	$16.50	$15.50
Ground beef, one 10-pound package	$22.50	$21.75	$22.00	$23.00
Tilapia, 24 count, 4 ounces each, frozen	$27.00	$26.75	$26.00	$27.25
Total	$134.50	$127.15	$134.95	$129.00

A. If buyers use the multiple source of supply method, list the products they would buy from each vendor.

B. If buyers use the bid method, list the products they would buy from each vendor.

C. If buyers use the prime vendor method, which vendor would you assume they would use?

Exercise 3-15

Complete the following exercise on the companion website:
www.g-wlearning.com/culinaryarts/

15. Ben is the manager of Main Street Grill. The restaurant's owner, Brian, requires Ben to calculate and track his inventory turnovers on a monthly basis. Brian set a goal for Ben of 3.0 inventory turns per month.

A. Use the information in the following spreadsheet to calculate Ben's inventory turns for January through April.

	Jan	Feb	Mar	Apr
Beginning Inventory	$15,000			
Food Purchases for Month	$22,000	$17,000	$21,000	$19,000
Ending Inventory	$10,000	$8,500	$11,000	$10,500
Cost of Food Sold				
Inventory Turns				

B. Has Ben achieved the goal for number of inventory turns that Brian established?

C. What actions can Ben take to improve his inventory turns?

Course Project

The Course Project is a full case study on controlling costs in a foodservice operation. Each chapter presents one component of the project. Refer to other completed components to answer the following questions.

16. From the menu developed for the course project, list the items that must be purchased to produce the menu. Determine the number of vendors that will be used to buy these items and the reasoning behind the decision.

17. Select one entrée item from the menu. Write a product specification for the main ingredient.

18. Do a value analysis comparing two different products. Select the best one to meet the needs of the menu and the type of foodservice establishment.

Chapter 4

Cost Control from Production to Waste Management

Learning Outcomes

After studying this chapter, you will be able to

- describe the five most common types of production systems used in foodservice operations.
- describe the physical regions of a food production area.
- list the information contained in a standardized recipe.
- explain the roles of forecasting, production sheets, and standardized recipes in production control.
- describe how standard portion sizes are determined and implemented.
- explain the five serving styles used in foodservice operations.
- state and describe two areas of waste management.
- explain how food safety and sanitation can impact cost control.
- list three examples of supply related expenses and state how each can be controlled.

Managers of successful operations understand that cost-control efforts do not end when the preparation stage begins. Cost-control efforts are essential during the stages from production to waste management, **4-1**. During these stages, an operation's goals are to

- prepare and serve appealing, wholesome menu items
- produce menu items in consistent, planned portions
- produce menu items in the needed quantities
- use efficient production methods
- use an appropriate style of service
- generate minimal waste

Establishing controls in production, portioning, presentation and service, and waste management are critical to controlling costs. Following food safety and sanitation guidelines are also essential to preserve the quality of food supplies and menu items, and to minimize the risk of foodborne illness.

Production

Food production is the process of converting purchased foods into finished menu items to serve to the customer. Understanding production systems, food production areas, and production controls will aid the foodservice operator in controlling costs.

Production Systems

A **production system** refers to the type of operation that is used to produce the menu. Production systems can range greatly in size and complexity. The most common production systems include

- cook-serve
- cook-chill
- commissary
- ingredient room
- kitchenless

Cook-Serve

A *cook-serve* kitchen is the most common system used today. In a **cook-serve system**, the food is prepared from the raw state and served with minimal delay or hold time between preparation and presentation. This system is similar to the one used in most people's homes. Food is prepared for the scheduled daypart (breakfast, lunch, or dinner), served, and then cleared away. The kitchen is cleaned and readied for the next daypart. Most of the discussion in this book assumes a cook-serve environment.

Cook-Chill

In a **cook-chill system**, food is prepared on the premises, quickly cooled to a safe temperature, then packaged and refrigerated. This system is found in some large hospitals and foodservice environments that use a cycle menu and prepare large quantities of product at one time. Food may be plated and assembled in the chilled state on serving trays. A tray may include foods that need to be reheated as well as foods that are served chilled. Before reheating, the chilled foods are either removed from the tray or wrapped to protect it from heat. The entire tray is then heated until the menu items are brought to the desired serving temperature while the cold food items remain at refrigerated temperatures. In other operations, the food items are delivered in bulk to an alternate location while still chilled. Once the food arrives at its destination, it is reheated and served.

Commissary

A *commissary* can use either cook-serve or cook-chill. In a **commissary** setting, the food is prepared in mass quantities and delivered to various locations for service. Food is delivered in individual packages, assembled meal trays, or in bulk for heating and assembly at the alternate location. Operations that use this system include school systems, large colleges and universities, hospitals with multiple sites, vending services, and concessions.

What Impacts Food and Supply Costs?

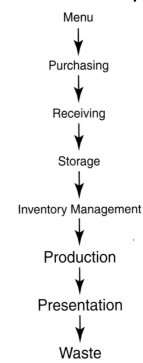

Menu
↓
Purchasing
↓
Receiving
↓
Storage
↓
Inventory Management
↓
Production
↓
Presentation
↓
Waste

Figure 4-1. This illustrates the path that food and supplies take through a typical foodservice operation.

Ingredient Room

Ingredient-room systems were once common, especially in the hospital setting. An **ingredient room** is an area in the kitchen where employees weigh and measure all of the ingredients for the recipes to be produced that day or the next. The cook obtains the pre-weighed and assembled ingredients needed to prepare the day's menu items.

Kitchenless

A *kitchenless system* is a convenience operation. In the **kitchenless system**, food is purchased in a prepared state from an outside source. The kitchenless kitchen simply serves the meals as delivered, or assembles and serves the meals to its customers. Basically, no food production occurs. Senior centers serving congregate meals and some school systems may use this system. Foodservice operations undergoing renovation may take this approach as well.

Figure **4-2** summarizes a few advantages and disadvantages of these production systems. Although they all offer opportunities to control costs, the cost savings are generated in different areas. To determine the best system for cost control, a manager must understand the needs of the operation and the environment in which it operates.

For example, if the operation has ready access to labor and the wages in the region are reasonable, a cook-serve operation may be the best option. This system requires more labor to produce and serve meals and to clean and sanitize the kitchen and dining areas following each meal service. However, in an area where labor is expensive or difficult to find, a kitchenless or mass-production system—such as cook-chill or commissary—may be preferable. These systems enable the operation to serve meals with minimal or streamlined labor. Food costs will be higher in the kitchenless system. Ultimately, the operation must select the production method that allows it to produce and serve meals at the desired quality and the least cost. The cost of food must be balanced against the cost of labor.

Trend

Mobile Food Trucks

Food trucks, mobile units that sell food, are hot, according to the National Restaurant Association. Until recently, they were most commonly found in large cities such as Los Angeles and New York City. Now they can also be found parked alongside sidewalks in rural areas and on college campuses.

Many food trucks contain standard kitchen equipment including refrigerators, freezers, fryers, ovens, and griddles. This allows operators to prepare food onsite. Other trucks sell food that is produced in commercial kitchens, and then loaded onto the trucks for distribution. Some restaurant owners are even taking their menus on the road to expand their business.

Food truck fare is not limited to meals of hot dogs, chips, and soda. Chefs and entrepreneurs are delivering affordable, gourmet food. These offerings include ethnic fare such as Austrian schnitzel, Indian parathas, and Mexican tamales. Some operators are selling unique grilled cheeses, organic vegan choices, and specialty desserts.

Food trucks are popular with consumers because they provide convenient, inexpensive food choices. They are popular with entrepreneurs because they cost less to open and operate than brick-and-mortar restaurants and because of lower labor costs. However, operators must follow government regulations and obtain the appropriate licenses to operate a food business in their state.

Advantages and Disadvantages of Production Systems		
Production System	**Advantages**	**Disadvantages**
Cook-Serve	Perception of fresh food	Skilled labor is required for all meal production times
		Kitchen experiences peaks and valleys in activity levels based on mealtimes
Cook-Chill	One work shift for production each day	Equipment is costly, requiring large amounts of capital dollars
	May decrease labor	Quality of some menu items may suffer due to the chill and rethermalization process
	One-meal cleanup	
Commissary	Similar to cook-serve or cook-chill, depending on system used	Similar to cook-serve or cook-chill, depending on system used
	Minimal equipment and skilled labor needed at alternate sites	Inflexibility at alternate sites
		Food quality may decrease during transfer
Ingredient Room	Strict adherence to standardized recipes	Additional space and storage requirements
	Consistent products	May require additional labor for recipe assembly
		Availability of quality convenience products decreases need for "from scratch" recipes
Kitchenless	Minimal labor	High food costs
	Minimal skilled labor	Less flexibility with menu
	Simplified purchasing	Products may be unavailable
	Limited inventory	Less variety
	Minimal equipment	High refrigeration and freezer needs

Figure 4-2. Foodservice operations produce food using a variety of production methods. This chart lists the different types of production systems along with their advantages and disadvantages.

Food Production Areas

The food production area, which consumes a large part of the kitchen, is where the food and recipes are prepared. The design of the area determines what happens where. A well-designed area helps an operation control costs because the menu can be prepared with the greatest efficiency. On the other hand, a poorly designed food production area results in inefficiency and higher costs. The production area is typically divided into sections or physical regions. Each section serves a particular function based on the needs of the operation. These needs include the

- types of food or menu items produced
- operation's size
- menu's complexity

The organization of the food production area ranges from simple to elaborate. In a simplified system, the area is partitioned into three regions—hot food production, cold food production, and beverages. In an elaborate system, the hot food production area may be further divided into separate areas for pre-preparation, entrées, and vegetables. The cold food area may be divided into separate production areas for salads, sandwiches, and dessert or bakery items.

An advantage to dividing up the production area is that the equipment and supplies necessary to produce like items can be conveniently located for the production staff. A disadvantage is that some equipment may need to be duplicated in separate production areas. For example, both hot food and cold food production require a slicer and mixer to produce their respective recipes.

The key to controlling costs in production area design is to ensure that the setup provides the greatest efficiency in the preparation of the menu. The design will mostly depend on the size of the operation and the type of menu produced. The menu should drive everything—from production-area setup, to equipment selection, to labor used. A review of the menu is the best place to start.

For each meal, the operator should determine

- what equipment is needed
- which staff will use the equipment
- how often the equipment will be used

For example, is it more efficient to have two slicers—one in the hot food preparation area and one in the cold food preparation area—or will one slicer suffice? No one kitchen design is right for all operations. The foodservice manager is responsible for ensuring that the production area is efficiently run on a daily basis so that the menu is produced and ready for service in a timely manner.

Production Controls

Strong control systems must be in place to control costs during food production. Foodservice operations that lack production controls, or do not enforce them, will experience increasing costs and decreasing profits. Essential tools for production control include standardized recipes, forecasting, and production sheets.

Standardized Recipes

Effective and efficient foodservice operations develop and use standardized recipes. A **standardized recipe** is a set of instructions to produce a consistent food product—including the amounts of the ingredients used and the preparation method necessary, **4-3**. When a standardized recipe is used, each product prepared using that recipe should be consistent as to taste, yield, quality, cost, and nutrition. Menu items can be prepared with less supervision. The over- or underproduction of menu items is less likely. Menu items are prepared with standardized amounts and with specifications for food items to be purchased. How does a standardized recipe assist in controlling food costs? Consider the following scenarios.

Scenario One: Catherine hires a new chef. For three consecutive days, he decides to jazz up the Basil-Buttered Salmon by adding a little of "this and that" to the recipe. What are some possible results? The food cost of the item increases with each added ingredient, but the selling price remains the same. The chef utilizes ingredients that were purchased for other purposes, requiring the buyer to scramble at the last minute for additional items. The menu item on day two is too spicy for the customers and many send it back to the kitchen and refuse to pay for it. They state, "This is not the same salmon that I had the last time I was here."

```
┌──────────────────────────────────────────────────────────────────────┐
│                        Standardized Recipe                             │
│ Basil-Buttered Salmon Steaks                                           │
├─────────────────────────┬────────────────────────┬────────────────────┤
│                         │                        │ Yield: 4-24 oz.    │
│ Cooking Time: 7 minutes │ Oven Temp: 500°F       │ Portions: 4-6 oz.  │
└─────────────────────────┴────────────────────────┴────────────────────┘
```

Ingredients & Instructions

Coho salmon fillet	4-6 oz. fillet
Bulk salted butter	1½ oz.
Basil leaf	1 Tbsp.
Parsley Ital fresh	1 Tbsp.
100% lemon juice	2 tsp.

Wash hands.
Soften butter.
Mix together basil, parsley, butter, and lemon juice.
Place salmon on broiler rack.
Lightly brush with spice mixture.
Broil 4 inches from heat for 4 minutes.
Turn salmon.
Brush side with spice mixture.
Return to broiler. Broil about 3 minutes, or until internal temperature reaches 145°F.

Figure 4-3. Standardized recipes ensure a consistent product, both in quality and price, is made each time. This is an example of a standardized recipe for basil-buttered salmon steaks. *Courtesy of Gordon Food Service*

Scenario Two: Catherine's Café had the same chef for five years. She never used a recipe; she just "knew" how to prepare all the items, and did so fairly consistently. The chef developed a health problem and was unable to work for a period of time. The operation's manager did not have recipes to duplicate the chef's products. Food waste and customer complaints result.

If both chefs had used standardized recipes, problems could have been avoided. A standardized recipe should include the following:

- recipe name
- recipe number for indexing
- yield or number of portions
- portion size
- portion utensil, pan size, or equipment used, if necessary
- ingredients
- amount of each ingredient needed
- preparation instructions
- date the recipe was tested or revised

Determining Ingredient Amounts

Before the portion cost and the menu price can be determined, the manager needs to ensure that the cost of each ingredient is appropriately determined. The manager needs to consider the form in which each ingredient was purchased. The form of the ingredient will impact the recipe, the standardization of it, and then the yield. Put another way, the form will impact the amount of the ingredient needed for the recipe, and in turn, the portion cost. Three methods are used to determine the ingredient amount used—cost per unit, the yield test, and cooking loss.

Cost per Unit

Cost per unit is used when the item is purchased and served as is. For example, an apple pie purchased already prepared and baked, is ready to serve once it is cut into serving sizes. To determine the portion cost, the purchase cost is simply divided by the number of servings.

$$\frac{\text{Purchase Unit Cost}}{\text{Number of Units}} = \text{Cost per Unit}$$

Using an apple pie as an example, if the cost to purchase the pie is $10, and the pie will be cut into eight slices, the cost per slice is:

$$\frac{\$10}{8 \text{ slices}} = \$1.25 \text{ per slice}$$

Yield Test

The yield test is used when an item is purchased in its raw form and will need to be trimmed before it can be used in a recipe. This is commonly the case for fresh fruits and vegetables. For instance, suppose an apple pie recipe calls for fresh apples. The apples need to be peeled, cored, and sliced before they are used in the recipe. The weight of the peel and the core—which are considered food waste—needs to be considered prior to costing out the recipe. In the yield test, the raw portion (the whole apple) is broken down into the edible portion (the apple slices) and the waste portion (the peel and core). The result is the edible yield available. If raw apples have an edible yield of 75 percent, then for every pound (16 ounces) purchased, only 75 percent of that pound, or 12 ounces, is usable in the recipe.

Cooking Loss

The cooking loss test is similar to the yield test, except it is used for products that lose edible portion due to cooking. This is very common in meats. For example, suppose a taco recipe calls for 10 pounds of cooked ground beef. How much fresh ground beef should the operator purchase to have enough cooked ground beef for the recipe? Tables giving standard yields for meats and other foods can help managers calculate a product's yield after cooking loss. These tables can be found on government websites, such as that of the US Department of Agriculture (USDA), and in many cooking books. If a standard-yield table states that one pound of fresh ground beef yields 69 percent cooked ground beef, then the operator can use the formula to figure out how much ground beef to purchase. The following formula is used:

$$\text{Product Yield \%} = \frac{\text{EP Weight}}{\text{AP Weight}}$$

$$69\% = \frac{10 \text{ lbs. (EP weight)}}{x \text{ (AP weight)}}$$

$$0.69x = 10 \text{ lbs.}$$

$$x = 14.49 \text{ lbs. (round to 14.5 lbs.)}$$

The operator would need to purchase 14.5 pounds of the ground beef if the recipe calls for 10 pounds. If the cost per pound of the ground beef is $3.00, then the ingredient cost for the 10 pounds of cooked ground beef is $43.50—not $30.00. This will impact the final cost of the tacos and the selling price that is needed for the item to be profitable.

There are several sources of standardized recipes. Many operators use existing standardized recipes as the basis for their own recipes. They modify them to suit their operation's image, level of quality, and uniqueness. The right recipe for an operation meets its product cost and quality requirements and can be produced with the labor and equipment available.

To develop a standardized recipe, a foodservice manager needs to

1. decide what ingredients will be used
2. develop the specifications for the ingredients and how they are to be assembled
3. specify the best cooking method to achieve the desired result
4. test the recipe and adjust it if necessary until the desired taste and quality requirements are met
5. calculate the cost to make the recipe, once it is final, so a menu price can be determined

A key to successful management of the production area includes ensuring that standardized recipes are readily available in the kitchen. Another key is ensuring that the right equipment—such as measuring tools and scales—are available for use. This will be discussed later in the chapter. Finally, the staff must know how to use the recipes and equipment.

Forecasting

Proper forecasting is essential for both food purchasing and production control. Forecasting is used to determine the amount of a particular menu item to produce based on historical data. When done well, forecasting results in minimal over- or underproduction of food. The chance of running out of menu items early in a meal service—which can drive down customer satisfaction—is less likely to occur. By curtailing the overproduction of food, forecasting can reduce leftovers. Food waste contributes to higher food costs.

In institutional settings where the menus are cyclical and the customer count is steady, forecasting the amount to produce can be done after one or two menu cycles. For instance, suppose a nursing home uses a four-week menu cycle and serves 100 residents each day. On Monday of the first week, meatloaf is the entrée. Based on the initial forecast, the kitchen prepares 110 servings of meatloaf. After the meal, 20 servings remain. Some residents either chose not to eat the meatloaf or were not at the nursing home that day. The manager records this information.

Four weeks later, when the meatloaf is served again, the manager will forecast the amount of meatloaf to serve. This estimate will be based on the amounts produced and served four weeks ago (110 servings produced and 90 servings used). Twenty extra servings were produced. The manager may consider forecasting 90 servings this cycle. However, to avoid running out of the meatloaf, an estimate of 95 servings may be better, allowing for a slight pad to the amount used last cycle. After meatloaf is served for the second time, the manager once again compares the amount produced to the amount remaining to further refine the amount to forecast for the following cycle.

Unlike an institutional setting, a typical restaurant forecast requires a daily review of the number of menu items produced and served. While the menu may stay the same from day-to-day, the number of customers varies. However, by maintaining accurate records, the manager can continually refine the amount to produce until an acceptable ratio of production to leftovers is achieved. Fortunately, computer software can track usage and forecast amounts to produce.

Production Sheets

Production sheets are the road maps for the food production area. A **production sheet** is a form used to communicate to production staff. It lists the types and amounts of food items to produce for each meal. A production sheet should include the following:

- day and date
- meal or daypart (breakfast, lunch, dinner)
- total meals served
- name of each menu item
  - forecasted amount to produce
  - amount actually prepared
  - amount left over
  - amount served or sold
  - percentage the menu item represents of the total meals served
  - discrepancy (difference between the amount sold plus the leftovers, to the amount produced)
  - comments

For instance, Catherine's Café is a small French restaurant that serves a limited menu for lunch. Catherine forecasts the amount of each menu item she would like to produce for Tuesday, June 20th, and prepares a production sheet, **4-4**. The cooks prepare the menu items and note how many servings are produced on the production sheet. Following the meal service, the quantity of each item served is recorded. The cook can simply total up the amount served of each menu item. The number can also be obtained from a software program that records the number of each menu item sold through the cash register system. In addition, the amount left over, the discrepancy, and any explanation of the discrepancy are noted. Finally, the quantity of each item served is recorded as a percentage of the total number of meals served.

Catherine can use the completed production sheet to improve her lunch production for the next service. First, she should verify that the cooks served the proper portion size for the casserole to determine the cause for the leftovers and the discrepancy. Additionally, she must learn the reason for the burned salmon cakes. Is there a problem with the oven? Was it due to the cook's error? Should the cooking time on the recipe be adjusted? Next, she should consider increasing the number of Asian Flank Steak to prepare to 70 or 75 servings. Finally, Catherine should determine why the cooks overproduced the shrimp and the pork. Possible reasons could be the recipe, the size of the roast, or an error by the cook.

Portion Control

The production staff and manager work to control costs during the production process. After production, food is ready to be plated for service. Ensuring that the correct portion is served is the critical next step in cost control. Therefore, a strong portion control system needs to be in place. **Portion control** is the process of ensuring that the amount of food in a serving of a menu item is equivalent to the amount of food specified in the standardized recipe. If a recipe for Basil-Buttered Salmon Steaks produces four six-ounce servings, the operation must ensure that only six-ounce portions are produced—no more, no less.

Day and Date: Tuesday 06/20/20XX

Meal: Lunch

Total meals served: 261

Menu Item	Forecast	Prepared	Leftover	Served	Percent of Total Meals Served	Discrepancy	Comments
Artichoke Spinach Casserole with Chicken	75	75	7	63	24.14	5	
Baked Stuffed Shrimp	45	50	5	45	17.24		
Salmon Cakes with Dill Sauce	25	25	0	22	8.43	3	Burned 3 cakes
Honey-Bourbon Grilled Pork Tenderloin	70	75	9	66	25.29	0	
Asian Flank Steak	65	65	0	65	24.90	0	Ran out 12:30—server had 10 additional requests
Totals	280	290	21	261	100.00	8	

Figure 4-4. Production sheets are a means for managers and the production staff to communicate. They list the recipes used for each meal and the quantities that should be produced. The cook records what was produced, what was left over or what was short. The manager can use this information to adjust the production schedule to more accurately reflect the amounts to produce the next time.

Portion control is essential for controlling costs. Portion control is also important because it

- ensures that meals meet regulatory requirements, including nutritional adequacy
- ensures customers receive consistent-size servings
- reduces waste and leftover food
- minimizes the possibility of running short of food during meal service
- provides a guide when ordering food from the vendor

For a foodservice operation, good portion control practices can mean the difference between having a profit or a loss. It can also determine whether customers are satisfied or unhappy.

Portion Size Determination

Before the recipe is written or the portion controlled, a manager determines the best portion size for each item on the menu. Three factors used to decide portion size are—quantity expectation, cost, and regulatory requirements.

Quantity Expectation

Customers typically expect that the amount of food they are served will be appropriate for the price charged. This quantity expectation is one method operations use to determine portion size. Information can be obtained by surveying customers to learn if they find a menu item to be an acceptable value.

Another way to evaluate whether or not portion sizes meet customer expectations is to observe what comes back on their plates. If plates are coming to the dishroom still covered with food, the portion sizes may be too large. On the other hand, when plates come to the dishroom nearly clean, the portion sizes are either acceptable to customers, or possibly too small.

The popularity of a menu item can help a manager assess whether or not the portion size is acceptable to customers. Typically, customers express their acceptance of a menu item's portion size by continuing to purchase it. Managers should consider the portion sizes of the best-selling items on the menu.

These methods of assessing quantity expectation can be subjective—what one customer considers a hearty portion, another customer may consider skimpy. However, repeat business and minimal complaints mean customers are satisfied.

Cost

The cost of the menu item can be used to establish portion size. For example, assume that the cost for an operation to produce one pan of lasagna is $48.00. What should the portion size be to achieve the desired $4.00 per portion food cost? Using the cost per unit method, this operation's portion size for lasagna would be ¹⁄₁₂th pan.

$$\frac{\$48.00 \text{ unit cost}}{x \text{ portions}} = \$4.00 \text{ desired portion food cost}$$

$$x = 12 \text{ portions}$$

Cost can establish portion size in another way. A manager may set a selling price for a menu item based on what the competition charges for the same or similar item. For example, suppose a manager uses the food cost percentage method to calculate the selling price of a serving of lasagna. If this price is higher than the price charged by the competition, the manager may have to decrease the portion size. This decreases the food cost of the item per serving. The menu price becomes competitive with the prices charged by other operations.

Regulatory Requirement

Regulatory requirements make portion size determination easy. Foodservice operations in government funded and regulated establishments—including healthcare facilities, schools, senior meal programs, and jails—are required to serve specific portion sizes. Many states require that long-term care facilities serve entrées that contain at least 14 grams of protein and vegetables that are four-ounce servings. These regulations dictate the minimum portion size the operation must serve.

Some operators consider nutrition when determining portion size, even when it is not required by law. As more and more consumers become aware of the relationship between nutrition and health, the consumers are asking for "healthy" options and portion control on the menu. To accommodate these consumers, some operators are serving smaller portions of menu items to meet designated calorie levels. For instance, a menu item may be prepared with the restriction that it contain under 500 calories. Serving smaller portions also reduces the amount of a specific nutrient in the item, such as the grams of fat or the milligrams of sodium.

Implementing Portion Control

Once portion sizes are determined, an operation must ensure that menu items are served in the correct portion sizes. Employees must be trained in the importance of portion control, and in correct portion sizes and portioning techniques. The operation must have the proper equipment for measuring portions, including scales, scoops, and ladles. The manager should frequently check plates leaving the kitchen for accurate portion size.

Food supplies also need to match the specifications written in recipes. For instance, if four-ounce salmon fillets are ordered, rather than the six-ounce fillets called for in the recipe for Basil-Buttered Salmon Fillets, serving the proper portion will be difficult.

Presentation and Service

All of the stages, from purchasing through portion control, lead to this moment—the food is now ready to move from the kitchen to the customer. This stage presents another opportunity to control costs. If the presentation and service are not acceptable, the customer will not return.

Presentation

Presentation refers to the plating and serving of menu items to the customer. The goal is to present the food in an attractive manner. In the past, a standard placement of food items on the plate was popular throughout the industry. In this type of presentation, the entrée is placed at the six o'clock position, with the starch and vegetable on either side. The entrée, starch, and vegetables are placed equidistant from the center and the edges of the plate in this standard triangle design.

Today, many operations are using more creative means of presenting the food to the customer. One such method is the stacking method. The starch is placed in the center of the plate. The entrée rests on the starch at a 45-degree angle, and the vegetables are placed near the starch item. This adds eye appeal to the plate, and keeps the food warmer.

Other ideas include altering the traditional shapes of menu items to create an interesting look. For example, instead of scooping or spooning rice onto a plate, cooks may pack rice into a cup and invert the cup onto the plate. This creates a different look. These and other creative plate presentations are cost-effective and require no more labor than the traditional triangle design.

An attractive plate can be presented while still controlling costs. Garnishes are used to enhance the appearance of a plate. A garnish should be edible and complement the food in both color and texture. Traditional garnishes include fruit and vegetable wedges. Plates are also garnished by sprinkling with herbs, drizzling with oils, and "painting" with sauces. These add great eye appeal without significant cost or skill.

Service

Foodservice operations can be classified by the serving styles they use to provide meals to their customers. Each serving style has cost savings advantages and requires measures to control costs, **4-5**. These include

- over-the-counter
- cafeteria
- buffet
- full-service (seated service)
- drive-through and take-out

Most people have experienced all of these styles of meal delivery. The following serves as a quick review.

Over-the-Counter

Over-the-counter service is typically associated with fast food. The customer approaches the serving area, places an order, and receives his or her meal in a bag or on a tray. The customer pays for the meal before leaving the counter. The service is quick and the menu is standardized.

An operation that delivers meals in this way often uses an assembly line method for food production and meal service with workers assigned to various stations. Food costs are low, as the menu is standardized, and there are fewer items to inventory. Labor costs are low because this type of service does not require specialized culinary skills. In addition, waitstaff is not needed to serve customers at their tables. However, supply costs are higher since disposable items are needed to package and serve meals.

Serving Styles	Cost-Saving Features	Cost Control Measures
Over-the-Counter	• Requires less labor • Control over portion sizes served • Menus typically require smaller inventory	• Monitor disposables • Portion control • Control condiments
Cafeteria	• Requires less labor	• Monitor serving portions • Monitor over- or underproduction of menu items • Monitor temperatures of products displayed over meal service
Buffet	• Requires less labor	• Ensure right serving utensils are used to control portion size • Monitor over- or underproduction of menu items • Monitor temperatures of products displayed over meal service
Full-Service	• Control over portion sizes served	• Monitor tableware • Monitor server and cashier for cash-handling accuracy
Drive-Through and Take-Out	• Service requires less labor • Control over portion sizes served	• Monitor disposables

Figure 4-5. This chart summarizes the cost-saving features of different serving styles and how they can be implemented.

Cafeteria

In a cafeteria setting, food is presented both in bulk and individual servings. Many of the cold-food items, such as desserts and salads, are individually plated for the customer. The hot-food items are placed on steam tables in bulk. Customers follow a straight line through various serving stations. Cafeteria staff portion and serve the menu items to customers. Preplated items may be offered, which are items customers can select and serve themselves. All customers proceed through a cashier station to pay for their selections before entering the dining area.

Some cafeterias do not require customers to proceed along a straight-line path. By using a scatter system, various food stations are scattered throughout the serving area. Customers only visit the stations serving items they need. They do not need to proceed through an entire line to obtain their menu choices.

When trying to control costs, the main advantage of using a cafeteria-style service is labor savings. Similar to the over-the-counter service, waitstaff is not needed.

Buffet

A buffet is similar to a cafeteria. The difference is that the food is generally all self-serve. This method reduces labor costs, requiring fewer servers. However, food costs may be higher because customers may serve themselves more than a standard portion.

Full-Service

In a full-service restaurant, customers are first seated before servers take their orders. The food is delivered to the table. In this setting, plate presentation has the biggest impact. This service method results in higher costs due to the increased labor needed to provide table service.

Drive-Through and Take-Out

In today's fast-paced world, drive-through and take-out are becoming mainstays of the foodservice industry. Drive-through is typically seen in fast-food restaurants. Take-out is offered at all types of operations, from local diners to five-star, white-tablecloth restaurants. Both offer foodservice operators opportunities to capture additional customers without the additional labor costs to serve them tableside. By capturing additional customers, the operator can realize an increase in sales.

A growing number of operations are using online delivery services. Websites provide customers with menus from participating restaurants. The customer places the order with the delivery service, which then picks up the food and delivers it to the customer.

Waste Management

Waste management involves controlling costs by maximizing the edible portions of the product during preparation and plating (*product maximization*). It also involves minimizing the amount of the product that is left over (*leftover management*).

Product Maximization

Product maximization refers to processes that enable an operation to gain the largest possible yield (edible portion) from a food item. This is achieved by proper trimming and cooking of a raw product and by complete removal of the product from its container.

For example, suppose Catherine's Café purchases whole cantaloupes to make melon wedges. The rind and seeds are removed before each cantaloupe is cut into wedges for serving. The goal of product maximization is to obtain the greatest EP, or edible portion, by trimming away only as much of the rind as necessary. This minimizes the loss of edible portion when the rind is thrown away. This principle also applies to food items that must be removed from containers, such as canned pudding or tomato sauce. Product maximization is accomplished by ensuring that all of the product is removed from the can before the can is thrown away.

Technology

Food Trucks and Social Media

Mobile food truck operators are using social media to promote their businesses and build their customer base. They post, blog, or tweet information about the locations of their trucks, as well as their cuisine, menus, and daily specials. By using social media, operators can advertise at no cost and stay engaged with customers. They can also respond to specific customer requests and complaints. Some operators use social media to interact with customers in creative ways. For example, in a blog post, one food truck operator promised free waffle toppings to customers who showed up imitating peacocks.

Saving small amounts of edible portion may appear inconsequential. However, as the following scenario illustrates, saving small amounts can add up to savings on food costs. Suppose Catherine's Café purchases a case of fresh cantaloupe at $40.50, and there are 18 cantaloupes in a case.

$$\frac{\$40.50 \text{ per case}}{18 \text{ cantaloupes}} = \$2.25 \text{ per cantaloupe}$$

As purchased, each cantaloupe costs $2.25. Next, suppose that with careful trimming and seed removal, Catherine gets six 1.25-cup servings from each melon. What is her cost per serving?

$$\frac{\$2.25 \text{ per cantaloupe}}{6 \text{ servings per cantaloupe}} = \$0.38 \text{ per serving}$$

If Catherine sells each serving for $2.50, how much can she make per serving and per case?

$2.50 selling price − $0.38 serving cost = $2.12 contribution per serving

$2.12 contribution per serving × 6 servings per melon × 18 melons per case = $228.96 contribution per case of cantaloupe.

Now, suppose that Catherine's prep cook arrives late for work one day and has limited time to prepare a case of cantaloupes for the lunch service. As a result, she scoops out edible fruit with the rind and seeds and loses about one serving, or 1.25 cups, per cantaloupe. This is a loss of about 18 servings per case. How will this loss of product impact Catherine's sales and profit?

$2.50 selling price per serving × 18 servings = $45.00 in lost sales

$2.12 contribution per serving × 18 servings = $38.16 in lost contributions

If 18 servings of cantaloupe were thrown away every day, Catherine's Café could have up to $13,928.40 per year in lost contributions.

Waste Not/Bookmark This

Creating a Food Waste and Recovery Program

Food waste is costly for foodservice operations. Costs include payments for solid waste pickup, water and sewage, and electricity used by waste-disposal equipment. A foodservice operation can reduce these costs by creating a waste reduction and recovery program. The U.S. Environmental Protection Agency (EPA) provides guidance in "Putting Surplus Food to Good Use: A How-to Guide for Food Service Providers." A food recovery hierarchy lists methods of reducing food waste from the most to the least important.
- Reduce the amount of food waste produced.
- Donate extra food to feed the hungry.
- Donate food scraps to local farmers or zoos for animal feed.
- Investigate industrial uses for waste oils and scraps.
- Consider food composting.
- Send food waste to landfills or incinerators only as a last resort.

The guide gives managers suggestions as to how each method can be implemented. This resource and others can be accessed at the EPA's website.

Leftover Management

Leftover management is the second aspect of waste management. The best way to manage leftovers is to have none. This is unrealistic in a foodservice operation. **Leftover management** refers to the processes an operation uses to minimize the amount of leftovers and to creatively utilize leftovers that remain. Some leftovers can be incorporated into other menu items. For example, leftover vegetables and meats can be used for soups, casseroles, and stews. Other leftover items can be reworked to create tomorrow's "Cook's Choice" entrée.

To minimize waste due to leftovers, a manager can

- ensure that standardized recipes are followed
- ensure that production sheets are followed and completed at the end of the meal service
- base forecasting on information obtained from the production sheets
- require that employees get approval before disposing of leftovers
- rework or incorporate leftovers into other menu items
- provide the proper number and types of containers to encourage proper storage of leftovers
- ensure staff uses safe-food handling procedures when dealing with leftovers

Controlling Costs by Practicing Food Safety and Sanitation

Ensuring that proper food safety and sanitation are practiced is the responsibility of every employee in a foodservice operation. Other courses will cover food safety and sanitation in detail. This text focuses briefly on the impact food safety and sanitation can have on cost control efforts.

Following food safety and sanitation guidelines helps to prevent foodborne illness. A **foodborne illness** is a disease caused by consuming food contaminated with biological, chemical, or physical hazards. The Centers for Disease Control and Prevention (CDC) estimate that nearly 76 million illnesses, 325,000 hospitalizations, and 5,000 deaths occur in the United States each year as a result of foodborne illness. These illnesses also cost the country billions of dollars each year. According to the National Restaurant Association, one incident of foodborne illness can cost a foodservice operation up to $75,000. This can put many operations out of business. If the business does not fail right away, the negative word of mouth will damage its most important asset—its reputation.

Following proper food-handling practices can prevent foodborne illness and help minimize waste from food spoilage. Food spoilage due to negligence is an unnecessary cost for the operation. Practicing food safety and sanitation can help control costs at every step in a foodservice operation.

Controlling Other Costs

A foodservice operation needs more than food to do business. Many other supplies and services are necessary to produce the food that is served. As with foods, these supplies must be purchased, received, stored, and issued into use.

Supplies

Many of the same methods used to control food costs apply to the control of supply costs. However, a few cost-control methods are unique to supply costs. Many foodservice operations purchase and use disposables, china, silver, utensils, and office supplies. Following a few preventive measures can help control costs in these areas, **4-6**.

Chemical Products

Chemical products allow foodservice operations to comply with food safety and sanitation guidelines and prevent foodborne illness. Having a clean, sanitary workplace

Preventative Measures to Control Supply Costs
Disposables
• Only use disposable items when absolutely necessary for service.
• Properly secure all disposable items after each meal period, particularly lids and napkins that tend to fall on the floor and ultimately in the trash.
• Use the correct product for the application. For example, use beverage napkins—not full-size dinner napkins—for snack service.
• Place only what is needed in the service areas.
• Keep all supplies secure in cabinets to prevent pilferage.
• Make sure that goods provided reflect the needs of the menu. For example, do not provide spoons for coffee service when coffee stirrers are acceptable.
• Pick up unused items immediately at the end of the service, and store properly. Napkins, cups, and other items that are left out frequently end up in the trash.
• Instruct the staff to return unused items to the proper storage areas.
China/Silver
• Reduce breakage by training staff in proper handling techniques.
• Randomly check trash receptacles for china/flatware being discarded by staff.
• Use correct dish racks/storage to prevent breakage.
Kitchen/Dining Room Utensils
• Provide production staff with tool kits/knives at hire. Replace annually, if necessary. Inform staff that replacement of lost/damaged utensils is their responsibility.
• Create tool kits for all serving areas. Inventory after each service by assigned staff.
• Properly store pots/pans to prevent damage.
Office Supplies
• Place office supplies in a secured location. Consider the use of requisition slips to obtain supplies. These steps can reduce pilferage by 60 to 70 percent.
• When checking off new items from packing slips, sequentially number and date the individual packets.
• Paper stock can be dated and numbered to help prevent reams of paper from "walking" out the door.

Figure 4-6. Supply costs contribute to the overall expenses of a foodservice operation. This chart lists areas a manager can review to control supply costs.

benefits both workers and customers. Chemicals are generally categorized as a supply cost. They may be purchased through a specialty company or through a foodservice broad-line distributor. As with any cost, the cost of chemicals must be controlled. Proper management of chemical usage can reduce this cost by 5 percent or more.

Factors to consider when selecting chemicals are the mineral content of the water supply and the type of food soil generated in the operation. The chemical supplier can be a great resource for information and recommendations, as well as staff training. Following guidelines for effective chemical use helps control costs and contributes to more effective cleaning and sanitizing, **4-7**. The proper training of the staff not only improves usage and decreases costs, but also decreases the number of chemical-related injuries.

Chemical Cost Control
Warewashing
• Ensure water temperatures are correct. Temperatures below specifications can result in excessive detergent and rinse agent use.
• Change water regularly since detergent is dispensed based on predetermined levels of concentration. (Rule of thumb—change water after every two hours of use.)
• Properly scrape and rinse dishes prior to washing. This will reduce the amount of food particles in the water, thus reducing the amount of chemical dispensed.
• Use proper dish racks. Racks are designed for maximum water flow and, therefore, maximum washing efficiency. Do not place dishes into racks in a manner that reduces the flow of water through the racks.
• Only operate the machine when full racks are ready.
• Presoak flatware prior to washing.

• Perform machine maintenance on a regular basis. Check for
  • lime build up (if excessive, consider a water softener)
  • proper functioning rinse agent
  • cleaning of wash/rinse arms each time water is changed
  • proper chemical calibration
  • proper drain function

• Train staff to be aware of normal chemical usage so they can spot malfunctions in chemical dispensing.
Pot and Pan Washing
• Change water on a regular basis.
• Remove heavy soil prior to putting pots and pans into wash water.
• Presoak as many items as possible.
• Ensure that dispensers are properly calibrated.
• Do not dispense chemicals manually.
General Sanitation
• Train staff to always use the correct chemical and correct quantity for the job.
• Keep cleaning schedules current and posted.
• Keep floors swept as frequently as possible. Surface dirt is easier and less costly to remove than ground in dirt.
• Properly clean and store mops and buckets. Clean equipment reduces the need to go over areas more than once.

Figure 4-7. Controlling the cost of chemicals will positively impact an operation's bottom line. Here is a list of ideas to consider in controlling chemical costs.

Professional Services, Fees, and Other Costs

Even expenses that account for a small portion of the overall expense of the foodservice operation need to be scrutinized by a manager. These include fees for licenses, travel and education expenses, and the costs of professional services, uniforms, and decorations. Hood cleaning, pest control, and knife sharpening are professional services. The manager needs to take necessary steps to control these costs to ensure that funds are properly utilized, 4-8.

Other Expenses	
Travel and Education	While a conference in Hawaii in January may be enticing, similar information may be obtained at a local or state meeting. Determine the cost to attend against the benefit received.
Purchased Services	Compare the cost of the service to the cost of performing the task in-house. Are the equipment, skills, and time available? Also, obtain pricing from more than one vendor.
Uniforms	Determine if employees should purchase their own uniforms, or if uniforms should be an employee benefit. If the operation purchases them, ensure that policies are in place to control their use.
Decorations	Obtain quotes from suppliers for items used. Determine if fresh or artificial decorations are best for the ambiance of the operation.
Licenses	Most of these are obtained at a set fee. Ensure that the operation has only what is required to operate the business.

Figure 4-8. While not as significant as the cost of food, other expenses need to be controlled. The chart lists some examples of these expenses and how their costs can be controlled.

Key Terms

food production
production system
cook-serve system
cook-chill system
commissary

ingredient room
kitchenless system
standardized recipe
production sheet
portion control

presentation
waste management
product maximization
leftover management
foodborne illness

Recap

- Production systems include cook-serve, cook-chill, commissary, ingredient room, and kitchenless.
- The three cost-control tools of food production are forecasting, production sheets, and standardized recipes.
- Standardized recipes help foodservice operations produce consistent products.
- Three methods are used to determine the ingredient amounts used—cost per unit, the yield test, and cooking loss.
- Production sheets are the road map for foodservice production areas.
- Portion control can be determined by quantity, cost, and regulations.
- Food presentation involves plating, eye appeal, and garnishing.
- The five basic types of service are over-the-counter, cafeteria, buffet, full-service (seated service), and drive-through and take-out.
- Waste management through product maximization and leftover control impact food costs.
- Food safety and sanitation guidelines can prevent foodborne illness.
- Nonfood costs, including supply costs, require monitoring by the manager.

Review Questions

1. True or false: The only type of production system used in a commissary is a cook-chill production system.
2. Standardized recipes provide consistency in ____, ____, ____, ____, and ____.
3. Describe three ways to determine portion size.
4. Why is forecasting important?
5. Name the components of a production sheet.
6. Compare and contrast the yield and cooking loss tests.
7. Describe two ways to present food on the plate.
8. Explain the differences between the cafeteria and the buffet serving styles.
9. List three things a manager can do to limit food waste due to leftovers.
10. Proper control of chemicals can reduce their costs by what percentage?
11. Name two examples of other supply costs and suggest one way to control the cost of each.

Applying Your Knowledge

12. Obtain a recipe from home. Rewrite it in a standardized recipe format.

Exercise 4-13

Complete the following exercise on the companion website:
www.g-wlearning.com/culinaryarts/

13. Rachelle is the purchasing manager of Red River Diner, which is known for its outstanding pot roast. Even though the invoice prices would be higher, Rachelle's sales representative suggests that Rachelle would be better off buying the ingredients ready-to-use.

A. Use the information given to complete the spreadsheet and answer the questions.

Recipe	AP Measures	Directions
beef chuck, raw boneless	6 lbs.	Trim and brown beef in oil.
cooking oil	3 Tbsp.	Add beef broth to pot, cover, and simmer for 1 hour.
broth, beef	1.5 c.	Peel, trim, and cut vegetables. Add to beef.
potatoes, peeled and quartered	3 lbs.	Cover and simmer for 45 minutes or until tender.
carrots, peeled and cut into 3-inch pieces	3 lbs.	Transfer meat and vegetables to serving pan.
onions, peeled and cut into 8 wedges	1 lb.	

Price Information	AP Price	Product Yield
beef chuck, raw boneless	$1.95/lb.	65%
pre-cooked pot roast	$3.05/lb.	100%
potatoes, whole	$0.40/lb.	85%
carrots, whole	$1.30/lb.	85%
onions, whole	$1.40/lb.	90%
pot roast vegetables, ready-to-use	$1.50/lb.	100%

Recipe Costing Spreadsheet

Ingredient	Recipe Amount (lb.)	Product Yield %	EP Amount (lb.)	AP Price/lb.	Recipe Cost
beef chuck, raw boneless	6	65.00%		$1.95	
pre-cooked pot roast		100.00%		$3.05	
potatoes, whole	3	85.00%		$0.40	
carrots, whole	3	85.00%		$1.30	
onions, whole	1	90.00%		$1.40	
pot roast vegetables, ready-to-use		100.00%		$1.50	

B. What is the cost difference between the raw and pre-cooked pot roast?
C. What is the cost difference between the whole and ready-to-use vegetables?
D. Which purchase decision should Rachelle make based on price only?
E. Name two benefits to buying the pre-cooked pot roast and pre-cut vegetables.

Course Project

The Course Project is a full case study on controlling costs in a foodservice operation. Each chapter presents one component of the project. Refer to other completed components to answer the following questions.

14. Select one entrée and one side from the menu you developed for the Course Project and do the following:

A. Write a standardized recipe for the entrée.
B. Diagram a plate presentation of the two items.
C. Define the production area(s) needed to prepare the items.
D. Create a production sheet for the entrée.

Chapter 5
Labor Cost Control

Learning Outcomes

After studying this chapter, you will be able to

- identify payroll and non-payroll labor costs.
- explain why orientation and training of employees is important.
- describe a supervisor's responsibilities.
- explain how employee turnover impacts an operation's costs.
- list factors that affect the amount of labor required.
- describe the importance of completing a job analysis.
- identify the purpose of a position control sheet.
- calculate how much labor a particular position requires.
- calculate labor analysis ratios and explain their implications.

Labor is one of the largest expenses for most foodservice operations. In non-commercial settings, it is not unusual for labor costs to consume 50 to 60 percent of an operation's total expense budget. For commercial operations, the median for labor expense is 35 percent. While automation and computers have replaced the need for some labor, foodservice still relies heavily on employees to meet the needs of its customers.

However, unlike computers and almost everything else a foodservice manager purchases, labor is not a product. The human element of this expense must be considered as well. The wise manager knows that the success of his or her operation is dependent on people—customers and employees. Both must be highly valued and treated with respect.

To be profitable, a foodservice establishment must have effective labor cost control measures in place. This is achieved through strong labor management. For any business, strong labor management can be summarized in one sentence: Having the right people, at the right times, in the right places, with the right knowledge and skills. This chapter will discuss how a foodservice manager can accomplish this.

Foodservice Labor Needs

According to the US Department of Labor's Bureau of Labor Statistics, the foodservice-and-drinking-places segment of the economy generated more than 9.6 million jobs in 2008, making it the country's third largest industry. The job outlook for the industry is above average through 2018. Growth is being driven by increases in the overall population and the number of aging baby boomers who enjoy dining out. As a result, foodservice managers will face an increasing need for more staff.

The need for labor is also high because of employee turnover. In comparison with other industries, turnover is high in foodservice operations. For example, consider a factory where cars are assembled. Employees arrive at the same time each day and go to their assigned locations on the assembly line where the components they need are located. Each worker adds his or her component to the car as it passes his or her station. Cars are produced throughout the day in a continuous process. At the end of the shift, a certain number of cars have been assembled. A portion of them are sold to car dealers. If only 15 of a total of 20 cars produced are bought, the five remaining cars can be kept in inventory. When the inventory gets too large, the production of cars and the scheduling of employees can be changed.

Contrast this to how most foodservice operations work. The activity level is not constant, but varies based on time of day and customer traffic. An operation is busy for the few hours around a standard mealtime. Then activity slows down as customer traffic lessens. It peaks again for the next meal period and dwindles once again. Foodservice operations also produce a wide variety of products, or menu items. Food items, unlike automobiles, cannot be stored in inventory until sales pick up. Their quality will decrease rapidly and they will eventually spoil.

To cope with the peaks and valleys in activity, foodservice managers tend to hire part-time employees or stagger employee start times. These strategies and others will be discussed in a later section about scheduling. Employees tend to be part-time, young, and temporary. In 2008, about three in five people who worked in foodservice and drinking places were between the ages of 15 and 19—about five times the proportion for all industries, according to a Bureau of Labor Statistics survey. Also, about two in five foodservice employees worked part-time—more than twice the proportion for all industries. Many view the work as something to do while they attend school or wait for other career opportunities. The majority of the jobs require minimal education and skills, are low-paying, and involve working long and sometimes odd hours. As a result, managers must frequently train new workers to replace those who leave.

Foodservice jobs can offer workers some unique advantages. Though hours can be odd, they also tend to be flexible. This enables employees to undertake other pursuits and responsibilities, such as schooling and child care. Foodservice jobs are rewarding in other ways. They can provide great satisfaction to people who enjoy creating products, or meals. Employees who work with customers are privy to their feedback about the products. The feedback—if it is positive—can be rewarding as well.

Labor Costs

The terms *labor cost* and *payroll cost* are not interchangeable. An operation's labor cost is higher than its payroll cost. Payroll refers to the payments the operation makes to employees in exchange for their labor or services. Foodservice employees are paid either wages or salaries. Labor cost includes payroll cost, plus the costs of employee benefits and payroll taxes.

A *wage* is a payment for work that is usually computed on an hourly basis. A worker may be paid a wage of $10 an hour. Hours worked must be tracked. Workers receive their wages every week, every two weeks, or every month. By law, when hours worked exceed 40 hours a week, workers must receive overtime pay. Overtime pay is based on a higher hourly wage that is at least 1½ times the regular hourly rate.

A *salary* refers to fixed payments that employees—including managers—receive on a regular basis. It is usually expressed as an annual figure, such as $40,000 a year. The amount of the salary is broken up into equal payments that are made to a worker over the year. Salaried employees are generally not paid overtime.

The Fair Labor Standards Act (FLSA), which covers most workers, stipulates a minimum wage that employers are required to pay qualified workers. The *minimum wage* is the lowest wage an employer can pay an employee. It is usually set by federal and state governments and is periodically raised. An employee who is covered by both a federal and a state minimum wage requirement is entitled to the higher rate. Foodservice operations can pay a lower minimum wage to employees who receive tips on a regular basis. *Tips* are a form of income received by many foodservice workers, especially those who work in operations that provide table service. Patrons customarily tip workers to reward them for good service. Some foodservice workers receive most of their income from tips. A tip is usually calculated as a percentage of a meal's price. In some operations, workers pool the tips they receive during a shift.

Since they are paid by customers, tips are not included in an operation's payroll costs. However, if the sum of a worker's wage and tips is lower than the federal minimum wage, the employer must make up the difference. Managers should be familiar with laws regarding the minimum wage and tipped employees.

Employee Benefits and Payroll Taxes

Payroll costs, or the wages and salaries that operations pay workers, are only part of what it costs to employ them. Non-payroll costs include employee benefits and payroll taxes. These are significant labor costs and may include payments for the following:

- sick leave
- vacations and holidays
- health insurance premiums
- worker's compensation
- unemployment compensation
- retirement savings plans and profit sharing
- employee meals (if not subtracted from employees' paychecks)
- educational expenses
- federal and state income taxes
- Social Security tax (both employers' and employees' contributions)
- Medicare tax (both employers' and employees' contributions)

Employers must withhold payments for Social Security and Medicare as required by the *Federal Insurance Contributions Act (FICA)*. FICA is a payroll tax imposed by the federal government that is used to fund the Medicare and Social Security programs. Employers are taxed as well as employees.

Selecting and Retaining Staff

Jim Collins, who researches business and management practices, examined companies that set themselves apart from their competition. He asked what made these companies great while others were simply good. His answer repeats an often-quoted truism in the business world: Success comes from "getting the right people on the bus." According to Collins' book, *Good To Great: Why Some Companies Make the Leap…and Others Don't*, great companies have the right people with the right knowledge and skills on board. Employees who are not the right fit are not kept on.

The success of an operation depends on the quality of its employees. Since they are an operation's most valuable resource, the manager must do a good job recruiting and hiring staff. The following sections will briefly cover the responsibilities of hiring, training, and supervising employees as it relates to labor cost control. An in-depth look at human resources can be found in other management or business coursework.

The Job Description

Before a manager can begin the recruiting process, a *job description* must be in place. The creation of an accurate, complete, and up-to-date job description for each job in the operation is the first step in managing labor. A **job description** lists the requirements and essential functions of a position, **5-1**, and includes the

- position title
- person to whom the worker reports
- basic purpose or summary of the position
- essential functions of the position

Job Description			
Position Title:	Foodservice Worker	**Job Code:**	1234
Reports To:	Kitchen Manager	**Revised:**	3/20XX
Position Summary			
Performs a variety of food preparation and kitchen sanitation tasks used in the preparation and serving of guest meals.			
Essential Functions			
1. Prepares or assists in preparation of foods for guest meals. 2. Sets up serving line. 3. Waits on tables, as assigned. 4. Cleans and sanitizes work area according to established procedures. 5. Stores food and supplies according to operation procedures. 6. Performs other duties as assigned.			
Minimum Requirements			
1. High school graduate or successful completion of the GED. 2. Previous foodservice experience preferred, but not required. 3. Must be able to lift 20 lbs., repeatedly. 4. Must be able to stand for long periods of time. 5. Must be able to use various kitchen equipment.			

Figure 5-1 A job description defines the qualifications an applicant needs to be considered for a position. The above statements are not intended to be an exhaustive list of all duties and skills of persons in this position. *Reprinted with permission of Dietetics in Health Care Communities*

- physical and mental requirements of the position
- minimum qualifications for the position (education and experience)

The essential functions of a job are the most-important duties. If an essential function were to be eliminated, the job would be fundamentally changed. When creating a job description, managers list the job's essential functions to be in compliance with Title I of the **Americans with Disabilities Act (ADA)**. The ADA prohibits discrimination against qualified individuals with disabilities in the following areas of employment—job application, hiring, firing, advancement, and pay. It applies to employers with 15 or more employees. Before rejecting a job applicant in the belief that a disability would keep him or her from performing a job function, the employer must show that the function is essential to the position. An accommodation may have to be made to enable the applicant to perform the essential function, if doing so is not overly difficult or expensive.

For instance, suppose a person has a physical disability and cannot stand for long periods of time. In a large operation, this person may be able to fill the cashier's position with the use of a chair. However, in smaller operations the cashier may fulfill other roles—server, bus person, dishwasher, and so forth. An accommodation may not be possible. Listing the physical requirements of the position in the job description makes position expectations clear to the applicant. Once the job description is written, the recruiting process begins.

Recruiting

In a large organization, *recruiting* is a function of the human resources department. In smaller operations, it may rest on the shoulders of the foodservice manager. **Recruiting** is the process of locating applicants for a job opening. Organizations recruit both internally and externally, depending on the position and the skill set desired. Recruiting resources include

- classified ads
- professional newsletters and meeting announcements
- educational institutions
- employment agencies
- current staff network, friends, relatives
- industry colleagues
- help wanted signs
- company websites, social media

Based on the position, one resource may be better than another. For most foodservice positions, classified ads—online or in print—are the most common means of advertising open positions. A second great resource is people—both customers and current employees. Word-of-mouth advertising is free and effective. The majority of job seekers surf the Internet looking for employment. Employers would be remiss if they did not utilize this cost-effective and far-reaching recruiting tool.

The Job Application

Depending on the position to be filled, applicants can be asked to fill out a job application, submit a résumé, or both. Applications can be provided on paper or online. An application should request the following information:

- applicant's name
- date
- position applied for

- date the applicant is available to work
- social security number
- contact information—address, phone number(s), and e-mail
- education and training (name of school and dates attended, degree or certification received)
- languages spoken besides English
- names of current and former employers (dates worked, contact information, job title and responsibilities, reason for leaving)
- references (names, titles, and contact information)
- signature after statement attesting to the truthfulness of the information

Since applications contain information that can be used to commit fraud, such as identity theft, if they fall into the wrong hands, completed applications should be kept in a secure location or carefully disposed of.

Interviewing

The hiring manager contacts the most promising job applicants for interviews. The interviewing process begins with a *screening interview*, usually by phone. In larger operations, the human resources department generally performs this interview. A **screening interview** is conducted to determine if an applicant meets the basic qualifications for a position.

Once a list of candidates for the position is generated, face-to-face interviews are scheduled and conducted. Having a standard interview format, and sticking to it, makes the process more efficient and allows for the comparison of one applicant to another. For the hiring manager, a typical process may include the following:

- Develop a list of open-ended questions to determine the applicant's ability to handle the position and fit into the culture of the operation.
- Use the same questions for all applicants for easy comparison, **5-2.**
- Choose a quiet location for the interview.
- Ensure that the applicant is comfortable and at ease (offer water, coffee, and so forth).
- Schedule 30 to 60 minutes for the interview.
- Have an up-to-date job description available.
- Inform the applicant that notes will be taken.
- Ask what the applicant knows about the operation or organization.
- Describe the position to the applicant. Be clear on the details of the position, including the type of work involved, the physical work environment, the hours, and weekend and holiday expectations.
- Ensure that federal civil rights laws are followed.
- Request at least two references from the applicant.
- Provide the applicant with an opportunity to ask questions.
- Inform the applicant of any drug screening, background check, or pre-employment test that will be required.
- Inform the applicant when and how he or she will be contacted regarding a decision.

Following the completion of the face-to-face interview process, the manager chooses the applicant or applicants who appear to be the best fit for the position. Before hiring someone, the manager should check his or her references. Since verification of employment dates is all a former employer can legally provide, character references from others may provide more detail. Most applicants only list references who will speak highly of them.

Sample Interview Questions
How would you describe yourself?
Why did you leave your last job?
What do you see yourself doing five years from now? Ten year from now?
How would your best friend describe you?
Describe the best job you ever had.
Describe the best supervisor you ever had.
What would your last boss say about your work performance?
Why should I hire you?
What do you like most about your current job?
What do you like least?
Describe a typical day at your current position.
Do you prefer to work as an individual or as part of a team? Why?
What do you look for in a supervisor?
In what areas do you need to improve?
What do you know about our company?
Why do you want this position?
What hours are you available to work?

Figure 5-2 These basic interview questions are appropriate for most foodservice positions. The list was adapted from information given in the *Pocket Resource for Management*, 2011 edition.

Background checks are required for some positions and the use of these checks is gaining in popularity. The signed consent of the applicant may be required by law. Internet programs are available, for a small fee, to conduct basic background checks, especially for criminal records and citizenship status. Since the foodservice industry employs a large number of immigrants, ensuring that people are in the country legally can prevent potential legal and financial penalties.

Just prior to making a formal job offer, many employers require applicants to be screened for illegal drug use. This function is usually outsourced to a local drug-screening company. Expenses associated with conducting the drug screen are borne by the employer. For this reason, it is generally the final step in the hiring process.

Once the references and background checks are complete and the drug screen results are received, a formal job offer is made. Now it is time for orientation and training.

Orientation and Training

The orientation and training of a new employee is essential. Unfortunately, many businesses fail to provide this. Instead, they throw a new hire into the operation to either sink or swim. Considering the time and money already spent to hire a new employee, it makes sound business sense to ensure that he or she is well trained. This way, the employee is more likely to be productive and content. The extent of orientation and training depends on the size of the operation, the complexity of the position, and the previous work experience of the new hire.

The general goal of orientation is to incorporate new employees into the operation. It consists of introducing new hires to the operation, easing their fears, making them feel welcome, and quickly making them contributing members of the team. If done correctly, orientation increases an employee's job satisfaction, motivation, productivity, and retention. An orientation checklist helps ensure that nothing is missed and that the employee's initial experience will be a good one. Prepared by a manager, it may include tasks scheduled as follows.

Prior to the new employee's start date:

- Notify the new hire of the start date, time, location, person to meet, dress code, parking locations, and so forth.
- Create a welcome packet that includes pertinent "getting started" and benefits information. The packet may include a job description, schedule, organizational chart, payroll and direct deposit information, telephone list, company mission and vision statements, and so forth.
- Communicate the new hire's name, position, and start date with current employees.
- Schedule meetings with team members during the first few days of employment. Arrange for any technology training, such as e-mail, POS, recipe programs, and so forth.
- Ready the new hire's workstation/locker—include access, supplies, and so forth.

On the first day:

- Welcome the new hire.
- Provide an overview of the first week.
- Introduce the team.
- Review the welcome packet.
- Tour the work area. Point out locations of supplies, and the policies, procedures, and safety manuals.
- Review key policies, such as those concerning dress code, safety, emergencies, and so forth.
- Review break and meal schedules and policies. Provide a meal for the employee on his or her first day.
- Complete benefits and human resources forms (W2, direct deposit, and so forth).
- Review payroll system and time card.

One to 12 weeks after start date:

- Schedule training.
- Review technology training, organizational chart.
- Review operation's goals, objectives, mission and vision statements and how the new employee fits into those.
- Ensure all personnel forms are complete.
- Touch base on overall progress.

Three to six months after start date:

- Discuss performance goals and performance appraisal.
- Check in weekly to see how the employee is adapting.
- Provide corrective guidance where needed.

It is important that a new hire receive the training necessary to successfully perform his or her duties and that the training is documented. The initial training takes place during the orientation and on-boarding process. The employee should understand company policies and procedures, as well as food safety and sanitation requirements. The training record includes documentation of training outside of job-task-specific training, such as diversity training or emerging leader courses. Once again, the extent of the training required depends on the employee's previous work history.

The operation should establish and use a training checklist to ensure that each employee learns and understands the requirements of his or her position. The checklist

Bookmark This

Youth Worker Safety eTool

According to government statistics, young and inexperienced workers are more likely to suffer workplace injuries and illnesses than older workers. The foodservice industry, which employs many young workers, is associated with a high percentage of these problems. The Occupational Safety & Health Administration created a tool to help foodservice operators comply with labor laws and keep young workers safe on the job. The Youth Worker Safety in Restaurants eTool provides

- information about laws that protect young workers and restrict their workplace activities.
- information about potential hazards and what employers and employees can do to minimize them. For example, instead of allowing employees to lift heavy trays above shoulder height—a sprain and strain hazard—employers can provide carts.
- downloadable stickers to mark equipment young workers should not operate.
- information about protection equipment.
- safety posters.
- games and quizzes to enhance safety training.

More information about this program can be found at www.OSHA.gov/

is also a means of keeping track of the employee's progress, and can be incorporated into the employee's training record. The training records of employees are often requested by regulatory agencies. Having them available is critical to passing any inspection. In addition, training records provide evidence that employees received the training required for their positions and can help exonerate the employer if legal action is taken against the operation.

For example, suppose that an employee is seriously injured when using a meat slicer to make deli sandwiches. The employer would likely be held responsible if the employee was not trained in the proper operation and cleaning of the machine or was not made to demonstrate competency in using it. Workplace accidents can be expensive for both employer and employee. An injured employee may become temporarily or permanently disabled. He or she may need medical care, be unable to work, and require time off. Additional labor hours will be needed to cover this employee during his or her recovery.

Creating and maintaining a safe work environment is primarily the manager's responsibility. Accident prevention is a critical part of this function. An employee safety and accident prevention program should be a significant component of the training process. What are some ways managers can ensure that they have a safe work environment?

- Train employees in the proper use of all equipment, knives, and chemicals.
- Train employees in safe-lifting techniques.
- Have procedures in place to minimize food and liquid buildup on the floors.
- Have wet floor signs and use them.
- Establish and train employees on emergency preparedness procedures, including the use of fire-fighting equipment.
- Conduct random and routine safety inspections of the operation. Take corrective action immediately.

When an employer is committed to workplace safety, employees know that their well-being is valued. Employees who are well trained are better able to complete their job duties effectively, efficiently, and with confidence. They are also more likely to be satisfied with their jobs.

Supervision

Once employees are oriented and trained, ongoing supervision helps to ensure their continued success. Managers should understand supervision as overseeing the productivity and progress of employees—not as watching over employees' shoulders as they work. Supervision involves

- conducting ongoing training of staff
- managing the work performance of employees
- providing direction and corrective action as needed
- developing the skill set of each employee

A good supervisor is a coach, an advocate for the employee and the employer, and a mentor. When managers provide adequate supervision, their workforce is more productive, which is essential in controlling labor costs.

Performance Appraisal

A formalized process called *performance appraisal* is a tool used to manage employees. A performance appraisal is a process by which a manager and employee review the employee's work performance to determine if it meets the requirements of the position. The employee's work performance is rated based on an established scale and criteria. Positive achievements, as well as areas that need improvement, can be noted.

While a formalized performance appraisal should be completed at least annually, a manager should ensure that employees receive routine feedback on their work performance.

Retention

Once the right people are brought on board, the goal of the manager is to keep them on board. This is retention, or the ability of an organization to keep its employees. The cost of replacing a skilled employee—recruiting, interviewing, hiring, and training a replacement—is high. Also, when a skilled employee leaves an operation, productivity for the operation is typically lowered for a period of time. These costs vary between operations and depend on the position being replaced. Many industry sources cite the cost to replace a front-line worker at as much as 30 percent of the annual salary for that position. It can run anywhere from 15 to 200 percent of annual salary for management staff.

What can mangers do to keep their employees? Is it enough to pay competitive wages and offer generous benefits packages? While these things are important and necessary, researchers have found that employees desire other less tangible things. The Hay Group, a management consulting firm, surveyed employees about what they sought from their employers. The top three things employees listed were: open communication, meaningful work, and the ability to have a balanced life. "More money" was near the bottom of the list.

What can managers learn from this research? They should do what they can to make sure employees feel they are part of the operation. Employees should understand

- the mission and vision of the organization
- the short- and long-term goals of the organization
- how they fit into the mission, vision, and direction of the company

The dishwasher in a hospital foodservice operation should understand that the hospital's mission is to improve the health of its patients. By providing patients with clean and sanitary dishes, the dishwasher contributes to the hospital's mission. By doing his or her job well, the dishwasher can prevent the spread of disease-causing microbes that can sicken patients.

An operation often benefits when managers share information with employees about how the operation stands vis-à-vis its short- and long-term goals. If the operation's food costs are over-budget, for example, the manager must find ways to rein them in. One of the best sources of practical cost-cutting ideas is employees who work with the food every day. Employees are more likely to feel they are a part of an operation when they are kept informed of their employer's growth plans. Such plans may include adding more seats in the dining room or opening a new restaurant on the other side of town. Employees-in-the-know tend to be more productive and more likely to stay with their employers. Increased employee productivity and retention decrease labor costs and contribute to cost savings.

Employee Turnover Rate

A management tool used to measure the retention of employees is the *employee turnover rate*. Employee turnover rate refers to the speed with which employees leave an organization and are replaced. It can be calculated for a year, a month, or for any other time frame depending on the policies and needs of the operation. A high turnover rate is undesirable since it increases labor costs. A manager's goal is to minimize turnover.

Employees leave or are separated from an operation for a variety of reasons. Factors that cause an employee separation include termination or firing by the employer, the offer of a new job, a career change, relocation, and job dissatisfaction. Some turnover is inevitable, no matter how good managers are or how satisfied employees are with their jobs. An employee turnover rate for a year can be calculated using the following formula.

$$\text{Employee Turnover Rate} = \frac{\text{Employees Separated During Year}}{\text{Average No. of Employees on Staff During Year}} \times 100$$

Suppose a foodservice operation has an average of 35 employees and loses 10 employees during a year. The turnover rate would be calculated as follows:

$$\text{Employee turnover rate} = \frac{10}{35} \times 100$$

$$\text{Employee turnover rate} = 28.57\%$$

Waste Not

Reducing Employee Turnover

Employee turnover is high across much of the foodservice industry—and it is costly. Foodservice operations spend millions of dollars a year training new employees. After an employee leaves, they must often pay their remaining employees higher overtime wages to work longer hours and pick up extra shifts. Better screening of job candidates is key to reducing turnover.

Another key is a focus on employee retention. Many foodservice operators find inexpensive and creative ways to retain employees and keep them happy. Some ideas include

* providing employee mentoring programs and improved training
* offering flexible work schedules
* interviewing employees to find out what they like about their jobs and what employers can work to improve
* rewarding employees for achieving sales and productivity targets with prizes, such as electronic devices or gas cards
* creating employee newsletters to boast about employee accomplishments
* celebrating employee birthdays and work anniversaries
* conducting team-building activities, such as after-hours bowling contests or barbeques
  Many employers find that these and other low-cost measures can reduce costly turnover.

Once the operation's baseline turnover rate is calculated, a manager can compare it against subsequent years to note changes. If employee turnover is worsening, the manager needs to look for ways to get from the actual rate to an acceptable one.

Determining Labor Needs

The number of employees working at any given time, and the tasks that they are completing, drive labor costs up or down. The amount of labor needed depends on several factors. Recall the discussions in other chapters about how labor needs vary with the menu, the type of operation, the food purchased, and the food production and serving methods employed. Figure **5-3** captures these and other factors that affect the amount of labor needed, or available to use in the operation.

Once these external factors are taken into consideration, it is time to determine when and where employees are needed, and what they will do while there. This is accomplished through:

- job analysis
- job routines
- work simplification studies
- organizational charts
- position control sheets

Job Analysis

A **job analysis** is the process of conducting a detailed study of the responsibilities and requirements of a job in order to improve the performance of the operation and its workers. A manager can begin a job analysis by writing down everything that must be done from the beginning to the end of the day. For instance, the manager of a restaurant that is open for breakfast and lunch, may list the following tasks:

- open the doors
- get out the ingredients and prep them for the omelets
- make the oatmeal and coffee
- ensure that the dining room is set
- make sure juice and milk are on hand
- prep items for the lunch recipes
- greet and serve the guests
- wash dishes
- clean the kitchen
- receive the deliveries
- order the food
- manage the bookkeeping

Job Routines

Once these tasks are written down, the manager assigns each to a job position, and determines the time frame in which each task must be completed. The breakfast cook may open the restaurant at 5:00 a.m., get the food out for the breakfast meal and do any pre-prep, make the oatmeal, cook breakfast, and begin the lunch production. At 5:30 a.m., a waitstaff person may begin work. This person checks the dining room's readiness for service, makes the coffee, ensures that the beverage station is set up, unlocks the front door at 6:00 a.m., and greets the first guest of the day.

Factors Affecting Labor Needs	
Factor	**Impact on Labor Needs**
Operation size	The larger the operation, the more staff may be needed.
Menu	Complex menus require a larger staff.
Food production system • Scratch versus convenience items • Commissary • Cook-chill • Cook-serve	Scratch cooking requires more production staff. Produce large volumes of food with less staff overall; food is delivered to various locations for service. Produce large volumes of food with less staff; food can be plated and assembled in the chilled state and rethermalized later. Requires more staff as the coordination of the food preparation and service is critical to its success.
Serving method(s) • Self-serve • Buffet • Table service • Trayline	Minimal service staff is needed. Minimal service staff is needed. More staff is required to wait on customers. Requires fewer staff than table service since meals are assembled similar to a manufacturing environment.
Layout and design of kitchen/ serving areas	When inefficient, more employees are needed to produce and serve meals; they must take more steps to accomplish tasks.
Available equipment	If equipment is not available, or if employees must wait for others to use it, they will take longer to complete their job duties.
Purchasing and receiving methods	The more orders placed and the more deliveries received, the greater the number of employees that will be needed.
Technology versus manual operations	Labor efficiencies can be gained through the use of technology; this can reduce the need for labor.
Union versus nonunion	At times, a union environment can add to labor requirements. Union contracts may limit the duties one employee can perform based on his or her job classification.
Job opportunities and unemployment rate	When the unemployment rate is low and job opportunities abound, operations may be forced to function with fewer staff, or be more generous with wages and employee benefits.
Amount of overtime allowed	Fewer positions are needed if overtime is an accepted practice. However, the manager should check overtime costs against the cost of hiring more staff.
Staff morale	Higher morale is associated with higher productivity.

Figure 5-3 Foodservice operations do not need the same number and types of employees. This list states factors that affect labor requirements.

This is the framework of a *job routine*. A **job routine** lists the tasks an employee is to complete and the time at which each task should be started and completed, **5-4**. A job routine ensures that all tasks are assigned, and that the work is appropriately divided among employees based on each person's time and skill set.

Work Simplification Study

Once tasks are identified and job routines sketched out, a foodservice manager should complete a *work simplification study*. A **work simplification study** is a process in which managers analyze how jobs are being done with the goal of finding easier ways to complete them. Consultants may be hired to conduct motion studies and workflow analyses. However, an experienced foodservice operator, with the help of an experienced staff and a stopwatch, can often accomplish a work simplification study internally.

Job Routine	
Food Service Aide 1	
6:30 AM–3:00 PM	
6:30 AM	Clock in. Wash hands. Set up Beverage Station: 　Brew 3 gallons regular coffee and 1 gallon decaf coffee. 　Pull cup lowerator to line. Gather lids. 　Get milk from walk-in cooler. Place in refrigerated unit on line.
6:50 AM	Work beverage station. Place beverage items on tray per menu. Brew additional coffee if needed.
8:15 AM	Break down station. Return leftover milk to cooler.
8:25 AM	15 minute break
8:40 AM	Work loader station in dishroom.
10:15 AM	Lunch break
10:45 AM	Set up Beverage Station: 　Brew 3 gallons regular coffee and 1 gallon decaf coffee. 　Pull cup lowerator to line. Gather lids. 　Get milk from walk-in cooler. Place in refrigerated unit on line.
11:00 AM	Work beverage station. Place beverage items on tray per menu. Brew additional coffee if needed.
12:30 PM	Break down station. Return leftover milk to cooler.
12:40 PM	Work loader station in dishroom.
2:00 PM	Clean dishmachine, including all curtains.
2:25 PM	Complete assigned cleaning (see daily schedule).
3:00 PM	Clock out.

Figure 5-4 For each position in a foodservice operation, a job routine states the activities that need to be completed and the timeframe in which they need to be done.

Consider this simple task: An employee needs to cut and plate 48 servings of apple pie. A pie yields 8 servings. The employee proceeds as follows:

1. Go to the refrigerator.
2. Get out one pie.
3. Walk back to the workstation.
4. Walk to the clean plate rack.
5. Obtain eight plates.
6. Walk back to the workstation.
7. Cut one piece of pie.
8. Place it on a plate.
9. Wrap it in plastic wrap.
10. Take it to the pie station.
11. Go back to the workstation.
12. Repeat steps 7 to 11 for the remaining 7 pieces of the pie.
13. Repeat steps 1 to 12 five more times until all the pieces are cut and plated.

If the manager observed the employee completing this task, what suggestions could he or she make to streamline this process? There is an easier way to accomplish it. Consider the following alternate series of steps.

1. Obtain a cart.
2. Go to the dish storage location.
3. Obtain 3 bun pans, 48 pie plates, a knife, and a pie server.
4. Proceed to the refrigerator.
5. Add 6 pies to the cart.
6. Go to the workstation.
7. Place a bun pan on the table.
8. Place 16 pie plates on the pan in a single layer.
9. Place the second bun pan on top of the first.
10. Place 16 plates on the pan in a single layer.
11. Repeat for the last pan.
12. Place two pies on the table and cut each into eight equal pieces.
13. Using the pie server, remove each piece of pie and place it on a plate on the top pan.
14. Cover the pan with plastic wrap.
15. Place the pan on the cart.
16. Repeat steps 12-15 two more times.
17. Take the cart with the pans of plated pie pieces to the designated refrigerator.
18. Place the pans in the refrigerator.

Which method sounds more efficient? The answer is the second. A work simplification study can help managers identify easier ways for employees to complete their tasks. It can also help the manager ensure that the layout of the kitchen and its equipment is most conducive to efficient motion, and that the employees have the equipment and tools they need to complete the tasks at hand.

Consider the pie-cutting steps described above. A manager doing a work simplification study may ask the following questions:

- How is the workstation located in relation to the dish storage area and the refrigerator? Could these areas be closer together to decrease the number of steps employees must take without causing traffic jams?

- What about the availability of the cart and pans at that time of day? Does the kitchen have an adequate number of them so this task can be completed while other activities are going on?
- Would it be more efficient for the employee to use a pie cutter instead of a knife?

In summary, a work simplification study helps managers examine the flow of the entire operation, in addition to the individual tasks of each employee. The manager's goal is to minimize steps for the employees and to find the most efficient way to complete all tasks. This improves workflow and the productivity of the staff.

Organizational Chart

An **organizational chart** is a diagram that illustrates the structure of an organization in terms of the relationships and relative rank of its employees. The chart usually depicts the position titles and the departments that make up an organization. It shows relationships between staff members, including the direct relationship between the supervisor and the workers he or she supervises. It represents the relationship between different departments on the same level. The organizational chart of a large company can be complex. Therefore, it may be broken up into a series of smaller charts—one or more for each department in the organization, **5-5**.

An organizational chart is a tool that can help operations control labor costs and improve productivity. It defines decision-making authority and provides employees with a map to navigate their organization. Employees are more productive when they can obtain information and direction from one particular individual, a supervisor. An organizational chart also helps supervisors understand their level of authority and decision-making.

Position Control Sheets

Position control sheets are useful labor-management tools, especially for larger operations. A **position control sheet** is a form that lists

- each position in a foodservice operation
- the job classification of each position
- the hours the employee holding the position works
- the total hours worked per pay period

Note that a job classification is similar to a job title. Cook, waiter, dishwasher, and manager are job titles. They have different job classifications. Each position has a corresponding number, **5-6**. The purpose of a position control sheet is to formalize the staffing for the operation. Positions are filled based on specific needs. Employees are hired for a specific job with specific hours assigned—not on a "where-needed"

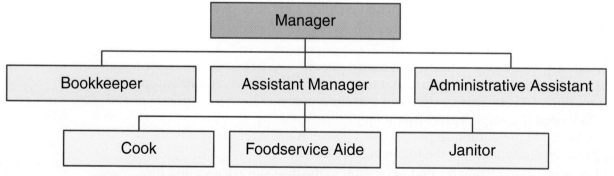

Figure 5-5 An organizational chart illustrates who reports to whom. Employees are informed about the chain of command and where they can go for assistance.

basis. Therefore, hired hours are controlled, labor costs are better monitored, and the operation runs more productively.

For example, suppose a bartender is paid a wage of $9.00 per hour. This bartender, who works 25 hours per week, wants to work more hours. When a janitor's position opens up, the bartender is allowed to pick up those hours, which add up to 10 hours a week. The janitor's position pays an hourly wage of $7.30. If the manager allows the bartender to work the janitor's position at a bartender's wage of $9.00 per hour, the actual wages paid will exceed the budgeted amount. While the bartender is working "where-needed," the wages exceed the amount budgeted for the position. The manager should either hire a janitor at the designated rate, or pay the bartender at the lower rate during the hours he or she works as a janitor.

Calculating Labor Requirement of a Position

How much labor does a particular position require? An operation needs more than one person to fill each full-time position because a person working an eight-hour shift does not work 365 days per year. The employee does not work every day that the operation is open either. For many positions, a substitute is required when the full-time person is on vacation, is sick, or has days off in the week. This staff-relief value can be determined with a simple formula using historical worked and non-worked hours.

Consider the following: An operation is open Monday through Friday, or five days a week. To determine how many days it is operational during a year, five is multiplied by 52, the number of weeks in a year. The operation has 260 available workdays per year.

A full-time employee generally works five days a week, or 260 days a year. In many operations, a full-time employee receives paid days off. Assume that during the previous year, the employee took off 10 days of vacation and five days of sick time. The employee also received seven holidays off and one day for jury duty. Last year, this employee was off 23 days and worked a total of 237 days—not 260 days. How much staff relief is necessary to fill this position? Or, how many full-time positions are needed to fill this one role? This can be calculated by taking the number of available workdays and dividing it by the number of actual workdays for this position.

$$\text{Full-time positions needed to fill job} = \frac{260}{237}$$

$$\text{Full-time positions needed to fill job} = 1.097, \text{ or } 1.1$$

This can be translated into hours by multiplying 1.1 by the number of hours worked per week.

$$1.1 \times 40 = 44.0$$

Subtracting 40 from 44 yields 4 hours. To be fully staffed, this position needs someone to work an additional 4 hours per week.

Scheduling Labor

When the job analysis and work simplification studies are completed, and the tasks are assigned to different positions, it is time to schedule the employees. **Scheduling** is the process of assigning employees to specific working hours and workdays. Schedules can be written to cover any length of time, but they typically cover a one- or two-week period.

When scheduling is done poorly, a foodservice operation loses money. One type of scheduling problem is understaffing. This occurs when a manager does not adequately staff the operation or when too few workers show up for a scheduled shift. When an operation is not adequately staffed, customers must wait longer to be served. This can lower customer satisfaction and result in fewer customers in the future. Understaffing also results in fewer table turnovers, or turns. Table turns refer to the number of times a table is used for a new guest or group of guests during a time period, such as a shift or a day. For instance, suppose a manager wants to know how many turns occur at a table during lunch. If four separate sets of guests dined at the table during lunch, that is four turns. The greater the number of turns, the greater the number of potential sales.

Understaffing can be costly for other reasons. Since the immediate needs of customers take precedence, employees may ignore or only partially complete their other tasks. Typically, cleaning, stock rotation, and paperwork are left for another time. There are consequences when these tasks are done poorly, or not at all. When stock is not rotated, product loss can occur. When cleaning schedules are not followed, unsanitary and dirty conditions can drive away customers or lead to citations by sanitation inspectors.

Can a busy operation ever have too many employees? Yes—at a certain point, adding staff is counterproductive. To illustrate why this is so, consider a restaurant that operates at maximum capacity—every table full—from opening to closing. The manager decides to add staff, thinking the extra employees will increase productivity. Instead, the manager observes employees trying to avoid bumping into each other. Employees complain of longer waits for shared equipment, such as trays and carts. The additional labor ends up being nonproductive. The manager pays for labor that is, in a sense, not working. Since the restaurant is already operating at full capacity, no more customers can be served in the same time period, so revenue does not increase. Therefore, the addition of labor can reach a point of diminishing returns. Both overstaffing and understaffing can cause an operation to lose money.

Factors That Affect Scheduling

The position control sheet is the main tool to use in plotting out the schedule, **5-6**. Consideration must be given to the anticipated activity of the operation during the time frame covered by the schedule, as well as employee time-off requests. Anticipated activity can be estimated by forecasting. A manager can forecast the operation's staff coverage needs by looking at current activity, historical trends, and future knowledge.

Trend/Technology

Labor Management Systems Aid Scheduling

The success of a foodservice operation depends on a manager's ability to have the right people in the right places at the right times. When scheduling is done with paper and pencil, inefficiencies can be hard to overcome. For example, papers get lost, communication between managers and workers can be cumbersome, and changes are difficult to make. A growing number of managers are using software systems to create and maintain their schedules and reduce inefficiencies.

One such system allows managers to create and transmit schedules to employees electronically. Employees can use their smartphones, laptops, tablets, or other devices to view schedules and request time off. The requests are received by managers on their electronic devices and can be easily approved or denied. Employees are instantly notified when managers change the schedule. Employees can use the system to communicate with one another if they need to switch schedules.

Many systems have built-in cost-control features and allow managers to specify targets. Targets can be set for labor costs and overtime pay. When costs threaten to go over targets, managers are alerted. They can then modify the schedule before it is transmitted to employees. The systems also report labor costs in real time.

Position Control Sheet		
Position	**Scheduled Time**	**Hours per Pay Period**
Manager	Varied	80
Assistant Manager	Varied	80
Adm. Asst.	8:00 AM–4:30 PM	80
Bookkeeper	10:00 AM–6:30 PM	80
Cook 1	5:00 AM–1:30 PM	80
Cook 2	8:00 AM–4:30 PM	80
Cook 3	11:00 AM–7:30 PM	80
Cook, Relief	Varied	64
Aide 1	6:00 AM–2:30 PM	80
Aide 2	6:00 AM–2:30 PM	80
Aide 3	6:30 AM–3:00 PM	80
Aide 4	6:30 AM–3:00 PM	80
Aide 5	6:30 AM–3:00 PM	80
Aide 6	10:30 AM–7:00 PM	80
Aide 7	10:45 AM–7:15 PM	80
Aide 8	4:15 PM–7:30 PM	32.50
Aide 9	4:15 PM–7:30 PM	32.50
Aide 10	4:15 PM–7:30 PM	32.50
Janitor	11:30 AM–8:00 PM	80
Janitor	5:00 PM–10:00 PM, pt	10
Bartender	4:00 PM–12:30 AM	80
Bartender	Varied	25
Aide 11	Varied	80
Aide 12	Varied	48
Aide 13	Varied	64
Aide 14	Varied, pt	42
Aide 15	Varied, pt	25.75

Figure 5-6 A position control sheet should be completed before a schedule is written. It tells the manager which positions are needed, and at which times. It also gives the number of hours employees in those positions need to work each pay period. In the example, there are four cook positions—three full-time (8 hours) and one part-time. Each cook is assigned different work hours.

As described earlier in this chapter, foodservice operations have fluctuations in their staffing needs during the day. For example, not all employees are needed when the restaurant opens or first thing in the morning in a noncommercial setting. As activity picks up during the day, more employees are needed. Staggering the staff's start and end times is a common practice for managers in scheduling, as seen in **5-7**. This enables them to control the amount and cost of labor, while meeting the needs of the operation.

Note how the positions are assigned a number in each job classification (Cooks 1, 2, and 3). The number assigned to the cook is placed on the schedule on the days that the cook works. When an employee is out, his or her number is written in the schedule next to the worker who will fill in. For example, when a relief cook takes the place of Cook 1, the "1" is noted on the relief cook's schedule. On Thursday of week one, the relief cook is working for Cook 1, whereas on Friday, he or she is working for Cook 3.

Note, also, how positions may be combined on days when sales or guest counts are lower. For a hospital, weekends may have fewer cafeteria guests, so, positions can be combined. For example, on the first Saturday, Cook 1 will work his or her normal scheduled time, 5:00 a.m. to 1:30 p.m., but, will cover the duties of both Cook 1 and Cook 2. One less cook is needed for the weekend.

Also note that the relief cook works one of the aide positions twice during the pay period. The manager needs to weigh whether this is an appropriate use of labor. Refer back to the discussion on position control sheets. There, the manager determined that the bartender's wage was too high compared to the janitor's wage, and the bartender should not pick up the hours of the janitor. Here, the manager should weigh whether the hours assigned to the relief cook should be removed and another aide hired, or, if it is more cost-effective and provides more schedule flexibility to allow the relief cook to work the 16 hours for the aide.

The number designation also allows the manager to quickly note whether he or she has scheduled all needed positions. Aide positions 1 through 10 must be filled each day. The manager can quickly review each day's schedule to be sure that it shows Aide positions 1 through 10 on the schedule.

Foodservice operations also use part-time employees to help them get through the peaks and valleys in activity during the day. A popular dinner spot will need more waitstaff between 5:00 to 9:00 p.m. than between 1:00 to 5:00 p.m. If the restaurant is only staffed with full-time workers, most of them would be idle or nonproductive during the four-hour lull in activity. The same is true in a noncommercial operation that serves three meals per day. A full-time employee cannot cover all three meal periods without working more than eight hours. It is typical for a noncommercial operation to employ part-time workers to cover either the first meal of the day or the evening meal.

Staffing Fluctuations over Blocks of Time

Staffing needs also fluctuate over longer periods of time. Staff coverage may need to change based on seasons, weather, and other factors. Studying historical trends can help managers forecast staff coverage. Suppose, for instance, that a hospital in northern Michigan runs an average daily census of 200 patients during most of the year. Between December and the end of February, census rises an average of 35 additional patients per day. A number of ski resorts are located nearby. During snow and ski season, the foodservice director needs to plan for the additional workload, and staff accordingly. A restaurant located in Sarasota, Florida, may also see an increase in traffic during the winter months as people travel south to escape the cold. This restaurant's foodservice director will also need to anticipate an increased workload at this time and add temporary or seasonal staff.

Staggered Schedule		M	T	W	Th	F	Sat	Sun	M	T	W	Th	F	Sat	Sun
Manager	Varied						X	X						X	X
Asst. Manager	Varied						X	X						X	X
Adm. Asst.	8–4:30						X	X						X	X
Bookkeeper	10–6:30						X	X						X	X
Cook 1	5–1:30	1	1	1	X	1	1&2	X	1	X	1	1	1	1&2	1&2
Cook 2	8–4:30	2	2	2	2	2	X	1&2	2	2	2	2	2	X	X
Cook 3	11–7:30	3	3	3	3	X	3	3	3	3	3	X	3	X	X
Cook, Relief	Varied	X	X	7	1	3	X	X	7	1	X	3	X	3	3
Bartender	4–12:30				X			X				X			X
Bartender	Varied	X	X	X		X	5:30–10	X	X	X	X		X	5:30–10	X
Aide 1	6–2:30	X	1	1	1	1	X	X	1	1	1	1	X	1	1
Aide 2	6–2:30	2	2	2	X	2	2	2	2	X	2	2	2	X	X
Aide 3	6:30–3	3	X	3	3	3	X	X	3	3	X	3	3	3	3
Aide 4	6:30–3	4	4	4	4	X	4	4	4	4	4	X	4	X	X
Aide 5	6:30–3	5	5	X	5	5	X	X	5	5	5	5	X	5	5
Aide 6	10:30–7	6	X	6	6	6	X	X	6	6	X	6	6	6&7	6&7
Aide 7	10:45–7:15	7	7	X	7	7	6&7	6&7	X	7	7	7	7	X	X
Aide 8	4:15–7:30	8	8	X	8	8	X	X	8	8	8	8	X	8	8
Aide 9	4:15–7:30	9	9	9	X	9	9	9	X	9	9	9	9	X	X
Aide 10	4:15–7:30	10	X	10	10	10	X	X	10	10	10	X	10	10	10
Aide 11	Varied	1	3	5	X	4	1	1	X	2	3	4	1	X	X
Aide 12	Varied	X	X	7	X	X	5	5	7	X	X	X	X	4	4
Aide 13	Varied	X	6	X	2	X	3	3	X	X	6	X	5	2	2
Aide 14	Varied, pt	X	10	8	X	J	8	8	9	J	X	10	8	9	9
Aide 15	Varied, pt	X	X	X	9	X	10	10	X	X	X	X	X	J	J
Janitor	11:30–8	J	J	J	J	X	J	J	J	X	J	J	J	X	X
Janitor	5–10, pt	X	X	X	X	X	X		X	X	X	X	X	X	

Figure 5-7 In most foodservice operations, all employees do not arrive and leave at the same time. A staggered schedule is essential to controlling costs. Only employees needed at any given time during the day are scheduled.

Scheduling can easily be adjusted to cover increased staffing needs during large blocks of time, such as months. However, foodservice managers must often anticipate other situations that impact staffing needs. For many restaurants, Mother's Day is the busiest day of the year. A wise manager brings in additional staff to cover the increase in patrons on this day. If the street on which a restaurant is located undergoes major repairs, a manager should anticipate that the customer count may decrease. Potential customers may avoid the construction area or the restaurant may be temporarily hidden by scaffolding and other obstructions. He or she should decrease staffing during this time.

For all of the reasons noted above, many operations prepare a unique schedule each week rather than use the same schedule from week to week. This is sometimes referred to as *zero-based scheduling*. Each week, the manager creates a schedule based on anticipated sales for the coming week and his or her targeted labor budget. So, an employee's schedule may not be routine. For example, an employee may normally work on Monday, Tuesday, Thursday, Friday, and Saturday, from 12:00 to 8:00 p.m. But this schedule may vary based on the anticipated needs of the operation for the coming week.

In summary, to prepare a schedule, a manager must understand an operation's core crew needs, based on the position control sheet. Employees' time off, historical trends, and anticipated needs must be reflected in the schedule. The goal is to complete the workload using the minimal number of work hours, while maintaining the desired level of service. If too many employees are scheduled, productivity is low compared to labor costs and money is wasted. If too few employees are scheduled, customers' needs might not be met. This, in turn, affects profits if these customers choose not to return.

Analyzing Labor Costs

How do foodservice managers determine how efficiently their operations are running, how productive their employees are, and how well they are doing their jobs? Managers can use a variety of ratios—or productivity indices—to answer these questions. Each index conveys a different piece of information and each has its strengths and weaknesses. This process is referred to as **labor cost analysis**.

Using labor cost analysis, the various factors that contribute to an operation's labor costs can be teased out and calculated. To get the best picture of an operation, managers should use more than one measure. They can then compare the numbers to those derived from subsequent analyses to determine the tipping point of their labor requirements. The tipping point is the threshold at which the labor used meets the service needs of the operation. This occurs when goals are no longer met and when service levels suffer because labor is too low. Common ratios used include:

- labor cost percentage
- covers per labor hour
- labor cost per cover
- labor cost per labor hour

In noncommercial operations, the following are commonly used:

- labor cost per meal
- meals per productive labor hour

Total labor cost may be defined differently from one operation to another. An operation may or may not include the cost of employee benefits and payroll taxes in its total labor cost. Also, the salaries of managers may or may not be included in an operation's total labor cost.

Labor Cost Percentage

Labor cost analysis generally begins with the calculation of labor cost percentage. The labor cost percentage is derived from information found in an operation's monthly financial reports. **Labor cost percentage** is defined as the total labor cost divided by the total sales in a given time period. The formula is:

$$\text{Labor Cost \%} = \frac{\text{Labor Cost}}{\text{Sales}} \times 100$$

For example, Jack's Chicken Joint spent $5,000 on labor costs and generated $40,000 in sales during one week. The cost of labor to total sales would be calculated as:

$$\text{Labor cost \%} = \frac{\$5,000}{\$40,000} \times 100$$

$$\text{Labor cost \%} = 12.5\%$$

As a measure of overall labor productivity, especially labor productivity over time, the labor cost percentage has its drawbacks. It does not take into account many variables that can change the percentage, but have nothing to do with labor productivity. If Jack's Chicken Joint generated $50,000 the following month, using the same amount of labor, the labor cost percentage calculation would be.

$$\text{Labor cost \%} = \frac{\$5,000}{\$50,000} \times 100$$

$$\text{Labor cost \%} = 10\%$$

At a labor cost percentage of 10 percent, is Jack's staff more productive than they were the previous month? Not necessarily. Other factors, besides labor productivity, may be at play. The increase in total sales revenue may have been caused by price increases on popular menu items. Assuming that the number of customers served was the same, the staff did not increase their productivity—the sales revenue simply increased.

The labor cost percentage can also shift with increases and decreases in labor costs. Suppose a few employees go on vacation and Jack must bring in staff to cover their schedules. Labor costs will increase because both the employees on vacation and the replacement workers are paid. The employees are not less productive as the higher ratio would indicate.

How can a manager use labor cost percentage to provide a better analysis?

- Separate calculations can be made for different job classifications, days of the week, and meal periods.
- The measure can be generated weekly, if not daily, to respond to fluctuations in the ratio.
- The measure can be used as an indicator. In addition, a manager can determine what may be causing a change in this ratio besides an increase or decrease in staff productivity.

Covers per Labor Hour

A **cover** is an industry term for a customer. **Covers per labor hour** is the number of customers served per labor hour worked. This is also expressed as a simple ratio. The formula is:

$$\text{Covers per Labor Hour} = \frac{\text{Covers}}{\text{Labor Hours}}$$

Therefore, suppose 240 customers patronize a restaurant on a given day. Eight employees work that day for eight hours each, for a total of 64 hours.

$$\text{Covers per labor hour} = \frac{240 \text{ covers}}{64 \text{ hours}}$$

$$\text{Covers per labor hour} = 3.75$$

Therefore, 3.75 customers were served for each labor hour worked. This ratio is the best measure of labor productivity because it is not influenced by changes in wages and selling prices.

Labor Cost per Cover

A manager can determine how many labor dollars it took to serve each customer. **Labor cost per cover** is the total labor cost during a period of time divided by the number of covers for the same time period. The formula is:

$$\text{Labor Cost per Cover} = \frac{\text{Labor Cost}}{\text{Covers}}$$

For example, if the total labor cost over a week was $5,000 and 1,680 people were served, the calculation would look like this:

$$\text{Labor cost per cover} = \frac{\$5,000}{\$1,680}$$

$$\text{Labor cost per cover} = \$2.98$$

During the week, the operation spent $2.98 in labor costs to serve each customer. A drawback to using this measure is that it depends on the price paid for labor, which can vary.

Labor Cost per Meal

In a noncommercial operation, the labor cost per meal ratio is similar to the labor cost per cover ratio. **Labor cost per meal** is the total labor cost divided by the number of meals served during a given period of time. The formula is:

$$\text{Labor Cost per Meal} = \frac{\text{Labor Cost}}{\text{Meals Served}}$$

Suppose a senior living community has 100 residents. They serve three meals per day, and provide meal service only to the residents. Therefore, the number of meals served per day is 300 (100 residents multiplied by 3 meals). Assume that eight employees work full time and the total labor cost per day is $608. The labor cost per meal would be calculated as follows:

$$\text{Labor cost per meal} = \frac{\$608}{300}$$

$$\text{Labor cost per meal} = \$2.03$$

The problem with this measure is that it cannot be used to compare worker productivity over time because it depends on labor costs, which can vary from one day to another. For instance, if an employee is away for a week, it would be unfair to criticize the remaining employees for decreased productivity during that time. Also, if a manager must hire a replacement, plus pay the employee on vacation, labor costs would rise, as would labor cost per meal. Does this indicate that employees are less productive because it costs more to serve each meal? Not necessarily. To get a better measure of labor productivity over time, the manager would want to factor out labor costs due to employee absences, and so forth.

Labor Cost per Labor Hour

Labor cost per labor hour is defined as the total labor cost divided by the total labor hours used. It is most effective when performed on a single job classification at a time, such as waitstaff or cooks. It is a good way to see the wage differences between job classes, and to establish wage ranges within each classification. The formula is:

$$\text{Labor Cost per Labor Hour} = \frac{\text{Labor Cost}}{\text{Labor Hours}}$$

Suppose the total labor cost for the cooks at a foodservice operation during one week is $2,000. First, the total labor hours would be calculated. Four cooks are employed full time for a total of 160 hours (4 cooks multiplied by 40 hours each). The ratio would be expressed as:

$$\text{Labor cost per labor hour} = \frac{\$2,000}{160}$$

$$\text{Labor cost per labor hour} = \$12.50$$

Now, assume that there are 12 full-time waitstaff employed each week. The total labor cost for this classification is $3,500. The total labor hours would be 480 hours (12 waitstaff multiplied by 40 hours each). The ratio would be expressed as:

$$\text{Labor cost per labor hour} = \frac{\$3,500}{480}$$

$$\text{Labor cost per labor hour} = \$7.29$$

The cooks make an average of $12.50 an hour compared with the waitstaff who each earns an average of $7.29 an hour. Using this information, the manager can decide if this is a good differential between the two positions.

The labor cost per labor hour can also be used by a manager to evaluate the wage spread within a job classification. Managers use labor cost per labor hour as a tool to ensure that employees are paid fairly in relation to each other. For example, a manager can determine the pay range for cooks by identifying the hourly wages of the highest- and the lowest-paid cooks. The manager determines where the pay range falls in relation to the average labor cost for cooks of $12.50 an hour. The manager can ask him- or herself if the spread is a good one based on the experience of the employees, the job market, and so forth.

Meals per Productive Labor Hour

Refer to the example of a foodservice operation in a senior living community. On a typical day, eight employees work full time (64 hours) and serve 300 meals. The meals per labor hour would be calculated as follows:

$$\text{Meals per labor hour} = \frac{300 \text{ meals}}{64 \text{ hours}}$$

$$\text{Meals per labor hour} = 4.69$$

Now, assume that the next day, two employees are out—one is on vacation and the other called in sick. The manager calls in other workers to fill both positions. So, for that day, the total number of labor hours would be 80 hours (64 regular hours plus 8 vacation hours and 8 sick leave hours). Now, the meals per labor hour would be:

$$\text{Meals per labor hour} = \frac{300 \text{ meals}}{80 \text{ hours}}$$

Meals per labor hour = 3.75

Are the employees less productive than those who worked the previous day? After all, they served 3.75 meals per hour versus the 4.69 meals per hour served the previous day. Comparing these numbers can be misleading because the second calculation factored in the nonproductive hours of vacation and sick time. The manager cannot control the cost of benefits granted to employees. So the best method of determining meals per labor hour uses only productive labor hours, or hours "on the clock."

The *meals per productive labor hour* ratio is used in noncommercial operations. **Meals per productive labor hour** is the number of meals served divided by the number of productive hours worked in a given period of time. The formula is:

$$\text{Meals per Productive Labor Hour} = \frac{\text{Meals Served}}{\text{Productive Labor Hours}}$$

This is a truer measure of worker productivity and how well a manager manages labor hours.

Analyzing and Benchmarking Results

After the ratios are generated, they are analyzed by the manager. This is achieved by *benchmarking*. **Benchmarking** is the evaluation of an operation's processes in relation to the industry's best practice, the operation's own experiences, or a standard set by law. An operation may choose to benchmark a measure—such as covers per labor hour—against the value that is considered to be the best in the industry. Or it can set its own acceptable target number and benchmark against that number.

If a ratio increases or decreases, the manager needs to identify what caused the change. If it is something that can be remedied, the manager should do so, note the result with the next set of ratios, and continue the practice if it proves to be positive. Take, for example, labor cost percentage, which was described earlier. Many operators calculate the labor cost percentage on a weekly, or even a daily basis. They may use it to determine the staffing or scheduling needs for a coming week.

To determine the labor cost percentage for a particular day, a manager divides the day's labor costs by total sales. A manager may choose to benchmark the labor cost percentage against the industry average, which is between 16 and 20 percent, according to the Uniform System of Accounts for Restaurants, published by the National Restaurant Association. Or the manager may use a labor cost percentage that the operation determined to be desirable—22 percent, for example.

If that percentage is higher than desired—say 23 percent—the manager can adjust the schedule for the coming week. Scheduled hours can be decreased, for example. The following week, the manager can look at the ratio of the total labor cost to total sales and once again determine the labor cost percentage. If the labor cost percentage is now at the desired level, the manager would create the schedule for the following week using a similar number of hours.

All of this, of course, must take into consideration the total sales anticipated based on historical data and anticipated sales for the following week. If the labor cost percentage is too high, the manager needs to determine the possible causes. Did the manager over-schedule? Are the employees being unproductive, resulting in fewer table turnovers and causing potential customers to leave? Are employees clocking in ahead of their scheduled time, or are they staying over when it is not necessary? Benchmarking allows the manager to keep close tabs on the operation, make timely adjustments, and monitor the success or failure of those adjustments.

Benchmarking is generally an ongoing process, as the manager attempts to move closer and closer to the benchmarking goal. Sources for industry benchmarks are available through trade groups, such as the National Restaurant Association (NRA), the Association for Healthcare Foodservice (AHF), or through government agencies.

Limits of Labor Analysis

The measurement of labor cost through labor cost analysis is important, but fails to tell the whole story. The ratios are impacted by a variety of factors, some of which managers do not control—including the weather, employee benefits, natural disasters, and road construction. Labor cost analysis also does not directly measure the impact on service levels when labor is significantly reduced. In other words, an operation's ratios or numbers for a particular day may look good, but customers waited too long to be served or the restaurant was dirty. Although these problems will not affect the day's labor ratios, their impact may be seen down the road. Customers may not return to a restaurant with poor service or an unsanitary dining room.

The foodservice manager must find the point at which customer expectations are met or exceeded while the least amount of labor dollars are spent. Analysis of labor costs is important to control the bottom line. However, the wise manager takes the words of Albert Einstein to heart: "Not everything that can be measured counts, and not everything that counts can be measured."

Key Terms

payroll	job analysis	cover
job description	job routine	covers per labor hour
American with Disabilities Act (ADA)	work simplification study	labor cost per cover
	organizational chart	labor cost per meal
recruiting	position control sheet	labor cost per labor hour
screening interview	scheduling	meals per productive labor hour
performance appraisal	labor cost analysis	
retention	labor cost percentage	benchmarking
employee turnover rate		

Recap

- Ensuring that an operation has the right people, at the right times, in the right places, with the right knowledge and skills, is essential to labor cost control.
- The nature of foodservice operations makes labor management and cost control especially challenging.
- Labor costs include payroll, employee benefits, and payroll taxes.
- Management responsibilities include hiring, training, and supervising employees, and ensuring they have a safe work environment.
- The employee turnover rate is a measure of employee retention; higher rates result in higher labor costs.
- Job analyses, job routines, and work simplification studies are used to determine what tasks need to be completed, which employees should complete them, and how to train employees to ensure the tasks are completed efficiently.
- An organizational chart defines decision-making authority.
- A position control sheet is a useful tool to manage labor; it is used to complete employee work schedules.
- Proper scheduling is a key to successful labor cost control.
- Labor cost analysis ratios measure productivity and labor costs.
- In benchmarking, managers evaluate ratios against some standard—an industry best practice, the operation's own experience, or a standard set by law.
- A foodservice manager must find the point at which customer expectations can be met or exceeding using the least amount of labor dollars.

Review Questions

1. Define the terms *labor cost* and *payroll cost* and explain the difference between them.
2. List five actions a manager can take to ensure a safe work environment for employees of a foodservice operation.
3. Explain the relationship between employee retention and cost control. Describe aspects of the foodservice industry that make employee retention especially challenging.
4. Calculate the annual turnover rate of an operation given the following: Fifteen employees were separated from the operation during the year and the average number of employees was 45.
5. State how kitchen layout and design affect labor cost.
6. Explain the difference between a job analysis and a work simplification study.
7. Explain why an establishment needs more than one person to fill each full-time position.
8. What is the advantage of a staggered schedule in a foodservice operation?
9. Describe the limitations of labor cost analysis.

Applying Your Knowledge

10. Using the information in the chart, calculate the following ratios for a foodservice operation. Then explain what each calculation means and its limitations, if any. (In this example, labor cost is equal to total payroll.)
   A. labor cost to total sales
   B. covers to labor hours
   C. labor cost to covers
   D. labor cost to labor hours for cooks
   E. labor cost to labor hours for waitstaff
   F. meals served to productive labor hours

Expense Type per Day	
Total payroll	$1,100 (cooks $400, waitstaff $400, bus person $50, manager/owner $250)
Total revenue	$11,000
Number of customers	250
Number of employees	10 (3 cooks, 5 waitstaff, 1 manager, 1 bus person)
Hours per employee	8.0 hours
Breaks per employee	0.5 hour

Exercises 5-11 and 5-12

Complete the following exercises on the companion website:
www.g-wlearning.com/culinaryarts/

11. Malcolm was recently promoted from lead cook to manager at Pat's Pub. Pat, the owner, told Malcolm his goal was to maintain labor costs at or below 20 percent. Unfortunately, Malcolm does not know how to calculate labor cost percentage.

   A. Complete the spreadsheet to calculate Malcolm's labor cost percentages for each day, as well as for the week. (Assume employees are paid $7.50 per hour.) Use this information to answer the questions that follow.

Pat's Pub								
	Hours Worked							
Employees	**Mon**	**Tues**	**Wed**	**Thurs**	**Fri**	**Sat**	**Sun**	**Total**
Sally	8	8	8	8	8			
Mark	8	8		8		8	8	
Kathy	6	7	7	6	5		8	
Dana	7		9	6		8	8	
Sarah	6	6	6		8	6		
Sharon	8		8		8	8	8	
Ashley	5	5		5	8	8	8	
Michelle	6	6	6			5	8	
Jessica	8		8	8	8	8		
Bethany		8		7	8	8	8	
Total Hours Worked								
Labor Cost Percentage Calculation								
Total Sales	$2,000	$1,250	$1,300	$1,500	$2,500	$2,700	$2,000	
Labor Cost								
Labor Cost Percentage								

   B. Is Malcolm achieving the labor cost percentage goal? Please explain.
   C. What can Malcolm do to decrease his labor cost percentage?
   D. Identify possible customer-service issues that might result from the current staffing pattern.

12. Pedra is the foodservice director at Park Grove Senior Living Center. The administrator is concerned about the turnover rate of the foodservice employees and asks Pedra how Park Grove's rate compares to other senior living centers in the area. Pedra belongs to a trade association that provides benchmarking information on all aspects of a foodservice operation. Pedra checks the benchmarking information and discovers that 39 percent is an average turnover rate for operations such as Park Grove.

   A. Complete the spreadsheet below to calculate Pedra's turnover rate for the past three years and use the information to answer the questions that follow.

Employee Turnover			
	Year 2012	Year 2013	Year 2014
Average number of employees during the year	38	40	41
Number of employees separated from employment	24	20	18
Turnover rate			

   B. How does Pedra's employee turnover rate compare with industry benchmarks?
   C. Pedra wants to maintain 41 employees on staff for 2015. What is the maximum number of employee separations that can occur if she wants to meet the industry benchmark?

Course Project

The Course Project is a full case study on controlling costs in a foodservice operation. Each chapter presents one component of the project. You may have to refer to other completed components to answer the following questions.

13. The chapter on menu planning required you to write a lunch menu for your foodservice establishment. Assume an average customer count of 200 for lunch, an average check of $10, and total sales of $2,000. Estimate the staffing needs for your operation. Write a position control sheet for lunch.

14. Based on wages in your area, assign a wage to each position. Assume the cost of employee benefits and payroll taxes are 20 percent of employees' wages.

15. Write a one-week schedule.

16. Calculate the labor cost percentage for the week.

Chapter 6
Beverage Cost Control

Learning Outcomes

After studying this chapter, you will be able to

- define the four types of beverage service systems.
- explain the difference between purchasing food and purchasing beverages.
- name three things that need to be verified during the receiving process.
- list the storage temperature requirements for the different types of alcoholic beverages.
- create a count sheet for four types of beer at the bar.
- list the variables to consider in determining the selling price of an alcoholic beverage.
- describe the beverage control systems used in serving.
- define dramshop liability.

Many foodservice operations offer alcoholic beverages to their patrons. These beverages are the featured menu items at some operations—bars, for example. At other operations, they are listed along with many food items. Selling alcoholic beverages can be more profitable than selling food alone. It requires minimal equipment and labor and can be easy to control if the proper systems are in place.

However, serving alcoholic beverages is not without its challenges. Due to its desirability, the theft of alcoholic beverages by employees and customers is often a problem. In addition, operations can be liable if they allow customers to consume too much alcohol or if alcohol is served to underage customers. Strong control systems are necessary to prevent these problems and to generate the greatest profit. Most operations separate beverages into the alcoholic and the nonalcoholic. Nonalcoholic beverages are considered with food costs. This chapter focuses on the control of alcoholic beverages.

Types of Beverage Services

To control beverage costs, managers need to understand the various types of beverage service. There are generally four types—bar service, server service, guest service, and special-purpose service.

Bar service is a type of beverage service in which beverages are ordered, prepared, and served from the bar. Bar service is sometimes referred to as *front service*. The bartender prepares the drink, and either the bartender or a server delivers it to the customer. Or a guest may sit at the bar. Bar-service costs can be the most difficult to control. A customer often has the option of running a tab and locating the customer when the bill is due can sometimes be difficult.

Server service is a type of beverage service in which drinks ordered by customers are prepared and served by the waitstaff. With the *point-of-sale systems* commonly used in foodservice operations today, this type of beverage service provides the best control on costs. **Point-of-sale system (POS)** refers to the hardware and software used for placing orders and generating bills for customers. POS systems can be very simple or quite sophisticated. Many can also track inventory. The server enters the sale into the system and the customer receives the bill.

Guest service is a type of nonalcoholic beverage service in which guests dispense their own drinks at beverage stations. They receive cups or glasses when they place their orders. Guest service is only used with nonalcoholic beverages and is most commonly used in the fast-food industry. The disadvantage of guest service, in relation to cost, is that a customer may dispense a refill without paying for it.

Special-purpose service is used to supply beverages to guests during events—such as receptions and banquets—that often require a portable or temporary bar setup. A bartender prepares and serves the drinks. The agreement made between the provider of the beverage service and the event host determines whether or not guests pay for the drinks. For instance, guests typically do not pay for their drinks at a wedding reception. The host pays for the beverage service.

At many fundraising or organization-sponsored events, guests are asked to purchase their own drinks from the bar. This is commonly referred to as a *cash bar*. To control costs, guests may be required to purchase drink tickets in advance or to pay the bartender when placing their orders. However, a method of recording purchases should be in place, otherwise, a bartender may provide free drinks to some guests. In the contract, the operator can establish that the event sponsor will pay for all alcohol consumed. This will help cover costs.

Beverage Classification

Alcoholic beverages are classified into three groups—beer, wines, and spirits. Beer is produced through a fermentation process. Grain, such as malted barley, wheat, corn, or rice, is fermented using yeast. The beer is flavored with hops, which are also a natural preservative. Fruit and herbs can be added to produce a distinct taste.

Beer can be either lager or ale. Lager, the most common beer, is fermented using a bottom-fermenting process, which produces a clean-tasting beer. It is fermented at a lower temperature and for a longer time period than ale. Ale is produced using a top-fermenting process. It is fermented at a higher temperature and for a shorter period of time. This yields a sweeter, fuller beer.

Wine is an alcoholic beverage made through the fermentation of fruit, such as grapes and berries, **6-1**. Yeast consume the sugar in the fruit and turn it into alcohol. The label on a wine bottle provides a wealth of information about the wine itself. Label content is regulated by the country in

Wine Category	Examples
Table	Red, white, rosé
Sparkling	Most champagne
Sweet (Dessert)	Sugar is added during fermentation, or sweeter grapes are used to produce the distinct taste
Fortified	Liqueurs, such as port, vermouth, sherry; alcohol is added during fermentation
Wine Coolers	Wines blended with fruit juices

Figure 6-1 Wine continues to grow in popularity among consumers. This illustrates the five basic wine categories and provides examples of each. Some operations will offer all five, while others may offer none or the basic table wine.

which the wine is made. A varietal wine is named after the type of grape used to make it, such as chardonnay or pinot noir. A red burgundy wine is made from pinot noir grapes and is produced in France. Regional wines are named after a place of origin—a large region or a small vineyard, for example. Chianti wine, which is produced in the Chianti region of Tuscany, Italy, mainly uses the Sangiovese grape.

Beer and wine are produced through fermentation. Spirits are produced when the products of fermentation are distilled. During distillation, the liquid is evaporated, condensed, and collected. This results in a product with increased alcoholic content. Vodka, bourbon, whiskey, and gin are examples of spirits.

Knowing the ingredients of various alcoholic beverages can be helpful to a manager in controlling costs. Like the cost of food, the price of beverages can be influenced by the cost of the ingredients. For instance, if a significant drought hit the wine-producing areas of California, the cost of wine from those regions may increase. In addition, the other wine-producing regions of the country may see an increase in demand for their products to offset the lower supply from California. The cost of American wine may increase during this time period. Anticipating an increase in the cost of wine, a manager may seek out less-expensive wines or increase prices charged customers.

Purchasing

Beverage costs can be controlled through a sound purchasing system. Beverages are easier to purchase than food for several reasons. First, unlike food, beverages generally do not spoil quickly. Also, their availability is not dependent on the season.

Unlike food, beverages are more uniform in pricing due to strict regulations of the alcohol trade. In most states, the purchasing and invoice prices of alcoholic beverages are highly regulated. Some states require operations to purchase their beer, wine, and spirits from designated distributors. Other states control the number and locations of distributors, so there are often few distributors of alcoholic beverages in a given geographical region. Since the prices for a particular product are usually about the same between vendors, it is often not possible for operations to receive competitive bids or to seek vendors or distributors that offer better pricing.

As with the purchase of food, establishing controls in the purchase of beverages is an important managerial function. Having purchasing controls ensures that an adequate inventory of alcohol is maintained by the operation and that purchases are made at an optimum price. It also ensures that the quality of the products purchased is adequate for their intended use and meets customer expectations.

In determining a purchasing schedule for beverages, consideration should be given to the following factors:
- available storage space
- vendor delivery schedules
- minimum order requirements of vendors
- price specials or volume discounts offered by vendors
- availability of items

The shelf life of alcoholic beverages is a consideration when determining the amount to purchase at a given time. The shelf life of beer, the most perishable type of alcoholic beverage, depends on how it is packaged or sold. Kegs are the cheapest per ounce, but require a tap and have a shorter shelf life. An untapped keg can be stored for about 45 days, but should be used within several days once it is opened. A bottle or can of beer has a longer shelf life than a keg. As a general rule, lagers retain their quality for about four months and ales for about five months. There is no legal mandate for beer to carry freshness or expiration dates, but it has become a common practice.

Trend/Waste Not

Growing Popularity of Boxed Wines

In the United States, most wines come in glass bottles. However, in many European countries, wine—even high-end wines—also come in cartons. These boxed wines are beating out bottled wines in international wine competitions. Given the many advantages of the box packaging format over bottle, the sales of boxed wines is trending up in the United States.

Boxes are more economical because the packaging costs less to manufacture and transport. Unlike glass containers, the lightweight boxes are easy to handle and store, and they do not shatter. Boxed wines have a longer shelf life than bottled wines. Box packaging is also environmentally friendly. It requires less energy to produce and less fuel to transport than heavier bottles. The boxes are made of recyclable materials and can easily be folded flat and stored until recycled.

The quality and taste of boxed wines can be good and sometimes better than that of bottled wines. Wine can degrade in bottles because glass does not fully protect the wine from UV light, which affects its quality and taste. Also, once opened and poured, a bottle fills up with oxygen, which can also degrade the wine. Boxed wine is held in an inner bag inside the box. When wine is dispensed, the bag collapses on itself, leaving little room for oxygen to enter. Although more high-end wines are being sold in cartons, aged wines must still be sold in bottles.

Wines are purchased for both consumption and cooking. The wine used for both purposes can be bought from the same vendor. The quality of a cooking wine does not have to be as high as the quality of a wine sold for drinking. The extent of the wine list, as well as the amounts and types of wine purchased, varies from one type of establishment to another. The manager should establish a wine list that fits the operation and the expectations of its customers.

The shelf life of a wine depends on the type of grape and the production method used. A wine's vintage date is the date it was bottled. In general, white wines should be consumed within one to three years from the vintage year shown on the label, and red wines within two to five years. Some wines are suitable for aging and may be at their best 15 to 30 years after the vintage year. An establishment that wishes to offer aged wines should consult a wine specialist about proper storage and aging to ensure that the quality is preserved.

Spirits have an extremely long shelf life. When purchasing spirits, decisions must be made about which varieties to stock. Variety is determined by the menu. Of course, the spirits needed to make the cocktails offered must be available. Since product quality can vary, operations must also make decisions about the quality they desire. Operations serving alcoholic beverages generally select a house brand for the various liquors sold. The house brand, also called a **well brand**, is a lesser-quality brand. If a customer orders a drink and does not specify a type of liquor, the bartender uses the well brand. The selection of the well brand gives the operation an opportunity to control costs. The well brand is generally less expensive than the *top shelf* and *call liquors*.

Depending on the operation, several tiers of liquor may be offered to customers. A **call brand** is a spirit that a customer requests by its brand name. A **top-shelf liquor**, also called a **premium liquor** or top-tier liquor, is the highest quality product of a particular type of liquor that an operation stocks.

In addition to controlling costs through the selection of brands to stock, an operation can take advantage of volume-purchasing discounts. However, volume purchasing may not make sense for small operations, or for operations with little or no storage space.

The most common method of maintaining beverage supplies is through the use of *par levels*. The operation establishes the minimum amount of each type of beer, wine, and spirit that should be kept on hand at any given time. A general rule of thumb is that the amount on hand should be equal to 1½ times the amount that is usually served. For instance, if a bar usually serves 300 bottles of wine on Friday and Saturday nights, the bar would maintain an inventory of 450 bottles of wine. When placing an order, the manager inventories the liquor and orders the amount needed to bring each one back to the par level. For example, if the par level for vodka is five bottles and two bottles are in inventory, the manager will order three bottles to bring the operation back to par.

Receiving

The system used for receiving alcoholic beverages is similar to that used for food. With a copy of the invoice in hand, the receiving person checks the delivery to ensure that ordered products are received and priced correctly. The product shelf life should be checked, including the freshness date of beer and the vintage year of wines.

The receiving person should also check that the correct brand is delivered based on the order sheet. The bottles should be examined for breakage. Some operations weigh in cases to verify that bottles are full when received. When receiving alcoholic beverages, it is critical to ensure that products are secured immediately following arrival to deter theft.

Storage

Like food, alcoholic beverages must be stored at the proper temperatures. Since beer in kegs is not pasteurized, it should be stored cold at between 36°F and 38°F. To maintain this temperature and to prevent temperature fluctuations, access to the refrigerator or walk-in cooler should be limited. Bottled beer should be stored in a clean, dark, and dry location. Exposure to light can cause it to take on an undesirable flavor and aroma. Canned beer is not as affected by light, but exposure to heat may change its taste.

Different types of wines also have temperature requirements. All wines should be stored at a cool, but not cold, temperature. The ideal temperature is 55°F, but a temperature between 53°F and 60°F is acceptable. Humidity can also degrade the quality of a wine. When humidity is too low, the cork in a bottle of wine may dry out. This allows wine to leak out and oxygen to enter the bottle and spoil the wine. A humidity range between 75 and 95 percent is good. Bottles should be stored on their sides so the wine remains in contact with the cork, keeping it moist. As with beer, wines should be stored in a dark room to prevent degradation by exposure to ultraviolet light.

When organizing storage locations, it is a good idea to store like items together. Items should be stored in a standard location to aid in the inventory and receiving processes. Storage locations should be kept clean. Wines should be stored away from chemicals or strong odors. Odors in the air can enter a bottle through the cork and alter the flavor. Proper product rotation is also necessary so that wines and beer are served before their quality is diminished. As always, storage areas should be secured and access to them restricted.

Issuing

The issuing of alcoholic beverages should be completed under tight control to limit pilferage. Without controls, an operation may lose product and revenue. In most establishments, a requisition is used to issue alcoholic beverages from the storage area to the bar or kitchen, **6-2**. Most operations issue alcohol at the beginning of a shift. At this time, the bartender inventories the items at the bar to determine what is needed. A requisition is completed and the amount requested is issued out to the bartender. The person issuing the product and the person receiving it should sign the requisition. In most cases, the manager issues out the alcoholic beverages.

In addition, liquor bottles are closely tracked from delivery to disposal. A system commonly used to control issues of alcoholic beverages is the *empty bottle return*. The bartender returns empty bottles to the manager before new bottles are issued. The bottles bear a unique and difficult-to-remove identification to indicate they were purchased by the operation. This ensures that the drinks sold by the bar are made from liquor bottles from the operation's inventory. Otherwise, bottles can be brought in from the outside and the money collected from customers can be pocketed by the bartender. This could be done without showing a discrepancy between the count sheet and the sales on the register.

As a means of inventory control, no more than one bottle of each type of liquor should be available at the bar at any given time. The quantity of beer and wine on hand will be greater because these beverages are consumed at a faster rate during a shift. Finally, many operations break empty liquor bottles before they are thrown out. This prevents people from manipulating the inventory by refilling the bottles with cheaper liquor which they then sell for their own profit.

Inventory

Conducting an accurate inventory enables a manager to determine how much product to order and stock at the bar. An accurate inventory allows the manager to calculate beverage costs, control expenses, and maximize profits from alcohol sales. To increase accuracy and decrease the likelihood of pilferage, at least two people should take the inventory.

Either a physical or a perpetual inventory may be used for food. The same is true of alcoholic beverages. When a physical inventory is used, products are counted at a certain point in time. For instance, an operation may perform a physical inventory every Thursday afternoon. At that time, all alcoholic beverages on hand are counted and the amounts are recorded.

Liquor Requisition Form					
Item	**Brand**	**Quantity**	**Size**	**Cost**	**Extension**
Wine	Columbia Crest Merlot	5	750 mL	$8.00	$40.00
Bourbon	Jack Daniel's	1	750 mL	$30.00	$30.00
Authorized: MFL	Filled: JBC	Received: MEL			

Figure 6-2 A liquor requisition form is commonly used in beverage operations to control the removal of liquor from the inventory. It serves as a record of what was requested, what was issued, and by whom. This example shows that five bottles of Columbia Crest Merlot were issued out to MEL by JBC, with authorization from MFL.

Technology

Energy Efficient Ice Machines

A foodservice operation can cut costs by replacing an older commercial ice machine with a newer ENERGY STAR qualified model. Annual water usage can be reduced by 2,500 gallons and utility costs can be cut by $110 per year, according to the U.S. Environmental Protection Agency (EPA). The EPA's ENERGY STAR program identifies and promotes products that are energy efficient.

The machines are air-cooled and use less water than standard water-cooled machines. Since many are programmable, managers can choose how much ice to make based on demand. Some machines detect the hardness level of water and remove minerals to speed up the ice making process. A number of them require fewer labor hours for cleaning because they have built-in antimicrobial protection.

Foodservice operators must weigh the advantages and disadvantages of buying utility efficient ice machines. Paying lower utility bills and using less water may offset a higher purchase price.

A perpetual inventory involves the continuous counting of the product on hand. The inventory is updated each time a bottle is removed or added. At any given moment, the manager can find out exactly how much of each product is available. Generally, a computerized system is necessary to accomplish this. While a perpetual inventory provides a higher degree of accuracy than the physical inventory, it is more costly and time-consuming. Before choosing a perpetual system, a manager should weigh the value of the information obtained against the time and cost.

The open bottles at the bar should also be included in either the opening or the ending beverage inventory. There are different ways of measuring the amounts used. Some operations weigh the bottles. Others measure the liquid remaining in the bottles with a ruler. Some operations perform a visual estimate of the volume left in the bottles. Regardless of the method used, managers need to be consistent from one inventory to the next.

The inventory is organized by beverage types—wine, beer, and spirits. For additional detail, some operations inventory by individual products. For instance, an inventory may separate spirits into bourbon, whiskey, vodka, gin, and so forth. When even greater detail is desired, inventories are organized and counted by brand name. Managers must weigh their desire for accuracy against the time and cost of detailed reporting.

Inventory Control Methods

Control systems must be in place to ensure that beverage sales are profitable. Several types of control systems are used. While many operations use automated dispensing systems to improve control, any system can be beneficial as long as it is followed and monitored.

Count Sheet

A **count sheet** is a document a manager uses to keep track of inventory. It is a valuable tool that managers can use to quickly identify and correct discrepancies. The count sheet can be formatted as a spreadsheet or a table document, **6-3**. Using this system, bartenders count and record each item at the bar at the beginning of their shift. They repeat the process at the end of the shift. The difference between the beginning and ending inventory is recorded as the amount used. The amount sold during the shift is also recorded. The difference between the amount used and the amount sold is recorded.

Count Sheet						
Product	Beginning Inventory	(+) Additions to Inventory	(−) Ending Inventory	(=) Amount Used	Amount Sold	Variance Over/(Under)
Budweiser	25		3	22	22	0
Bud Light	20		5	15	15	0
Miller High Life	30	24 (manager initials)	13	41	39	−2
Samuel Adams Light	22		4	18	18	0
Coors	35		8	27	26	−1
Corona Extra	26		2	24	24	0

Figure 6-3 Alcoholic beverages are costly, profitable, and easy to pilferage. Keeping close tabs on the product once it is available for service ensures a profitable bottom line. A simple count sheet, as illustrated here, can easily be developed and implemented for any size operation.

For instance, in the example given in **6-3**, the beginning inventory for Miller High Life® was 30 bottles. During the shift, 39 bottles were sold and the manager added 24 bottles to the inventory. The manager noted this on the count sheet and initialed the addition. The ending inventory was 13 bottles. However, the manager notices a discrepancy. If there were 30 bottles on hand at the beginning of the shift, and the manager added 24, the total available for sale for the shift is 54 bottles. But according to the sales receipts, 39 bottles were sold. If 54 bottles were available and 39 were sold, 15 bottles should be left in the ending inventory—not 13. Two bottles are "missing."

What could be the reason for this discrepancy? Perhaps the bartender broke two bottles or miscounted either the beginning or the ending inventory. Perhaps the manager added only 22 bottles to restock the inventory rather than the 24 recorded. A third possibility is that someone removed the bottles without recording a sale. It is up to the manager to investigate discrepancies and to take action to prevent them from happening again.

Bottle Weighing

While a count sheet is a great tool, its use is limited to whole bottles or whole cans of product. What type of control system can be used for items that are sold as part of a whole, such as glasses of wine or mixed drinks? Some operations used the bottle-weighing system. Instead of being counted, bottles are weighed at the beginning and at the end of a shift. During a shift, the number and types of drinks sold are recorded. Based on this information, the manager determines how much of each product should have been used. This can be a cumbersome process if done manually.

Some systems use bar codes from the bottles as tracking devices. The bar codes are scanned and the bottles are weighed. The system records the weights of the bottles. At the end of the shift, the process is repeated. This system links to a register that records the number and types of drinks sold. For each product, the system calculates the difference between the amount sold and the weight of the liquid remaining in each bottle. For instance, suppose a bottle of vodka weighs 52.8 ounces at the beginning of a shift. At the end of the shift, the same bottle weighs 17.6 ounces. The difference between the weight of the vodka at the beginning and at the end of the shift is 35.2 ounces. Therefore, the number of drinks that would use 35.2 ounces of vodka should have been sold.

The cash register recorded the sales of 16 vodka-containing drinks. Since each drink is made with 2 ounces of vodka, 32 ounces of vodka was sold. The difference between the weight of the product that was poured from the bottle and the weight of the product sold is 3.2 ounces. The missing amount could be the result of spillage or overpouring. Although small, the amount should be noted by the manager. If a particular bartender habitually uses more alcohol than indicated by sales, the manager should investigate.

Calculating the Cost of Beverages Sold

Conducting an accurate inventory is important—not only to determine how much product to order or how much to stock at the bar—but also to have a means to determine the beverage cost. Knowing the beverage cost can assist the manager in controlling expenses as well as realize greater profits from the sale of alcohol. *Beverage cost percentage* is the ratio of the cost of beverages sold to the total beverage sales. It is similar to the food cost percentage. It is calculated for a specified time period—usually one month. Beverage cost percentage is calculated using the following steps:

1. Calculate the cost of beverages sold using the formula:

Cost of Beverages Sold = (Beginning Inventory + Purchases) − Ending Inventory

Beginning inventory is the ending inventory figure from the previous month. *Purchases* refers to the total cost of all beverages purchased from vendors during the month. *Ending inventory* is the amount of inventory at month's end.

2. Total all beverage sales during the time period.
3. Divide the cost of beverages sold from step 1 by the total sales from step 2. Convert the result to a percentage by multiplying it by 100.

$$\text{Beverage Cost \%} = \frac{\text{Cost of Beverages Sold}}{\text{Beverage Sales}} \times 100$$

For instance, assume that an operation had beverage sales of $34,000 during a particular month. The operation bought $8,000 of product from vendors during that month. The beginning inventory was $500 and the ending inventory was $100. What is the beverage cost percentage? It is calculated using the steps described above.

Cost of beverages sold = ($500 + $8,000) − $100 = $8,400

Since the total beverage sales for the month was $34,000, the beverage cost percentage is calculated as follows:

$$\text{Beverage cost \%} = \frac{\$8,400}{\$34,000} \times 100$$

Beverage cost % = 24.7%

This translates into the following: Each dollar taken in for beverage sales cost the operation about $0.25. The beverage cost percentage of a typical operation is between 22 and 28 percent.

Once a manager calculates the beverage cost percentage, that number should be compared with industry averages for similar types of operations. The Uniform System of Accounts for Restaurants, published by the National Restaurant Association, provides industry averages for beverage cost based on operation type. Beverage cost percentage varies with the type of beverage served and the volume each type generates. According to the 2012 Uniform System of Accounts, beverage cost percentages were as follows:

- 24 to 28 percent for bottled beer
- 15 to 18 percent for draft beer
- 35 to 40 percent for wine
- 18 to 20 percent for spirits

Beverage cost can also be assessed by comparing the beverage cost percentage from one month to the next. A month's actual beverage cost can be compared with its budgeted amount. The manager should note if a beverage cost remains stable, or if adjustments need to be made to bring costs in line to increase the operation's profitability. By careful monitoring—including the regular calculation of beverage cost percentage—managers can maximize profits and decrease losses.

Effect of Sales Mix on Beverage Cost Percentage

A manager can calculate an overall beverage cost percentage for all of the types of beverages purchased and sold at an establishment. However, to truly understand the impact of beverage sales on the bottom line, a manager should determine the beverage cost percentage of each beverage type—beer, wine, and spirits. Once the manager has this information, he or she can determine how the current sales mix of beverages impacts the operation's gross profit. Adjustments can be made to try to increase profits.

The *sales mix* refers to the purchasing decisions made by customers that determine the beverage cost percentage. If customers are offered a choice of beverages, their selections determine the sales mix. However, a manager can manipulate the sales mix to generate greater revenue.

An example of an operation's sales mix is shown in **6-4**. Cost percentages are shown for each beverage type—beer, wine, and spirits. The cost percentages show that the operation makes its greatest profit by selling spirits at a 20 percent cost percentage, and the least by selling wine at a 30 percent cost percentage.

A manager can determine the sales mix each month and compare the results of the mix on the bottom line. This can help the manager work toward the most profitable mix of beverage sales. In another example, suppose the manager at McCarthy's Pub determines the sales mix for two previous months. The first month, the Pub sold 500 bottles of beer, 350 glasses of wine, and 200 glasses of spirits. This sales mix generated a total profit of $5,250.

The second month, the Pub sold the same number of drinks, or 1,050. But the sales mix was different. The Pub sold 800 bottles of beer, 100 glasses of wine, and 150 glasses of spirits. It sold significantly more beer, and less spirits and wine. This sales mix generated a total profit of $5,038.

The gross profit per sale, which is the total profit divided by the number of drinks sold, dropped from $5.00 to $4.80. Compared with what it made on beer, the Pub made more money on each glass of wine and spirits it sold. In the second month, more beer was sold to total sales, resulting in less total profit. Knowing this, what can the manager do to manipulate the sales mix to generate more revenue?

The manager could raise the price of beer to decrease the beverage cost percentage and increase the profitability it contributes. However, as discussed earlier in the chapter, the purchase price of alcohol is highly regulated. Operations often cannot significantly influence the price of a particular brand of vodka, wine, or beer. Also, the manager does not want to charge more than the market will bear.

Therefore, to control costs and impact profitability, the manager must find a way to decrease the beverage cost percentage or to influence the sales mix of beverages sold. The manager could also focus on increasing the sales of spirits and wine. Beer customers can be tempted to buy wine or spirits through marketing, or by having the bartender or waitstaff use up-selling tactics. The operation could also purchase a less expensive house wine to decrease the purchase costs to sales volume.

	Purchases	Sales	Beverage Cost %
Beer	$1,250	$5,000	25.0%
Wine	$6,000	$20,000	30.0%
Spirits	$3,000	$15,000	20.0%
Total	$10,250	$40,000	25.6%

Figure 6-4 The sales mix is the relative proportions in which an operation's products—beer, wine, and spirits—are sold.

A manager may take this one step further and determine the beverage cost percentages for various drinks offered. The beverage cost percentage of a Manhattan can be compared with that of a whiskey sour. If Manhattans have a lower beverage cost percentage, the manager may decide to promote them to increase sales. The manager could also increase the sale price of whiskey sours to gain a better beverage cost percentage. Similarly, the beverage cost percentage of a bottle of beer can be compared with that of a mug or a pitcher of beer. Similar scenarios can be used to create the most profitable sales mix of wines, beer, and other spirits by adjusting prices or by promoting items with a lower beverage cost percentage.

Pricing

Pricing methods used to price food items may also be used for beverages. These include the beverage cost percentage method, and the contribution margin and prime cost methods.

Beverage Cost Percentage Method

Operations that use the beverage cost percentage pricing method, base the selling price of a beverage on the cost of the products used to make it, or the beverage cost. The manager decides that the beverage cost should represent X percent of the selling price; X is a fraction of the selling price. This goal is the desired beverage cost percentage.

$$\text{Selling Price} = \frac{\text{Beverage Cost}}{\text{Desired Beverage Cost \%}}$$

Suppose the beverage cost for wine is $2.50 per glass and the desired beverage cost percentage is 40 percent. The cost of the wine purchased should represent 40 percent of the wine's sale price.

$$\text{Selling price} = \frac{\$2.50}{0.40}$$

$$\text{Selling price} = \$6.25$$

Using a related pricing method, called the *factor system*, the beverage cost is multiplied by a pricing factor to determine the selling price. The pricing factor is derived from the desired beverage cost percentage.

$$\text{Pricing Factor} = \frac{100\%}{\text{Desired Beverage Cost \%}}$$

Again, suppose a restaurant manager has a goal of 40 percent beverage cost for wine. The pricing factor is determined as follows:

$$\text{Pricing factor} = \frac{100\%}{40\%}$$

$$\text{Pricing factor} = 2.5$$

The manager then uses the pricing factor to calculate a selling price that results in a 40 percent beverage cost.

$$\text{Selling Price} = \text{Beverage Cost} \times \text{Pricing Factor}$$

$$\text{Selling price} = \$2.50 \times 2.5$$

$$\text{Selling price} = \$6.25$$

Again, the manager would sell the glass of wine for $6.25. The disadvantage to using the beverage cost percentage method is that it only considers beverage cost. It does not consider labor cost, overhead cost, or the market value of the item.

Contribution Margin Method

The beverage cost percentage method determines the selling price of a beverage item based on the beverage cost. When the contribution margin method is used, the beverage cost—as well as everything else needed to produce and sell the beverage—is considered. The contribution margin is the dollar amount remaining after variable costs—including the beverage cost—are subtracted from the selling price. It is the amount available to pay for fixed costs and provide for any profit. The formula for contribution margin is

Contribution Margin = Selling Price – Variable Costs

The beverage selling price must be high enough so that money made from its sale can help pay for the operation's overhead and also contribute to the operation's profit. A manager can determine the selling price by adding a desired contribution margin to the beverage cost. The desired contribution margin comes from the manager's assessment of the potential sales for the operation, fixed costs that must be paid, and the costs of items such as glassware, beverage napkins, and stirrers.

Selling Price = Beverage Cost + Desired Contribution Margin

Refer to the glass of wine in the previous example. The cost of the wine is $2.50 per glass. Suppose the manager's desired contribution margin is $3.00. Then, the selling price for the wine would be:

Selling price = $2.50 + $3.00

Selling price = $5.50

If the operation is an upscale restaurant located on the 25th floor of a metro downtown hotel, the contribution margin would need to be higher to help cover the higher operating costs. If the manager desires a contribution margin of $7.00, the selling price would be:

Selling price = $2.50 + $7.00

Selling price = $9.50

Prime Cost Method

The prime cost method is similar to the beverage cost percentage method because it uses the cost of the beverage in the calculation. However, it also includes wages, employee benefits, and payroll taxes.

Prime Cost = Beverage Cost + Wages + Employee Benefits and Payroll Taxes

Suppose that the labor cost is $1.00, and that benefits and taxes equal 26 percent of wages. The Prime cost would be calculated as follows:

Prime cost = $2.50 + $1.00 + ($1.00 × 0.26)

Prime cost = $3.76

To arrive at a selling price using this pricing method, the prime cost is divided by the operation's desired prime cost percentage.

$$\text{Selling Price} = \frac{\text{Prime Cost}}{\text{Prime Cost \%}}$$

For instance, if the desired prime cost percentage is 45 percent, the selling price for the wine would be calculated as follows:

$$\text{Selling price} = \frac{\$3.76}{0.45}$$

Selling price = $8.36

As is the case with food pricing, determining the prices for various alcoholic beverages can be challenging. It is driven by the cost of the ingredients, but also by what the market will bear. If a drink is priced too high, it will not sell. If it is priced too low, potential revenue from its sale will be lost. The price should also reflect the establishment's decor, service level, entertainment value, theme, and location. For instance, a gin and tonic may cost $4 in a neighborhood bar in a rural area, $6 in an establishment in a metropolitan area, and $10 in an upscale club. A bar that features entertainment can ask a higher price for a drink than a bar that does not.

When pricing an alcoholic beverage, it is important to consider the additional costs associated with the drink. For instance, a fine wine requires proper care in storage. The cost of holding this wine is higher than that of other beverages. The cost of special glassware needs to be considered, along with any extras required to prepare and serve a drink. Those extras may include the colored salt for the rim of a margarita glass, the umbrella for a tropical drink, or the olives served in a martini.

Serving

Much of beverage cost control occurs during serving. Controlling the dispensing of the alcohol is critical. Over-portioning will add significantly to the beverage cost. Consideration must also be given to the legal issues related to beverage sales. Operations can face expensive fines if they fail to control the amount of alcohol sold to individuals. Fines are also levied on operations that fail to control to whom the alcohol is sold. The following are examples of serving controls commonly found in beverage operations.

Standardized Recipes

Similar to the standardized recipes used in the kitchen, a bar should have and follow standardized recipes for the drinks they serve. Standardized recipes are more important in the bar because the overuse of alcoholic beverages can be costly to an operation's bottom line. By following a standardized recipe, the ingredients and amounts used can be monitored and controlled. Ensuring that the right ingredients in the correct amounts are used each time is important to controlling the cost of the drink and the inventory on hand. In addition, the use of standardized recipes creates a consistent product for the customer. For example, if McCarthy's Pub is known for its Dubliner cocktail, each one should taste just like the last one to ensure customer satisfaction. Most bars keep their drink recipes in a file or in a recipe book located in the bar area.

What if a customer orders a drink not commonly sold at the bar, or a drink made to his or her specifications? Most bars have a "free" or customized option or key on their point-of-sale system or cash register. The server or bartender uses it to enter in the ingredients and the system generates a price. The manager, or a bartender with input from a manager, sets the price based on similar drinks served.

Point-of-Sale Systems

Point-of-sale systems are a computerized approach to controlling costs. A POS system can be a valuable tool for controlling beverage costs. The bartender or server enters the drink order into the POS. The order is recorded and an order ticket is printed. The bartender receives the order electronically and fulfills the request. The system also generates a bill for the customer.

Specifications for each drink on the operation's menu are programmed into the POS system. When the server or bartender presses the key for a particular drink, the system records the order. The system generates a report that indicates the type of drink ordered and the amount of each ingredient needed to fill that order. At the end of the shift, information about the drinks sold can be used to calculate how much of a particular alcoholic beverage was used.

For instance, suppose the POS system at McCarthy's Pub recorded the sale of 25 Manhattans during a shift. Each Manhattan contains 2.50 ounces of whiskey and 0.75 ounces of sweet vermouth. The amount of whiskey used during the shift should have been 25 multiplied by 2.50 ounces, or 62.50 ounces. If 70 ounces of whiskey was used instead, the manager may wish to investigate the discrepancy.

Guest Checks

One function of the POS system is the printing of guest checks which are used by many operations as a means of control. When an order is entered into the POS system, a guest check is printed. This ticket may be placed in front of the guest at the bar, indicating that an order has been placed and for what drink. Each time a drink is ordered by the guest, a new ticket is generated. As a control mechanism, the manager can pick up a ticket in front of a customer and check that the drink ordered is the drink that was placed in front of the customer. If the ticket reads "beer," and the customer is drinking a premium mixed drink, the manager can quickly investigate the discrepancy.

Dispensing Systems

Various dispensing systems are available on the market that control the amount of alcohol used in making a drink. These systems often interface with a POS system. One popular dispensing system works as follows:
- A pouring spout is affixed to the bottle of liquor.
- The spout is sealed to the neck of the bottle with a heat gun so it cannot be removed.
- When a drink is ordered, the bottle is attached to a portioning device that is preset for varying amounts. (Typically, preset amounts are 0.5-ounce, 1.0-ounce, and 2.0-ounce portions.)
- The bartender presses the button for the desired preset amount and the correct amount is dispensed from the bottle.
- The amount dispensed is recorded in the POS system.

The liquor cannot be dispensed if it is not attached to the portioning device. Even when a bottle is upended, no alcohol is released until the device is attached. This ensures that all pouring activities are recorded.

Standardized Glassware

The use of standardized glassware is a means of controlling costs by portion control. Each drink can have a designated glass in which to serve it. The glass used can control the volume of the drink served. A drink recipe should include the type of glass to be used. Although wine glass size may vary from bar to bar, each bar uses a consistent style. The bartender will pour wine to a certain level on the glass—the level indicates the portion. The same can be said for beer. If a bar uses draft beer, a beer that is drawn from a tap, the bar may offer different glass sizes at different prices. When a "tall" beer is ordered, the beer is served in the glass designated for a tall beer.

Serving Responsibly

An operation needs to have strong controls in place to ensure that alcohol is not served to minors. One of them is an identification-checking policy that clearly states the criteria used to verify that a patron is of legal drinking age. It should include a list of acceptable identifications for verifying age—such as a state-issued driver's license or photo identification card, a military identification, or a current passport. The policy should identify who should be asked for identification. Most establishments require patrons who appear to be under 30 years of age to present an ID. Some operations require that everyone ordering an alcoholic beverage be asked for identification.

Bookmark This

ServSafe Alcohol® Training Program

Since operations that serve alcoholic beverages take on financial and other risks, they are wise to invest in alcohol safety training and certification for their employees. The ServSafe Alcohol Training Program was developed by the National Restaurant Association. Employees learn about regulations that govern the sale of alcohol in their area. They are taught how to assess alcohol intoxication levels, confirm customers' identification, and deal with other potentially difficult situations. Upon passing an exam, employees receive the alcohol safety certification. The course is taught online or in a classroom setting. Print materials are available in English and Spanish. Visit the ServSafe website to learn more about this program.

Dramshop Liability

Dramshop is a term referring to a bar, tavern, or a similar operation where alcoholic beverages are sold. The term *dram* means a small amount of liquid. **Dramshop liability** refers to laws that establish the responsibilities of commercial establishments that serve alcoholic beverages. The laws vary from one state to another. Many states impose liability on bars that serve minors and intoxicated persons—especially when these people subsequently injure themselves or others. When one of these customers causes a death or injury—an alcohol-related car crash, for example—the operation, and sometimes the employee who served the individual, can be held responsible. Many municipalities have their own regulations concerning alcoholic beverages, such as those that govern a business's hours of operation. These regulations may be more restrictive than state laws. Business owners who sell alcoholic beverages in their establishments should be knowledgeable about the regulations in their state, county, and municipality.

The cost to an operation for violating a state's dramshop laws can be severe. Therefore, alcohol-serving establishments must have strict policies in place. The staff should be trained to identify and refuse service to minors and visibly intoxicated adults. They should receive the full support of the manager when refusing to serve these customers. Finally, situations in which a customer is refused service due to age or intoxication should be documented. An operation should also document incidents in which they must contact law enforcement or arrange a customer's transportation home. Such documentation may prove invaluable if a lawsuit is filed against the establishment.

Dramshop laws were created to protect the general public from hazards that may be caused by alcohol consumption. However, some critics claim the laws give short shrift to the individual's responsibility for his or her actions

Key Terms

bar service	special-purpose service	premium liquor
server service	well brand	count sheet
point-of-sale system (POS)	call brand	dramshop
guest service	top-shelf liquor	dramshop liability

Recap

- With a strong control system in place, the sale of alcoholic beverages is profitable for a foodservice operation.
- The four main types of beverage service are bar, server, guest, and special purpose.
- Alcoholic beverages are classified into three groups—beer, wines, and spirits.
- Beverage classification impacts decisions made in purchasing, receiving, storage, inventory, and dispensing of alcoholic beverages.
- Beverage cost percentage can be used by managers to control expenses and generate greater profits from alcoholic-beverage sales.
- By manipulating the sales mix, a manager can improve profitability.
- Beverage operations must be aware of regulations governing the purchase, pricing, and sale of alcoholic beverages in their area.
- Managers must ensure that their employees are aware of the liability associated with serving underaged and intoxicated patrons.

Review Questions

1. Describe how beer, wine, and spirits are produced.
2. List three reasons that make the purchase of beverages less burdensome than the purchase of food.
3. Describe the steps in the receiving process for alcohol.
4. List factors that should be controlled when storing beer and wine to maintain product quality.
5. Describe the difference between a perpetual inventory and a physical inventory.
6. What factors are considered when setting the selling price of an alcoholic beverage using the contribution margin method?
7. Briefly explain the following beverage serving control systems:
   A. weighing the bottle
   B. empty bottle return
   C. standardized recipe
   D. dispensing system
8. Define *dramshop laws* and give two examples of the areas they regulate.

Applying Your Knowledge

9. During one week, a foodservice operation used 500 ounces of whisky. One bottle of whisky weighs 25 ounces and each drink made used one ounce of whiskey. The total sale for drinks made with whiskey was $1,000.
   A. How many bottles of whiskey were used?
   B. Calculate the sales value for each bottle of whiskey.

10. Complete the variance column in the count sheet that follows. Explain what steps (if any) the manager should take based on the results of the bottle count sheet analysis.

Count Sheet						
Product	Beginning Inventory (bottles)	(+) Additions to Inventory	(−) Ending Inventory	(=) Amount Used	Amount Sold	Variance Over/ (Under)
Bud Lite	15		8	7	6	
Budweiser	7		3	4	3	
Coors	16	12 (ML)	3	25	26	
Corona Extra	20	12 (ML)	10	22	22	
Miller High Life	20		5	15	12	
Samuel Adams Light	25		11	14	14	

Exercises 6-11 to 6-13

Complete the following exercises on the companion website:
www.g-wlearning.com/culinaryarts/

11. Dana is reviewing her beverage sales for the month. Results for her current sales mix are given in Table 1 (Sales Mix 1). While she is somewhat happy with her overall beverage cost percentage and profit, Dana wonders if a different sales mix would provide her with higher profitability.

Table 1. Sales Mix 1							
	Sell Price	Cost	Beverage Cost %	Sold	Total Sales	Beverage Cost	Profit
Chardonnay	$7.00	$3.00	42.9%	200	$1,400	$600	$800
Beer	$8.00	$1.80	22.5%	300	$2,400	$540	$1,860
Gin & Tonic	$9.00	$1.70	18.9%	100	$900	$170	$730
Totals			27.9%	600	$4,700	$1,310	$3,390

A. Use the information that follows to complete Tables 2 and 3 below.

	Sales Mix 2	Sales Mix 3
Chardonnay	300	100
Beer	200	450
Gin & Tonic	100	50

Table 2. Sales Mix 2							
	Sell Price	Cost	Beverage Cost %	Sold	Total Sales	Beverage Cost	Profit
Chardonnay	$7.00	$3.00					
Beer	$8.00	$1.80					
Gin & Tonic	$9.00	$1.70					
Totals							

Table 3. Sales Mix 3							
	Sell Price	Cost	Beverage Cost %	Sold	Total Sales	Beverage Cost	Profit
Chardonnay	$7.00	$3.00					
Beer	$8.00	$1.80					
Gin & Tonic	$9.00	$1.70					
Totals							

B. Complete Table 4 to evaluate the three sales mix scenarios.

Table 4. Evaluation of Sales Mix						
	Sold	Total Sales	Total Cost	Profit	Beverage Cost %	Gross Profit
Mix 1	600	$4,700	$1,310			
Mix 2	0					
Mix 3	0					

C. Which sales mix scenario provides Dana with the best profitability?

12. The owner of Johnny's Restaurant and Bar purchases his wine and spirits from the beverage distributor in the next town. Johnny has identified the following factors regarding beverage pricing for his operation:

Beverage cost percentage goals are 19% for spirits, 35% for wine, and 25% for beer
Servers' wages account for $0.75 for each drink served
Benefits are 20% of wages
Johnny's desired contribution margin is $3.00

A. Complete the following spreadsheet to calculate the beverage cost per serving.

Beverage	Purchase Unit Cost	Serving Size	Purchase Unit Size (in serving size units)	Servings per Purchase Unit	Beverage Cost per Serving
Beer	$12.00	12 oz. bottle	24 12-oz.bottles	24	
Gin, well brand	$20.00	2.25 oz.	50 oz.	22	
Gin, premium brand	$35.00	2.25 oz.	50 oz.	22	
Chardonnay wine	$108.00	150 mL	12 750-mL bottles	60	
Shiraz wine	$144.00	150 mL	12 750-mL bottles	60	
Bourbon, well brand	$25.00	2.25 oz.	50 oz.	22	
Bourbon, premium brand	$38.00	2.25 oz.	50 oz.	22	

B. Determine the selling price for a bottle of beer and a glass of chardonnay using the beverage cost percentage method and the information given earlier.

Beverage	Beverage Cost %	Pricing Factor	Beverage Cost per Serving	Selling Price
Beer				
Chardonnay wine				

13. Johnny had $23,400 in beverage sales this month. He performs his month-end inventory and counts 8 cases of chardonnay, 3 cases of Shiraz, and 18 cases of beer.

A. Calculate the beverage cost percentage based on the following spreadsheet and sales information.

Chardonnay $8,000
Shiraz $8,700
Beer $3,300

Beverage	Cost per Case	Cases Purchased	Beginning Inventory Value	Value of Purchases	Ending Inventory Value	Cost of Beverages Sold	Beverage Cost Percentage
Chardonnay	$108	30	$648				
Shiraz	$144	25	$864				
Beer	$12	100	$180				
Total							

B. Is Johnny meeting his beverage cost percentage targets of 35 percent for wine and 25 percent for beer?

Course Project

The Course Project is a full case study on controlling costs in a foodservice operation. Each chapter presents one component of the project. You may have to refer to other completed components to answer the following questions.

14. Based on the foodservice operation you selected for your course project, list three beverages from each beverage category—beer, wine, and spirits—that will be available for purchase. For each beverage category, describe procedures that can be used to control costs in inventory, issuing, and serving.

Chapter 7

Facilities Management as a Cost Control Tool

Learning Outcomes

After studying this chapter, you will be able to

- explain facilities management and its role in cost control.
- list nine areas in which utility costs can be controlled, and give an example of each.
- explain four ways that an operation can decrease the energy use of equipment.
- state the components of a preventive maintenance program.
- list the steps in a preventive maintenance cycle.
- create a preventive maintenance schedule for a piece of equipment.
- list the six steps in the risk management process.
- state the four areas foodservice operations typically cover with insurance.

In addition to food, beverages, labor, and equipment, other expenses must be considered and controlled when operating a foodservice business. These include expenses related to managing the facilities. **Facilities management**, sometimes referred to as *maintenance*, is the monitoring and controlling of costs related to the building, equipment, and utilities. It focuses on three areas—the monitoring and controlling of utility costs, preventive maintenance for buildings and equipment, and the implementation of a risk-management plan. Facilities management can decrease expenses by minimizing the possibility that people will be injured in the establishment. It also minimizes the likelihood of service interruptions. This chapter discusses the important role of facilities management in controlling the overall costs of a foodservice operation.

Utility Cost Control

More than other types of businesses, foodservice operations rely on stable and inexpensive sources of water, gas, and electricity. According to the Smart Energy Design Assistance Center at the University of Illinois, a typical restaurant spends between 3 to 5 percent of its budget on energy costs. Increases in these costs can quickly impact a restaurant's bottom line.

Among commercial businesses, foodservice operations are some of the highest energy users. According to the Environmental Protection Agency's *ENERGY STAR®️ Guide for Restaurants*, restaurants use between five and seven times more energy per square foot than other commercial buildings. *BTUs* are used to measure the energy content of different types of fuels. A **BTU**, or British thermal unit, is the quantity of heat required to raise the temperature of 1 pound of water by 1°F.

In the past, individuals and businesses had one choice when it came to a utility provider. This has changed in many states. Laws have been adopted that allow licensed utility suppliers to compete with one another for business. Foodservice managers need to research the laws of the state in which the operation is located. If there is more than a single licensed utility supplier, the manager should compare the rates they charge. The goal is to find the supplier that offers the lowest rate, while providing adequate service.

Once a supplier is chosen, managers can implement utility-cost-control measures. **Utility cost control** is the process of managing and controlling the costs related to utility usage. It involves

- monitoring the amount of water and energy used
- identifying ways to decrease the amounts used
- implementing steps to reduce usage
- checking to see if those steps produce the desired results

The following sections identify ways that foodservice operations can reduce the waste of utilities and lower utility costs. Before these energy saving strategies are discussed, different types of energy sources will be described, along with how each is purchased.

Types of Energy

Natural gas and electricity are two types of energy commonly used in foodservice operations. Natural gas is measured by volume or in cubic feet (cu. ft.). It is sold by the *therm*.

**1 Therm of Natural Gas = Approx. 100 Cu. Ft. of Natural Gas =
Approx. 100,000 BTUs of Heat Energy**

Electricity use is measured in a unit of energy called the kilowatt-hour (kWh). The cost of electricity is based on how much is used and when it is used. Costs can vary greatly from one location to another. Charges are based on the price charged per kWh. However, many utilities use a demand charge, or a tiered-rate system. Higher rates are charged for electricity used during times of peak demand.

To control utility costs, a foodservice manager may need to decide which source of energy is the most cost effective—natural gas or electricity. A manager needs to determine which energy source is less costly in a particular area and for the particular operation. To determine which is more economical, monthly utility bills are studied. The manager can find the amount of gas or electricity used from the bills. The manager calculates the energy cost based on the assumption that all of the energy used was natural gas. Next, the manager calculates energy cost based on an assumption that all of the energy used was electricity. The following formula can be used to convert from one to the other and compare the costs.

1 Therm of Natural Gas = 29.3 kWh of Electricity

Energy usage and cost also needs to be considered before an operation buys a piece of equipment. Federal law requires that appliance manufacturers disclose the average utility cost of using an appliance for one year. Buyers can use this information to compare different models and select the one that costs less to operate.

Sometimes a piece of equipment comes in both a gas and an electric model. Energy usage and cost of the utility should play a role in deciding which model to buy. An operator can ask manufacturers to specify how many BTUs are used for the gas appliance and how many kWh are used for the electric model. Then, using the actual cost of the energy source derived from monthly utility bills, the operator can determine the estimated cost of running the appliance.

Controlling Utility Costs

For guidance and recommendations in controlling utility costs, foodservice operations can turn to a growing number of resources. One of these is **ENERGY STAR**, a government program that rates the energy efficiency of products and provides guidance in energy conservation practices. It is a joint program of the U.S. Environmental Protection Agency and the U.S. Department of Energy. Operations that use the program can reduce utility costs from 10 to 30 percent. These small decreases can result in big cost savings. For example, some experts say a 20 percent reduction in energy use is equivalent to a 5 percent boost in sales. To control utility costs, foodservice managers should look at the following areas:

- equipment purchases
- equipment usage
- food production methods
- equipment sanitation and maintenance
- refrigeration
- hoods and vents
- lighting
- water usage
- heating, ventilation, and air conditioning (HVAC)

Trend

Utility Costs Rising

Since foodservice operations use so much water and energy, they are especially vulnerable to changes in the supply of water and energy. Water and energy are increasingly in short supply. This is partly due to the rising demand for resources, especially energy, around the world. As the economies and populations of other countries grow, more resources are needed. As a people's standard of living goes up, they consume more. Rising demand pushes prices upward.

Climate plays an important role. Parts of the United States are experiencing frequent droughts, power outages, and electrical brownouts. A brownout is a lowering of alternating current power voltage for a period of time and causes light flickering and dimming. Drought is often followed by water shortages and rationing. During these times, foodservice operations may have to cut their operating hours or temporarily shut down.

Technological advances are also driving the growing demand for energy in foodservice. Though still heavily dependent on human labor, many foodservice operations have turned to technology to improve efficiency. The need for energy increases as more of these devices are used. This results in rising costs.

Utility costs are beginning to play a major role in the daily management of business operations and in the design of buildings and equipment. For example, more foodservice equipment is being designed with energy efficiency and water conservation in mind.

Equipment Purchased

More than 35 percent of a foodservice operation's daily energy use is spent in food preparation. Manufacturers have been working to improve the energy efficiency of foodservice equipment. For instance, the newest, most efficient gas fryers are twice as energy efficient as the older baseline models, according to Pacific Gas & Electric's Food Service Technology Center. The newer models run more efficiently than older models. Manufacturers have improved temperature consistency and oil filtration systems to extend the life of the oil. An operation that replaces a gas fryer with an energy efficient model can save up to $400 a year in energy costs. Likewise, newer models of dishmachines use less water and less energy to clean dishes because of heat recovery systems and increased insulation.

Foodservice operations can reduce energy costs by buying ENERGY STAR-qualified equipment whenever possible. Foodservice equipment recommendations can be found on the ENERGY STAR program website. To receive an ENERGY STAR rating, the equipment must incorporate advanced technologies to reduce energy and water usage. Although the purchase price of the equipment may be higher than that of standard-model counterparts, they save money over the long run. When comparing prices, a manager needs to also consider the projected utility-cost savings over the life of the equipment.

There is another important benefit to purchasing ENERGY STAR-qualified equipment. By doing so, foodservice operations keep approximately 130,000 metric tons of greenhouse gas emissions from entering the atmosphere annually. This is equivalent to the output of about 25,000 cars.

Use of Equipment

Wasteful practices push energy costs higher in many foodservice operations. For example, in foodservice operations, energy is expended to both create and remove heat. Heat that is generated for cooking must be removed so food and the kitchen can cool down. It takes energy to create and remove the heat. Less energy is needed for heat removal if food is cooked as quickly as possible and the amount of heat emitted is kept to a minimum. Here are some ways this can be accomplished:

- Cover pots, pans, kettles, and so forth when heating foods in them. The food will heat faster and less heat will be released into the surroundings.
- Do not turn on cooking equipment until it is needed. Many operations turn everything on at the beginning of the day and leave it on all day. This is wasteful. Programmable timers can be used to turn on equipment when needed.
- Use equipment when it is filled to capacity. The same amount of water and energy is used whether a dishmachine is full or only half full. Using it when filled to capacity conserves resources. When baking, energy can be saved by putting several items into an oven to bake at the same time.
- Use equipment that is the appropriate size for the task at hand. A food processor may be able to do a job currently performed by a buffalo chopper. The less-powerful machine runs on less energy.
- Avoid opening oven doors to check on cooking food because it allows heat to escape. Foodservice operations should invest in ovens that have glass windows on the doors.
- Turn down exhaust fans when grilling stops. Leaving them running wastes energy.

Food Production Methods

The amount of energy used also depends on the food production method used. Energy efficient cooking methods include steaming, microwaving, baking, and stir-frying. Foodservice operations can reduce energy usage during food production in the following ways:

- Use individual burners rather than flat-top cook surfaces. A smaller area is heated which uses less energy.
- Cook foods at lower temperatures for longer periods of time.
- Purchase precooked foods that require less time and energy to heat.
- Review recipe instructions for utility-cost savings. For example, if a recipe calls for adding frozen vegetables to a base, the vegetables can be thawed out first. This reduces the amount of energy needed to heat the soup.
- Limit the preheating of equipment, especially ovens. An exception is when preheating the oven is necessary to get the product to rise appropriately.
- Turn off the oven a little early. The food will finish cooking with the heat that remains. Experimentation may be necessary to determine if a product cooked this way will still be of an acceptable quality.

Equipment Sanitation and Maintenance

For a cooking method to be energy efficient, the heat must reach the food. Anything that inhibits heat transfer increases the amount of energy needed. For instance, cooking food on dirty, food-encrusted coils uses 25 percent more energy than cooking it on clean coils. Cleaning equipment on a regular basis is important.

Maintaining equipment in good working order is also important. This includes making sure it is properly calibrated. To *calibrate* something means to check or adjust it, or to compare it against a standard. The standard can be provided by a quantitative measuring instrument, such as a thermometer. Calibrating burners and ovens ensures that the right amount of energy is used for cooking. Equipment maintenance is covered in more detail later in the chapter.

Refrigeration

Refrigeration requires a lot of energy. It is another potential area of energy waste. Refrigerators consume less energy if they are kept full with adequate space for air circulation around the food and beverages inside. In larger operations, using walk-in refrigerators can save money because they are more energy efficient than reach-in types. When the door is open, a barrier of plastic strips installed at the entrance can prevent the warmer outside air from entering and keep the cooler air inside. It is also important to keep the lights off in a walk-in whenever possible. Besides using electricity, lights emit heat that increases the temperature inside a walk-in.

As with all equipment, regular maintenance can boost a refrigerator's energy efficiency. Coils should be free of frost. Compressors and condensers need to be cleaned and maintained. Doors with gaskets should be cleaned regularly and checked to ensure a good seal when the door is closed.

Hoods and Vents

Hoods and vents use energy to operate and can also allow energy to escape. As stated earlier, vent fans should only be used when necessary. A double-walled hood is more energy efficient than a single-walled hood. Single-walled hoods pull air-conditioned air out of the kitchen, which is wasteful, especially in the summer during the peak use of cooking equipment.

The hood exhaust pulls the air rising from behind the equipment. The Food Service Technology Center recommends that the equipment be placed as close to the wall as possible. Better yet, they suggest that a stainless-steel ledge be placed between the equipment and the wall to seal off the airflow. Hoods and vents should be cleaned regularly to minimize fire hazards. This also enables them to operate at their greatest efficiency.

Lighting

Technological advances have led to the creation of new, energy efficient ways to light homes and businesses. Ninety percent of the energy used by traditional incandescent lightbulbs is given off as heat. By 2020, these bulbs will be phased out by the Energy Independence and Security Act of 2007. The legislation sets standards for the amount of energy lightbulbs can use. Following are some energy efficient alternatives:

- **Energy-saving incandescent bulbs** use 25 percent less energy and can last up to three times longer than traditional incandescent bulbs.
- **Compact fluorescent lightbulbs (CFLs)** use 75 percent less energy and can last up to 10 times longer than traditional incandescent bulbs.
- **Light-emitting diode bulbs (LEDs)** use 75 to 80 percent less energy and can last up to 25 times longer than traditional incandescent bulbs.

Operations that use energy saving bulbs with energy efficient light fixtures save energy and money in the long run. Since the bulbs last longer, they do not have to be replaced as often.

Other steps can be taken to decrease the energy used to light a foodservice operation. Of course, turning the lights off when they are not needed helps. Timers or motion sensors can turn lights off when no one is in a room. Also, less energy is needed to light up a room when the walls and ceilings are white or another light color. These colors reflect light and make a room appear brighter.

Water Usage

Droughts in parts of the United States have led to an increased emphasis on water efficiency. Foodservice operations can waste lots of water, mostly due to inefficient equipment or leaking faucets. The U.S. Environmental Protection Agency's WaterSense®

Bookmark This

Rebates and Other Incentives

The government and utilities offer businesses incentives to conserve resources. A source of information about these incentives is the Database of State Incentives for Renewables & Efficiency (DSIRE). The database is funded by the U.S. Department of Energy. It provides information on state, local, utility, and federal incentives and policies that promote renewable energy and energy efficiency.

The ENERGY STAR rebate locator provides information about available rebates for the purchase of energy efficient equipment. Rebates or discounts are offered to operations that implement energy saving programs or use high-efficiency equipment. Many states and municipalities have their own programs. Foodservice operations in New York can tap the New York State Energy Research and Development Authority (NYSRDA). It offers services including audits, benchmarking, loans, and financial incentives to help operations save energy.

In the San Francisco Bay Area, water agencies implemented the "Water Saving Hero" program with the goal of helping residents and businesses cut water use. Their website contains information on rebates for water-saving products and equipment. It also provides conservation tips for foodservice operations.

program helps consumers and businesses conserve water by identifying the most water-efficient faucets, showerheads, toilets, and other equipment. For example, ENERGY STAR-qualified commercial dishmachines are about 25 percent more energy and water efficient than similar commercial dishmachines. When buying equipment, it pays to look for the ENERGY STAR and the WaterSense labels.

Foodservice operations can conserve water by ensuring that all sources of water are functioning properly. Leaks in sinks and toilets must be fixed, for instance. According to the Food Service Technology Center, a small leak of just 0.2 gallons per minute can waste up to 100,000 gallons of water per year. The use of low-flow, pre-rinse spray valves at all sinks can produce a savings of $1,000 per year. The spray valves save significant amounts of water. They also save energy because less hot water is used for dish rinsing and other tasks.

Foodservice operations should test their water to determine the hardness level. Hard water contains calcium and magnesium that builds up in water pipes and equipment, such as dishmachines and laundry facilities. The deposits reduce water flow to taps and appliances, and must be removed to maintain water efficiency. The removal is time-consuming and requires the use of costly chemicals. The installation of water-softening equipment is an added expense, but one that is offset by reduction in costs over time. By preventing deposits from forming, costs related to chemical usage, utilities, and labor are reduced. In addition, soft water requires less detergent to get items clean.

Heating, Ventilation, and Air Conditioning (HVAC)

Taking steps to conserve energy inside a building can be a great cost saver. For example, energy can be conserved while maintaining a comfortable room temperature. An ambient temperature of 68°F is considered comfortable. Decreasing the heating temperature by 1°F can cut energy consumption by 1 percent. Increasing the thermostat by 1°F can cut cooling costs by 3 percent.

To conserve energy, an operation should ensure that

- the building is free of leaks
- the windows are tightly sealed
- insulation is adequate
- ducts are not blocked so that air circulates efficiently

Utility Cost Control Audit

Monitoring and implementing a solid utility cost control program is a big project. Operators can use two approaches to get started. In the first approach, a manager determines where the bulk of the energy is used. This is where the biggest impact can be made to reduce utility use. Following are the typical areas of energy use in a full-service restaurant . The percentage of the total energy used in each area is also given.

- Food preparation—35 percent
- HVAC—28 percent
- Sanitation—18 percent
- Lighting—13 percent
- Refrigeration—6 percent

Looking at these percentages, a manager can see that the food preparation area consumes more energy than any other area of the operation. He or she may wish to start here when implementing an energy conservation program.

The second approach involves a utility cost control audit. The manager develops a checklist based on the areas noted earlier (lighting, food preparation, and so forth). The checklist may include the following:

- Check for water leaks, especially hot water leaks, and repair them.
- Check and replace dirty filters in air conditioners.
- Check that dishmachine racks are fully loaded before running.
- Check the condenser coils of the refrigerator and clean them if needed.
- Check thermostat settings.
- Check refrigerator door gaskets for damage and repair them if needed.
- Check strip curtains for damage and repair them if needed.
- Check that appliances are under their exhaust hoods.
- Check for leaks in gas lines and valves and have them fixed if found.

Using this checklist, the manager routinely walks through the operation and notes areas where utility use can be decreased. He or she then implements the steps necessary to produce the desired result.

Preventive Maintenance Programs

Every operation, regardless of its size, needs a preventive maintenance program. **Preventive maintenance** involves periodic inspections of equipment and building areas to ensure that they continue to operate efficiently. This assures that the operation will continue to run smoothly and without interruption. Manufacturers specify the maintenance their products need and when it should be completed. Managers who adhere to these recommendations are more likely to have operational equipment when they need it most—during dining service hours, for example.

Preventive maintenance reduces operational costs in other ways. It extends the life of equipment and ensures that it is running efficiently to save on utility costs. Minor repairs are less costly than major ones because they can usually be made in less time and with little or no interruption in an operation's functioning. For example, consider the financial impact on an operation of closing for a day because the air-conditioning

Waste Not/Technology

Benchmarking Energy Usage

The first step to reduce utility costs and conserve resources is to conduct an energy audit. An energy audit is a formal assessment of a facility's energy needs and energy efficiency. Some operations hire consultants to perform energy audits of their facilities. Others conduct their own using tools such as the ENERGY STAR Benchmarking Starter Kit. Using this interactive energy management tool, a manager can

- create a profile of the facility that identifies its energy usage, water usage, and carbon emissions
- devise a plan of action, using the profile, to make the facility more energy efficient
- benchmark the facility, or compare its energy costs against the national average for similar facilities

ENERGY STAR provides many additional resources, including information on energy efficient foodservice equipment. To learn more visit www.energystar.gov/

stopped working or the dishmachine is broken. A preventive maintenance program also controls costs by safeguarding the employees who could be injured by defective equipment or unsafe working conditions. To begin a preventive maintenance program, a manager lists all the pieces of equipment in the operation. For each piece of equipment, the following is noted:

- equipment type
- model number
- date purchased
- dates of maintenance checks
- preventive maintenance schedule (when filters need to be replaced, and so forth)
- repair history

All equipment in the operation should be placed on a preventive maintenance schedule to ensure that they perform at their peak for as long as possible. A preventive maintenance schedule for a hood vent is shown in **7-1**. According to the manufacturer, the filters should be replaced each month and the belts need to be changed annually. The coils and the fan should be checked and cleaned quarterly.

A preventive maintenance cycle typically consists of the following steps:

- Install the equipment and establish the maintenance schedule based on the manufacturer's recommendations.
- On the scheduled date, complete the maintenance check.
- Document the completion of the maintenance check and note any recommendations for repair.
- Take necessary repair action.
- Document the completion of the repair.

In addition to equipment, a preventive maintenance program covers the building and grounds. It includes a walk-through of the operation, in which a manager notes the condition of the roof, windows, walls, landscaping, and furnishings. Fire hazards and needed repairs and refurbishing would also be noted.

The Occupational Safety & Health Administration (OSHA) is a federal program that sets and enforces standards concerning workplace safety and health. Some states, working with OSHA, develop their own workplace safety and health programs. Checking these areas during an audit is good business practice. Included are checks for adequate lighting, ventilation, and a comfortable working temperature.

Preventive Maintenance Schedule												
Hood Vent												
	Jan	Feb	Mar	Apr	May	Jun	Jul	Aug	Sep	Oct	Nov	Dec
Replace Filters	X	X	X	X	X	X	X	X	X	X	X	X
Change Belts	X											
Clean Coils	X			X			X			X		
Clean Fan	X			X			X			X		

Figure 7-1. This illustrates a preventive maintenance schedule for a hood vent. Note that the coils should be cleaned on a quarterly basis.

Contracting Preventive Maintenance

Preventive maintenance programs may be completed by staff in house. Or it can be contracted out. Some operations do some of the maintenance themselves and hire contractors to perform the rest. The success of a program that uses outside service contractors depends on choosing the right one.

A good place to begin the search for a reputable contractor is the equipment manufacturer. They should provide a list of authorized service agents for their equipment in various locations across the country. In evaluating service providers, managers should consider more than the price charged. Contractors should be bonded and insured; licensing may be required as well. Managers must ensure that contracted companies can meet their needs. For instance, if an operation has a large volume, the contracted company must be able to handle it.

Once a service contractor is selected, the foodservice operation should establish a good relationship with the contractor. The service agent should be considered a member of the operating team. They must be given information about the equipment in the operation, the service needs of that equipment, and the service expectations desired. It is a mistake to first contact a service agent for assistance when a piece of equipment breaks down on a Saturday night.

The manager should contact the manufacturer and obtain a list of "must have" spare parts for the equipment to keep in inventory. A copy of the warranty should also be available and shared with the service provider. The service provider should be included in any training programs offered by the manufacturer. The responsibility of tracking the preventive maintenance of the equipment will fall to the service agent.

Risk Management

Risk refers to the possibility of loss, injury, failure, disadvantage, or destruction. What are some potential risks to a foodservice operation? A water main may break and flood a restaurant or a fire may break out above a range. Risks also include things that can happen to customers. For example, a customer can slip on a patch of ice in a restaurant's parking lot and break a leg.

Risk management is the process of analyzing exposure to risk and deciding how to best handle such exposure. It requires a manager to assess the operation's exposure to various risks and to use methods and tools to manage those risks. One of those tools is insurance. This section begins with a discussion of overall risk management, and then covers the insurance aspects.

Steps in Risk Management

Risk management is a proactive process. It involves anticipating what might go wrong and putting a plan into place to prevent it from happening or to minimize loss if it does. Risk management should be an ongoing, everyday process. A best-practice approach to risk management includes the following steps:

- Identify possible risks and their causes on a continuous basis.
- Evaluate the likelihood that each risk may occur, and the consequences should it occur.
- Prioritize the risk management effort. Rank risks in order of the most to the least important.
- Develop a plan or a strategy to manage each risk.
- Implement the strategies to deal with those risks.
- Track the outcomes of the risk management efforts, and modify procedures if necessary.

An operation without a risk management program in place can suffer serious consequences. Generally, the manager will be unprepared when a problem arises. A small problem may quickly escalate into a crisis. The service recovery time may be extended.

For example, fire is the most serious threat to a foodservice operation. A small fire can quickly grow into one that can reduce a thriving business into a total loss. An operation must have a sufficient plan in place to handle fires. This plan will have many components, some required by law. One part of the larger plan would address the inspection and maintenance of fire extinguishers.

A successful risk management program is one in which risks are continuously identified and analyzed for relative importance. Risks are mitigated, tracked, and controlled. Problems are prevented before they occur. Some actions to take to minimize an operation's exposure to risk are listed in **7-2**. Risk management is not a silver bullet. However, it can improve decision making, help avoid surprises, and improve chances of succeeding.

Ways to Manage Risk

In a foodservice operation, there are two main types of risk—retail and manufacturing. Retail risks involve customer exposure. Manufacturing risks involve risks, such as the risk of equipment failure. Managing risk can involve any or all of the following:

- risk avoidance
- loss control
- risk retention
- risk transfer

The rest of the chapter will briefly describe these four options and give some examples of each.

Minimizing Risk Exposure

- Ensure that entrances to the operation are secure.
- Scheduling fire-alarm tests at least twice a year to make sure fire-protection systems are fully functional.
- Arrange adequate covering for electrical equipment that can be damaged from water seepage if overhead sprinklers open up.
- Conduct building inspections twice a year that include the following:
  A. inspect floors for ripped carpets
  B. note if cables or wires are lying on the floor
  C. note any electrical outlets blackened with soot (indicates electrical shortages)
  D. ask staff if their work space is sufficient (appropriate table height, sufficient lighting)
  E. note any heavy items on or near the floor that staff must stoop to lift
  F. ensure all doors have fully functional doorknobs
  G. ensure there is a well-stocked first-aid kit available
  H. post emergency numbers on the wall near the central phone
  I. ensure adequate ice removal during the winter
- Schedule a few minutes during staff meetings to assess the risk exposure of the facility and staff members. Staff safety is covered in more detail in the chapter on labor cost control.

Figure 7-2. This chart describes ways a manager can minimize the operation's exposure to risk. Note that the activities focus mainly on security and safety.

Risk Avoidance

Risk avoidance is asking the question, "What can be done to prevent a problem or disaster from happening?" To eliminate the risk of fires breaking out in the dining room because of tipped-over candles, a manager could remove open-flame candles from dining room tables.

Loss Control

Loss control is another risk-management strategy. It involves preventing or minimizing a potential loss due to an accident or disaster. As discussed earlier in this chapter, implementing a preventive maintenance program is a loss-control strategy for a foodservice operation. The program limits losses associated with damage to and failure of equipment, or the damage to buildings and grounds.

Risk Retention

Risk retention is a risk-management strategy in which a business owner assesses risk and then decides on self-insurance or no insurance. In self-insurance, the owner sets aside funds to use if a loss occurs. For instance, some companies do not contract with an insurance company for the health insurance of their employees. Rather, they set aside funds each month to cover the cost of the medical bills for their employees. The thought is that the company can invest those funds and, possibly, save money. The operator retains the risk of a loss within the business. An operation may also choose retention if the chance of a loss does not merit the cost of insurance.

Risk Transfer

Risk transfer is the strategy of shifting risk away from the individual or company. For some operations, one form of risk transfer is to form a limited liability corporation, or limited liability partnership (LLP). A **limited liability corporation (LLC)** is a legal entity that limits an owner's liability should the company fail or suffer a financial setback. If an LLC fails, the most an owner can lose is the amount of his or her investment in the company. He or she will not be personally responsible for the debts of the company—that risk is transferred from owner to the LLC or LLP.

Insurance is the most common form of risk transfer. Risk is transferred to insurance companies. **Insurance** is a financial arrangement that protects individuals or businesses against financial loss. The insurance policy, which is sold by insurance companies, provides the details of this financial arrangement to the policyholder. The policy protects the policyholder by providing a certain amount of money if the policyholder suffers a loss. The policyholder pays a certain amount on a regular basis, or a premium, for the insurance policy. Many types of insurance are marketed to foodservice operations. Most foodservice operations purchase the following types of insurance.

- *Business property insurance* pays for loss of or damage to assets, such as buildings, inventory, and personal property (fixtures, materials, furniture, and so forth). In its basic form, it covers losses due to explosions, fires, hail, vandalism, accidents, burglary, and arson. For example, if a hailstorm damages the siding and the roof of the restaurant, the insurance company may pay to have them replaced.
- *Business liability insurance* covers claims against an operation that are generally filed as lawsuits. For example, customers may sue a restaurant if they suffer confirmed cases of food poisoning after dining there. Employees can also sue the operation if they are injured or if their personal belongings are damaged on the premise.

- *Business crime insurance* pays for losses due to crimes such as theft, embezzlement, arson, or forgery. In some policies, theft and arson are covered by property insurance.
- *Business interruption insurance* is purchased as an additional covered item in a business insurance policy. The insurance company will pay for the cost incurred when the operation is temporarily closed, or can only provide minimal service. For example, if the city tears up the street in front of a restaurant and customers cannot get to it, the restaurant may need to temporarily close. The insurance would reimburse the restaurant for the lost revenue.

When insurance is purchased, the coverage should be adequate for the value of the property and other assets. The coverage should be checked again when the policy is renewed. Any changes in the value of the property and additions of equipment can be noted and the insurance coverage changed to meet the needs of the operation. This is also a good time to note any steps taken to decrease the risk of a loss, which can decrease the insurance premium. The installation of a security system or sprinkler system can lower the premium.

In summary, establishing a strong risk management program and ensuring that the operation has adequate insurance coverage are important functions of facilities management. Both are necessary in order to control costs for the operation.

Key Terms

facilities management
BTU
utility cost control

ENERGY STAR
preventive maintenance
risk management

limited liability
   corporation (LLC)
insurance

Recap

- Facilities management focuses on three areas—the monitoring and controlling of utility costs, preventive maintenance for buildings and equipment, and the implementation of a risk management plan.
- Among commercial businesses, foodservice operations are some of the highest energy users.
- Energy and water conservation can positively impact the bottom line of a foodservice operation.
- Utility cost control audits can help reduce utility costs.
- Every operation should have a preventive maintenance program.
- Preventive maintenance programs can be completed in-house or contracted out.
- Risk management is a proactive process, but not a silver bullet. Adequate insurance coverage is important to ensure that assets are protected.

Review Questions

1. State the two types of energy used in foodservice operations.
2. List three ways that a manager can control the cost of utilities.
3. Define ENERGY STAR, and explain how its use can decrease costs in a foodservice operation.
4. Suggest modifications to the following recipe to decrease energy use:

Tex-Mex Chicken Soup with Split Peas	
chili powder	2 tsp.
coriander	¼ tsp.
pepper	⅛ tsp.
ground red pepper	⅛ tsp.
garlic powder	⅛ tsp.
frozen chicken breasts	1 lb.
olive oil	1 tsp.
frozen, diced peppers	10-oz. package
sliced onions	1½ c.
chicken broth	2 c.
water	2 c.
split peas	½ c.
bottled salsa	½ c.

Directions

Thaw chicken in refrigerator.

Combine spices in a shallow dish. Dredge chicken breasts in spices.

Heat oil in skillet. Cook chicken 6 minutes on each side until done. Remove chicken from pan.
   Cut into ½-inch pieces.

Add peppers and onion to skillet. Sauté 3 minutes.

Add broth, water, chicken, and peas. Bring to boil, cover, and simmer 30 minutes.

Add salsa and simmer 10 minutes.

5. State three ways to reduce energy use in refrigeration.
6. A restaurant has its thermostat set at 70°F year-round. It currently spends $2,000 per month on heating and cooling costs. What amount would the restaurant save annually if its thermostat is lowered to 68°F for six months in the winter, and increased to 71°F for six months in the summer?
7. In implementing a utility control audit, what is the first area in which a manager may wish to start and why?
8. How does a preventive maintenance program control costs?
9. Not implementing a risk management program has several negative consequences. Name two.
10. Which type of risk management strategy—risk transfer, risk retention, risk avoidance, and loss control—does each of the following exemplify?
    A. preventive maintenance programs
    B. insurance policy
    C. self-insurance
    D. flameless candles in the dining room
11. Name the four types of insurance coverage that foodservice operations often purchase.

Applying Your Knowledge

12. Conduct a utility control audit of your home, apartment, or dorm room. List the areas where energy conservation can be implemented.
13. Explore the website of the Food Service Technology Center (www.fishnick.com).
    A. Identify two tools on the site that can help a foodservice operator conserve energy.
    B. Watch a video from the site. Write a brief paragraph summarizing the video content and state two key points you learned.
14. Go to the websites of two commercial dishmachine manufacturers. For each manufacturer, select a conveyor dishmachine model and answer the following questions.
    A. What does the manufacturer state about the energy efficiency of the dishmachine?
    B. Is the dishmachine ENERGY STAR qualified?

Course Project

15. Write a preventive maintenance schedule for three pieces of equipment needed to produce the Course Project menu. Search the Internet or contact the manufacturer to obtain the information about recommended maintenance.

Chapter 8

Operating Budget and Performance Reports

Learning Outcomes

After studying this chapter, you will be able to

- describe what is included in a *budget*.
- list the advantages and disadvantages of planning a budget.
- state and explain the five steps in budget planning.
- state the difference between an operating budget, a cash budget, and a capital budget.
- read and interpret an operating budget.
- state the differences between a fixed and a flexible budget.
- analyze a monthly performance report and describe how sub-optimal performance can be corrected.

Previous chapters have stressed the importance for an operation to control costs to maximize profit. Making a profit is the main purpose of any operation, whether it is a commercial business, such as a restaurant, or a noncommercial operation, such as a nursing home. Businesses cannot continue to operate if expenses consistently exceed revenues resulting in ongoing losses. Businesses need profit to keep owners or investors happy, supply funds for maintenance or expansion, and provide raises or bonuses for employees. To be profitable, an operation must have a strong financial management system. Budgets and performance reports, which are covered in this chapter, are key tools in this system.

Budgets

A **budget** is a plan for the availability and use of funds to pay for the activities of an organization, a company, or an individual. A budget is created for a given period of time. In the case of a business, funds come from the sales, or revenues, the business generates. There are three basic types of budgets: operating, cash, and capital. Operating and cash budgets will be covered in this chapter. The capital budget is a financial plan for the purchase of assets that have a life expectancy of one year or more. Capital budgets are covered in another chapter.

Budgets help operations stay viable. Budget preparation

- helps managers establish financial controls
- provides managers with a clear direction and with guidelines for the operation in the upcoming year
- encourages managers to establish and prioritize goals, and monitor progress toward those goals
- guides managers in assigning responsibility and accountability for meeting goals
- helps managers coordinate activities across departments or divisions in larger organizations
- encourages operations to plan for the future, rather than react to the present

Budgeting has disadvantages as well. Budgets take time to prepare. The information used to prepare them must be collected or recorded, which also takes time. In the case of large operations, budgeting requires cooperation from all budget-planning team members to ensure that funds are appropriately allocated and spent. Also, budgets are only as good as the information used to prepare them. If a manager relies on forecasts that are inaccurate, or does not account for unforeseen circumstances, the usefulness of the budget is diminished.

The Operating Budget

An **operating budget** is a financial plan that includes projections of sales, expenses, and profit for a period of time. It lists the revenues a business or organization anticipates receiving. Also listed are the expenses that will be necessary to run the operation during that time.

Typically, a budget covers a one-year period. The time frame is based on the company's fiscal year. A **fiscal year** is an organization's 12-month accounting period. The fiscal year may or may not coincide with the calendar year. For instance, the government has a fiscal year that begins in October and ends the following September. Many businesses use July 1st as the start of their fiscal year. Restaurants often begin their fiscal year with their opening date. An example of an operating budget for an upcoming fiscal year is given for Pat's Pub & Grub, **8-1**. Following are descriptions of the line items in an operating budget. Many operations follow the format recommended in the "Uniform System of Accounts for Restaurants," published by the National Restaurant Association.

Sales

In an operating budget, the word *sales* refers to the payments a company expects to receive from the sale of goods and services. For a foodservice operation, sales are broken down into food, beverages, and sometimes merchandise. For example, for the month of July, Pat's Pub & Grub projects total sales of $84,500, 8-1. Food sales are projected to make up $69,700 of that. Beverage sales are projected at $14,000, and merchandise at $800.

Cost of Sales

Cost of sales refers to the dollars spent for the food, beverages, and merchandise that are sold to customers. Again, in a budget, these numbers are projections. In July, Pat's Pub & Grub expects the cost of food sales to be $20,910. This is the projected value of the food that will be used to generate food sales. This number does not reflect other costs, such as labor, that are associated with producing, marketing, and selling the menu items.

Pat's Pub & Grub — 20XX Budget

	July	Aug	Sept	Oct	Nov	Dec	Jan	Feb	Mar	Apr	May	June	Total
Sales													
Food	69,700	72,500	71,000	71,500	70,000	76,000	70,000	70,000	79,000	71,000	71,500	71,500	863,700
Beverage	14,000	14,100	14,000	14,200	14,000	14,300	14,000	14,700	17,500	14,000	14,200	14,200	173,200
Merchandise & Other	800	800	800	800	800	800	800	800	800	800	800	800	9,600
Total Sales	84,500	87,400	85,800	86,500	84,800	91,100	84,800	85,500	97,300	85,800	86,500	86,500	1,046,500
Cost of Sales													
Food	20,910	21,750	21,300	21,450	21,000	22,800	21,000	21,000	23,700	21,300	21,450	21,450	259,110
Beverage	2,800	2,820	2,800	2,840	2,800	2,860	2,800	2,940	3,500	2,800	2,840	2,840	34,640
Merchandise & Other	200	200	200	200	200	200	200	200	200	200	200	200	2,400
Total Cost of Sales	23,910	24,770	24,300	24,490	24,000	25,860	24,000	24,140	27,400	24,300	24,490	24,490	296,150
Labor													
Salary	5,000	5,000	5,000	5,000	5,000	5,000	5,000	5,000	5,000	5,000	5,000	5,000	60,000
Wages	9,100	9,100	9,100	9,100	9,100	9,100	9,100	9,100	9,100	9,100	9,100	9,100	109,200
Employee Benefits	2,820	2,820	2,820	2,820	2,820	2,820	2,820	2,820	2,820	2,820	2,820	2,820	33,840
Total Labor	16,920	16,920	16,920	16,920	16,920	16,920	16,920	16,920	16,920	16,920	16,920	16,920	203,040
Prime Cost	40,830	41,690	41,220	41,410	40,920	42,780	40,920	41,060	44,320	41,220	41,410	41,410	499,190
Other Controllable Expenses													
Direct Operating Expenses	1,000	1,000	1,000	1,000	1,000	1,000	1,000	1,000	1,000	1,000	1,000	1,000	12,000
Music & Entertainment	300	300	300	300	300	300	300	300	300	300	300	300	3,600
Marketing	120	120	120	120	120	120	120	500	500	120	120	120	2,200
Utilities	800	800	800	800	800	800	800	800	800	800	800	800	9,600
General & Administrative	500	500	500	500	500	500	500	500	500	500	500	500	6,000
Repairs & Maintenance	150	150	150	150	150	150	150	150	150	150	150	150	1,800
Total Other Controllable Expenses	2,870	2,870	2,870	2,870	2,870	2,870	2,870	3,250	3,250	2,870	2,870	2,870	35,200
Controllable Income	40,800	42,840	41,710	42,220	41,010	45,450	41,010	41,190	49,730	41,710	42,220	42,220	512,110
Noncontrollable Expenses													
Occupancy	1,900	1,900	1,900	1,900	1,900	1,900	1,900	1,900	1,900	1,900	1,900	1,900	22,800
Equipment Leases													
Depreciation	100	100	100	100	100	100	100	100	100	100	100	100	1,200
Total Noncontrollable Expenses	2,000	2,000	2,000	2,000	2,000	2,000	2,000	2,000	2,000	2,000	2,000	2,000	24,000
Operating Income	38,800	40,840	39,710	40,220	39,010	43,450	39,010	39,190	47,730	39,710	40,220	40,220	482,640
Interest Expense													
Other (Income)/Expense													
Income before Income Taxes	38,800	40,840	39,710	40,220	39,010	43,450	39,010	39,190	47,730	39,710	40,220	40,220	482,640
Net Income	38,800	40,840	39,710	40,220	39,010	43,450	39,010	39,190	47,730	39,710	40,220	40,220	482,640

Figure 8-1. Although each operation uses its own format, this is a typical set-up of an operating budget. Note that the revenue, or sales, and expenses are listed on the left. The months covered by the budget are listed across the top. The dollar amounts projected for the revenue and expense items are then recorded for each month of the budget.

Labor

Labor is a significant cost to an operation—the greatest single expense, in some cases. Total labor includes payroll, or salaries and wages, and the costs of benefits and payroll taxes that must be paid. In an operating budget, the manager projects these costs. Salaries are paid to managers and wages are paid to hourly employees to compensate them for the hours they work. In addition, these expenses include vacation pay and bonuses. This is called payroll expense.

Employee benefits and payroll taxes include the dollars paid for labor-related costs other than salary or wages. Examples of these costs include

- health insurance premiums
- worker's compensation
- social security (both employer and employee contributions)
- Medicare (both employer and employee contributions)
- federal and state income taxes
- unemployment taxes

Operations may offer other employee benefits. For example, free meals may be provided to employees. Some operations provide tuition reimbursement. These expenses would be reflected in this line item.

In creating budgets, operations may calculate employee benefits and payroll taxes as a percentage of wages and salaries. For example, at Pat's Pub & Grub, benefits and payroll taxes are estimated at 20 percent of payroll. The employee benefits line is calculated as follows:

$$\text{Employee benefits} = (\text{salary} + \text{wages}) \times 0.20$$

$$\text{Employee Benefits} = (\$5,000 + \$9,100) \times 0.20$$

$$\text{Employee Benefits} = \$2,820$$

Trend/Technology

Financial Management Tools in POS Systems

Point-of-sale (POS) systems have replaced cash registers at many foodservice operations. In addition to cash drawers, these systems consist of a computer, computer software, and peripheral devices. They may include a bar code scanner, touch-screen monitor, receipt printer, debit-and-credit-card reader, signature-capture device, and a PIN pad. The systems can be customized to meet the needs of an operation and offer many powerful financial management tools. For example, POS systems allow foodservice managers to

- store and retrieve customer and sales data
- track production costs, sales, and inventory in real time
- pinpoint problems and make adjustments to keep performance on track
- make revenue and expense projections
- easily calculate profit margins and other performance indicators
- generate financial reports

Web-based POS systems are being used by a growing number of foodservice operations, particularly those that have multiple units. The POS system software resides on the Internet instead of on each operation's computer system. Since it can be accessed by all managers of a multiunit operation, information can be easily shared and collected throughout the organization. Large amounts of data can be stored and used to generate budgets and performance reports. The central office can compare the costs and revenue generated by different units.

Prime Cost

Prime cost reflects the ability of a manager to control the two largest drivers of the business—the cost of sales and the cost of labor. The foodservice industry has established benchmarks to guide managers in identifying where operational changes may be needed to improve profitability. This prime-cost benchmark varies with the type of business, but is generally between 60 and 70 percent. Controlling the prime cost is a critical function of management. Decreasing the prime-cost percentage without sacrificing quality or service, leaves more money for other expenses and/or profit. Prime cost is the sum of the cost of sales and the cost of labor.

Prime Cost = Total Cost of Sales + Total Labor

What is the projected prime cost for September at Pat's Pub & Grub? It can be calculated as follows:

Prime cost = $24,300 + $16,920

Prime cost = $41,220

Other Controllable Expenses

A **controllable expense** is an expense over which a manager has direct influence. For example, the cost of sales and wages are controllable expenses. This section includes other operating expenses that a manager has some control over. Typically, controllable expenses are broken down into the following categories.

Direct Operating Expenses

Expenses such as linens, china, glassware, and other tabletop items are captured in this category. In addition, employee uniforms and disposable supplies would be recorded here.

Music and Entertainment

Depending on the operation and its brand, this category can be a minimal expense (piped in music), or a significant expense (live bands every weekend).

Marketing

Marketing includes expenses used to advertise or promote the business. All forms of media advertising would be included here, including costs associated with the use of social media. In addition, sponsorship of outside events is considered marketing. Those donations or sponsorship dollars would be accounted for on this line.

Utilities

The costs of water, gas, electricity, as well as waste removal are captured in the utilities expense line. In addition, lightbulbs, engineering supplies, and ice and refrigeration supplies are accounted for in this category. Many managers fail to consider utility expenses when calculating the cost of doing business. However, these expenses must be controlled because foodservice operations use greater amounts of utilities in comparison to other types of businesses.

General and Administrative

General and administrative costs are expenses related to running the business, as opposed to expenses that are directly related to serving guests. These expenses include

- telephone service
- postage
- liability and other general insurance coverage
- credit card fees
- information technology processing
- legal or accounting fees
- provisions for cash shortages
- provisions for accounts receivable the operation cannot collect

In a foodservice operation, there are not many accounts receivable as most sales are paid for with cash or a cash equivalent, such as a debit or a credit card.

Repairs and Maintenance

These expenses include equipment parts, service on the equipment, and so forth. It includes charges for preventive maintenance and equipment repair. It also includes costs associated with maintaining the physical plant, such as landscaping and maintaining signage and parking lots. The cost of service contracts, such as a hood-cleaning service, is a repair and maintenance expense.

Controllable Income

Controllable income is the revenue that remains after all of the controllable expenses have been paid. This value is often used to assess a manger's performance and to determine compensation—salary and bonus. Subtracting the cost of sales, labor, and other controllable expenses from total sales yields the controllable income. This is expressed as follows:

Controllable Income = Total Sales – (Total Cost of Sales +
Total Labor + Total Other Controllable Expenses)

Or

Controllable Income = Total Sales – (Prime Cost + Total Other Controllable Expenses)

Noncontrollable Expenses

Controllable expenses were defined as those costs that a manager has the ability to influence. **Noncontrollable expenses** do not relate directly to the day-to-day operation of a business. They are costs related to the investment in the business. Noncontrollable expenses are typically outside the manager's sphere of influence. Occupancy costs, equipment leases, depreciation, and corporate overhead are noncontrollable expenses.

Occupancy

This includes rent paid, any real estate taxes that may be due, and property insurance. It includes costs that are necessary to make a property ready to be occupied by the business.

Equipment Leases

This section covers equipment that is leased over an extended period of time. For example, an operation may lease, rather than purchase, a point-of-sale system or certain kitchen equipment.

Depreciation

Depreciation means the value of the asset—a piece of equipment, for example—is spread out over the anticipated useful life of the asset. For example, suppose a business purchases and installs a steamer for $4,500. Since expenses should be applied to the sales they help to generate, it would be inaccurate to apply the entire $4,500 expense to the year it is purchased. Therefore, the expense is spread out over the life expectancy of the steamer.

The budget for Pat's Pub & Grub shows a monthly depreciation expense of $100, 8-1. Depreciation is discussed further under the topic of the capital budget.

Operating Income

Operating income is the difference between controllable income and noncontrollable expenses.

Operating Income = Controllable Income – Total Noncontrollable Expenses

To arrive at a projected operating income figure for the October budget, the manager of Pat's Pub & Grub can perform the following calculation:

Operating income = $42,220 – $2,000

Operating income = $40,220

Corporate Overhead

If an operation is a single unit, this item will not appear on the statement. It reflects the costs associated with running a corporate office—the costs of corporate office staff and office equipment. Some corporations allocate this expense to each of its units. Since Pat's Pub & Grub is a single-unit operation, corporate overhead does not apply.

Interest Expense

The interest expense reflects the dollar amount that is paid to cover the cost of borrowing money. This includes interest on a mortgage, if the operation owns property. Interest paid on loans used to purchase equipment would also appear on this line.

Other (Income)/Expense

This line captures any income or expense that is not typically part of an operation's activity. For example, some operations sell grease to people who convert it to fuel. Others sell food scraps to farmers to use for animal feed. The income generated from these activities would be noted here. Also noted would be income received from the sale of an asset, or the expense associated with settling a lawsuit.

Bookmark This

Federal Reserve Beige Book

To prepare a budget for a foodservice operation, a manager needs to look at past revenues and expenses. The manager should also consider current and forecasted economic conditions in the region and in the broader economy. One source of this information is the Federal Reserve, the central bank of the United States.

A Federal Reserve report, commonly referred to as the *Beige Book*, comes out eight times a year. Each of the 12 Federal Reserve banks across the country collects information about current economic conditions in their areas. The information is presented in the report which also summarizes trends and growth in many industries, including foodservice. A manager can use the information to forecast future sales and growth potential. The latest report can be found on the Federal Reserve's website.

Income before Income Taxes

This is the last line on the operating budget of some types of operations. Many businesses are structured so that taxable income or losses are noted on the owners' tax returns. If an operation must pay income taxes, a line for the projected income tax is given on a following line in the budget. *Net income* is what remains after all expenses, including income taxes, are subtracted from sales. It is often referred to as the *bottom line*.

The Budgeting Process

During the budgeting process, the manager forecasts how much revenue the operation will earn during the budget period. Next, he or she decides how these funds should be allocated to realize the planned revenue and desired profit. To create an effective budget, a business or an organization follows a series of steps.

Step 1: Establish a Timeline

Preparing a budget takes time. The first step in creating a budget is to establish a time line. Managers need to determine what has to be completed and by what date. This allows them to devote adequate time to gathering and evaluating the information needed to develop a realistic budget.

Step 2: Consider Goals

The purpose of a budget is to allocate funds for the provision of supplies and services the company will need to do business for a given period of time. To understand what supplies and services will be required, goals for the period must be considered. For instance, suppose a restaurant owner plans to add a take-out area to increase sales in the coming budget year. During the budget process, the owner should consider how this goal will impact expenses. For example, additional staff may be needed, which will raise labor costs. The owner needs to allocate funds for the additional staffing in the budget. Adding a take-out area will increase the use and cost of disposable take-out containers. The owner needs to allocate funds for this expense in the budget.

Considering goals also involves forecasting the operation's level of activity for the coming year. Does the operation anticipate that sales will increase, decrease, or stay the same? Is there a plan to increase capacity? These and similar questions must be answered before funds can be allocated.

Step 3: Gather Data

To project an operation's future needs, a manager needs to study internal and external data. Internal data refers to the operation's historical financial information. It includes past financial reports, prior-year budgets, and analyses of financial performance. This information can help managers answer questions such as those that follow.

- What was the cost of food last year? last January?
- What was the number of covers?
- How many hours of labor were used to serve meals?
- Were the operation's financial goals achieved?
- What should be adjusted to improve financial results?

This is also a good time to evaluate the menu data. Unpopular and less profitable menu items may need to be eliminated, be given new prices, or undergo recipe changes to reduce food and production costs. This is part of menu engineering, which was covered in another chapter. These changes may impact the budget.

External data can also be used to make sound projections during the budgeting process. Operations should investigate and consider factors that may influence the operation's activities or expenses. These may include

- inflation projections
- business trends in the community
- the consumer price index
- wage scales and trends
- foodservice trends
- community growth or decline

For example, suppose the government increases the minimum-wage requirement. If a restaurant fails to anticipate and account for the wage increase in its budget, its projected labor expense will be understated. This will result in actual labor expenses being over budget all year, with profits being under budget. However, if the increase in minimum wage is accounted for, the business can adjust the budget to balance the higher labor costs and preserve the profit. For instance, the manager could evaluate ways to decrease food costs by using less-expensive ingredients or by decreasing portion size. Or the manager could evaluate current labor expenses for possible savings that would not sacrifice customer service.

Step 4: Determine Level of Costs

After considering goals, historical financial information, and external data, the manager is ready to determine the level of costs. Each line item on the budget must be reviewed and calculated for the final budget. How is this done? The following scenarios illustrate how the manager of Pat's Pub & Grub can make projections and adjust an operating budget.

Scenario 1

Pat's Pub & Grub experienced a decrease in sales last July. The inaugural season for the community's "Music in the Park" series began and concerts were held every weekend in July. Unfortunately for Pat's Pub & Grub, this event was held on the other side of town. Many of Pat's loyal customers spent their weekends—and their food and beverage dollars—enjoying the music series. The community plans to make the series a permanent addition to the summer events calendar. For this reason, sales projections for July will be decreased accordingly in the next fiscal year budget.

Scenario 2

Historically, Pat's Pub & Grub has experienced increased sales during December due to business from holiday parties. A revamped catering menu and e-mail promotion is expected to generate more revenues in the upcoming year. As a result, additional sales are budgeted for December.

Scenario 3

The chamber of commerce is planning a St. Patrick's Day celebration next year. The parade route and many of the events will occur within walking distance of Pat's Pub & Grub. The manager is planning a promotion to coincide with the parade. Food and beverage sales are projected to exceed that of a typical month. The anticipated increase in revenues as well as the extra advertising expense will need to be accounted for in the budget.

Scenario 4

The manager's goal is to maintain a 30 percent food cost and a 20 percent beverage cost. Historically, labor costs have averaged 18 to 20 percent of revenue. Benefits have been 20 percent of the labor cost. The manager can calculate these expenses based on the projected food and beverage sales.

Some expense items, such as occupancy costs, equipment leases, and administrative and general, are not linked to the amount of sales. These expenses are allocated equally each month.

Once projections are made based on internal and external data, the budget can be examined for opportunities to improve the bottom line, or profit. For instance, to circumvent losses in an upcoming July due to the "Music in the Park" series, the Pub could satellite meals to the location. They could run a picnic-basket promotion to encourage customers to pick up meals on their way to the park. Another approach may be to decrease labor below the usual 18 to 20 percent of sales during the slow months. This may be accomplished by decreasing the hours of service.

Step 5: Submit Budget for Approval

The final step is the completion of the budget form and the submission of the budget for approval. This can be either a simple or an involved process. In a single-unit operation, the owner approves the budget. In a large organization, the budget may have to be submitted to a budget committee that reviews budget submissions from all departments or divisions. The manager may be asked to supply additional information. The committee may ask the manager to cut or increase funds based on the overall budget needs of the organization. The budgets from all departments are combined into one overarching budget, which may require approval by a board of directors.

Cash Budgets

Businesses typically prepare a monthly *cash budget*. A **cash budget** projects cash flow—how much money will come in and how much will go out— in the short term, **8-2**. It is used to determine if additional funding will be needed during a month. This is based on the projections for revenues and expenses in the operating budget.

A cash budget is similar to the budgets individuals create for their personal spending. When preparing a budget for a coming month, anticipated income during the month is noted, such as paychecks or student stipends. Next, anticipated expenses during the month— rent, car payments, utilities, food, and so forth—are noted. The expenses are then subtracted from the income. If cash remains after expenses are paid, it can be used to pay down debt or buy new clothes. It can be deposited into a savings account or invested. If additional money will be needed to pay for anticipated expenses, an individual can take steps to prevent the cash from running out. These steps may include decreasing expenses, working extra hours, or taking out a small loan.

Businesses also establish cash budgets. For a smaller operation, an accountant would prepare this statement. In a noncommercial operation, or a large restaurant corporation, the controller or vice president of finance would prepare the cash budget. In a large corporation, the cash budget determines funding requirements for the entire company, not only for the individual departments or divisions.

A cash budget starts with an opening balance. The opening balance is the amount of cash that was on hand at the end of the previous month. In Figure 8-2, the opening cash balance for August is carried forward from the closing cash balance for July. Anticipated sales for the month are added to the opening balance. These sales figures are obtained from the operating budget, 8-1.

Pat's Pub & Grub			
20XX Cash Budget			
	July	Aug	Sept
Opening Balance	35,000	74,610	117,510
Cash			
Sales	84,500	87,400	85,800
Loans	1,200	1,200	1,200
Total Cash	120,700	163,210	204,510
Expected Cash Expenses			
Food	21,300	20,910	21,750
Beverages	2,800	2,800	2,820
Merchandise & Other	200	200	200
Labor	16,920	16,920	16,920
Direct Operating Expenses	1,000	1,000	1,000
Music & Entertainment	300	300	300
Repairs & Maintenance	150	150	150
Marketing	120	120	120
Utilities	800	800	800
General & Administrative	500	500	500
Interest	-	-	-
Occupancy	1,900	1,900	1,900
Depreciation	100	100	100
Total Cash Expenses	46,090	45,700	46,560
Cash Increase (Decrease)	74,610	117,510	157,950
Expected Cash Balance	50,000	50,000	50,000
ST Loans Needed	0	0	0
Cash Available for Dividends, Capital Expenditures, Investments, Savings	24,610	67,510	107,950

Figure 8-2. A cash budget starts with an opening balance. Note that the opening balance for August is the closing balance for July. The operating and cash budgets are interrelated. For example, note that the monthly sales amounts listed in the cash budget matches the projected amount of total sales given in the operating budget in Figure 8-1.

In this example, the sales projections for food, beverages, and merchandise that appear in the July operating budget were used to obtain the sales figure of $84,500 for July's cash budget. Pat's Pub & Grub may need to take out a small business loan each month to pay its bills during leaner times. If so, the loan amount would be considered cash received. It would be added to the beginning balance and the anticipated sales amount to give the projected total cash available. *Cash* refers to more than the revenue received from the sale of food and beverages. Cash, in a cash budget, is both cash (sales) and cash equivalents (loans).

The cash budget also projects the amount of cash needed to pay for expenses over the course of the month, or the *cash outflow*. Typically, the expected food and beverage expense on the cash budget differs from that on the operating budget. Cash-budget expenses often lag behind operating-budget expenses by about one month. The delay exists because bills are not paid until the month following a food delivery. In other words, the cash budget reflects when the dollars are actually paid out for an expense, rather than when the expense is incurred as planned in the operating budget. The August cash budget in Figure 8-2 shows payment of $20,910 for the food purchases projected in the July operating budget. This is not the case if a vendor requires the restaurant to pay cash on delivery.

The outflow of cash, or total cash expenses, is deducted from the total cash available for the month to arrive at the closing cash balance, or cash increase (decrease).

Fixed and Flexible Budgets

Two types of budgets are commonly used in businesses today. A **fixed budget** is a budget that bases the amounts of line items on a static level of business activity. In other words, the amounts budgeted for various expenses are based on a set level of revenue. An example of a fixed budget is the operating budget in 8-1.

A **flexible budget** is a budget that bases the amounts of line items on a range of business activity levels. It is similar to establishing a fixed budget for two, three, or more activity levels. A simplified version of a flexible budget is based on 90 percent, 100 percent, and 110 percent of an estimated activity level.

If the activity level at 100 percent is 5,000 meals, the expenses are projected based on what is needed to serve 5,000 meals. If the business uses a 30 percent food cost and sales for the 5,000 meals is projected to generate $40,000 in revenues, then the cost of food sold (or food expense) would be $12,000 for the month.

$40,000 sales × 0.30 food cost = $12,000 budgeted food expense

---

Waste Not

EPA Food Waste Calculator

In 2010, Americans generated more than 34 million tons of food waste, according to the U.S. Environmental Protection Agency (EPA). Foodservice operations produce a lot of food waste and much of it is disposed of in landfills. This results in financial losses and environmental problems.

The EPA offers an online tool that can help operations compare the financial and environmental impacts of the different forms of waste disposal. These forms include donating, recycling, and composting. Operators enter information into a spreadsheet and the program calculates the costs of various food waste management options.

For more information on food waste and to access the Food Waste Cost Calculator, visit www.epa.gov/

How much would the same operation budget for food expense based on a 90 percent activity level? First, sales at the 90 percent level would have to be calculated. This is done by multiplying the sales at 100 percent activity by 90 percent.

$$\$40,000 \times 0.90 = \$36,000$$

Now the food expense for this lower sales amount can be projected.

$$\$36,000 \text{ sales} \times 0.30 \text{ food cost} = \$10,800 \text{ budgeted food expense}$$

This process can be used to calculate the budget for a 110 percent activity level, as well as the other line-item expense amounts. While this is a simple way to create a flexible budget, it is not completely accurate because not all of the expenses are directly proportional to sales. For instance, fixed and semi-variable expenses will require further consideration when developing a flexible budget, **8-3**. A flexible budget is more accurate than a fixed budget, but it does require additional planning.

Regardless of the format used, a budget is only a plan and should be adjusted if situations change during the year. It is through the monthly monitoring of the budget that these situations may come to light. This monthly monitoring is the purpose of the performance report.

Types of Expenses
Fixed Expenses
Costs that are minimally impacted by changes in an operation's sales volume. Examples: Rent, property taxes, insurance premiums, management salaries
Variable Expenses

Costs that increase or decrease in direct proportion with changes in an operation's sales volume, or number of customers.
Examples:
  Food cost. When sales volume increases, the cost of food purchased will increase. When sales volume decreases, as when fewer customers are served, less food needs to be purchased.
  Wages. When sales volume increases, the wages earned by hourly employees should increase. When it decreases and there are fewer customers to be served, wages should decrease proportionately.

Semi-Variable Expenses

Costs that have elements of both fixed and variable costs. They are also called mixed expenses. A semi-variable expense rises and falls with the sales volume, but not in direct proportion to it.
Examples:
  Electricity and other utilities. An electric bill has elements of both fixed and variable costs—a service charge that remains the same each month, and a charge for the amount of electricity used during a particular month.
  Total labor cost. It consists of both salaried and wage-earning workers. A restaurant can serve an increasing number of customers with its current level of labor. However, at a certain sales volume, more labor must be scheduled to maintain appropriate service levels.

Figure 8-3. Expenses are categorized as fixed, variable, or semi-variable. This chart explains what distinguishes each type of expense.

Performance Reports

Once the yearly budget is developed, a manager can use it to monitor an operation's performance to make sure it continues to meet goals. By doing so, timely adjustments can be made to correct performance that is veering off course. Typically, a business establishes a system to monitor how it is doing on a monthly basis. The system usually centers on a monthly *performance report*, also called an operations report.

A **performance report** is a statement of an operation's actual numbers or results compared with some standard—such as the budgeted numbers. It covers a specific period of time. The line items are the same as those appearing in the operating budget. A performance report for Pat's Pub & Grub is shown in **8-4**. For the month of September, the figures in the *Actual* column show the operation's real financial data for the month. The dollar figures in this column reflect the amount of revenue received and the amount paid for expenses during September. These numbers are compared with the budgeted amounts and the differences are noted in the *Variance* column.

$$\text{Variance \$} = \text{Actual} - \text{Budget}$$

A variance of actual to budget can be either positive or negative. When it is positive, the actual amount is greater than the budgeted amount. When it is negative, the actual amount is less than the budgeted. Negative variances are enclosed in parentheses. A negative variance can be favorable when the line item is an expense. In the case of revenue, a negative variance is unfavorable.

The next column shows the percent variance for each line item.

$$\text{Variance \%} = \frac{\text{Variance \$}}{\text{Budget}} \times 100$$

The comparison of actual to budget is also calculated based on totals for each line item at a certain point in the fiscal year, or year-to-date (YTD).

What can be learned from the performance report in Figure 8-4?

- Total sales in September was 13.81 percent over the amount projected in the budget.
- The costs of food and beverages increased as a result of the increased food and beverages sales. However, the cost of food increased 16.67 percent compared with the increase in food sales of only 15 percent. Additionally, the cost of beverages increased 12 percent compared with a 7.14 percent increase in beverage sales. Why did food costs increase at a greater rate than the sales? Perhaps the month ended with an extra delivery from the food vendor. Perhaps the kitchen prepared more food than was sold, or menu prices were decreased. Inflation may be hitting the industry. The manager must learn why these variances are occurring and take corrective action if needed.
- Labor expense was controlled using only a few additional hours to serve the increase in customers. Total labor increased by 2.11 percent compared to a 13.81 percent increase in total sales.
- Expenses for utilities and for the general and administrative categories were over budget which may or may not be warranted. It is the role of the manager to know why those two expense lines increased.
- The repairs and maintenance line item expense was budgeted for $150. However, only $100.50 was spent, resulting in a negative variance of 33 percent.
- There are no variances for occupancy and depreciation because these are fixed expenses and should not change as a result of increased business activity. However, as sales increase, the static nature of fixed expenses contributes to an increasingly greater total income before taxes than was budgeted. This is because the fixed expense is spread out over greater-than-expected revenue.

Pat's Pub & Grub								
September 20XX Performance Report								
	Month				YTD			
	Actual	Budget	Variance		Actual	Budget	Variance	
			$	%			$	%
Sales								
Food	81,650.00	71,000.00	10,650.00	15.00	225,565.60	213,200.00	12,365.60	5.80
Beverage	15,000.00	14,000.00	1,000.00	7.14	44,710.20	42,100.00	2,610.20	6.20
Merchandise & Other	1,000.00	800.00	200.00	25.00	3,100.00	2,400.00	700.00	29.17
Total Sales	97,650.00	85,800.00	11,850.00	13.81	273,375.80	257,700.00	15,675.80	6.08
Cost of Sales								
Food	24,850.71	21,300.00	3,550.71	16.67	68,008.67	63,960.00	4,048.67	6.33
Beverage	3,136.00	2,800.00	336.00	12.00	8,851.95	8,420.00	431.95	5.13
Merchandise & Other	250.00	200.00	50.00	25.00	700.00	600.00	100.00	16.67
Total Cost of Sales	28,236.71	24,300.00	3,936.71	16.20	77,560.61	72,980.00	4,580.61	6.28
Labor								
Salary	5,000.00	5,000.00	0	0	15,000.00	15,000.00	0	0
Wages	9,373.00	9,100.00	273.00	3.00	24,843.00	27,300.00	(2,457.00)	(9.00)
Employee Benefits	2,904.60	2,820.00	84.60	3.00	6,995.40	7,860.00	(864.60)	(11.00)
Total Labor	17,277.60	16,920.00	357.60	2.11	46,838.40	47,160.00	(321.60)	(0.68)
Prime Cost	45,514.31	41,220.00	4,294.31	10.42	124,399.01	120,140.00	4,259.01	3.55
Other Controllable Expenses								
Direct Operating Expenses	960.00	1,000.00	(40.00)	(4.00)	2,610.00	3,000.00	(390.00)	(13.00)
Music & Entertainment	300.00	300.00	0	0	900.00	900.00	0	0
Marketing	115.20	120.00	(4.80)	(4.00)	349.20	360.00	(10.80)	(3.00)
Utilities	900.00	800.00	100.00	12.50	2,472.00	2,400.00	72.00	3.00
General & Administrative	600.00	500.00	100.00	20.00	1,549.50	1,500.00	49.50	3.30
Repairs & Maintenance	100.50	150.00	(49.50)	(33.00)	396.00	450.00	(54.00)	(12.00)
Total Other Controllable Expenses	2,975.70	2,870.00	105.70	3.68	8,276.70	8,610.00	(333.30)	(3.87)
Controllable Income	49,159.99	41,710.00	7,449.99	17.86	187,538.49	128,950.00	58,588.49	45.44
Noncontrollable Expenses								
Occupancy	1,900.00	1,900.00	0	0	5,700.00	5,700.00	0	0
Equipment Leases								
Depreciation	100.00	100.00	0	0	300.00	300.00	0	0
Total Noncontrollable Expenses	2,000.00	2,000.00	0	0	6,000.00	6,000.00	0	0
Operating Income	47,159.99	39,710.00	7,449.99	17.86	181,538.49	122,950.00	58,588.49	47.65
Interest Expense								
Other (Income)/Expense								
Income before Income Taxes	47,159.99	39,710.00	7,449.99	17.86	181,538.49	122,950.00	58,588.49	47.65
Net Income	47,159.99	39,710.00	7,449.99	17.86	181,538.49	122,950.00	58,588.49	47.65

Figure 8-4. The monthly performance report is a tool that allows managers to perform a routine "checkup" of the annual budget. This report compares actual activity to the planned activity given in the operating budget. Note that the revenue and expenses found on the performance report appear in the same location on the operating budget.

The YTD information indicates that Pat's Pub & Grub is having a good year so far. The operation had a great month in sales, growing 13.81 percent compared with YTD of 6.08 percent. However, the prime cost for September was significantly higher, 10.42 percent compared with 3.55 percent YTD. This impacted the bottom line, with the percent variance for income before taxes at 17.86 percent for September compared with 47.65 percent YTD. Although sales were great in September, the manager may need to look at a stronger control on expenses to bring more dollars to the bottom line.

Financial Ratios

The monthly performance report can be further analyzed to assess an operation's performance and to correct sub-optimal performance. Managers use financial ratios to help pinpoint problems. Some financial ratios were discussed in the labor cost control chapter. Similar ratios using historical data and number of meals served can be used to assess performance. For example, suppose Pat's Pub & Grub served 4,700 meals in September and 13,000 meals YTD (July through September). The manager can use a variety of ratios to obtain a more complete picture of the operation's performance, **8-5**. The ratios can then be used to benchmark against numbers generated by other operations in the industry.

	September	YTD
Meals Served	4,700	13,000
Food Cost per Meal	5.29	5.23
Beverage Cost per Meal	0.67	0.68
Total Cost of Sales per Meal*	6.01	5.97
Labor Cost per Meal	3.68	3.60
Prime Cost per Meal	9.68	9.57
Total Sales per Meal	20.78	21.03
*Includes merchandise & other.		

Figure 8-5. Several financial ratios are used to evaluate how an operation is performing against what was planned. These ratios can be compared between months and between a month and YTD. If a ratio is off, a manager can try to pinpoint what needs to change to bring it back into line.

What should the given ratios tell the manager of Pat's Pub & Grub? The prime cost per meal was $9.68 in September, compared with $9.57 YTD. So, the manager incurred a higher labor and cost of sales per meal in September than what occurred YTD. Also, the total sales per meal numbers indicate that the average sale per customer was lower in September than YTD. The average customer spent $20.78 in September compared to $21.03 YTD. The manager should evaluate the sales history of each menu item to determine if there is a way to increase the average check amount. Perhaps increasing the price of a few menu items will help increase the average check amount without adversely impacting the number of meals served. Or, the manager may wait to see if this trend continues in October before making any changes.

Reviewing and evaluating information on the monthly performance report is an essential function for a foodservice manager. It enables the manager to identify issues and make corrections, or improvements, to guide the operation to achieve its goals.

Key Terms

budget	controllable expense	fixed budget
operating budget	controllable income	flexible budget
fiscal year	noncontrollable expenses	performance report
cost of sales	cash budget	

Recap

- Planning a budget has both advantages and disadvantages.
- A good budget planning process includes the following steps. A time line for completion is set. An operation's goals and projected level of activity are considered. Internal and external data are collected. Amounts are assigned to each line item on the budget. The budget form is completed and submitted for approval, if necessary.
- The operating budget is a plan for the anticipated revenue and expenses necessary to run an organization or company for a period of time.
- Businesses plan a cash budget to determine if they have adequate funds to support the operation on a monthly basis.
- A fixed budget establishes line-item amounts based on a static level of business activity. A flexible budget is based on a range of business activity levels.
- A monthly performance report assists operations in monitoring how well they are performing compared with the planned budget.

Review Questions

1. Define the following:
   A. budget
   B. fixed budget
   C. cash budget
2. Data gathering is one step in the budget-planning process. State the two main categories of data and give an example of each.
3. How are the amounts for variance and percent variance calculated in a performance report?

Applying Your Knowledge

4. Create a personal cash budget for next month using a spreadsheet program.
   A. What is your anticipated balance at the end of next month?
   B. If you are anticipating a positive balance, what are some things you can do with the extra income?
   C. If you are anticipating a negative balance, what steps can you take today to minimize or eliminate the negative balance?

Exercises 8-5 to 8-8

Complete the following exercises on the companion website:
www.g-wlearning.com/culinaryarts/

5. James is the general manager of a new chain restaurant opening in July. He must use the following monthly projections from the corporate office to prepare an operating budget for July through October. Use this information to prepare the operating budget.

      Food Sales: $30,000 the first month; will increase 5% each subsequent month
      Beverage Sales: 20% of food sales
      Food Cost Percentage: 30%
      Beverage Cost Percentage: 25%
      Labor Expense: $20,000 initially; for each additional $5,000 in sales, an additional employee must be scheduled at $1,200 per month
      Direct Operating Expenses: $1,000
      General & Administrative: $500
      Utilities: $500
      Occupancy: $800
      Interest: $1,000
      Repairs & Maintenance: $200
      Marketing: $4,000 the first month, $1,000 the second, then $250 a month

	July	Aug	Sept	Oct
Sales				
Food	30,000			
Beverage				
Total Sales				
Cost of Sales				
Food				
Beverage				
Total Cost of Sales				
Labor				
Salary and Wages	20,000	20,000	20,000	21,200
Prime Cost				
Other Controllable Expenses				
Direct Operating Expenses				
Marketing				
Utilities				
General & Administrative				
Repairs & Maintenance				
Total Other Controllable Expenses				
Controllable Income				
Noncontrollable Expenses				
Occupancy Costs				
Equipment Leases	0	0	0	0
Depreciation	0	0	0	0
Total Noncontrollable Expenses				
Operating Income				
Interest Expense				
Other (Income)/Expense	0	0	0	0
Income before Income Taxes				
Net Income				

6. After two months of business, James is ready to prepare a performance report for the restaurant in the previous problem. Use the following two months of financial data to prepare monthly performance reports for July and August.

	July				August			
	Actual	Budget	$	Variance	Actual	Budget	$	Variance
Sales								
Food	31,000	30,000			34,000	31,500		
Beverage	5,600	6,000			6,000	6,300		
Total Sales	36,600	36,000			40,000	37,800		
Cost of Sales								
Food	9,300	9,000			10,200	9,450		
Beverage	1,400	1,500			1,500	1,575		
Total Cost of Sales	10,700	10,500			11,700	11,025		
Labor								
Salary and Wages	19,500	20,000			19,800	20,000		
Prime Cost	30,200	30,500			31,500	31,025		
Other Controllable Expenses								
Direct Operating Expenses	900	1,000			950	1,000		
Marketing	4,300	4,000			1,200	1,000		
Utilities	540	500			520	500		
General & Administrative	560	500			490	500		
Repairs & Maintenance	210	200			190	200		
Total Other Controllable Expenses	6,510	6,200			3,350	3,200		
Controllable Income	(110)	(700)			5,150	3,575		
NonControllable Expenses								
Occupancy Costs	800	800			800	800		
Equipment Leases	0	0			0	0		
Depreciation	0	0			0	0		
Total Noncontrollable Expenses	800	800			800	800		
Operating Income	(910)	(1,500)			4,350	2,775		
Interest Expense	1,000	1,000			1,000	1,000		
Other (Income)/Expense	0	0			0	0		
Income before Income Taxes	(1,910)	(2,500)			3,350	1,775		
Net Income	(1,910)	(2,500)			3,350	1,775		

7. Assume that James' restaurant served 1,500 meals in July and 1,600 in August.

   A. Using the actual numbers, fill in the chart and compute the given ratios.

	July	August	YTD
Food Cost			
Beverage Cost			
Labor Cost			
Total Sales			
Total Meals Served	1500	1600	
Average Check			
Food Cost/Meal			
Beverage Cost/Meal			
Labor Cost/Meal			

   B. Write a brief analysis to explain your results.

8. Taryn Smith is the foodservice director at Boomerville Senior Living Community. She has submitted the following first four months of a proposed annual budget for the Garden Terrace Café, one of the dining venues offered at Boomerville. The Garden Terrace has always operated at a loss because it was considered a benefit for the residents. The new owner no longer wants to subsidize the Terrace and has instructed Taryn to revise her four-month budget to achieve breakeven by October. The owner is clear that he does not want to reduce staffing and that Taryn should concentrate her efforts on gradually increasing sales and decreasing food cost percentage. Taryn decides she will adjust her budget as follows:

   1) Increase her food and beverage sales each month by 10% over the previous month.
   2) Decrease her food cost incrementally each month until she achieves 24% food cost.

   A. Complete the spreadsheet on the next page using Taryn's two-step plan and answer the questions that follow.

   B. Did Taryn achieve breakeven ($0 Income before Income Taxes)?

   C. If you were Taryn, what recommendation would you make regarding the labor expense?

Course Project

9. The performance report for the foodservice operation described in the Course Project shows a problem. For the past two months the operation's food costs have been over-budget, while the check average has remained steady. Discuss three possible steps to take to bring the food costs back at or below budget. Explain how the manager can monitor the results.

2015 Budget				
	July	**Aug**	**Sept**	**Oct**
Sales				
Food	5,000			
Beverage	500			
Merchandise & Other	350	350	350	350
Total Sales				
Cost of Sales				
Food	1,500			
Beverage	100	110	121	133
Merchandise & Other	200	200	200	200
Total Cost of Sales				
Labor				
Management	1,000	1,000	1,000	1,000
Staff	4,000	4,000	4,000	4,000
Employee Benefits	1,000	1,000	1,000	1,000
Total Labor	6,000	6,000	6,000	6,000
Prime Cost				
Other Controllable Expenses				
Direct Operating Expenses	300	300	300	300
Music & Entertainment	150	150	150	150
Marketing	120	120	120	120
Utilities	150	150	150	150
General & Administrative	75	75	75	75
Repairs & Maintenance	75	75	75	75
Total Other Controllable Expenses	870	870	870	870
Controllable Income				
Noncontrollable Expenses				
Occupancy Costs	200	200	200	200
Equipment Leases	0	0	0	0
Depreciation	100	100	100	100
Total Noncontrollable Expenses	300	300	300	300
Operating Income				
Interest Expense	0	0	0	0
Other (Income)/Expense	0	0	0	0
Income before Income Taxes				

Chapter 9
The Capital Budget

Learning Outcomes

After studying this chapter, you will be able to
- describe the differences between a capital budget and an operating budget.
- list the steps in the capital budget process.
- explain why preplanning for a renovation or an equipment purchase is important.
- state three situations that require the purchase of a capital asset.
- state the considerations in determining equipment requirements.
- calculate the annual depreciation of an asset using the straight-line method.
- conduct a comparison of capital purchase options.
- differentiate between the options used to acquire a capital asset.

A previous chapter discussed the annual operating budget. Foodservice establishments use the operating budget to project their anticipated sales, profits, and expenses for a given period of time. The operating budget helps managers plan for expenses that are necessary to run an operation during the time period. Expenses include the purchase of items that have a relatively short useful life, such as food, beverages, and dishmachine chemicals.

However, a foodservice operation also needs to budget for purchases that have a longer useful life. These *capital assets* are part of an establishment itself. They include equipment, fixtures, buildings, and land. Since they are generally costly, an operation needs a means to plan for these purchases. As part of this plan, a method to prioritize various purchases is also required.

Capital Assets

An **asset** is cash or anything that has monetary value. **Capital budgeting** is the process of planning for the expenses of assets that are expected to last longer than one year. In addition, the costs of renovations or improvements—including installation and down-time costs—are often included in capital budgets. In this chapter, most examples of capital assets will refer to foodservice equipment.

Operations also use cost to define capital assets. In many operations, a capital asset is an asset that costs a minimum of $500. Others may use $1,000 or $2,000 as the minimum cost.

Another difference between a capital budget and an operating budget is that operating expenses are funded by the revenues or sales generated by the operation. Capital expenditures are paid for out of retained earnings, new equity, or borrowed funds (debt). Capital budgeting also involves strong record keeping of current equipment and its anticipated life. This enables the operation to establish proper internal controls and to prepare financial and tax reports. Unlike operating budget expenses, capital expenditures are *capitalized*—they are recorded on an operation's balance sheet and tracked throughout their useful life. At the end of their useful life, their disposition must be documented appropriately. With the exception of land, capital assets are also depreciated.

To create an effective capital budget, a manager must think strategically about the future needs of the operations. The manager must exercise strong fiscal management to meet the operation's capital needs over the next few years. Many operations base their capital budgets on a five-year plan period. Others choose a plan length of three or ten years. Despite these differences, the steps in the capital budget process are the following:

1. preplanning
2. determining need
3. capital investigation
4. justifying the request
5. prioritizing all requests
6. purchasing or leasing the capital asset

Each of these steps will be described on the following pages.

Preplanning

Since capital assets tend to be costly, an operation needs to plan these purchases. Problems can result from either spending too much or spending too little. Overspending can deplete an operation's funds or create excessive debt. However, spending too little can cause problems as well. For example, an operation may lack the equipment it needs to meet current or future operational needs. It may be unable to proactively respond to changing trends in the marketplace. By failing to acquire labor- or energy-efficient equipment, an operation may continue spending too much in these areas. Also, equipment may require costly repairs if it is not replaced quickly enough.

Planning for capital expenditures should be a part of an operation's *strategic planning process*. The **strategic planning process** is a process an organization uses to assess where it is at, where it wants to go, and how it can determine its future direction. For example, if an operation's strategic plan calls for growth, it may need to purchase additional buildings, equipment, and so forth. It is important that these needs be noted and scheduled out in the appropriate years.

Determining Need

How do managers determine which capital assets their operations need? At times, this is simple. For example, if an operation's only oven breaks down and is irreparable, a new one is needed immediately. However, determining an operation's capital needs

Waste Not

LEED for Retail Building Certification

Some foodservice operations have remodeled their facilities to meet LEED green building certification. Others have moved into new, LEED-certified buildings. LEED, short for Leadership in Energy and Environmental Design, is a program developed by the U.S. Green Building Council (USGBC) in 2000.

To qualify for LEED certification, an operation must meet USGBC program standards for the design, construction, operation, and maintenance of its facilities. Point values are earned for employing sustainable building and design practices, such as
- using renewable energy sources and ENERGY STAR kitchen equipment
- using paints, cleaners, and flooring made from low-emitting materials
- installing water-collection devices and using water-efficient landscaping
- reducing light pollution

The total number of points an operation earns determines its level of certification.

Achieving this certification can be expensive. However, the costs can be offset by the benefits, including a reduced environmental impact. Compared with other foodservice establishments, LEED-certified operations have lower utility costs and provide healthier environments for workers and customers. In addition, operations can use the certification in their marketing and advertising.

More information about the LEED program and retail settings can be found in "LEED 2009 for Retail: New Construction and Major Renovations."

is often a more involved process that requires proper preplanning. Managers need to step back from their day-to-day responsibilities to assess whether or not they have the right equipment, the proper aesthetics, or adequate space to meet long-term goals. Before investing in new capital assets, a manager should consider the following questions.

- What can the operation use to improve the flow of food from menu development and purchasing through waste management?
- What might assist in improving food quality?
- How much labor is available? What types of labor skills are available? What might be used to reduce the amount of labor needed and improve labor productivity and the skill set of workers?
- Is the amount and type of equipment adequate? Is it properly organized? Is there equipment on the market that could increase efficiency?
- What is the anticipated life of the equipment on hand? When will it need to be replaced? How long are the warranty periods? Is equipment frequently in need of repair? Are certified, licensed technicians available?
- Can service be improved with additional or different equipment, remodeling, or other types of capital? If so, how will the new capital asset impact the HVAC system, the cost of utilities, and the operation's layout and use of space?
- How will a new capital asset impact the operation's ability to comply with food safety and other regulatory requirements? Will new building permits be needed?
- Should a new product line or service be added that will require new equipment or additional space?
- What sources of funding can be used to acquire new capital assets?
- Does the operation anticipate growth or decline? If growth is expected, can it be accommodated by the current layout and equipment?

From here, the manager can generate a list of capital needs he or she hopes to meet during the capital budgeting period, **9-1.** Spreadsheet programs are often used to create these lists. Listed items should be organized so they are easy to reference. They should be easy to update so the list stays current. Each item should include the anticipated year the capital need will be met and its urgency. Urgency can be labeled "critical," "essential," and "desirable," for example. The critical and essential items should have the highest priority and should be investigated first.

For example, suppose a restaurant is experiencing a surge in the number of customers. Michael's On Main is an established, white-tablecloth restaurant located in the heart of a city. Over the past year, developers renovated several buildings near the restaurant into one- and two-bedroom condominiums. As a result, Michael's has enjoyed an increase in business and established a consistent following.

When he saw the developers coming, Michael, the owner and manager, anticipated the increase in traffic and the need to plan for a larger customer base. Since further expansion of the space the restaurant occupies is not feasible, Michael decides to add a broiler to expand his cooking capacity. Currently, the steamer must be located under the ventilating hood. Since the added broiler must also be located under the hood, Michael must reconfigure the equipment in the kitchen. He reviews his five-year capital expenditure plan and notes that his current steamer is beyond its warranty period. It has recently required several repairs and is on the "essential" list for capital expenditures in two years. With the increase in customers, the steamer is being pushed to capacity and may need to be replaced in one year.

Michael attends an equipment trade show and sees a few ventless steamers that do not require hood ventilation. Such a steamer can be located outside the hood system, and a new broiler could replace the current steamer under the hood. The ventless steamers are more expensive than the standard types that need venting. However, if Michael chooses another standard steamer, he will need to budget for additional duct work which will add to the steamer's expense. Michael will investigate both options for his next capital budget.

Capital Needs					
Asset	**Purchase Date**	**Useful Life**	**Replacement Year**	**Estimated Cost**	**Urgency**
Oven	2006	7	2013	$6,000	critical
Steamer	2010	5	2015	$5,000	essential
Dishmachine	2005	12	2017	$15,000	essential
Cooler One	2003	10	2013	$10,000	critical
Cooler Two	2003	10	2013	$11,000	essential
Freezer	2009	8	2017	$15,000	critical
Future Capital Needs					
Dining Room Renovation			2014	$50,000	essential
Take-Out Area Expansion			2013	$15,000	desirable
Bake Shop Addition			2016	$40,000	desirable

Figure 9-1. A manager may maintain a prioritized list of capital needs that can be referred to during the capital budget planning process.

This example illustrates the importance of understanding the current state of the operation. Keeping detailed records on equipment and having a strategic plan for the future are key tools in effectively managing capital needs.

Capital Investigation

After identifying a capital asset need, a manager should determine all of the requirements for the capital purchase. For example, which features will be necessary, and which ones are only desirable? What dimensions must a piece of equipment have so it may fit into the available space? If a dining room renovation is planned, what type of flooring should be installed? Of what quality should the materials be? The manager can explore the various options available to meet these needs. Basically, this is the shopping phase. It is similar to the process consumers should use to purchase high-ticket items.

Capital Requirements

Before a manager shops for new equipment or engages a contractor for a renovation, the needs of the operation must be considered. For instance, if new equipment is being purchased, how will it be used and what requirements must it meet? The following questions should be considered.

Menu

- For which menu items will the equipment be used?
- How often do these items appear on the menu and how popular are they?
- What capacity must the equipment have to meet current operating needs and plans for future expansion?
- How will a new acquisition impact production time?

Utilities

- What are the utility requirements of a piece of equipment?
- How much will utilities cost—the cost of gas versus electric, for example?
- Where are the equipment's lines, outlets, drains, or vents? Will this allow it to be placed where it needs to be located?

Equipment Design

- What functionalities are needed? What supplemental parts?
- How durable must the equipment be?
- What materials should it be made from?
- Should the equipment be compatible with other pieces of equipment in the kitchen?

Safety

- What safety features are required?
- What is required by OSHA (Occupational Safety & Health Administration)? or by the U.S. Food and Drug Administration's Food Code?
- If a capital asset is a product, is it certified for quality and safety? Does it have NSF certification? Does it meet the standards of groups such as Underwriters Laboratories® (UL), AGA, or ASME?

Sanitation

- What are the sanitation requirements for the equipment?
- How much time is available for cleaning?

Equipment Complexity

- What is the skill set of the kitchen staff? What skill set must they have to operate the equipment?
- How much time and money will be needed to train the staff to use and maintain the equipment?

Additional Costs

- Beyond the cost of the equipment, what other costs need to be considered? installation? maintenance? repairs? warranties? licensing? training?
- Does it require customized pans? smallwares? other supplies?
- What will be the financial impact on labor and on quality?
- For renovations or additions, how much space is desired? What are the aesthetics, quality, and type of materials needed?

Sources of Information

After the operation's capital needs are defined, a manager can investigate what the market has to offer. The following sources can provide information:

- primary food vendors—they often employ equipment or design specialists
- corporate specialists or engineers, if an operation is a multiunit operation
- trade journals

Trend/Technology

Chip-and-PIN Technology

When a new technology comes along, businesses can be forced to invest in costly equipment and software. For example, when credit card companies began to replace magnetic-stripe cards with chip-and-PIN smart cards, businesses had to upgrade their POS systems or purchase new ones that could accept the cards.

Chip-and-PIN, also called EMV (EuroPay, MasterCard and Visa), is the preferred payment processing technology in Europe, Canada, and other parts of the world. An EMV card looks like a traditional credit or debit card, which stores data on a magnetic stripe. However, an EMV card contains an embedded microprocessor chip that can hold much more data, including software applications.

Credit card companies prefer the new technology because it reduces the risk of fraud. Instead of signing for a purchase, cardholders enter a personal identification number or PIN. Some EMV cards are contactless, meaning a card can be read without physical contact with a card reader. EMV technology also paves the way to new mobile payment technologies, which are already being used. Consumers pull out their smartphones instead of their wallets to pay for purchases.

The main disadvantage of EMV payment processing technology is that it requires capital investments for many businesses. To be able to accept EMV cards for payment, foodservice operations must upgrade their POS systems or purchase new ones. This can be expensive. Since the magnetic-stripe cards are being phased out, operations that do not upgrade will be unable to accept credit card payments. They may also be held liable for financial losses that occur due to fraud. Credit card companies plan to pass those costs down the line. Experts say noncompliant businesses will eventually be responsible for those losses.

- brochures and websites of individual manufacturers, interior designers, or contractors
- manufacturers' associations, such as the North American Association of Food Equipment Manufacturers (NAFEM)
- groups such as the not-for-profit testing organization NSF International, (founded as the National Sanitation Foundation)
- trade shows
- networks of industry contacts

The best source of information is often another foodservice operation. If an operation plans to purchase a piece of equipment, the manager should contact or visit a foodservice operation that uses it. If a renovation is being planned, the manager should contact an operation that recently completed similar construction. Feedback can be obtained from managers and employees at the other operation. A manager can be referred to these operations through manufacturer's representatives, construction companies, or from someone in his or her industry network.

Earlier in the chapter, the owner and manager of Michael's On Main visits an equipment trade show to look at steamers. The trade show is an excellent venue for Michael. In one place, he finds models of foodservice equipment from different manufacturers. Representatives are on hand to answer his questions and to explain and demonstrate how the equipment works. Suppose he stops by a booth and picks up a brochure on a 6-pan, ventless, countertop unit that appears to meet his needs. It can handle the increased customer demand he anticipates and offers potential savings in utility costs. Also, it does not have to be located under the hood system. A portion of a specification for a similar type of steamer is shown in **9-2**.

Michael is also considering purchasing a standard convection steamer like the one he already uses. One of the best sources of information about this product would be the manufacturer that sold him his current steamer. At the trade show, Michael can also meet with that manufacturer's representative.

Buying New versus Used

Michael can either buy a new steamer or investigate purchasing a used one. Before he solicits bids for a steamer, he should weigh the advantages and disadvantages of buying new versus used.

The major disadvantage of buying new equipment is its higher cost. If it needs to be built or customized to the operator's specifications, the wait time could be lengthy. However, that is offset by the many advantages of buying new. When buying new, an operator can obtain equipment to his or her exact specifications and take advantage of depreciation. In the early life of equipment, repairs, and the downtime necessitated by repairs, are usually minimal. Also, new equipment usually comes with a guarantee. The seller will reimburse purchasers if a product is defective or does not perform as stated. New equipment usually comes with a full warranty and a maintenance service agreement. During a stated warranty period, the seller or manufacturer will repair it under certain conditions if it is defective. A warranty does not guarantee that the purchaser will be reimbursed for the cost of the purchase if it is defective or does not meet anticipated performance.

The advantages of buying used equipment include lower cost and immediate availability. Used equipment can sometimes be purchased "like new" if the seller has gone out of business or is no longer in need of the equipment. The disadvantages of buying used equipment may include

- limited or no warranty
- limited or no service agreements
- accelerated depreciation

Intek Steamer model XS

Model XS

**6 Pan Capacity
Stainless Steel
Pressureless,
Connectionless Steamer**

**Table Top
Self-Contained
Electric Heated**

Short Form
Groen Intek XS 6-pan connectionless countertop steamer unit is available as 208, 240 or 480 volt, single or three phase, 6, 8, 12, or 14kW (12 and 14kW available in three phase only) steam cooker with a pan capacity of 6 pans (2.5" deep 12" x 20") or 4 pans (4" deep 12" x 20"). Unit must be capable of producing steam at 212°F with no water or drain connection required. Unit must be a NSF approved holding vessel. 4" stainless steel adjustable legs with flanged feet. Unit is to have inverted convection fan technology and includes a 1 year parts and labor warranty. Unit to be NSF and UL listed and manufactured in the U.S.A.

Model Numbers
XS-208-6-1 (208V, 6kW, 1-Phase)
XS-208-8-1 (208V, 8kW, 1-Phase)
XS-208-8-3 (208V, 8kW, 3-Phase)
XS-208-12-3 (208V, 12kW, 3-Phase)
XS-208-14-3 (208V, 14kW, 3-Phase)
XS-240-6-1 (240V, 6kW, 1-Phase)
XS-240-8-1 (240V, 8kW, 1-Phase)
XS-240-8-3 (240V, 8kW, 3-Phase)
XS-240-12-3 (240V, 12kW, 3-Phase)
XS-240-14-3 (240V, 14kW, 3-Phase)
XS-480-12-3 (480V, 12kW, 3-Phase)

Description
The Intek XS connectionless countertop steamer unit has a pan capacity of 6 pans (2.5" deep 12" x 20") or 4 pans (4" deep 12" x 20"). Unit must be capable of producing steam at 212°F with no water or drain connection required. Unit is to have inverted convection fan technology and includes a 1 year parts and labor warranty. NSF listed as both steamer and holding cabinet. UL listed.

Construction
- 14 gauge reinforced stainless steel cavity
- Insulated cavity and double door panel
- Heavy refrigeration style door handle with magnetic latch
- Stainless steel wire racks positioned to support 2.5", 4", or 6" deep pans

Operation
- Inverted flow convection fan in cooking chamber
- NSF approved holding cabinet
- Open door while cooking
- Heating element external to compartment and not exposed to water
- 3 gallon capacity water reservoir

Options/Accessories
- ☐ Stand w/Bullet Feet for Single or Double Stack
- ☐ Casters for Stand
- ☐ Flanged Feet for Stand
- ☐ Door Hinged Left
- ☐ Correction Package
- ☐ Auto Water Fill
- ☐ Drain Line
- ☐ Trivet

Origin of Manufacture
Steamer shall be designed and manufactured in the United States.

Applications
Pasta
Rice
Vegetables (Fresh & Frozen)
Seafood (Fresh & Frozen)
Poultry
Potatoes
Eggs
Meats
Reheat Cook-Chill & Prepared Foods

**Groen Intek, Page 2
XS REV F**
Updated 08/11

Figure 9-2. Brochures provided by manufacturers give detailed information about products. Managers can use these to compare the features and benefits of like items of capital. This is a page from a product specification of a Groen Intek Steamer.
Used with permission from Unified Brands®

- an increased likelihood of needing repairs
- the need to modify the equipment or space to meet operational needs or kitchen location
- the operator's lack of expertise in determining the equipment's true value or potential faults
- increased operating expenses if the used equipment is not as energy efficient as a newer model

Calculating Depreciation

The financial health of a company is reflected in its income, expenses, and net income over a given year. Suppose a foodservice operation buys an expensive piece of equipment or renovates its dining room. If the entire cost of that capital investment is listed in the year it was purchased, the financial health of the company during that year will be understated. In the following years, the equipment will still provide value to the company as an asset, but expenses for the equipment will not be recorded. This results in the financial health of the company being overstated. To truly measure the cost of an asset, only a portion of its total cost should be recorded for the year.

Determining the exact value a capital asset provides to an operation each year can be difficult. It can also be extremely time-consuming if the operator has purchased multiple assets over the years. **Depreciation** is an accounting method that is used to distribute the cost of an asset—minus its salvage value—over its anticipated useful life. Accounting principles give managers a few acceptable methods to determine how much to depreciate an asset over its useful life. The most basic method is called *straight-line depreciation*.

Using straight-line depreciation, the salvage value of an asset is subtracted from its cost. The difference is then divided by the useful life of the asset, or the depreciation period. The depreciation period varies by the asset, but the typical depreciation period is five to seven years.

$$\text{Annual Depreciation} = \frac{\text{Asset Cost} - \text{Salvage Value}}{\text{Anticipated Useful Life in Years}}$$

For instance, suppose a company buys a piece of equipment for $8,000. Its anticipated useful life is five years and its salvage value is expected to be $500. Using straight-line depreciation, the annual depreciation of the equipment would be calculated as follows:

$$\text{Annual depreciation} = \frac{\$8,000 - \$500}{5 \text{ years}}$$

$$\text{Annual depreciation} = \frac{\$7,500}{5 \text{ years}}$$

$$\text{Annual depreciation} = \$1,500$$

Other depreciation methods are more complicated and are typically calculated by a financial manager. They are beyond the scope of this text.

Soliciting Bids

After evaluating the pros and cons of buying new versus used, suppose that Michael decides to go with a new steamer. His next step would be the solicitation of bids. During the capital investigation process, managers solicit bids from qualified contractors or vendors. The names of qualified contractors and vendors often come from other people in the foodservice industry or from local equipment dealers in larger urban areas. Managers can get referrals to highly regarded professionals by tapping into their own network of contacts. Qualified contractors or vendors can also be found exhibiting or presenting at major industry trade shows. Contractors should be bonded, insured, and licensed. Before making a hiring decision, managers should ask for references and then check out the references.

Contractors should be given sufficient time to respond. Managers often request quick turnarounds on bids which can drive up costs. When given insufficient time, contractors and vendors may increase their estimates. Furthermore, on large projects, managers may consider hiring professionals or consultants. They can help managers determine their actual needs and the costs of design, construction, and equipment.

Once bids are received from contractors and vendors, they should be studied carefully. The bids should fulfill the operation's requirements. Managers also need to make sure all parties bid on the same piece of equipment or on the same renovation requirements. In some cases, a substitute may be acceptable.

Justifying the Request

At this point in the capital budget process, the manager has determined the need for a capital asset. Information has been gathered. This may include brochures, journal advertisements, equipment specification sheets, customer testimonials, and bids. It is now time for the manager to complete a capital request.

Businesses generally use a standard capital request form. In completing the form, the manager identifies all the costs related to the purchase of the equipment or the completion of the project. The savings that may result from the capital expenditure is estimated. If more than one option is presented, information on each one should be included. The manager will recommend one over the other in the final presentation. This is referred to as *equipment justification* or *project justification*.

Revisiting the earlier example, Michael has identified two options for a new steamer. One is the ventless steamer he saw at the trade show. The other is a newer model of the standard convection steamer he currently uses. Michael's next step is to do a comparison of the two steamers. He needs to determine the equipment cost, justify the need, and identify any realized savings. Then he can calculate the impact the purchase of each steamer will have on the restaurant's bottom line. A form, such as the "Comparison of Capital Purchase Options" form, **9-3**, can be helpful. In filling out the form, Michael determines that the ventless steamer will cost $5,600—$5,000 for the steamer and an additional $600 for a stand to hold it. The standard convection steamer will cost $5,400—$3,900 for the steamer and an additional $1,500 for a hood that would need to be added.

Comparison of Capital Purchase Options	Standard Convection	Ventless
Cost of Unit	3,900	5,000
Hood (standard convection steamer)	1,500	
Stand (ventless steamer)		600
Shipping	100	100
Taxes (6%)	324	336
Asset Cost	5,824	6,036
Salvage Value	390	500
Life Expectancy in Years	8	10
Annual Operating Cost		
Electrical	3,304	630
Water	462	17
Maintenance	200	100
Total	3,966	747
Operating Cost over Life Expectancy	31,728	7,470
Total Cost	37,162	13,006
Annual Savings over Current Steamer*	1,034	4,253
Payback Period	5.6	1.4

*Assumes a $5,000 operating cost for the aging convection steamer

Figure 9-3. To decide what to purchase, a manager compares products on the market. This is an example of a comparison of two steamers. Note that the payback period for the standard convection steamer is 5.6 years, and 1.4 years for the ventless steamer.

The annual cost of operating each steamer includes annual maintenance costs and the costs of water and electricity. From the manufacturer, Michael finds the annual cost of operating the ventless steamer is an estimated $747. The new standard convection steamer will cost $3,966 to operate each year. These costs are better than his current steamer's annual operating cost of $5,000. Both steamers result in savings, but the ventless model is much less expensive to operate. The annual operating cost can be multiplied by the life expectancy of each steamer to give the operating cost over its projected useful life.

Operating Cost over Life Expectancy = Annual Operating Cost × Life Expectancy in Years

For a new standard convection steamer, operating cost over life expectancy is calculated as follows:

Operating cost over life expectancy = $3,966 × 8

Operating cost over life expectancy = $31,728

For the new ventless steamer, operating cost over life expectancy is calculated below:

Operating cost over life expectancy = $747 × 10

Operating cost over life expectancy = $7,470

The total cost line is calculated by adding the operating cost over life expectancy to the cost of the asset. Then the salvage value is subtracted from that sum. The total cost line for each steamer is calculated using the formula:

Total Cost = (Asset Cost + Operating Cost over Life Expectancy) – Salvage Value

The total cost of a new standard convection steamer is calculated as follows:

Total cost = ($5,824 + $31,728) – $390

Total cost = $37,162

The total cost of a new ventless steamer is derived as follows:

Total cost = ($6,036 + $7,470) – $500

Total cost = $13,006

Calculating Payback Period

Michael can calculate the impact the purchase of each steamer will have on the restaurant's bottom line. The **payback period** is the amount of time it will take to recover the cost of the purchase. After the payback period, the operation begins to see a return. The option with the lowest payback period is generally the best choice. First, the annual savings in utility costs is calculated.

Annual Savings = Current Operating Cost – Operating Cost of New Equipment

New standard convection steamer:

Annual savings = $5,000 – $3,966

Annual savings = $1,034

New ventless steamer:

Annual savings = $5,000 – $747

Annual savings = $4,253

To find the payback period, the cost of the equipment is divided by the annual savings. A 6 percent sales tax and a $100 freight charge are added to the cost of each steamer. This brings the total cost of the convection steamer to $5,824 and the total cost of the ventless steamer to $6,036. Sales tax may not always apply.

$$\text{Payback Period} = \frac{\text{Asset Cost}}{\text{Annual Savings}}$$

New standard convection steamer:

$$\text{Payback period} = \frac{\$5,824}{\$1,034}$$

Payback period = 5.6 years

New ventless steamer:

$$\text{Payback period} = \frac{\$6,036}{\$4,253}$$

Payback period = 1.4 years

Michael will recoup his investment in 1.4 years if he buys the ventless steamer, as opposed to 5.6 years if he purchases the other. Based on this comparison, Michael will recommend the ventless steamer.

Completing a Request for Capital Asset Form

After making his choice, Michael completes a request for capital asset form, **9-4**. The form serves as a cover letter for detailed information that will be attached. This information includes vendor quotes and a capital equipment justification form, **9-5**. The capital equipment justification form includes

- the initial cost of the equipment
- a written justification for the purchase
- annual savings, if any
- the payback period

Michael gives the initial costs and any annual costs. Then, he documents the annual savings he expects from decreased utility costs.

Prioritizing Requests

When an operation is sizable—a restaurant that is large or part of a chain—several capital requests may be under consideration simultaneously. In an institutional setting, such as a hospital or school, capital requests from the foodservice department would be considered alongside those of other departments, such as surgery or the athletic department.

Request for Capital Asset	
Requested date	2/02/____
Requested by	Michael L.
Asset title	Steamer
Description/Purpose	Company X Model 12345 Steamer. Ventless steamer needed to meet increased customer volume, and replace aging convection steamer.
Account code	8000-10
Purchased asset (total cost, including shipping/tax, installation)	$6,036
Fees (licensing, etc.)	$0
Is this a replacement for existing equipment?	Yes
Describe old asset	Convection steamer model #54321
Supporting documentation attached?	Yes
Comparison of Capital Purchase Options form completed?	Yes
Vender quotes attached?	Yes
Capital Equipment Justification form completed?	Yes
Approval	

Figure 9-4. This is an example of a capital asset purchase request. Each operation has its own format. The request contains the information managers should obtain before requesting funds to purchase capital.

Capital Equipment Justification	
Date	2/02/____
Equipment requested	Ventless Steamer
Requestor	Michael L.
Cost	$6,036
Justification	Will increase steamer capacity. Will replace old steamer that has excessive repairs and is beyond warranty. Requires no venting. Can be placed outside hood system.
Payback period	1.4 years
Total annual operating expenses	$747
Salvage value	$500
Annual savings	$4,253
Action to take if not purchased	Current steamer may not last with anticipated increase in customers. Will not be able to provide menu items to meet demand.
Additional resources required	None
Comments	

Figure 9-5. A manager must justify why capital dollars should be spent on a particular capital asset. The manager must supply decision makers with the information they need to determine whether or not a purchase will be a good investment.

Generally, a set amount of funds is provided for capital purchases in a given year. There is a maximum amount of dollars that can be spent by the company. Since capital is a limited resource, the people who determine where capital dollars are spent look at each request. For example, suppose that two requests for funds are submitted by managers in an operation. One manager requests a piece of equipment that will lower labor costs and is expected to pay for itself in five years. The other manager requests funds for a piece of equipment that is needed to produce a new product line. Although the profit from this product line may take seven years to realize, it will generate far more profit in 10 years time than the first piece of equipment. Which is the better long-term investment for the company? How much annual return is necessary, or how much profit must be made, to justify the purchase of the equipment? Can this amount of profit be achieved? To answer these questions, the people evaluating capital requests for an operation run various standard accounting scenarios. These are beyond the scope of this text.

Purchasing or Leasing the Asset

After approval is received on a capital budget request, the asset can be acquired. The information gleaned during the capital investigation step is used to complete an order form. An operation can

- purchase the asset outright
- borrow funds for the purchase
- use hire purchase
- enter into a lease agreement

Purchasing Outright

When an operation purchases an asset outright, payment is made using cash on hand and the operation takes ownership of the asset immediately. This is similar to what consumers experience when they go to an electronics store and pay cash for a new television.

There are advantages and disadvantages to funding an asset in this way. Operations can save money because they avoid fees added to the purchase price—such as interest or leasing fees. There is usually a tax advantage, since operations may be able to claim the asset on their tax returns. Foodservice operations can claim tax allowances, called capital allowances, on purchases or investments. They can reduce their taxes by deducting a portion of these costs from taxable profits.

The disadvantage of purchasing in this way is that cash is tied up in capital and cannot be used for other purchases. Also, the capital will most likely depreciate and may require insurance. When the item needs to be replaced, its disposal may be costly.

Borrowing Cash to Purchase

An operation may borrow cash to purchase an asset, including land or property. This is comparable to a consumer taking out a loan from a financial institution to buy a car or house. The borrower and the creditor—the financial institution or party making the loan—enter into a contract. The contract will require the borrower to pay back the loan in a series of regular payments, which come out of the operation's revenue.

The advantage of this method of capital purchase is that the operation has possession and use of the asset from the outset. It has less impact on the operation's cash flow. The interest paid on the loan may be tax deductible and a way that the operation can lower its tax liability.

The primary disadvantage of borrowing cash to make a purchase is that interest and fees—which can be substantial—must be paid to the creditor in addition to the amount borrowed. Also, if the operation fails to meet the loan agreement, it may have to pay a penalty or lose a down payment or collateral. Some creditors require borrowers to make a down payment or to provide some form of collateral, or security, when a loan is made. This provides the creditor with an asset if the borrower fails to meet the loan agreement.

Hire Purchase

In hire purchase, a party other than the operation purchases the asset. The operation makes regular periodic payments to that party over a set period of time. Eventually the operation takes ownership of the asset. This is similar to the rent-to-own arrangement used by consumers. Hire purchase is best used for assets with a medium to long life. Its main advantage is that the operation can use the equipment during the repayment period, and the purchase price is spread out over several payments.

A disadvantage is that the seller can reclaim the equipment if the buyer fails to make timely installments, and may not return the money already paid by the purchaser. In addition, the buyer does not own the equipment until the final installment payment is made.

Leasing

Another way an operation can fund capital assets is to enter into a lease agreement. This option is chosen when the asset has a short life or requires regular upgrading. For example, many operations choose to lease computers and software, products that are regularly upgraded. A lease can also be used to fund an asset that will be used for a period shorter than its anticipated life. A good example of this is the leasing of a car. The car is leased for a period of time that is less than its anticipated life. Once the lease is up, the car can be sold as a used vehicle.

The operator, or lessee, enters into an agreement with the *lessor*, or the owner of the asset. The operator pays the lessor a set rental rate over the life of the lease. Although it will never own the equipment, the operation has full use of it for the duration of the agreement. At the end of the lease period, the asset will be returned to the lessor.

While lease payments may be tax deductible, an advantage of leasing equipment is that it has less impact on an operation's cash flow than purchasing equipment outright. The lessee does not have the full cost of the capital tied up in cash. A disadvantage of leasing is that the leasing company owns the asset. Also, the lessee may have to commit to purchasing associated products. For example, as a condition of leasing a dishmachine, an operation may also have to buy dishmachine chemicals from the leasing company.

Weighing the Options

How do managers decide which of the four options is best for a particular capital purchase? An employee of a large company or corporation would be guided by company or corporate procedures. Managers sometimes consult financial experts. These professionals study an operation's past history and its usual approach to acquiring assets. They evaluate how a capital request may affect an operation's cash flow and its working capital requirements.

However, in the end, managers are responsible for finding the best solutions for their operations' capital needs. This involves researching possible options and stating the pros and cons from both operational and financial standpoints. After the justification process is completed, the best solution is presented. A request for capital funds to purchase the item follows.

It is important that the amount requested is accurate. Once a request is accepted, an item can be purchased at a cost that is less than or equal to the amount requested. If additional funds are needed, managers may need to submit a new capital budget request which may be rejected.

Key Terms

asset	strategic planning process	payback period
capital budgeting	depreciation	

Recap

- Capital budgeting is the process of planning for the expenses of assets that are expected to last longer than one year.
- Capital budgeting involves strong record keeping of current equipment and its anticipated life.
- Capital expenditures are paid for out of retained earnings, new equity, or borrowed funds.
- The steps in the capital budget process are preplanning, determining need, capital investigation, justifying the request, prioritizing all requests, and purchasing or leasing the asset(s).
- The capital requirements of an operation are determined by its menu, utilities available, equipment design, safety and sanitation requirements, equipment complexity, and additional costs of utilizing the equipment.
- Information about equipment is available through various sources.
- A capital asset purchase request includes a justification form and vendor quotes.

Review Questions

1. Describe the differences between an operating budget and a capital budget.
2. List the steps in the capital budget process.
3. When might it be necessary to purchase capital equipment?
4. Briefly describe how each of the following affects equipment requirements.
   - A. Menu
   - B. Utilities
   - C. Equipment design
   - D. Safety and sanitation requirements
   - E. Equipment complexity
   - F. Additional costs
5. Name four sources of equipment information.
6. Use straight-line depreciation to figure out the annual depreciation for a steamer with an anticipated useful life of 10 years, a salvage value of $300, and a cost of $4,500.
7. Explain hire purchase and state the advantage of funding capital purchases in this way.
8. What information is needed on a capital equipment justification form?

Applying Your Knowledge

Exercises 9-9 and 9-10

Complete the following exercises on the companion website:
www.g-wlearning.com/culinaryarts/

9. Tom's Taco Haven is in need of a new deep fryer. Tom has completed his research and gathered the following information:

Fat Fryer Brand:
Cost: $4,000
Useful life: 8 years
Salvage value: $250
Utility costs per year: $125
Estimated annual repairs: $75
Shipping: Included in asset cost
Tax rate: 6%
Annual operating cost of current fryer: $600

Greener Fryer Brand:
Cost: $5,000
Useful life: 8 years
Salvage value: $350
Utility costs per year: $75
Estimated annual repairs: $50
Shipping: $100
Tax rate: 6%

A. Use the information provided in the following spreadsheet to complete a capital purchase comparison of Tom's two fryer options and answer the questions that follow.

	Fat Fryer Brand	Greener Fryer Brand
Cost of unit		
Shipping		
Tax (6%)		
Asset cost		
Salvage value		
Life expectancy (years)		
Annual operating expenses (utilities + est. repairs)		
Operating expenses over life expectancy		
Annual operating expenses of current fryer		
Annual savings of new equipment over old		
Total cost (asset cost + operating expense over life) − salvage value		
Payback period (years)		

B. Based on financial considerations, which fryer should Tom purchase and why?

C. Tom is not happy with either bid and asks both vendors to submit new bids. Fat Fryer brand chooses to let their original bid submission stand. Greener Fryer's new bid decreases the cost of the fryer to $3,500 if Tom agrees to buy their frying oil for the next eight years at a cost of $50/case. All other aspects of the bid remain the same. Tom currently spends $48/case for oil and uses two cases per week. He decides to consider the cost of the oil in his annual operating expenses to see if Greener Fryer's offer is a good option for him. (Assume the current cost of oil remains constant over the next eight years.)

Second Round Bids		
	Fat Fryer Brand	Greener Fryer Brand
Cost of unit		
Shipping		
Tax (6%)		
Asset cost		
Salvage value		
Life expectancy (years)		
Annual operating expenses (utilities + est. repairs + cost of oil)		
Operating expenses over life expectancy		
Annual operating expenses of current fryer		
Annual savings of new equipment over old		
Total cost		
Payback period (years)		

D. Which fryer should Tom purchase based on the second round of bids?

10. Use the information in problem 9A to calculate the annual depreciation for both fryers using the straight-line method.

	Fat Fryer	Greener Fryer
Asset cost		
Salvage value		
Useful life (years)		
Annual depreciation		

Course Project

11. Select a piece of equipment that will be needed to produce the menu created for the Course Project. Obtain a manufacturer's specification and a purchase price for the equipment. Write a justification to purchase.

Chapter 10
Revenue Control

Learning Outcomes

After studying this chapter, you will be able to

- recognize the importance of revenue control in foodservice.
- describe how to establish a revenue control system.
- differentiate between intentional and unintentional revenue loss.
- list three job activities that give employees the greatest opportunities to steal funds.
- summarize steps that can be taken to prevent revenue loss due to employee theft.
- outline basic cash-handling and deposit procedures.
- summarize the corrective-action process.
- state three ways patrons can steal from foodservice operations.

In a foodservice operation, revenue is typically received in the form of cash or credit card payments from customers. As revenue flows through the operation, many people may have access to it. This underscores the need for a system to safeguard revenue. Organizations use control systems to measure expected results against actual results. **Revenue control** is the management function of measuring whether expected revenue is equal to actual revenue—or the revenue an operation recorded it received. For each sale, the purpose of revenue control is to ensure that the appropriate revenue is received and eventually deposited. Any deviation between actual and expected amounts should be corrected or minimized, and prevented from reoccurring. A strong revenue control system is essential to ensure an operation's sustainability and profitability.

Revenue Loss

Any loss of revenue results in lost profit. Revenue loss can result from actions that are intentional or unintentional. An *unintentional revenue deviation* or loss is caused by an employee error, or by a malfunction of the cash register or POS system. An employee who causes this type of deviation does not intend to steal from the company. An *intentional revenue deviation* or loss is most commonly referred to as *theft* or *pilferage*. It can be committed by an employee or a patron.

The larger the foodservice establishment, the more complex revenue control becomes. For example, suppose a hot dog vendor has 12 hot dogs to sell at the beginning of the day. At the end of the day, three hot dogs remain. The hot dogs sell for $1.50 each. The cash register should record the sale of nine hot dogs, and contain $13.50 more than it did at the beginning of the day. Revenue is fairly simple to control with only 12 items to sell and one cash register.

However, in larger operations, many transactions occur throughout the day on a variety of items. In addition, more people are involved in the selling process and in the exchange of cash and product. A revenue control system must be in place to ensure that the total sales recorded in the cash register match the cash or credit receipts on hand as well as the selling prices of the items sold.

As illustrated in the following scenario, an effective control procedure can be implemented using four basic steps, **10-1**. Cassandra is hired as the manager of Collins's Culinary Creations. One of her first actions is to evaluate the revenue controls of the operation. She notes that the restaurant is equipped with an antiquated, manual cash register. It does not offer a POS system or many of the security features needed to control cash, such as password controls for accessing the register. Cassandra requests that the owner purchase a new register system, which costs close to $6,000. The owner does not want to spend the money.

Cassandra decides to monitor the revenue received against the amounts of the guest checks. She notes that the restaurant is $400 short in just one week. She presents this information to the owner, and states that much of this loss can be tracked if a POS system is installed. The owner agrees and the new system is purchased.

Next, Cassandra writes a detailed policy and procedures manual for the use of the new register. She trains her staff on the functions of the register and the new policies and procedures. Over the next few months, Cassandra monitors how well the employees are following the new policies and procedures. She provides extra training and corrective action as needed. After two months, the difference between the revenue received and the guest check totals has dropped. It averages under $50 per week. Cassandra continues to tweak the process, looking for new ways to control the revenue loss.

Implementing a Control Procedure
1. Establish the procedure.
2. Train staff to follow the procedure.
3. Monitor performance and compare it against the procedure.
4. Take necessary action to correct deviations from the procedure.
Example: A manager wants to implement a count-sheet procedure to better track the inventory of beer bottles.
• *Procedure:* At the start of a shift, the bottles on hand are inventoried. The number is recorded on the count sheet. At the end of the shift, the bottles left are counted and the number is recorded.
• *Training:* The bartender is trained to follow the count-sheet procedure.
• *Monitoring:* The manager checks the count sheet against the actual sales recorded by the cash register. Discrepancies are noted, accounting for losses due to breakage, etc.
• *Action:* If the actual number of bottles sold varies from the expected number, the manager takes action to identify and correct discrepancies before the next shift.

Figure 10-1. The implementation of a procedure to control any asset—including revenue—can be carried out in these steps.

Trend/Technology

Hackers Target Foodservice Operations

Foodservice operations are the favorite targets of hackers. Approximately half of all reported data breaches involve food and beverage operations, according to firms that investigate these incidents. About 90 percent of the investigations find that criminals are after customers' payment card data. It is commonly stored on POS systems, computer networks, and websites.

Foodservice operations are targeted because their data security is often lax—passwords are weak, firewalls are nonexistent, or data security programs are outdated. Some foodservice establishments that provide Wi-Fi to their customers increase their vulnerability to attacks by linking the Wi-Fi to their POS systems. Also, foodservice operations are often parts of chains or franchises. After discovering a weakness in one establishment's payment system, thieves can exploit similar weaknesses at other operations in the chain.

The people who commit these crimes use increasingly sophisticated tools and methods. Some use wireless skimmer devices to secretly transmit credit card numbers and PIN codes to criminals. Other criminals, working thousands of miles away, hack into servers that businesses use to transmit payment card information. They install software programs that log customer data during transmission—from a restaurant POS system to a central office computer, for example. The data are often sold to criminal networks that use it to commit identity theft and fraud.

Data breaches can be very costly for a business. Many of the losses are not covered by standard liability insurance policies. Costs and losses in revenue may result from the need to

- identify and notify customers and employees affected by the security breach
- hire data security experts to find and fix the breach
- pay fines and penalties levied by governments
- pay for credit monitoring services for the business and for customers
- switch to a cash-only operation after having payment card privileges rescinded by credit card companies
- defend against lawsuits filed by customers whose data were compromised
- repair a damaged reputation
- shut down until the security problems are remedied

Hackers' activities are often undetected for months and even years. Operations are usually unaware of a data breach until they are contacted by law enforcement agencies or customers who are fraud victims. Experts stress that prevention is the best strategy for businesses that want to protect their operations and their customers. Prevention includes the implementation of basic, low-cost data security practices.

In foodservice operations, revenue loss is often caused by theft. Theft can occur when funds are entrusted to employees who wrongfully use it for their own benefit. Employees who work at the register, create deposits, or handle guest checks, have the greatest opportunity to steal funds. Most employee theft can be minimized or prevented by the careful selection of employees and by the implementation of strong cash-handling and guest-check procedures. Operations should also enact measures to prevent or minimize theft by patrons.

Employee Selection and Screening

Although many employees are honest and trustworthy, employee theft is common in many types of businesses. Employees who commit theft may take a pen home from the office, falsify their time cards, and steal food, equipment, and cash from their employers. According to the United States Chamber of Commerce, 75 percent of employees are capable of stealing, while one in three will do so repeatedly. In restaurants, employee theft accounts for about 75 percent of all inventory losses, according to the

National Restaurant Association. This equals about 3 percent of annual sales. If an operation has annual sales of $1,000,000, the loss due to theft could be $30,000.

When searching for a potential hire, a good screening process is essential. A job candidate should be screened for desirable traits, such as honesty, a strong work ethic, and a positive attitude. To ensure that an applicant does not have a history of theft, a background check may be necessary. Managers should check with local authorities for information about available screening resources.

An operation must have clear, established policies regarding employee expectations and disciplinary action related to theft. Managers should review these policies with new employees during the orientation process. Employees' signatures should be required to acknowledge that they received and understand the policies. Also, the policies must be applied consistently or employees will not take them seriously. If employees see coworkers committing theft without consequence, they will come to view stealing as an acceptable practice. The chapter on labor cost control covers employee screening and hiring in more depth.

Employee Bonding

Even the best employee screening practices and the most careful monitoring cannot prevent all employee theft. **Bonding** is a process in which employers purchase insurance to protect themselves from financial losses due to the actions of dishonest employees. The bonding agency guarantees payment to the employer in the event of these losses. The agency runs background checks on employees before writing a bond. Since an employee who cannot be bonded may have a problematic background, bonding can screen out problematic job candidates.

If an operation uses bonding and a theft occurs, the employer informs the bonding agency of the theft. The bonding agency reimburses the operation for the loss per the contract. The agency then works to recover the stolen assets. Police action needs to be considered.

Cash Handling Policies and Procedures

When working the cash register, some employees steal funds by manipulating transactions. This type of theft is known as *cash skimming*. **Cash skimming** is the theft of cash receipts before the receipts are recorded. Five techniques are commonly used by cash handlers to remove money from the system, **10-2**. To prevent or minimize the loss of revenue, strong cash handling policies and procedures must be established. These procedures can prevent both unintentional and intentional revenue deviations. Cash-handling policies need to address the following:

- separation of duties
- cash-drawer practices
- cashier job duties
- deposit practices
- using a safe

Separation of Duties

The *separation of duties* is important when establishing cash-handling procedures. Different employees are given responsibility for different steps in the process. For example, a cashier may close out the cash drawer, count the cash, and record the total amount. The supervisor may then reconcile the cash register receipts to the cash in the drawer, and record the amount to be deposited. The total receipts rung on the cash register should equal the cashier drawer total. This system of checks and balances can prevent theft.

Cash-Skimming Techniques	
No Ring	Cashier collects payment from the customer, but does not ring in a sale.
Underring	Cashier collects payment, but rings in a lesser amount for the sale.
Overring	Cashier rings in the sale for a greater amount, and collects payment.
Voids	Cashier rings in the sale, collects payment, and then voids the sale.
Discounts	Cashier rings in the sale, collects payment, and then discounts the sale amount.

Figure 10-2. The most common cash-skimming techniques used by employees to steal from cash drawers are listed.

Cash-Drawer Practices

Cash-drawer practices are important to prevent theft. A **cash drawer** is generally a compartment underneath a cash register that holds the cash from transactions. The drawer is usually divided into separate compartments for bills and coins. Each cashier should have his or her own drawer and be held accountable for all cash and the transactions associated with that drawer.

Each cashier should have his or her own cash bag, or *cashier's bank*, for use with the cash drawer. At the beginning of the shift, the cashier is given his or her bank which is placed in the cash drawer. The cashier's bank consists of a preset cash allocation, made up of different denominations of coins and currency. The amount in this bank should be based on the anticipated cash needed to make change during the cashier's shift. The bank should remain in the safe when not in use. In operations where servers ring in orders and make sales transactions, servers are issued a *server's bank*.

The register itself—particularly a POS system—is a great tool in controlling revenue deviations. Registers print a receipt for each transaction, which cashiers should be required to give to customers so they can check that they were properly charged. Menu prices are programmed into registers to ensure that the correct prices are charged and that prices cannot be manipulated by cashiers. Further control is achieved if a register is equipped with an automatic changer. It will generate the right amount of change and prevent employee error and theft.

As most cash registers are now computerized, cashiers and servers who access registers should have their own passwords or keys. Passwords are provided by managers to limit access to cash registers. The registers can record the key or user identification and print out a tape for auditing purposes. This is helpful when investigating revenue deviations. By examining the tape, or a digital record produced by the register, a manager can identify the employee who used the register at a particular time. A manager can also note whether discrepancies tend to be associated with a particular employee. The performance of each cashier should be tracked to detect patterns or frequent shortages.

Cashiers should be required to close the drawer between each transaction. Many registers are programmed to record the closing of the drawer as the end of the transaction. This prevents other transactions from starting until the drawer is closed and minimizes the possibility of cash removal.

Skimming creates an imbalance between the cash in the drawer and the data collected by the register. These imbalances can be detected when the cash balances are reconciled with the total receipts recorded by the register. If the register records all transactions, receipts can be compared to the cash in the drawer to verify that all sales have been recorded. If the register records transactions in numerical order, a missing record may indicate that a theft has occurred. Register reconciliations should be performed at mid-shift and at other unexpected times.

Employees may alter the register tape to match the cash in the drawer to prevent the manager from reconciling the cash to the transaction record. For example, an employee may use correction fluid to change the cash balance on the register tape. An employee may claim that the register tape was destroyed, or that the register malfunctioned and failed to produce it. The manager should carefully examine register tapes for correction fluid and other alterations. Many point-of-sale (POS) systems maintain back up records of transactions on hard drives.

To prevent register theft, a manager can also limit the amount of cash in registers by periodically removing some of it throughout the day. After taking a reading of the register, the manager or supervisor removes cash from the drawer and counts it in front of the cashier. The amount removed is recorded. This should be done at random times throughout the shift.

An operation's cash-handling policies should require that all voided or corrected transactions be approved by a manager or a supervisor. This prevents cashiers from skimming funds by reversing transactions. By creating fraudulent returns or voids on the register, they decrease the total receipts and are able to steal the difference in cash. An override code, input by a manager or a supervisor, can be required. The register may be programmed to shut down until approval is received.

Managers should look for telltale signs of cash skimming—such as the presence of paper clips, loose change, or other objects in or around the register. These objects are sometimes used by employees to remind them of the extra money in the cash drawer that they later intend to pocket. For instance, a penny may equal a $1.00 and a nickel may equal $5.00.

Cashier Job Duties

At the start of a shift, cashiers should count and verify the total amount of the bank for the cash drawer. They should be adequately trained and their work performance monitored. Training should be provided in the proper procedures for handling cash transactions with customers, **10-3**. These procedures can minimize revenue deviation and help resolve disputes with customers over payment amounts. For instance, suppose a customer's bill totals $15.65 and the customer pays with a $20 bill. The cashier should state to the customer, "Out of twenty dollars." The cashier should keep the $20 bill visible, obtain the change for the customer, and then verbally count out the change amount as it is returned to the customer. The cashier can say, "Fifteen sixty-five, seventy-five, sixteen dollars , seventeen, eighteen, nineteen and twenty," as the customer is given a dime, a quarter, and four one-dollar bills.

The same procedures for handling cash transactions should be followed by servers who accept cash payments at customers' tables. Bills should be kept visible on the table as change is counted out and placed on the table for customers. These actions confirm what the cashier or server received. For example, it can verify that the customer paid with a $20 and not a $50 bill.

With the increasing use of credit and debit cards for payment, proper handling procedures need to be established. Cashiers and servers need training to ensure that revenue controls are in place and followed. A credit or debit card payment is often made by sliding the card through a reader on a POS system, or by swiping it through a terminal supplied by the processing company. Newer systems can scan card information into the system without the use of a reader. A signature must appear on the back of a card and the cashier must check the expiration date. Some cardholders use a security feature that prompts the cashier to ask for identification. When prompted by the processing system, the customer should be asked for proper identification.

Cash Transaction Procedure

1. Cashier verbalizes the amount of the sale as shown on the guest check or the point-of-sale system (POS). For example, cashier states, "Fifteen dollars."
2. Upon receipt of the cash payment from the customer, the cashier verbalizes the amount received. For example, if a customer gives the cashier a $20 bill for a $15 sale, the cashier should say, "Out of twenty dollars." This confirms the amount the cashier received from the customer.
3. Employees who handle cash should be trained to detect counterfeit bills. Bills should be carefully examined by noting the quality of the paper, the sharpness of the images, and so forth. Marking bills with counterfeit detection pens can also help cashiers detect counterfeit currency. If a bill is counterfeit, the mark will turn dark brown or black. These pens are inexpensive, but may not detect all counterfeit bills.
4. If change is due, the cashier should leave the bill(s) received outside of the cash drawer until the transaction is complete. Therefore, if a customer claims to have given the cashier a larger bill, the bill the customer provided is still on top of the cash drawer.
5. The cashier should verbalize the change count back to the customer. For example, "Fifteen dollars is your bill and five dollars change equals twenty dollars." Should there be a dispute over how much the customer gave in payment, the cashier can easily refer to the cash that was received since it was not yet placed in the cash drawer. Assuming there is no dispute over the accuracy of the transaction, the bill(s) from the transaction can be placed in the cash drawer and the drawer closed.
6. The cashier should keep all large bills under the cash drawer in the register. This will aid in preventing a customer from claiming that he or she paid with a large bill. These bills will be out of sight and out of reach.

Figure 10-3. These cash-handling procedures are to be used by cashiers when receiving cash payments by customers and making change.

Cashier Checkout Form

At the end of a shift, the cashier needs to account for and record receipts. In the presence of the manager or a supervisor, the cashier counts the cash in the cash drawer. The following steps are taken to complete the cashier checkout form, **10-4**:

1. Complete the cash drawer section of the form. Note the beginning balance of the cashier's bank. Record any additions or removal of cash from the drawer by the manager during the shift. Record the amount of cash in the drawer at the end of the shift.
2. Record total sales from the cash register or point of sale system for each transaction type—cash, check, credit card, and gift card.
3. Calculate tips from the credit card tendered receipts. For each type of credit card, record tips charged. Total tips on all credit cards.
4. Set aside cash from drawer equal to credit card tips total. This money will go to servers.
5. Record cash owed for deposit:
   Cash Owed for Deposit = Cash Sales (from register) - Credit Card Tips Total
6. Record total owed for deposit:
   Total Owed for Deposit = Cash Owed for Deposit + Checks Owed for Deposit
7. Complete the actual cash for deposit:
   Actual Cash for Deposit = Total Cash Drawer - Credit Card Tips Total
8. Record the actual deposit:
   Actual Deposit = Actual Cash for Deposit + Actual Checks for Deposit

Cashier Checkout Form

Cashier/Server Name	Sally Jones
Date	March 14, 20XX
Shift	morning

Cash Drawer:

Beginning Balance	$ 200.00
Cash Additions During Shift	$ 75.00
Manager Cash Removal	$ -
Cash Drawer Returns	$ 275.00
Cash in Drawer at End of Shift	$ 773.00
Total Cash Drawer	$ 498.00

POS Receipt Totals:

		Tips on Credit Cards
Cash	$ 500.00	0
Checks Received	$ 12.00	0
Visa	$ 800.00	$ 133.34
MC	$ 400.00	$ 66.67
Amex	$ 500.00	$ 83.34
Gift Card Redeemed	$ 25.00	0
Total Receipts	$ 2,237.00	
Credit Card Tips Total		$ 283.35

Cash Owed for Deposit (Cash Sales Less Credit Card Tips)	$ 216.65
Checks Owed for Deposit	$ 12.00
Total Owed for Deposit	$ 228.65

Actual Cash for Deposit (Total Cash Drawer Less Credit Card Tips)	$ 214.65
Actual Checks for Deposit	$ 12.00
Actual Deposit	$ 226.65
Cash Over/Under	$ (2.00)

Cashier Signature: _____

Supervisor/Manager Signature: _____

Figure 10-4. The cashier's report provides the beginning and ending balances for the cash register drawer. It notes the amount that the cashier may be over or under in money when compared to the transactions recorded. This report is used by the manager to verify the accuracy of the drawer, and to track how well the cashier is doing in performing his or her duties.

This is the amount available for deposit to the bank. In the example given, note that the cash owed for deposit is two dollars more than the actual deposit. The cashier's count of the money in the drawer is two dollars less than the sales recorded on the register. Each operation should establish a standard amount by which the cashier may be over or under before corrective action occurs. A log of overages and shortages, by day and by cashier, may indicate deviations. When a discrepancy occurs, a review of the journal tapes from the register may pinpoint the error.

If a server has a bank, he or she also needs to complete a cashier checkout form. When the actual deposit is short, the server's tip amount can be deducted by the difference. In the example given, the server would receive $281.35 in cash for tips from credit cards instead of $283.35, 10-4. The final amount of cash deposited to the bank would be $228.65.

Deposit Practices

After a cashier closes out his or her register, someone must

- gather all transactions, separate them by cash and check; count the receipts
- reconcile the receipts with the register total
- note the amounts on the operation's deposit slip, **10-5**, and prepare it for the bank
- deliver the deposit to the bank
- reconcile the bank statement

An employee may attempt to take a portion of the money prior to its deposit into the company's bank account. In many small operations, a single person is responsible for all or many of these tasks. Money can easily be taken and the theft concealed. For instance, if a day's receipts are $1,000, an employee might fill out a deposit slip for $500 and pocket the other $500. The employee would then make the corresponding false bookkeeping entries, understating the day's receipts. This process creates a false balance in the company's records.

The separation of duties, which was discussed earlier in this chapter, is one way to deter this kind of fraud. The person who receives cash should not be the person who deposits it. Therefore, a cashier may balance the cash drawer, but a manager or supervisor should prepare the deposit. This process should be conducted in a secure location, away from customers and other employees. It generally takes place in an office with both the cashier and a supervisor (head cashier) or manager present. The manager or supervisor needs to verify the reconciliation and deposit amounts. The person who created the deposit slip should retain a copy of it. It will later be matched to a receipted deposit slip issued by the bank when the deposit is made.

Deposit Ticket	
ABC Bank Anytown, Any State	
Cash	585.15
Checks	
1	20.15
2	10.05
3	
4	
5	
6	
7	
8	
9	
10	
11	
12	
13	
14	
15	
Net Deposit	$615.35
Prepared by	
Date	
Bag #	

Total Items 2 — Account Number: XXXXXXX XXXXXXX — Joe's Bar and Grill, 100 Main St, Anytown, Any State

Figure 10-5. The deposit slip is a means of recording all the currency, coin, and checks received during the work shift or meal service. The cashier and the manager count the cash and checks. However, the manager completes this form to ensure a separation of duties.

The deposit slip itemizes receipts in the forms of currency, coin, and checks. The cash receipts and deposit slip should be placed in the bank's cash bag. The deposit slip should equal the cash register or point-of-sale system cash-tendered receipts for the deposit period. In addition, the credit-card-day-end summary report should equal the cash register, or point-of-sale system, credit-card-tendered receipts. This report is generated by whatever system the operation uses to receive credit card authorizations from the credit card company. In most places, this is done right at the POS.

The amount received via credit cards should be recorded on the cashier checkout form. An employee should be assigned the responsibility of taking the deposit to the bank, or to a drop box via an established pick-up arrangement.

It is recommended that at least one deposit be made each business day. This minimizes the amount of cash available at any one time. It also helps prevent *deposit lapping*. **Deposit lapping** is a method of theft concealment in which an employee steals the deposit from Day 1 and replaces it with the deposit from Day 2. The Day 2 deposit is replaced with the deposit from Day 3, and so forth. The deposits are always one day behind. This type of theft can go undetected for a period of time if no one demands an up-to-the-minute reconciliation of the bank statement and if daily receipts do not drop dramatically. To prevent losses that are concealed by deposit lapping, a bank deposit should be made every business day. In addition, the dates and amounts of deposits from receipted deposit slips should be compared with the bank statement to confirm that the deposits were properly made. The functions of making the deposit and reconciling the account balance should be separated. They should not be performed by the same person.

Another way to conceal a theft from a deposit is to explain the missing money as a *deposit in transit*. A **deposit in transit** is cash (currency, coins, checks, electronic transfers) a company has received and rightfully reported as cash on its balance sheet. However, it does not appear on the bank statement until a later date, due to normal processing delays. An employee may use this delay to prevent others from detecting stolen funds. Again, this type of scheme can be easily prevented or detected by separating the functions of making the deposit and reconciling the account balance. Also, the employee assigned to perform the reconciliation function should be instructed to account for all deposits in transit.

Proper record keeping is crucial to detecting and preventing fraud and errors, especially during the deposit stage. Copies of deposit slips, register or point-of-sale cash tendered receipts, credit card tendered receipts, checks, adding-machine tapes, and register or POS data should be assembled on a daily basis and filed in a secure location for future reference. This documentation can be used to research any issues regarding misappropriation of funds or deposit errors. Printed register tape, or POS data, can also be used to gather data such as menu popularity and customer counts.

Using a Safe

All cash and checks must be kept in a secure location within the operation until the deposit is made. If cash is not in the cash register drawer(s), it should be stored in a safe. For control reasons, it is recommended that an operation have only one safe. Cashier's banks and server's banks should be kept in locked bags and placed in the safe when not in use.

Depending on the size of the operation, the number of individuals who know the combination to the safe will vary. However, the number should be limited to those who absolutely need access to the safe on the various shifts. As an added precaution, the combination to the safe should be changed on a regular basis. Finally, employees accessing the safe should be required to sign a log noting the time, date, and reason. Each withdrawal from, or deposit to, the safe must be recorded. This discourages theft.

Waste Not

Green POS Systems

Many POS systems have features that prevent wasted energy and paper. For example, energy efficient terminals and computer servers reduce energy consumption and costs. These include ENERGY STAR qualified displays and back office equipment. To save even more energy, the power-management feature on terminals should be enabled.

Some POS systems offer paper-saving features, such as an electronic receipt option. Instead of printing out paper receipts, these systems can e-mail receipts to customers. This reduces paper use and allows the operation to save money. Forms and reports can also be filled out online and sent electronically.

Fraud Using Guest Checks

In a foodservice establishment, a guest check may be used by either an employee or a customer to intentionally deviate the revenue. A variety of schemes involve the use of guest checks. For example, an employee may write the correct order on a guest check and accept payment from the customer. Then, the employee alters the check to reflect a lower sale and keeps the difference. After collecting the guest check and the payment from the customer, an employee may withhold them from the business.

An employee may use his or her own guest check, accept payment from the customer, and keep the money. An employee may total the guest check for a higher amount, collect payment, and keep the difference. He or she then revises the guest check to the correct amount. Sometimes an employee and a customer work together to steal from an operation. A customer may be billed for an item with a lower price than the item actually ordered. Or an employee may write a guest check that does not include the food or beverage served to a customer.

Control elements should be in place when an operation uses paper guest checks. The operation should

- purchase paper checks that have a distinguishing feature. This prevents a customer or an employee from substituting a generic guest check for the operation's check. Generic checks are easy to obtain.
- have checks printed on paper that is erasure-proof so adjustments are apparent. Operations using a manual check system can use carbonized copies.
- require staff to use a pen for order taking. Errors would have to be crossed out, making alterations to the check apparent.
- require waitstaff to use a guest-check log. Each employee signs out a pack of numbered guest checks. At the end of a shift, all checks in the sequence must be accounted for.

The use of a POS system—for entering customer orders and generating guest checks or receipts—can control theft. POS systems have replaced the use of numbered guest checks in many establishments. While POS systems can deter theft, some clever employees have found ways around them. For example, an employee may enter in a menu item or beverage and receive payment from the customer. Then the employee voids out the sale and keeps the cash. The requirement that a manager or a supervisor approve all voids typically deters this type of theft.

Monitoring of Cash Handling

Revenue controls and procedures are only effective if they are monitored by the manager and if issues are addressed as they arise. Managers and owners should employ both direct and indirect monitoring.

Direct Monitoring

Direct cash monitoring involves the active steps a manager takes to check on the actions of the cashier. Direct monitoring includes:

- manager oversight
- random audits
- deposit verification
- visibility
- security cameras and mirrors
- mystery shoppers

Manager Oversight

The impact of manager oversight is readily apparent. Oversight requires the manager to be present and engaged in the activities of the operation. For example, by making frequent trips around the kitchen and dining areas, a manager can deter theft by employees. The times and routes of these trips should be varied to prevent dishonest employees from identifying the most opportune time to steal from the company.

Random Audits

A cashier anticipates that the manager or supervisor will count the cash drawer and compare it to the sales transactions at the end of the shift. Knowing this, a cashier may use certain techniques to steal from the drawer, intending to match sales and cash by the end of the shift. Any of the skimming activities listed in 10-2 can occur during the shift. The cashier would remove the cash before turning in the cash and the receipts at the end of the shift.

Random audits can deter this type of theft. To perform a random audit, the manager requests a cashier to close out his or her register at an unexpected time during the shift. A replacement cashier is assigned to avoid service disruption. The manager and the cashier proceed to the office where the drawer is counted and reconciled to the register readings.

Random audits should also be performed to check what employees are removing from the work environment. Potential hiding places for stolen food, flatware, and cash include dumpsters, garbage bins, and garbage bags. These and other areas should be checked often. Policies banning personal belongings such as purses and backpacks in the work area help to prevent theft. Employees can hide items in them and easily remove money or other assets from the business without detection. Some operations have switched to using only clear or opaque garbage bags so the contents are easily seen.

Deposit Verification

Internal controls are also used to monitor the activities of the management team. Generally, the manager or a supervisor signs off on the deposit for the day. He or she may also be responsible for making the deposit with the bank. Direct monitoring to verify deposits will help deter theft of cash assets by the manager or supervisor. Random inspections by the manager's peer or superior should be performed to verify deposit amounts with the deposit slips. It is critical that the person preparing the deposit slip also signs it indicating that the amount in the bag equals the amount on the deposit slip.

Visibility

The cash register should be in a location that is easily viewed by other people. Employees are less likely to steal if they feel they could be caught. However, it is important to ensure that the cash register and safe are secure, and only those authorized to access them may do so. It is best if the register displays what is being rung up so that the customer, the supervisor, or a manager can verify that the cashier correctly entered what was ordered.

Security Cameras and Mirrors

Locating security cameras and mirrors in the operation is a great deterrent to theft. Mirrors can be placed in areas that are hard to monitor, such as corners or L-shaped rooms. Security cameras should be located in areas where theft is highly likely. For example, a security camera should monitor the cashier's station. In addition, monitoring the entrances to the operation—both front and back—with a security camera can aid in preventing or catching a thief. While it is best to have the cameras monitored, this may not always be practical for small operations. However, operators should make sure that cameras are operational, and recordings should be reviewed regularly.

Mystery Shoppers

Mystery shoppers are used to ensure that the policies and procedures of the operation are being followed. A **mystery shopper** is a person hired to impersonate a shopper at a business or an operation. This tool is used by companies to measure quality of service, note discrepancies in policies, and so on. Instructions to mystery shoppers can include a script of behavior, questions to ask, complaints to give, purchases to make, and measures to record. For instance, they may be asked to record the time it takes to receive attention from an employee, or to receive responses to questions. A mystery shopper may be instructed to challenge the cashier or server when change is given. The shopper can verify if a cashier or server calls out the cash received and states the amount of the change returned. The shopper may be able to observe whether or not a cashier rings up sales correctly and whether or not skimming is occurring.

Bookmark This

Resources for Creating a Data Security Plan

Foodservice managers, even those who hire outside experts to manage their computer networks, should be familiar with data security laws and best practices. This includes having a data security plan in place. "Protecting Personal Information: A Guide for Business" outlines five key principles of a data security plan. A detailed checklist helps managers evaluate and improve their data security practices. An interactive tutorial is also available.

The guide and tutorial are offered by the Bureau of Consumer Protection's Business Center. The bureau is a part of the Federal Trade Commission (FTC) which provides information to consumers and businesses to prevent identity theft and other types of fraud. Resources are located at http://business.ftc.gov/

More information about data security for businesses is offered by the following groups:
- Payment Card Industry (PCI) Security Standards Council
- National Institute of Standards and Technology's Computer Security Division/Small Business Corner
- National Cybersecurity Center of Excellence
- United States Secret Service

Indirect Monitoring

Indirect monitoring of cash handling occurs behind the scenes. In order to do this successfully, the operation must have a second individual perform the following verification steps:

- confirm that deposits on bank statements agree with general ledger postings
- balance currency and coin in safe at least daily
- verify night-drop deposits at beginning of the following day
- make sure that deposits in transit are the first items to clear on the next statement
- perform daily bank reconciliation

Large or high-volume operations may employ coin and bill counters. The bank will send the reconciliation back to the operation indicating how much cash was in the cash bag, and how it compares to the deposit slip. Any discrepancies need to be acted upon immediately by the manager.

Corrective-Action Process

When errors or discrepancies are discovered, taking corrective action is an essential step in a revenue control system. Once corrective action is taken, the steps of planning, monitoring, and taking action are repeated. Steps in the corrective-action process are described below, along with examples of how each step can be applied.

- *Identify and define a problem.* Problem: At the end of a cashier's shift, the cash received does not match the totals from the cash-register receipts.
- *Investigate the discrepancy.* The manager confirms the cash count and reviews the register tape or transaction records for error.
- *Adjust control measures, policies, or training as necessary to return to desired results.* If the discrepancy occurred because a cashier did not count the currency correctly, the manager may choose to retrain the employee on the cash-counting policy and make a note in the employee's file.
- *Monitor action for effectiveness.* Following retraining, the manager audits the cashier's cash-counting performance to verify that it has improved.
- *Reinforce desired change with positive feedback.* If the cashier corrects his or her performance, the manager should acknowledge this with positive feedback.
- *Provide progressive disciplinary action when needed.* If the cashier's performance continues to fall short of standards, the manager should initiate an improvement plan with the employee. The manager communicates disciplinary implications if improvement does not occur.
- *Discharge employees caught stealing.* Managers must respond consistently and strongly to employees caught stealing within the constraints of the law. This will deter dishonest activity by other employees.

Patron Theft

Patron theft is more common than many managers realize. Means of patron theft include passing counterfeit currency, altering guest checks, stealing tips, and walking out without paying—or "dine and dash." Some customers take condiments, china, or glassware home as souvenirs. All of these actions create a loss of profit for the operation. Some customers do not consider their actions to be theft. For instance, a customer who uses a linen napkin as a doggie bag may not consider the cost of the napkin. He or she may not consider this theft. However, if many customers engage in this practice, the cost of replacing the linen napkins will add up.

An establishment may not be able to prevent all patron theft. However, implementing control systems will help minimize it. This requires an operation to follow the control steps listed earlier—establish policies and procedures, train staff to follow them, monitor activity against procedures, and take corrective steps to control repeat occurrences.

For instance, to limit the loss of linen napkins, waitstaff should be timely in the offering of doggie bags. If a customer is seen using a napkin for this purpose, the staff can be instructed to offer a doggie bag. Most customers who take china and glassware as souvenirs do so because it bears the monogram or logo of the restaurant. The best way to minimize this is to avoid the use of customized china or glassware. However, the use of a monogram is a great marketing tool. What many restaurants have done to counter this problem is to offer these items for sale or to give them away with the purchase of special drinks or dishes.

Some measures can be taken to prevent customers from altering their bills or from walking out without paying. The cashier and waitstaff should have training to make them more alert to these actions. Restaurants should have a clear policy that specifies where customers pay the bill—at the table or at the register. For the greatest security, the register should be located near the exit. Customers should stop at the cashier to pay on their way out. However, upscale operations often prefer that customers pay at the table. To decrease losses from dine-and-dash customers, the number of exits from the restaurant can be minimized while still complying with fire safety laws. In addition, the waitstaff should be alert to customers leaving their tables. Host staff should be alert to patrons leaving the building.

Banquets and Catered Events

Banquets and catered events often involve many people, patrons and employees. They often occur in venues that present limited opportunities to monitor people as they enter and exit. Theft can be minimized when waitstaff are instructed to bus tables frequently and to return china and silverware to the back-of-the-house operation. If security is not present, servers can be stationed near doors to catch guests who try to leave with supplies. If a guest is observed leaving with the operation's property, the server can simply offer to take the item off his or her hands.

Another opportunity for guest theft at banquets and catered events occurs when a cash bar is offered and a cash register is not present. A bartender may serve a guest without receiving payment, or a bartender may pocket the cash payment. To prevent this type of theft, an operation can set up a cash register station near the bar. Guests will purchase drink tickets at the cash station which they will exchange for drinks from the bartender.

This chapter has stressed the importance of managers continually monitoring activities and control systems to note problems and discrepancies. For instance, the monitoring of sales against receipts has been discussed several times. This is crucial to ensuring that payment is received for menu items ordered and served. Comparing the linen, glassware, and china inventory to usage can alert a manager to possible theft issues. As with all control systems, a revenue control system takes time and effort to implement and monitor. However, in return, the operation should experience a decrease in revenue loss, and, therefore, an increase in profit.

Key Terms

revenue control	cash drawer	deposit in transit
bonding	deposit lapping	mystery shopper
cash skimming		

Recap

- To ensure its sustainability and profitability, an organization must have a revenue control system.
- Intentional and unintentional revenue deviation results in lost profits.
- An operation can prevent or minimize employee theft by careful selection of employees and by implementing strong cash-handling policies and procedures.
- Systems of checks and balances—such as the separation of duties—can prevent cash skimming.
- By performing a register reconciliation, a manager can detect imbalances between cash in the register drawer and the cash register or point-of-sale cash tendered receipts.
- Control elements in deposit practices can prevent employees from diverting cash before it can be deposited into a company's bank account.
- Guest checks can be used by employees and customers to intentionally deviate the revenue.
- A revenue control system can reduce revenue loss due to patron theft.

Review Questions

1. Explain why a revenue control system is necessary in a foodservice operation.
2. Compare and contrast intentional and unintentional revenue loss and provide an example of each.
3. Which three activities give employees the greatest opportunities to steal funds from a foodservice operation?
4. For each of the three activities listed in previous response, give three steps an operation can take to minimize or prevent employee theft.
5. What practices and procedures can an operation follow during employee selection and screening to reduce the likelihood of employee theft?
6. Describe the procedures a cashier should use to make change.
7. Give one example of how a random audit is used.
8. List four ways to indirectly monitor cash handling.
9. Describe two ways patrons steal from a foodservice establishment, and the preventive steps an operation can take.
10. Briefly describe how a POS system lessens the opportunity to use the guest check for theft.

Applying Your Knowledge

11. What suggestions would you make for improving the process Cassandra followed to request and implement a POS system at the beginning of the chapter?

12. A manager has policies for proper handling of voids and overrings at the cash register, but suspects a cashier may be skimming from the cash drawer. Describe the steps the manager can take to determine if employee theft is occurring and how to prevent it.

Exercise 10-13

Complete the following exercise on the companion website:

www.g-wlearning.com/culinaryarts/

13. Given the following information, complete the cashier checkout form on the next page or on the website.
    ✓ Cashier's bank contained the following at beginning of shift:
    Currency $100
    Coin $15
    ✓ Transaction totals from POS:
    Cash sales $586.25
    Visa credit card sales $905.10
    MasterCard sales $765.15
    American Express sales $498.75
    Gift cards $50.00
    ✓ Manager supplied cashier with an additional $75 in change during the shift
    ✓ Two customers paid with personal checks in the amounts of $20.15 and $10.05
    ✓ All credit cards used had tips recorded at 20%
    ✓ Cashier's cash drawer contained the following at the end of shift:
    Currency $769.00
    Coins $6.66
    Checks $20.15 and $10.05

14. The operation in the previous problem allows for a $1.00 over/under discrepancy for cashiers. Should the manager take any action with the cashier described in the problem? If yes, what steps should be taken?

Course Project

15. For the foodservice establishment created for your Course Project, determine who patrons will pay—the server or a cashier. Explain the rationale of your decision as it relates to revenue control. Write a cash-handling procedure that includes the guest-check process, cash counting, and the bank-deposit steps.

Cashier Checkout Form

Cashier/Server Name	Sally Jones
Date	March 14, 20XX
Shift	morning

Cash Drawer:

Beginning Balance	
Cash Additions During Shift	
Manager Cash Removal	
Cash Drawer Returns	
Cash in Drawer at End of Shift	
Total Cash Drawer	

POS Receipt Totals:

		Tips on Credit Cards
Cash		0
Checks Received		0
Visa		
MC		
Amex		
Gift Card Redeemed		0
Total Receipts		
Credit Card Tips Total		

Cash Owed for Deposit (Cash Sales Less Credit Card Tips)	
Checks Owed for Deposit	
Total Owed for Deposit	
Actual Cash for Deposit (Total Cash Drawer Less Credit Card Tips)	
Actual Checks for Deposit	
Actual Deposit	
Cash Over/Under	

Cashier Signature: _____

Supervisor/Manager Signature: _____

Chapter 11
Financial Management

Learning Outcomes

After studying this chapter, you will be able to
- identify the three types of financial statements.
- interpret a statement of income.
- recall the balance sheet equation.
- differentiate between comparative and common-size analysis.
- compare and contrast trend analysis with financial analysis.

Financial management encompasses a whole host of activities that all businesses undertake. It begins with a gathering of an operation's financial data. The data are then analyzed using a variety of equations and ratios to determine how well the operation is performing. Finally, this performance is measured over time through the use of trend analyses. Both internal and external trend analyses are used in the industry. This chapter will cover the gathering of financial data and the various analyses used. It will also explain what the results mean in relation to the financial health of the operation.

Financial Statements

Management uses *financial statements* to prepare taxes, to apply for loans or credits, and to evaluate the financial status of an operation. Banks, investors, and creditors use them to decide if the organization is worthy of a loan or an investment of their funds. **Financial statements** are written reports that use quantitative data to provide insight into a company's financial health and describe changes in its performance. They are valuable tools for making economic decisions. Three types of financial statements are used in business operations—the statement of income, the balance sheet, and the statement of cash flows.

Statement of Income

To gauge how well an organization performed over a period of time, a manager can look at the amount of sales generated and the amount of expenses paid. The difference between these two numbers is the profit (or loss) the company generated over the set time period. The **statement of income** is a financial statement that measures

Trend

Growth Projected for Foodservice Industry

Despite difficult economic times, the National Restaurant Association (NRA) is bullish about the foodservice industry. Each month the NRA surveys restaurateurs throughout the United States about key industry indicators. These include current and anticipated sales (same-store), customer traffic, labor and capital expenditures. The feedback is used to create the Restaurant Performance Index (RPI), a composite index that provides a measure of the restaurant industry's health and the outlook for the following six-months. RPI values have consistently been over 100, indicating a positive outlook.

The NRA also releases a "Restaurant Industry Forecast" each year that examines economic, workforce, and other trends. The report is available to members and can be purchased by others.

Projecting over a longer period of time, the United States Department of Labor also predicts growth in the foodservice industry. The employment of foodservice workers is expected to increase 12 percent from 2010 to 2020, according to the Bureau of Labor Statistics.

the financial performance of an operation over a specific period of time. The period of time covered can be a month, a quarter, a year, or whatever accounting period the organization chooses to use. The statement of income is also called the *income statement* or the *profit and loss (P&L) statement*. The following equation summarizes the P&L statement:

Revenue – Expenses = Profit (Loss)

The data in Figure **11-1** represent the 12 months ending March 31, 2014. A statement of income could also be prepared for the quarter ending March 31, 2014, or for the month ending March 31, 2014. Each item in the P&L is stated as a dollar amount and as a percentage. The percentages can be used for benchmarking, or to compare an operation's performance with other operations in the industry. Following are descriptions of the line items in a P&L statement. The line items are the same as those found in operating budgets, which were covered in another chapter. Many operations follow the format recommended in the "Uniform System of Accounts for Restaurants," published by the National Restaurant Association.

Sales

Sales, or revenue, is the amount of payment a company receives from the sale of goods and services. A foodservice operation receives revenue from the sale of food and beverages. In the example given, food and beverage sales for the year ending March 31, 2014, were $750,000 and $225,000 respectively. Merchandise sales brought in another $25,000. Total revenue was $1,000,000.

Cost of Sales

Cost of sales refers to the dollars spent for the food, beverages, and merchandise sold to customers. In the case of food, it is the value of the food that was used to generate the food sales over the time period of the statement of income. In a discussion of cost control in purchasing, the cost of food sold for a time period was calculated as follows:

Cost of Food Sold = (Beginning Inventory + Purchases) – Ending Inventory

The same calculation is used to find the value of the beverages used to generate the sale of beverages for the fiscal year.

Cost of Beverages Sold = (Beginning Inventory + Purchases) – Ending Inventory

Pat's Pub & Grub		
Statement of Income **Year Ending March 31, 2014**		
	(in dollars)	**(% of total sales)**
Sales		
Food	750,000	75.0%
Beverage (alcoholic)	225,000	22.5%
Merchandise & Other	25,000	2.5%
Total Sales	1,000,000	100.0%
Cost of Sales		
Food	350,000	46.7%
Beverage (alcoholic)	45,000	20.0%
Merchandise & Other	5,000	20.0%
Total Cost of Sales	400,000	40.0%
Labor		
Salary	70,000	7.0%
Wages	175,000	17.5%
Employee Benefits	30,000	3.0%
Total Labor	275,000	27.5%
Prime Cost	675,000	67.5%
Other Controllable Expenses		
Direct Operating Expenses	50,000	5.0%
Music & Entertainment	2,000	0.2%
Marketing	10,000	1.0%
Utilities	38,000	3.8%
General & Administrative	38,000	3.8%
Repairs & Maintenance	18,000	1.8%
Total Other Controllable Expenses	156,000	15.6%
Controllable Income	169,000	16.9%
Noncontrollable Expenses		
Occupancy	60,000	6.0%
Equipment Leases	0	0.0%
Depreciation	10,000	1.0%
Total Noncontrollable Expenses	70,000	7.0%
Operating Income	99,000	9.9%
Corporate Overhead	0	0.0%
Interest Expense	700	0.1%
Other (Income)/Expense	(2,000)	(0.2%)
Income before Income Taxes	100,300	10.0%
Income Tax	0	0.0%
Net Income	100,300	10.0%

Figure 11-1. The statement of income is used to show the profit or loss of a company over a specific period of time. It lists the revenue received and the expenses incurred. This example shows a net income of $100,300 for the year.

In 11-1, the cost of food sold is determined by adding the amount of food purchased during the fiscal year (between April 1, 2013, and March 31, 2014), to the value of the ending inventory from the previous period (in this case, March 31, 2013). The value of the food inventory on hand on March 31, 2014, is then subtracted from this sum. For example, suppose the beginning food inventory on April 1, 2013, was $35,000 and $355,000 of food was purchased during the fiscal year, **11-2**. When the inventory is taken on March 31, 2014, the inventory on hand is valued at $40,000. What is the cost of food sold?

$$\text{Cost of food sold} = (\$355,000 + \$35,000) - \$40,000$$

$$\text{Cost of food sold} = \$350,000$$

The cost of food sold reflects only the cost of the food. It does not account for labor or any other costs associated with producing, marketing, or selling the products. Cost of food sold is used to calculate the food cost percentage.

$$\text{Food Cost \%} = \frac{\text{Cost of Food Sold}}{\text{Food Sales}} \times 100$$

$$\text{Beverage Cost \%} = \frac{\text{Cost of Beverages Sold}}{\text{Beverage Sales}} \times 100$$

Labor

Total labor expense includes payroll—salaries and wages—as well as the costs of benefits and payroll taxes paid.

Salary and Wages

Salary and wages are paid to employees as compensation for their labor. This is called payroll expense, and it also includes vacation pay and bonuses. Payroll expense is always less than labor expense because it does not include the benefits and taxes that must be paid. This line on the income statement represents the payroll expense for the stated time period.

Benefits and Payroll Taxes

Benefits and payroll taxes include the dollars paid for labor-related costs other than salary or wages. Examples of these costs include

- health insurance premiums
- worker's compensation
- Social Security (both employers' and employees' contributions)

Cost of Food Sold for Year Ended March 31, 2014		
	(in dollars)	
	April 1, 2013 Beginning Food Inventory	35,000
plus	Food Purchased During Period	355,000
	Cost of Food Available During Period	390,000
less	March 31, 2014 Ending Food Inventory	40,000
	Cost of Food Sold During Period	350,000

Figure 11-2. The value of inventory at the beginning and at the end of a time period is needed to calculate the cost of the product sold during that period.

- Medicare (both employers' and employees' contributions)
- federal and state income taxes
- unemployment taxes

This chapter covers a basic P&L statement. To get a more accurate picture of their true profit or loss, many operations delve deeper into their revenues and expenses. What is tracked on the P&L statement, and to what degree, will vary with the type, size, and sophistication of the operation and operator. For instance, an operation may record its food and beverage sales, and the corresponding cost of sales, for each separate dining venue, such as the bar, a patio, or a banquet room.

Meals offered to employees is another example of where an operation may choose to further break out the sales and the cost of sales from the meals sold to guests. Say that an operation offers meals to employees at a discount. The operation needs to capture the sale as revenue, but also needs to account for the discount and the expense of the food and beverages served. A common method used is to add the sale of the employee meals at full price to the total guest sales. Food cost is then based on total sales at full menu price. The discount offered is considered an employee benefit. So, the operation accounts for this discount as an expense, and records this value under labor costs.

Prime Cost

Prime cost reflects the ability of the manager to control the two largest drivers of the business.

Prime Cost = Total Cost of Sales + Total Labor

In the income statement in Figure 11-1, prime cost is the sum of $400,000 and $275,000, or $675,000. According to benchmarks set by the foodservice industry, prime cost is generally between 60 and 70 percent of total sales. It varies with the type of business. Decreasing the prime cost percentage without sacrificing quality or service, leaves more money for other expenses and/or profit.

Other Controllable Expenses

This section includes the other operating expenses over which a manager has some degree of control. Typically, it is broken down into the categories that follow.

Direct Operating Expenses

This category includes expenses such as linens, china, glassware and other tabletop items, employee uniforms, and disposable supplies.

Music and Entertainment

This category can be a minimal expense (piped-in music), or a significant expense (live bands every weekend). The line item for music and entertainment expense in Figure 11-1 is $2,000.

Marketing

This line item includes the expenses used to advertise or promote the business. The cost of media advertising is one of these expenses. Donations and money used to sponsor outside events are also included.

Utilities

The utilities expense line captures the costs of water, gas, electricity, and waste removal. In addition, lightbulbs, engineering supplies, and ice and refrigeration supplies are accounted for in this category.

Waste Not

Food Service Technology Center

Foodservice operations can save thousands of dollars in energy costs each year by having energy efficient kitchens. The Food Service Technology Center (FSTC) can help them get started. The FSTC, funded by Pacific Gas & Electric (PG&E), performs energy efficiency testing of commercial kitchen equipment. FSTC offers the following:

- energy saving tips
- results of energy efficiency testing of commercial kitchen equipment
- kitchen design ideas
- product rebate information
- equipment life cycle calculators
- industry best practices
- educational seminars
- professional consulting services
- facility design review
- technical training for employees
- interactive energy efficiency kitchen toolkit

To learn more, go to www.fishnick.com/

General and Administrative

These expenses include telephone service, postage, liability and other general insurance coverage, credit card fees, information technology processing, legal or accounting fees, cash shortages, and provisions for accounts receivable that the operation may not be able to collect. (In a foodservice operation, there are not many accounts receivable as most sales are paid for with cash or a cash equivalent such as a debit or credit card.) These are costs related to running the business versus costs directly related to serving the guest.

Repairs and Maintenance

These expenses include equipment parts and charges for both preventive maintenance and equipment repair. Also included are costs associated with maintaining the physical plant, such as the landscaping, parking lot, or signage, and any service contracts such as hood-cleaning services.

Controllable Income

Subtracting the costs of sales, labor, and other controllable expenses from total sales yields the controllable income. Controllable income is the income that remains after an operation pays the expenses a manager has direct influence over. Often, it is this value that is used to measure the performance, and, therefore, determine the salary and bonuses received by the manager.

Controllable Income = Total Sales − (Total Cost of Sales + Total Labor + Total Other Controllable Expenses)

Or

Controllable Income = Total Sales − (Prime Cost + Total Other Controllable Expenses)

Noncontrollable Expenses

This section includes expenses that do not relate directly to an establishment's day-to-day operation. These costs are related to the investment in the business and are typically outside a manager's sphere of influence. They include the following line items.

Occupancy Costs

This line includes the costs of rent, real estate taxes, and property insurance.

Equipment Leases

This line covers equipment that is leased over an extended period of time. Equipment may include POS systems and kitchen equipment.

Depreciation

The depreciation line item on the income statement is a total of the yearly depreciation for some of the business's assets. Some assets are depreciated, while others are not. In Figure 11-1, depreciation during the year ending March 31, 2014, was $10,000.

Operating Income

Operating income is the difference between controllable income and noncontrollable expenses.

Operating Income = Controllable Income – Total Noncontrollable Expenses

The operating income for the business in Figure 11-1 would be calculated as follows:

Operating income = $169,000 – $70,000

Operating income = $99,000

Corporate Overhead

If an operation is a single unit, this section will not appear on its P&L statement. This line reflects the costs associated with running a corporate office, including the costs of corporate office staff and office equipment. Many corporations allocate these expenses to their units and they appear in the P&L statements of the units. However, some corporations do not. Since Pat's Pub & Grub is a single unit, there is no corporate overhead cost.

Interest Expense

The interest expense is the cost of borrowing money. If an operation owns property and pays a mortgage, this line includes the interest paid on the mortgage. It also includes interest paid on loans used to purchase equipment.

Other (Income)/Expense

This line captures the income and expenses that are generated by activities that are not part of the operation's typical activities. For example, during the period covered by the P&L, Pat's Pub & Grub generated $2,000 in income from the sale of grease. This line also includes income received from the sales of assets and the expenses paid to settle lawsuits.

Income before Income Taxes

This line gives an operation's income after the expenses of corporate overhead, interest, and other (income)/expenses are subtracted from the operating income.

Income before Income Taxes = Operating Income – [Corporate Overhead + Interest Expense + Other (Income)/Expense]

A business can be structured so that taxable income and losses are noted on the owner's tax return and not by the businesses. Pat's Pub & Grub does not pay income taxes. Therefore, income before income taxes is the same as the net income.

Taxes and Net Income

If a business does pay income taxes, the income before income taxes line would be followed by a line for the tax. Then the net income would be calculated as follows:

Net Income = Income before Income Taxes − Income Tax

Net income is often referred to as a company's bottom line. It is the profit or loss an operation generates after paying the appropriate expenses. Put another way, net income is the amount of money that remains once expenses—such as salary, wages, and food and beverage purchases—are deducted from total sales. If the number is positive, a profit was generated. If it is negative, the operation lost money

Calculation of Percent Total Sales

Each item on a P&L statement has two corresponding numbers. One is a dollar amount and the other is a percentage. For most items, the figure in the percentage column measures the item's contribution to total sales. For these line items, the percent total sales is calculated as follows:

$$\text{Percent Total Sales} = \frac{\text{Amount (In Dollars)}}{\text{Total Sales}} \times 100$$

For example, in March 2014, the value for sales from food was $750,000 and the amount of total sales was $1,000,000. What percentage of total sales is $750,000? Sales from food is divided by total sales.

$$\text{Percent total sales} = \frac{\$750{,}000}{\$1{,}000{,}000} \times 100$$

$$\text{Percent total sales} = 75.0\%$$

In another example, the operation spent $10,000 on marketing. The percent total sales for marketing is calculated as follows:

$$\text{Percent total sales} = \frac{\$10{,}000}{\$1{,}000{,}000} \times 100$$

$$\text{Percent total sales} = 1.0\%$$

However, for the line items listed under cost of sales, percent total sales is calculated using an item's corresponding sales figure—not total sales.

$$\text{Percent Total Sales} = \frac{\text{Amount (In Dollars)}}{\text{Product Sales}} \times 100$$

For instance, the percent total sales for the cost of food sold would be calculated as follows:

$$\text{Percent total sales} = \frac{\$350{,}000}{\$750{,}000} \times 100$$

$$\text{Percent total sales} = 46.7\%$$

Likewise, the percent total sales for the cost of beverages sold would be found by dividing the beverage cost by beverage sales:

$$\text{Percent total sales} = \frac{\$45{,}000}{\$225{,}000} \times 100$$

$$\text{Percent total sales} = 20.0\%$$

The statement of income is also used by noncommercial foodservice operations. However, what is measured may be different. For example, they may not note rent payments. Noncommercial operations usually exist as departments within organizations. Interest and income tax are also not noted.

Balance Sheet

The *balance sheet* is the second type of financial statement used by all businesses, **11-3**. While the statement of income reflects a company's profitability over a period of time, the **balance sheet** summarizes an operation's assets, liabilities, and shareholders' equity on the date it was issued. A balance sheet is divided into three parts—assets, liabilities,

Pat's Pub & Grub		
Balance Sheet as of December 31, 2014		
(in dollars)		
ASSETS		
Current Assets		
Cash and Equivalents	47,500	
Accounts Receivable	8,000	
Inventories	70,000	
Prepaid Expenses	8,000	
Total Current Assets		133,500
Fixed Assets		
Land	110,000	
Building Improvements	800,000	
Furniture and Fixtures	380,000	
Less Accumulated Depreciation	(315,000)	
Operating Equipment and Uniforms	88,000	
Total Fixed Assets		1,063,000
Other Assets		45,000
TOTAL ASSETS		1,241,500
LIABILITIES		
Current Liabilities		
Accounts Payable	200,000	
Current Portion of Long-Term Debt	75,000	
Accrued Expenses	76,500	
Other Current Liabilities	90,000	
Total Current Liabilities		441,500
Noncurrent Liabilities		
Long-Term Debt (less current portion)	350,000	
Other Noncurrent Liabilities	80,000	
Total Noncurrent Liabilities		430,000
TOTAL LIABILITIES		871,500
SHAREHOLDERS' EQUITY		
Capital Stock	228,000	
Retained Earnings End of Year	142,000	
Total Shareholders' Equity		370,000
TOTAL LIABILITY AND SHAREHOLDERS' EQUITY		1,241,500

Figure 11-3. A balance sheet is another financial tool used by all businesses. It differs from the Statement of Income in that it reflects a specific window in time (in this example, a day). The assets and the liabilities are equal.

and shareholders' equity. As the name implies, each side of the balance sheet must equal out. So, the total assets must equal the total liabilities plus the shareholders' equity. This is described in the following equation:

$$\text{Assets} = \text{Liabilities} + \text{Equity}$$

Assets

An asset is anything of value that a company owns. Assets are categorized as current or fixed. A foodservice operation's **current assets** include cash, inventory on hand, accounts receivable, and any prepaid expenses.

- Cash includes cash in the bank and the cash held in an operation's safe and cash drawers.
- Inventory on hand includes food, beverages, and other items, such as candy or cigars, which can readily be turned into cash through sales.
- **Accounts receivable** are invoices, or bills, for which the company is awaiting payment. Foodservice operations do not normally have significant amounts of accounts receivable because they generally require payment at the time of service. A business may allow customers to charge meals to accounts and bill them on a monthly basis.
- Prepaid expenses are also considered an asset for the operation. Prepaid expenses include services for which the operation pays in advance. For example, an operation may pay for a year's worth of landscaping services. If the operation goes out of business halfway through the year, the landscaping company would need to reimburse it for the prorated amount.

Fixed assets are long-term assets that are not used up or sold during the normal course of business. They include land, buildings, furniture, equipment, and any improvements made to an operation's building or grounds. If a foodservice operation does not own land or a building, these assets would not appear on the balance sheet.

Liabilities

A **liability** is a debt or obligation owed by an operation that is settled by the transfer of goods, services, or cash. For example, a car is an asset, but a car loan is a liability. A consumer who purchases a car with a loan is liable to the creditor for the amount of the loan. In a foodservice operation, liabilities include current and noncurrent liabilities.

Current liabilities are debts that need to be paid within one year. For example, the current liability on a home purchased with a loan would be the amount of the loan that needs to be repaid during the current year. For a foodservice operation, current liabilities include accounts payable, accrued expenses, and the current portion of its long-term debt.

Accounts payable are an operation's unpaid bills. If the foodservice operation ordered food from a distributor, and the distributor issued an invoice, the money due to the distributor is a debt for the operation. It is an account that is payable to the distributor. Those funds must be accounted for, as they are a debt owed by the operation. Funds needed to pay that invoice appear as a liability for the operation.

Accrued expenses are expenses that are due, but that have not been paid. This includes payroll that is owed, but has not been paid. The wages employees earn for hours worked prior to payday are accrued expenses until the checks are distributed.

Noncurrent liabilities include long-term debt. A *long-term debt* is a debt that is owed minus what was accounted for under current liabilities. It is the remainder of a loan after the deduction of the current year's payments. It may also include long-term notes or equipment contracts that extend beyond one year. The sum of current liabilities and noncurrent liabilities (long-term debt) equals the amount of total liability for the operation.

Equity

The purpose of noting total assets and total liabilities is to determine the *net worth*, or *equity*, of the company. Depending on the type of operation, equity may include stock paid to shareholders or capital dollars paid to a sole owner. Some funds may also be "reserved" in the operation for future use versus being paid out as stock or capital dollars. These retained earnings are kept in the operation.

Noncommercial foodservice operations use balance sheets. However, the assets listed are different from those listed by a commercial company. Since the noncommercial operation is part of a larger organization, assets are usually not called out by department.

Statement of Cash Flows

A company's P&L statement may show a profit, but if cash is not available to pay expenses—such as what is owed to employees and vendors—the company may be unable to stay in business. Money may be tied up in investments, such as real estate or equipment, and not readily available for use.

A **statement of cash flows (SCF)** is a financial statement that summarizes the actual or anticipated movement of cash into and out of an operation over a particular period of time, **11-4**. It is used to determine whether a company has the cash on hand to pay

Pat's Pub & Grub	
Statement of Cash Flows **For Year Ending December 31, 2013**	
(in dollars)	
Cash Flow from Operating Activities	
Cash Receipts from Customers	1,000,000
Cash Paid to Suppliers	(400,000)
Cash Paid to Employees	(275,000)
Cash Paid for Other Operating Expenses	(156,000)
Interest Paid	(2,000)
Net Cash Provided by Operating Activity	167,000
Cash Flow from Investing Activities	
Equipment Sales Proceeds	2,000
Cash Payments for Leasehold Improvements	(40,000)
Cash Payments for Equipment Purchases	0
Net Cash Provided by Operating Activity	(38,000)
Cash Flow from Financing Activities	
Borrowing from Line of Credit	5,000
Dividends Paid to Owners	(20,000)
Loan Payment	(20,000)
Net Cash Provided by Operating Activity	(35,000)
Net Increase (Decrease) in Cash and Cash Equivalents	94,000
Cash and Cash Equivalents, Beginning of Period	(6,000)
Cash and Cash Equivalents, End of Period	88,000

Figure 11-4. The statement of cash flows, also known as the cash flow statement, is created from the income statement and the beginning and ending balance sheets for the period.

bills, make loan payments, and invest or provide dividends to investors. An SCF is created from a P&L statement and the beginning and ending balance sheets for a time period. There are four parts to a statement of cash flows—operating activities, investing activities, financing activities, and net increase or decrease in cash.

- Operating activities include the cash receipts from customer transactions and the cash outflows used to pay suppliers and employees. It also covers cash outflows to government agencies as taxes, and outflows to banks as interest payments.
- The investing activities section involves cash inflows from the sale of equipment. It also includes cash outflows for the purchase of equipment or buildings, and cash paid for building improvements. For instance, if an operation adds a patio to the back of a building it is leasing, that cost is considered a leasehold improvement. The operator cannot take the patio if the operation moves to another location.
- Financing activities generally reflect the sources of cash inflows and outflows related to borrowing money or purchasing stock.
- The last section shows the net cash increase or decrease for the period. It also shows the cash balance at the beginning of the period and the cash balance at the end of the period—the amount of cash available to the operation.

Financial Analysis

After financial information is gathered, it can be used to gauge the financial stability and health of an operation. Managers can determine if their operations are running efficiently and whether or not they can meet short- and long-term obligations. **Financial analysis** is the process of using financial data to monitor and evaluate an operation's performance, profitability, financing needs, and future growth. Financial analysis involves the use of various calculations to uncover areas of concern and to provide insight into what corrections need to be made.

Managers can compare an operation's performance to that of similar operations in the industry. Comparisons can be made involving an operation's overall performance or just the performance of specific line items. One reporting period can be compared to another or comparisons can be made within the same reporting period. Analyses commonly used include comparative analysis, common-size analysis, and a number of ratio analyses.

Comparative Analysis

A **comparative analysis** is a method used in the analysis of financial statements to uncover emerging trends. It involves the item-by-item comparison of two or more like items. It measures change—in both dollars and percent—for each line item on a financial statement across two or more periods or dates. A *comparative statement of income* measures change from one time period to another. A *comparative balance sheet* measures change between two or more dates.

To perform a comparative analysis, the dollar differences (Difference $) are calculated between items from the current and a previous year. The prior-year value is subtracted from the corresponding current-year value. Then the numbers from the Difference $ column are divided by the prior-year values to give the percent difference (Difference %). This is the percent change from the prior year to the current year.

$$\text{Difference \%} = \frac{\text{Difference \$}}{\text{Prior-Year Value}} \times 100$$

For example, the manager of Pat's Pub & Grub may want to perform a comparative analysis of the P&L statements for the current and previous fiscal years, **11-5**. Food sales were $750,000 in the current fiscal year, compared with food sales of $680,000 in the previous fiscal year. The difference between the two years is $70,000. The percent difference would be calculated as follows:

$$\text{Difference (\%)} = \frac{\$70,000}{\$680,000} \times 100$$

$$\text{Difference (\%)} = 10.3\%$$

Therefore, between the previous and the current fiscal years, food sales increased by $70,000, or by 10.3 percent.

It is also necessary to compare the cost of goods sold for each item to the sales for that item, and then note the percent difference from one year to the next. So, the cost of food sold as a percent to total food sales would be compared to the cost of food sold and the corresponding food sales for the next period. The last column in the comparative analysis statement of income is the percent change.

Percent Change = Current Period % – Prior Period %

In Figure 11-5, food sales increased 10.3 percent in dollars from one year to the next, with a 4.5 percent increase when compared with total sales. Yet, the cost of food as a percent of food sold decreased by 2.6 percent.

Beverage sales decreased sharply, falling $75,000 or 25 percent, and decreasing 7.8 percent when compared to total sales. The beverage cost remained the same over the two years, $45,000. However, the beverage cost as a percentage of beverage sales increased 5 percent, 11-5. Total sales increased $10,000 or 1 percent in dollars. The total cost of sales increased 4.7 percent, but the total cost percent only increased 1.4 percent.

What does this indicate? First, it is important to look at the change in dollars from one year to the next in all sales and cost categories (food, beverage, and so forth). However, it is also important to review the change in cost percent (% Change) compared to the specific category of sales. In other words, how did the cost of food purchased change in relation to the total sales? What contribution did it make and why? Perhaps menu prices were increased without an equal increase in food costs. It could also mean that the operation is buying more efficiently. For beverages, perhaps the customers are buying less expensive drinks. Or perhaps the cost of the alcohol has increased, but the operation has not raised its prices to offset that increase.

The beverage cost percent increased 5 percent while the food cost percent decreased 2.6 percent. So, beverages are dragging down the profitability of this operation. This analysis should lead the manager to investigate the beverage situation and take action to rectify it. In doing so, the profitability may improve.

Current year labor is actually lower as a percent to total sales than the previous year: 27.5 percent to 26.9 percent respectively. Prime cost is up, however, by 2 percent. This points to the cost of goods sold as a percent of total sales as the issue for the manager.

Other controllable expenses are up as a percent to total sales by 1 percent , with the driver of this being the increase in utilities. Controllable income is down as a percent to total sales by 3 percent. Further evaluation of controllable expenses indicates that some expenses increased over the past year. For example, the cost of music and entertainment increased 300 percent and the cost of marketing increased 33.3 percent. When compared to the percent to total sales, the music increased 0.1 percent as a percent to total sales and marketing increased 0.2 percent. If the manager's plan was to spend more money on live music and advertising to generate more beverage sales, the manager may want to rethink this decision. The strategy does not appear to be effective.

Pat's Pub & Grub						
Comparative Analysis of Statements of Income Years Ending March 31, 2013 and March 31, 2014						
	Current year ($)	%	Prior year ($)	%	Difference ($)	Difference (%)	% Change
Sales							
Food	750,000	75.0%	680,000	68.7%	70,000	10.3%	6.3%
Beverage	225,000	22.5%	300,000	30.3%	(75,000)	(25.0%)	(7.8%)
Merchandise & Other	25,000	2.5%	10,000	1.0%	15,000	150.0%	1.5%
Total Sales	1,000,000	100.0%	990,000	100.0%	10,000	1.0%	0.0%
Cost of Sales							
Food	350,000	46.7%	335,000	49.3%	15,000	4.5%	(2.6%)
Beverage	45,000	20.0%	45,000	15.0%	0	0.0%	5.0%
Merchandise & Other	5,000	20.0%	2,000	20.0%	3,000	150.0%	0.0%
Total Cost of Sales	400,000	40.0%	382,000	38.6%	18,000	4.7%	1.4%
Labor							
Salary	70,000	7.0%	67,000	6.8%	3,000	4.5%	0.2%
Wages	175,000	17.5%	170,000	17.2%	5,000	2.9%	0.3%
Employee Benefits	30,000	3.0%	29,000	2.9%	1,000	3.4%	0.1%
Total Labor	275,000	27.5%	266,000	26.9%	9,000	3.4%	0.6%
Prime Cost	675,000	67.5%	648,000	65.5%	27,000	4.2%	2.0%
Other Controllable Expenses							
Direct Operating Expenses	50,000	5.0%	47,000	4.7%	3,000	6.4%	0.3%
Music & Entertainment	2,000	0.2%	500	0.1%	1,500	300.0%	0.1%
Marketing	10,000	1.0%	7,500	0.8%	2,500	33.3%	0.2%
Utilities	38,000	3.8%	32,000	3.2%	6,000	18.8%	0.6%
General & Administrative	38,000	3.8%	38,000	3.8%	0	0.0%	0.0%
Repairs & Maintenance	18,000	1.8%	20,000	2.0%	(2,000)	(10.0%)	(0.2%)
Total Other Controllable Expenses	156,000	15.6%	145,000	14.6%	11,000	7.6%	1.0%
Controllable Income	169,000	16.9%	197,000	19.9%	(28,000)	(14.2%)	(3.0%)
Noncontrollable Expenses							
Occupancy	60,000	6.0%	60,000	6.1%	0	0.0%	(0.1%)
Equipment Leases	0	0.0%	0	0.0%	0	0.0%	0.0%
Depreciation	10,000	1.0%	11,000	1.1%	(1,000)	(9.1%)	(0.1%)
Total Noncontrollable Expenses	70,000	7.0%	71,000	7.2%	(1,000)	(1.4%)	(0.2%)
Operating Income	99,000	9.9%	126,000	12.7%	(27,000)	(21.4%)	(2.8%)
Corporate Overhead	0	0.0%	0	0.0%	0	0.0%	0.0%
Interest Expense	700	0.1%	690	0.1%	10	1.4%	0.0%
Other (Income)/Expense	(2,000)	(0.2%)	0	0.0%	(2,000)	0.0%	(0.2%)
Income before Income Taxes	100,300	10.0%	125,310	12.7%	(25,010)	(20.0%)	(2.7%)
Income Tax	0	0.0%	0	0.0%	0	0.0%	0.0%
Net Income	100,300	10.0%	125,310	12.7%	(25,010)	(20.0%)	(2.7%)

Figure 11-5. A comparative analysis compares two financial periods (year to year) using the Statement of Income, and shows the percent change between the two. Here, the net income in the prior year was greater than that of the current year.

The same analysis can be used to assess the increase in utility costs. What drove the percent increase? Perhaps the manager can conduct an energy audit to determine if this expense can be decreased going forward.

Common-Size Analysis

Using **common-size analysis**, each line on the financial statement is expressed as a percentage of either total assets or total sales, with the exception of cost of goods sold. Similar to the comparative analysis above, the cost of goods sold is expressed as a percent of the total sales of the respective item: the cost of food sold to food sales, the cost of beverages sold to beverage sales, and so forth. On a common-size balance sheet, total assets are given a value of 100 percent. Each line of assets, liabilities, and equities are then calculated as a percentage of total assets.

A common-size income statement calculates each sales and expense line item as a percentage of total sales. The percentages from different periods can then be quickly compared to see how sales or expenses changed from one period to the next and how profits were impacted. In the example, food sales increased from 68.7 percent to 75 percent. The cost of food sold decreased from 49.3 percent to 46.7 percent, while depreciation decreased from 1.1 percent to 1.0 percent, **11-6**.

Ratio Analysis

A number of ratios can be used to financially evaluate the operation. A ratio is a comparison between two related quantities. For example, if the ratio of waitstaff to tables is 1:6, then each server has six tables to serve.

In **ratio analysis**, ratios are used to determine how well an operation is performing financially. The numbers used in the ratios are obtained from the statement of income and the balance sheet. Once again, these tools are used to gather data that are later used for financial analysis. Generally, a ratio is compared to the same ratio using values from another time period (statement of income or balance sheet). It is then that the ratios have meaning for the manager.

The financial ratios that are most commonly used are: liquidity, solvency, activity or operating, and profitability. However, any type of ratio may be used and different organizations use ratios that are not discussed in this text. Since the focus of this text is on controlling costs in an operation, only the operating and profitability ratios are reviewed.

Operating Ratios (Activity Ratios)

Operating ratios use data from the income statement to assess how well costs are controlled and how efficiently a business is run. These ratios are then compared to ratios from another time period—the same period last month, last year, or any time period the operation chooses. They help managers gauge how well an operation is doing in the areas of sales, expenses, and profit.

It is important to look at percent changes in addition to dollars. For example, if a manager wants to know if food sales are increasing at a lower rate than beverages, he or she would need to compare the percentage rate change. In evaluating activities or operating ratios, it is most effective if these ratios are compared to one another by meal type as well. For example, an activity ratio can be used to calculate the amount of an average check.

$$\text{Average Check} = \frac{\text{Sales}}{\text{Customer Count}}$$

Common-Size Income Statement				
For Years Ended March 31, 2013 and March 31, 2014				
	(in dollars)		(% of total sales)	
	2013	2014	2013	2014
Sales				
Food	680,000	750,000	68.7%	75.0%
Beverage	300,000	225,000	30.3%	22.5%
Merchandise & Other	10,000	25,000	1.0%	2.5%
Total Sales	990,000	1,000,000	100.0%	100.0%
Cost of Sales				
Food	335,000	350,000	49.3%	46.7%
Beverage	45,000	45,000	15.0%	20.0%
Merchandise & Other	2,000	5,000	20.0%	20.0%
Total Cost of Sales	382,000	400,000	38.6%	40.0%
Labor				
Salary	67,000	70,000	6.8%	7.0%
Wages	170,000	175,000	17.2%	17.5%
Employee Benefits	29,000	30,000	2.9%	3.0%
Total Labor	266,000	275,000	26.9%	27.5%
Prime Cost	648,000	675,000	65.5%	67.5%
Other Controllable Expenses				
Direct Operating Expenses	47,000	50,000	4.7%	5.0%
Music & Entertainment	500	2,000	0.1%	0.2%
Marketing	7,500	10,000	0.8%	1.0%
Utilities	32,000	38,000	3.2%	3.8%
General & Administrative	38,000	38,000	3.8%	3.8%
Repairs & Maintenance	20,000	18,000	2.0%	1.8%
Total Other Controllable Expenses	145,000	156,000	14.6%	15.6%
Controllable Income	197,000	169,000	19.9%	16.9%
Noncontrollable Expenses				
Occupancy	60,000	60,000	6.1%	6.0%
Equipment Leases	0	0	0.0%	0.0%
Depreciation	11,000	10,000	1.1%	1.0%
Total Noncontrollable Expenses	71,000	70,000	7.2%	7.0%
Operating Income	126,000	99,000	12.7%	9.9%
Corporate Overhead	0	0	0.0%	0.0%
Interest Expense	690	700	0.1%	0.1%
Other (Income)/Expense	0	(2,000)	0.0%	(0.2%)
Income before Income Taxes	125,310	100,300	12.7%	10.0%
Income Tax	0	0	0.0%	0.0%
Net Income	125,310	100,300	12.7%	10.0%

Figure 11-6. The Common Size Income Statement expresses everything on the Income Statement as a percentage. The manager can then compare the change in percentage from period to period, and notes any corrective action that needs to be taken.

If total sales equal $3,000 and there were 350 customers, then the average check is:

$$\text{Average check} = \frac{\$3,000}{350}$$

$$\text{Average check} = \$8.57$$

In a ratio analysis, this average check ratio would be compared with the average check ratio from another time period to determine if it is increasing or decreasing. To perform a more precise analysis, a manager should compare the average check within different meal types. For example, the average check ratio for breakfast in period one should be compared to the average check ratio for breakfast in period two. Once the manager has the data, he or she can then compare one period to the next.

How can a manager explain an increase in the ratio? For example, what if the average check is now $9.00 instead of $8.57? Perhaps the number of customers or the sales dollars changed. If the number of customers stayed the same, but the average check ratio increased, then the customers spent more or the menu prices increased. The sales number would be $3,150 compared to $3,000 in the previous period. Figure **11-7** lists just a few of the operating ratios commonly used by foodservice operations. Most of them were discussed in other parts of this text.

Ratio Analysis	
Operating Ratios	
Sales	$\text{Average Check} = \dfrac{\text{Sales}}{\text{Customer Count}}$
	$\text{Seat Turnover} = \dfrac{\text{Customer Count}}{\text{Available Seats}}$
	$\text{Sales per Sq. Ft.} = \dfrac{\text{Sales}}{\text{Number of Sq. Ft.}}$
Expenses	$\text{Labor Cost \%} = \dfrac{\text{Labor Cost}}{\text{Sales}} \times 100$
	$\text{Food Cost \%} = \dfrac{\text{Cost of Food Sold}}{\text{Sales}} \times 100$
	$\text{Food Cost per Meal} = \dfrac{\text{Cost of Food Sold}}{\text{Number of Meals Served}}$
Profitability Ratios	
	$\text{Profit Margin} = \dfrac{\text{Net Income}}{\text{Sales}} \times 100$
	$\text{Profit to Assets} = \dfrac{\text{Net Income}}{\text{Assets}}$

Figure 11-7. This table lists the common financial ratios used in businesses.

Operating ratios can also be computed as percentages. These are often called cost percentages. They are useful in comparing one period to another and in identifying and analyzing trends. If percentages are rising or falling, the manager needs to look for the cause. For example, if an operation's food cost percentage is trending up over the past three months, and the customer count is stable, the manager needs to quickly determine the cause of the percentage increase. Have food costs gone up? Have the buying habits of the purchasing employee changed? Is the operation experiencing pilferage?

Profitability Ratios

To survive, a business must make a profit. Profit is the difference between sales (revenue) and expenses. However, shareholders and business owners want assurance that they are spending their investment dollars wisely. They may ask themselves if they could make more money by investing in another venture. Profitability ratios, such as those listed in 11-7, will aid in this assessment. Profitability ratios also assist in determining if the manager is using resources appropriately. They are a measure of a manager's business skills. **Profitability ratios** are measures that are used to determine whether or not an operation is making a profit in comparison to its expenses.

Profit margin is a common ratio that measures how much a business earns out of every dollar in sales. This is important to the ongoing survival of the business, and is the ratio a manager has much control over. Profit margin is calculated by dividing net income by total sales.

$$\text{Profit Margin} = \frac{\text{Net Income}}{\text{Sales}}$$

Bookmark This

Restaurant Industry Operations Report

The *Restaurant Industry Operations Report* is created by the National Restaurant Association and Deloitte LLP, a professional services firm. The report provides detailed information about the operating expenses of various types of foodservice operations. The operations are broken out by type, sales volume, region, menu theme, and other characteristics. The report includes the following:

- gross profits
- operating expenses
- seat turnover
- employees per seat
- pre-tax income
- average per-person check

Using the report, a foodservice manager can compare an operation's performance to that of similar operations, resulting in better management of budgets and expenses.

The manager has significant control over sales and expenses and, therefore, the manager's skill is reflected in the profit margin. The profit margin will vary depending on the type of foodservice operation. However, a profit margin between 2 and 6 percent is typical.

Profit to equity, more commonly called return on investment (ROI), profit to assets, and earnings per share, are other common profitability ratios used by business owners and investors. While important, these ratios are often not used by managers who must focus on the day-to-day running of an operation.

Trend Analysis

Financial analysis focuses on the comparison of one period to another. While these comparisons are useful, a truer picture of an operation's direction emerges when numbers are viewed over a longer period of time. This is referred to as *trend analysis*. **Trend analysis** uses various operating data and ratios to assess patterns over a period of time. Many trend analyses are performed using spreadsheets, graphs, or other means of tracking the data.

Trend analysis can be both internal and external. An internal trend analysis compares the operation against itself. An external trend analysis compares, or benchmarks, the financial ratios of an operation to those of other operations or to industry standards. It is a great way to determine if a manager is running an operation effectively and efficiently.

In an external trend analysis, the operations being compared should have similar characteristics. It is also important to ensure the criteria are the same and that the data are gathered in the same manner. External trend analysis is a great tool to assess where an operation sits in comparison to others. In fact, benchmarking aids in determining best practices in the industry. A manager can compare his or her numbers to those that are best in the industry and take steps to become an industry leader.

Key Terms

financial statement
statement of income
balance sheet
current assets
accounts receivable
fixed assets

liability
accounts payable
statement of cash
   flows (SCF)
financial analysis
comparative analysis

common-size analysis
ratio analysis
operating ratios
profitability ratios
profit margin
trend analysis

Recap

- The statement of income, balance sheet, and statement of cash flows are the three financial statements used by businesses.
- The statement of income is a report that shows whether an organization has gained or lost money over a specific period of time.
- The balance sheet reflects the financial health of a business on the date the statement was issued.
- The statement of cash flows shows whether a company has cash on hand to pay the bills, make loan payments, invest, or provide dividends to investors.
- Financial analysis is the process of comparing financial information to evaluate an operation's performance.
- Trend analysis uses various operating data and ratios to assess patterns over a period of time. Internal and external trend analyses aid in understanding how well a company is doing compared to itself and compared to best practices in the industry.

Review Questions

1. List two other names the statement of income is commonly called.
2. Explain the difference between the statement of income and the balance sheet.
3. Explain why controllable income is often used to assess a manager's performance.
4. Explain the difference between an income statement and a statement of cash flow.
5. A common-size income statement expresses each sales and expense line item as a percentage of what?
6. Describe the two types of trend analysis.

Exercises 11-7 and 11-8

Complete the following exercises on the companion website:
www.g-wlearning.com/culinaryarts/

Applying Your Knowledge

7. ABC Restaurant is a small diner open for breakfast and lunch. The restaurant does not sell alcoholic beverages. The following data was generated during the course of business for the month of March 2014.

Feb. 28, 2014 inventory (food)	$13,000
Mar. 31, 2014 inventory (food)	$22,500
Food purchases	$51,700
Food sales	$100,820
Manager's salary	$6,000
Hourly wages	$15,000
Benefits equal 30% of salary and wages	
General and admin. costs	$500
Utilities paid	$700
Repairs and maintenance	$500
Direct operating expenses	$4,000
Marketing costs	$300
Depreciation expense	$2,500
Occupancy cost	$900
Interest paid	$2,000

A. Use the information above to calculate the cost of food sold for the month of March 2014.

Cost of Food Sold for Month of March 2014		
	Beginning Food Inventory	
plus	Food Purchases During Month	
	Cost of Food Available During Period	
less	Ending Food Inventory	
	Cost of Food Sold During Month	

B. Prepare an income statement for ABC Restaurant for the month of March 2014.

ABC Restaurant		
Statement of Income **Month Ending March 31, 2014**		
(in dollars)		
Sales		
Food		
Beverage (alcoholic)	0	0.0%
Total Sales		
Cost of Sales		
Food		
Beverage (alcoholic)	0	0.0%
Total Cost of Sales		
Labor		
Salary		
Wages		
Employee Benefits		
Total Labor		
Prime Cost		
Other Controllable Expenses		
Direct Operating Expenses		
Music & Entertainment		
Marketing		
Utilities		
General & Administrative		
Repairs & Maintenance		
Total Other Controllable Expenses		
Controllable Income		
Noncontrollable Expenses		
Occupancy		
Equipment Leases		
Depreciation		
Total Noncontrollable Expenses		
Operating Income		
Interest Expense		
Other (Income)/Expense		
Income before Income Taxes		
Income Tax	0	0.0%
Net Income		

C. The owner of ABC Restaurant budgeted based on 37 percent food cost. Did the restaurant meet the budgeted goal for food cost percentage in March?

8. The owner of ABC Restaurant wants to compare the operation's performance in March to February's performance to be sure the business is moving in the right direction. The following data was generated during the course of business in February.

Jan. 31, 2014 inventory (food)	$14,500
Feb. 28, 2014 inventory (food)	$13,000
Food purchases	$41,300
Food sales	$97,700
Manager's salary	$6,000
Hourly wages	$14,450
Benefits equal 30% of salary and wages	
General and admin. costs	$535
Utilities paid	$700
Repairs and maintenance	$500
Direct operating expenses	$3,900
Marketing costs	$300
Depreciation expense	$2,500
Occupancy cost	$900
Interest paid	$2,000

A. Use the information above to calculate the cost of food sold for February.

Cost of Food Sold for Months of February and March		February	March
	Beginning Food Inventory		13,000
plus	Food Purchased During Period		51,700
	Cost of Food Available During Period		64,700
less	Ending Food Inventory		22,500
	Cost of Food Sold During Period		42,200

B. Prepare ABC Restaurant's comparative analysis for February and March.

ABC Restaurant Comparative Analysis						
Statements of Income for February and March 2014						
	March ($)	%	February ($)	%	Difference ($)	Difference (%)	% Change
Sales							
Food	100,820	100.0%					
Beverage (alcoholic)	0	0.0%	0	0.0%	0	0.0%	0.0%
Total Sales	100,820	100.0%					
Cost of Sales							
Food	42,200	41.9%					
Beverage (alcoholic)	0	0.0%	0	0.0%	0	0.0%	0.0%
Total Cost of Sales	42,200	41.9%					
Labor							
Salary	6,000	6.0%					
Wages	15,000	14.9%					
Employee Benefits	6,300	6.2%					
Total Labor	27,300	27.1%					
Prime Cost	69,500	68.9%					
Other Controllable Expenses							
Direct Operating Expenses	4,000	4.0%					
Music & Entertainment	0	0.0%	0	0.0%	0	0.0%	0.0%
Marketing	300	0.3%					
Utilities	700	0.7%					
General & Administrative	500	0.5%					
Repairs & Maintenance	500	0.5%					
Total Other Controllable Expenses	6,000	6.0%					
Controllable Income	25,320	25.1%					
Noncontrollable Expenses							
Occupancy	900	0.9%					
Equipment Leases	0	0.0%	0	0.0%	0	0.0%	0.0%
Depreciation	2,500	2.5%					
Total Noncontrollable Expenses	3,400	3.4%					
Operating Income	21,920	21.7%					
Corporate Overhead	0	0.0%	0	0.0%	0	0.0%	0.0%
Interest Expense	2,000	2.0%					
Other (Income)/Expense	0	0.0%	0	0.0%	0	0.0%	0.0%
Income before Income Taxes	19,920	19.8%					
Income Tax	0	0.0%	0	0.0%	0	0.0%	0.0%
Net Income	19,920	19.8%					

   C. Did the food cost percentage improve from February to March? Explain
       your answer.
   D. Did ABC Restaurant's bottom line (net income) improve from February to March?
 9. Refer to the comparative analysis statement of income in the chapter. List three
    steps the manager could take to improve his or her bonus opportunities.

Course Project

10. Prepare a statement of income for the restaurant you created for the Course
    Project. By researching similar types of restaurants, you can find numbers you can
    use to complete the statement.

Chapter 12

Controlling Costs through Technology

Learning Outcomes

After studying this chapter, you will be able to

- explain why the use of information technology is increasing in foodservice.
- list the advantages of using a computerized purchase order system.
- list the advantages of using an inventory software system.
- identify the key features of a menu, recipes, and production program.
- explain how a POS system can be used as a management control tool.
- list the office software systems commonly used by foodservice managers.
- define enterprise software systems and explain why corporations use them.
- list the advantages of using high-tech foodservice equipment.
- prepare a list of questions a manager should consider before purchasing technology.

Information technology (IT) is technology that involves the development, implementation, and support of computer-based information. In the past, many foodservice operators shied away from IT, thinking it was either too costly or too complicated to implement. However, in recent years, technology use in foodservice has grown as managers use it to curb costs and raise profitability and customer satisfaction. They see the benefits that the technology can offer and are more comfortable with the functionality of information systems. The greater use of the Internet and mobile devices by the general population, particularly by the technologically savvy generation entering the workforce, has also been driving this trend.

This chapter focuses on the application of information technology in various areas of foodservice operations—especially as it pertains to cost control. It discusses how managers can evaluate and match the needs of their operations with IT solutions. Some of the pitfalls in the uses of information technology will be discussed later in the chapter.

Computerizing Foodservice Operations

The term **management information system** refers to the people, technology, and procedures used to solve business problems. It involves the collection, storage, and distribution of information to better manage an operation. In other words, a management information system aids in the management functions of planning, control, and resource allocation.

Most, if not all, of the functions performed in a foodservice operation can be computerized. These include

- purchasing
- receiving
- inventory
- menu planning
- production
- point of sale
- human resource management
- office systems and financial management

Computers consist of two components—software and hardware. Software refers to the computer programs and applications that perform tasks or functions. Hardware is the equipment—the central processing unit, the monitor, the printer, and so forth—used to run the software.

A plethora of hardware and software products and services are available. They are packaged and sold in different ways. A manager may purchase a product to use in a single area of the operation, such as purchasing. Another manager may select a product that addresses multiple areas—purchasing, receiving, inventory, production, recipes and menus, point of sale, and financial management. A product may consist of components or modules from which a manager can pick and choose.

A technology tool commonly used in foodservice operations is a point-of sale system. When they place an order at most fast food restaurants, consumers see these in use. The hardware for the point-of-sale system includes the touch-screen monitor that the order taker uses to punch in the customer's request. Once the order is punched in, it transmits to another hardware device that the prep cook uses to prepare the menu item and deliver it to the customer. Point-of-sale system software includes the computer programs that record the order, send it to the prep cook, and store information for the tracking of sales. POS systems will be discussed in more detail later in this chapter.

Management information systems that offer *system integration* can be especially useful to a business that consists of a chain or a system of foodservice operations. **System integration** refers to the merging of various individual software programs used in an operation into a single system. The data and functionality can be shared and accessed at multiple locations and by multiple workers.

Purchasing

It is critical for a foodservice operation to establish an effective and efficient purchasing system. When done manually, the purchasing process is labor-intensive. All of the items needed to produce the menu and serve the guests must be listed. For each item, the quantity, cost, vendor, and so forth, must be noted. The manager phones in the order to the vendor, or a vendor's sales representative comes by to take the order. Unfortunately, changes to the order guide—or list of items needed to prepare and serve the menu—are difficult to make. If the menu changes, old items must be deleted and new ones added. If the list is lost, it must be recreated. Although this scenario sounds outdated, some foodservice operations continue to perform purchasing tasks manually. Since many vendors offer web-based purchasing systems to their customers at little or no cost, operators should convert to this method.

Technology

Using Cloud-based Services

Many foodservice operators use information technology to manage their businesses. For those with limited resources, technology costs can be prohibitive. A growing number of businesses are subscribing to cloud-based services, which tout lower costs and increased functionality. These services allow foodservice operations to move data and software from on-site computer networks and servers to the Internet. They can exploit powerful Internet features, including unlimited storage capacity and quick access to data at anytime and from anywhere.

The number of cloud-service providers is growing. Some are simply repositories for large amounts of data and simplify data sharing. Data can include large volumes of customer information collected by POS systems and huge files that are difficult to e-mail. Other services help subscribers create customized cloud environments akin to their own private social networks. They also promise a higher level of security and the services of a help desk. Clients can access hundreds of web-based software applications without having to buy and install them on multiple onsite computers. Money can be saved on the costs of new computer systems and system upgrades.

Cloud-based services can help franchise and multinational operations streamline and improve communication within their organizations. Employees in different locations can share resources, solve problems, and conduct training. Conducting meetings online helps these operations reduce travel costs. Instead of subscribing to a cloud service provider, some operations create their own cloud environments.

The use of technology can help an operation streamline and automate purchasing. The list of items to be purchased can be entered into a word-processing or a spreadsheet program. The ordering clerk can print off the list, determine what is on hand and what needs to be ordered, and generate purchase orders to the vendors. With Internet access and vendor-provided tools, many operations prefer to place their orders online. The manager simply opens the program, enters the order quantities, and presses the send button. The order is transmitted electronically to the vendor. Changes to an electronic order guide are easy to make and copies are easy to print out. This is the most cost-effective, quick, and efficient means of placing an order.

Another advantage of web-based ordering is that it takes much of the guesswork out of ordering and decreases the chance of error. The vendor can list each item with a description, item code number, and price. When ordering, the manager knows which product he or she is ordering and how much it costs. For example, instead of asking for three cases of chicken breasts, and leaving it up to the distributor to guess which product to send, the manager can order three cases of item number 999999. It is described as "six-ounce, boneless, skinless chicken breast, individually quick frozen" at $50 per case. With this order placed on the distributor's ordering system, the operation has a document listing what was ordered, which can be used to verify that the correct items are received at delivery. The operation will also know the total cost of the purchase order.

In summary, as a result of using technology in the purchasing process, an operation can have

- a current list of items to be ordered based on its menu and serving needs
- an order guide that includes item specifications and item code numbers to ensure accuracy of the order
- a simple means of updating the order sheet when an item changes

- the ability to place the order electronically versus via the telephone or sales representative
- a document listing what was ordered that can be used in the receiving process
- purchase history with the ability to print off reports
- up-to-date pricing on all items ordered

These efficiencies can decrease labor costs, increase order accuracy, and lead to savings in the costs of food and supplies.

Receiving

Information technology can also improve efficiencies in the receiving process. The goals of this process include ensuring that all ordered items are received in the right quantity, quality, and temperature. Then they are placed in the correct storage area in a timely manner. If completed manually, the receiving clerk compares the list of items ordered against the items received when a delivery arrives. Each item must be found and checked off the list before being delivered to its proper location. If an item is missing, an extra item is delivered, or another error occurs, it can be time consuming to rectify. How will the information be documented, and how will the vendor handle the credit to the operation?

Several technologies used today greatly simplify the receiving process. One of them is *bar-code technology*. A **bar code** is a code consisting of bars, numbers, and spaces that is used to label boxes, packages, and other objects. A bar code contains information that can be read with a handheld device and stored electronically in computer memory. A delivery person can scan a bar code to look up an item or an order to make sure the item, and the amount delivered, match what was ordered. The delivery is closed out when the customer signs the device screen. The advantage of the bar-code system is that the items ordered and the items delivered can be quickly matched up to ensure that all items have been received. The operation can use scanning devices to verify its orders as well.

A **radio frequency identification device (RFID)** reads information from a tag or a bar code and transmits it to a computer wirelessly and in real time. Unlike a bar-code system, a package and a recording device do not need to be in close proximity to each other. The RFID device may even be out of sight. These systems are found in food production and commissary facilities, hospital purchasing departments, and other large operations.

Today, many food manufacturers and foodservice distributors are moving to a common product identification code called Global Standards One (GS1). The code, or **Global Trade Item Number® (GTIN®)**, is a unique number that is assigned to each product and service. A GTIN for a product is encoded on RFID tags or printed on boxes, similar to bar codes. It is used by all industries and by all information systems within a supply chain. This enables faster identification and tracking of products as they move through the supply chain. This is especially helpful if a product is recalled for food safety reasons. It also controls costs, as all software systems read the same GTIN, eliminating the need to enter an item into a system multiple times. By 2015, the GS1 adoption rate across industries is hoped to be as high as 75 percent.

Inventory

Inventory activities and control can be almost completely automated by the use of software programs. The programs can be purchased from various software vendors or they may come as part of larger software systems. The first step in using a computerized inventory system is to generate a beginning inventory—a list of all the items currently in the inventory.

The beginning inventory can be created in several ways. A manager can complete a physical inventory, noting all the items in the storage units and what quantities are on hand. This information is entered into a software program. Otherwise, a manager can use an order guide that lists the items purchased from the vendor, item codes, and product descriptions. The manager verifies that the listed items are in the storage areas and records the quantities on hand. Items that are not listed are also recorded. Once completed, an up-to-date inventory is in the system and can be used as the beginning inventory.

Once the beginning inventory is recorded, the software system can be used to perform several functions. First, it can maintain the inventory control system. The inventory list can be printed off and used to record what is currently on hand and what needs to be purchased. Once the inventory is checked, the amount on hand is entered into the system, and once again, an accurate picture of the inventory is available. If the price of each item is recorded, the system can calculate the value of the inventory. Most inventory systems allow items to be sorted and listed by product type or storage location. All frozen items can appear together, for example. A manager can quickly determine how much of a particular item is on hand, and its value.

The inventory, purchasing, and receiving programs can be integrated, allowing data to be shared across all three areas. This creates even greater efficiencies and controls. Using a vendor's electronic ordering system, an operator can access the list of items ordered and their current prices. After using a bar-code scanner to scan all the items in inventory, the operator knows which items are on hand and which ones are needed based on prior purchase history. For each item, the purchasing program lists the amount that should be kept on hand, or *par level*, and the amount that should be ordered to serve the menu for the next order cycle.

For instance, suppose an operation's inventory system indicates that it has three cases of item 999999, which is a six-ounce, boneless, skinless chicken breast. According to the purchasing system, the next order cycle calls for six cases. The software program can automatically place an order for three cases of item 999999 with the distributor. When the order is delivered, the cases are scanned. The receiving system notes that three cases of 999999 were received. They are automatically added to the inventory program and the amount on hand is changed to six cases. In this example, the only manual process was the scanning of the initial inventory on hand. Significant labor savings and a decrease in human error add up to an overall cost savings for the operation. In addition, the manager can see what is available in the storage units at any given time by consulting the software program.

With integration of the inventory, purchasing, and receiving programs, errors can be found and corrected quickly. For example, suppose a cook begins to prepare the chicken breasts and finds five cases on hand, instead of six. Is the discrepancy due to an error or to pilferage? The manager can see that the operation ordered three cases and received three cases. The receiving clerk scanned in three cases of chicken using a bar-code scanner. An error may have occurred if the clerk missed a box when scanning. On the other hand, a case may have been stolen out of the inventory. Using an integrated system allows the manager to zero in on where the discrepancy occurred and to address the problem quickly.

The use of an inventory software system—especially a system tied to the receiving and purchasing systems—can bring increased efficiencies and cost control opportunities. These include

- an electronically maintained perpetual inventory.
- the means to monitor and control food and supply costs through accurate ordering and receiving.

- the ability to accurately cost out all recipes and menus through access to up-to-date ingredient costs.
- the ability to generate purchasing reports by product category, such as frozen, or by storage area, such as "Walk-in Refrigerator B." These reports can be used to conduct a physical inventory for ordering purposes or for inventory valuation in financial reporting.
- the generation of storage-area orders that include all items needed for the menu.
- bar coding inventory tracking systems. Operators scan a bar code on the shelf that identifies a product. They plug in the number of boxes in stock and enter the amount to be ordered or have the system order what is needed.

Menu Planning and Production

Since the menu drives all else in a foodservice operation, any efficiency gained in menu planning is beneficial to the operation. Recipe and menu programs are commonly used in the noncommercial foodservice arena—hospitals, long-term care communities, and educational institutions. However, many commercial operations also use recipe programs. Some operations only use software to publish or print their menus. This section explores some of the functionalities that menu, recipe, and production programs can deliver.

Recipe Programs

Many foodservice managers keep their recipes in software programs. These programs store recipe ingredients, ingredient amounts, preparation instructions, yields, and portion sizes. In addition, these programs allow a manager to identify critical control points in the recipe as part of a hazard analysis critical control points (HACCP) plan. The following are advantages of using recipe programs.

- When a cook needs a recipe for production, it is available. Recipes stored electronically are not as easily lost or damaged as those on paper.

Waste Not

Using Information Technology to Reduce Food Waste

At many foodservice operations, large amounts of food are thrown out. Food waste is costly. The main sources of food waste include

- the overproduction and overcooking of food by employees
- the expiration and spoilage of food before it is used
- customers who leave food on their plates after eating

Another problem is that many operations are unaware of how much waste they generate. This is where a computerized food waste management system can help. They can allow operators to track and manage their food waste more efficiently, thereby reducing costs.

In an operation using such a system, employees weigh the waste. They enter the item name, weight, loss reason, type of container, and service area into a preprogrammed touch screen system. The system tracks whether the food is pre-customer waste or uneaten by the customer. It also records whether the food will be thrown out, donated, or composted. Then it estimates the value of the lost food.

The data from a computerized food waste management system helps managers identify trends and problem areas that result in costly food waste. Upon analyzing the data, they can implement process changes to reduce it. Touch screen devices, scales, and software must be purchased. However, operations may find that costs are offset by a significant reduction in food costs and the operation's carbon footprint.

- Recipes can be easily modified or updated. A recipe may need updating when new ingredients become available, a new flavor profile is desired, the quantity produced changes, or a new piece of equipment is added.
- Nutrition information for the recipe is readily available. Some programs come with nutrition information for the items used.
- The overall cost of a recipe, and the cost of each ingredient, can be adjusted. If a recipe costs too much to produce, the ingredients can be adjusted using the software program until the desired price is obtained. This is more efficient than looking up the price of each ingredient, determining its cost in the recipe, and then performing the calculations to get to the desired recipe cost.
- If a recipe program is part of a prime vendor's software offerings, prices and available nutrition information are automatically updated by the vendor.

Menu Programs

Operators can lower costs by creating and printing their own menus using inexpensive desktop publishing programs. They can select paper of a certain color and quality to create the menu look they desire. There are two types of menu programs. One type gives managers the ability to create and publish menus in-house. After menu items are entered into the computer, managers specify how they would like the menu formatted. The computer program formats and prints the menus. Managers using this program can easily make menu changes and print out additional menus if needed. When outside services are hired to develop and print an operation's menus, they generally charge for each change to the menu and for each copy printed.

A second type of menu program is used by foodservice operations for production and reporting purposes. This menu program is integrated with the recipe program and can generate production reports. First, the operator must enter every item on the day's menu and the serving size of each. Each recipe—Quiche Lorraine, for instance—has a recipe number assigned to it. An item such as applesauce can be listed by its vendor item code number or description, **12-1**.

If a menu item has a recipe, the recipe number from the recipe program is listed. Now everything related to the recipe is also tied to the day's menu. All of the ingredients needed to produce the recipe are accounted for. In addition, the menu program lists all the items needed for the menu that are not a part of a recipe. The program creates a complete list of everything needed for the menu. Instead of manually recording every ingredient in a recipe, and then manually listing all the stand-alone items, a manager can use the computer program to generate a combined list.

Many programs can also generate production sheets based on the day's menu and recipes. The manager enters the number of servings needed for each item. Then the cook receives an accurate list of everything to produce, including quantities of each. The recipe program can adjust the yield and ingredient amounts to produce the needed quantity, **12-2.**

From here, the program can generate a forecasted count sheet. Once a meal is produced and served, the operation should note the amounts that were produced, served, and leftover. The information can be used to fine-tune production the next time the menu is used. The goal is to honor all orders without creating leftovers. Tracking this electronically can save the manager significant time and headache.

Menu Cycle: Spring				
Day: Sunday		Meal: Breakfast		
Item Code/ Recipe Number	Item	Portion Unit	Cost (dollars)	Nutrition Information Available?
R25	Quiche Lorraine	⅛th slice	0.95	Y
R306	Pancakes	2 each	0.15	Y
R305	French toast	2 each	0.24	Y
R200	Egg, fried	1 each	0.25	Y
231456	Bacon	3 slices	0.18	Y
221113	Sausage patty	1 patty	0.20	Y
543345	Banana	1 each	0.23	Y
342167	Applesauce	0.5 cup	0.10	Y
555433	Orange juice	6 oz	0.22	Y
R34	Coffee	8 oz	0.10	Y
775483	Milk	8 oz	0.25	Y
886884	Tea	8 oz	0.10	Y

Figure 12-1. This menu uses codes for the recipes (R25 for Quiche Lorraine) and vendor item codes for individual items (342167 for applesauce). This allows recipes and items to be commonly referenced and tracked through the various programs or modules in the kitchen.

A menu, recipe, and production program can offer the following features:
- HACCP-formatted recipes
- menu printing
- generation of production reports
- nutritional analysis
- forecasted production counts
- production sheets that can be sorted by preparation and dining locations
- recipe adjustments based on cost, nutritional requirements, and production needs

As stated earlier, inventory, purchasing, and receiving programs can be part of an integrated system. Recipe, menu, and production programs can also be integrated if they share the same system of codes. Again, each item used in a recipe or in a menu is identified by an item code number—usually a vendor item code. A can of green beans may appear in an inventory system with an item code number of 111222. In the purchasing and receiving systems, it will also be identified as 111222. Suppose that the green beans are used in recipe number 15, which is for a green bean casserole. In the recipe program, the green beans will be identified with the item code number of 111222. In the menu program, the green beans are part of recipe 15. If they are offered as a simple side dish on the menu, they would also be entered on the menu by the number 111222.

Production								
Date: March 8, 20XX **Meal: Breakfast**								
Comments (weather, holiday, etc.): major snow storm, many roads closed								
Estimated Count: 140 **Actual Count:**								
Temperature	**Item**	**Portion Size**	**Portion Cost (dollars)**	**Price (dollars)**	**Portions to Prepare**	**Actual Portions Prepared**	**Left-Over**	**Register Sales**
	Eggs	#8 scoop	0.25	2.50	80			
	Oatmeal	0.5 cup	0.10	2.25	125			
	Pancakes	2 each	0.15	1.50	50			
	Bacon	3 slices	0.18	0.95	100			
	Sausage	0.5 oz	0.20	0.95	40			

Figure 12-2. By keeping track of what is produced and what is leftover, a manager can continuously streamline the operation to control costs. Using a software program to do this makes storing data and sharing information easier. It also saves time.

Suppose that a manager determines that 50 portions of green beans and 75 portions of the green bean casserole will be needed for the menu. These amounts are generated on the production report. Based on the production report, the cook removes one case of green beans from the storeroom for the day's menu. The inventory will show one less case on hand. The inventory system will trigger the purchasing system to order a case of 111222. When the distributor delivers the order, the receiving system will scan in one case of 111222. The inventory will be updated and the process begins again. All of this is completed automatically, which saves time and minimizes human error. The computer-generated tracking system allows for cost control.

Point of Sale

All of the IT applications discussed so far are used in the back-of-the-house operation. Point-of-sale (POS) systems used in the front of the house, or the service side, are growing in popularity and sophistication. A POS system is a computerized cash register that is placed and used at the location of the transaction. As with most software solutions, a POS system can be very basic or highly sophisticated in its applications.

A transaction begins when a server receives the customer's order and enters it into the POS system. At some operations, the server, while still at the customer's table, enters the order into a handheld device. At other operations, the server goes to the POS station and enters the items ordered into the system. Either way, once in the system, each item is transmitted to the area within the operation charged with filling it.

For instance, suppose a customer orders salmon, rice pilaf, asparagus, tossed salad with blue cheese dressing, and a glass of Chardonnay. The server enters this order into the POS which generates three orders. The Chardonnay order is transmitted to the bartender. The orders for salmon, rice, and asparagus go to the hot production cook. The salad and dressing order is transmitted to the cold food station. Staff members at each location prepare their part of the order. When they are ready, the server delivers the complete order to the customer. It is stored in the system. If the customer decides to top off the meal with coffee and cheesecake, the server can easily amend the order and add the items to the bill. When the customer is finished, the server generates the bill from the POS, obtains payment from the customer, and completes the transaction.

The POS screen is generally a touch screen. Menu items are listed by a coding system and customers are identified by their tables and seat numbers. The POS system can track the sales of every item on the menu and ensure that the production and beverage staff receive customer orders quickly. It processes the sales transaction like a cash register.

Integrated systems can connect the POS to any and all of the operation's software systems. Suppose the operation that serves the green bean casserole uses an integrated system with POS. The manager will not need to enter the amount sold to generate the production and inventory information. The POS will add the amount sold to all the other programs. The operation will know the amount to produce the next time the menu is used based on the sales entered into the POS. The recipe, menu, production, inventory, purchasing, and receiving systems can all be updated with the information on the green bean sales generated from the POS.

Once again, this minimizes labor, human error, and time, and increases accuracy for the operation. In addition, it provides a means of tracking all aspects of the operation so the manager can maintain better control.

Labor Management

Two other functions common to the office are schedule writing and payroll. Software solutions for both are available on the market. Having a computerized scheduling system simplifies the tracking and reporting processes. The program can quickly calculate the number of *full-time equivalent (FTE)* employees scheduled and compare that to the number budgeted. FTE is a ratio of the total number of paid hours in a given period divided by the total number of full-time hours worked, usually 40 hours. For instance, if four workers work 110 hours in a given week, the number of FTEs would be found by dividing 110 by 40, or 2.75. Regardless of the number of people working—four people—it is the total hours required, or 110, that is key. Knowing this helps the manager decide whether the schedule needs modification and how best to do it. Also, once the schedule is posted, it can be easily updated. If an employee calls in sick and another employee fills in for him or her, the hours each employee worked is updated. The system can then generate the number of hours each employee worked for the time period, and transfer that information to the payroll system.

A payroll software system generates paychecks for employees based on the hours worked and the pay rates entered into the program. The system stores the numbers of hours worked and labor hours paid. This information can be used to complete the various financial ratios discussed throughout this text for operational control purposes. It can also be used to generate documents required by the government to show compliance with laws related to labor and taxes. Finally, a payroll software system can be used to electronically send employees' pay to their financial institutions for direct deposit into their accounts.

Office Systems and Financial Management

Desktop applications are commonly found in the offices of foodservice operations. Although these programs are not foodservice specific, they streamline office functions and create efficiencies in this area. Independent operations may choose which hardware and software products to use. However, corporations often mandate particular products for each of their locations to enable information sharing by various users and units.

Desktop applications include products that perform the following functions:

- word processing for creating documents, letters, memos, policies and procedures, job descriptions, and so forth
- spreadsheets for sorting data, preparing reports, drawing graphs, and performing quick calculations of data entered using formulas

Bookmark This

Robot-Staffed Restaurants

Some scientists predict that most foodservice jobs, particularly those in quick-service restaurants, will eventually be filled by robots. Robots will perform back-of-the-house tasks such as ordering, taking inventory, preparing menu items, and loading dishmachines. Robot cashiers will take payments and mobile robot waiters will deliver food to customers.

Although they are still a novelty, service robots are being used in some restaurants in Asia and Europe. For example, robot chefs prepare ramen noodles for customers in a restaurant in Nagoya, Japan. Diners at a restaurant in Jinan, China, are greeted by robot hostesses and served by robot waiters. The benefits of using robots include lower labor costs. Although they are costly to purchase, robots do not receive wages, tips, or benefits. They do not tire or need breaks. They do not pilfer or make mistakes.

Several sources of information about the industrial robotics industry are The Robotics Institute at Carnegie Mellon University and the International Federation of Robotics.

- desktop publishing for creating menu designs, signs, and newsletters
- presentation software for creating materials for training and marketing
- Internet connectivity for accessing online resources—including recipes, information about equipment and industry trends, vendor software, and e-mail

Financial Management

The financial management software solution for an operation may be a stand-alone program or an integrated system that includes many programs. For example, the financial functions of a foodservice operation are easier to manage with a basic accounting software program. The creation of balance sheets and income statements is greatly simplified with the use of spreadsheets or software programs designed for this purpose.

The use of accounting software simplifies the process of creating a yearly budget and generating monthly operations reports. Without it, a manager needs to manually enter in all of the information, make the calculations, and record the revised information. By setting up and using a software budgeting system, a manager can have the computer complete the calculations and report the new numbers.

One type of financial management software, called *scenario management*, allows the manager to create and test various scenarios to see the impact a decision may have on the operation. The advantage is that the system can calculate the data. The manager can save it as an example, then create another scenario, and compare the two.

Suppose a manager is purchasing a piece of capital equipment. Company A and Company B sell models that differ in purchase price and utility costs. The manager can enter these costs for Company A's model into a spreadsheet program, along with the formula that calculates payback period. Once the program calculates the payback period for the Company A model, the payback period for the Company B model can be easily computed. The manager only needs to change the price and utility costs on the spreadsheet. Then the manager can compare the two options. The more variables in the scenario, the more useful the software program becomes.

Other Business Office Functions

Software programs can assist with the various business office functions of a typical foodservice operation. Accounts receivable (AR), which is money owed to the operation, must be correctly accounted for and recorded on the accounting ledger. Accounts payable (AP)—or all of the invoices that must be paid—need to be accounted for, processed, and entered into the ledger. Setting up a software program to perform these tasks greatly speeds up these processes, improves accuracy, and provides a readily accessible record of all transactions.

Taking this one step further, many foodservice operations use *electronic funds transfer (EFT)*. **Electronic funds transfer (EFT)** is the transfer of funds from one account to another, or from one financial institution to another, via an electronic or computer-based exchange. It is similar to the online banking that many individuals use today. Before EFT, a manager received an invoice for a food delivery and then wrote and mailed a check to the vendor. The amount was recorded and the operator waited for confirmation from the vendor or bank that the check was received and deposited.

Using EFT, the operator has a few options for processing invoices and paying for them. Using one method, the operator reviews the invoice in the ordering system, verifies that the order was received, and electronically sends payment approval to the financial institution. The financial institution then transfers the payment from the operator's to the vendor's account.

Another method allows for automatic withdraw of funds by the vendor from the operator's bank account. The vendor sends an invoice or bill directly to the bank electronically. At the same time, the vendor sends an e-mail to the operator indicating that funds to cover the invoice will be removed from the operator's account on a specified date. Then the bank electronically transfers funds from the operation's account to the vendor's account. The manager can look up the account information online, or wait for the monthly statement. Of course, if the manager determines that some or all of the funds should not be withdrawn, he or she can take action once the e-mail notification is received. The manager can stop a payment withdrawal by contacting the financial institution. While efficient, this payment method may not be embraced by some operators who do not want to relinquish control of the payment process. Having the ability to transfer funds electronically, review accounts online, and determine when to transfer the funds, provides them with enough time-saving and record-keeping benefits.

Enterprise Software Systems

Enterprise software systems are business-oriented software systems designed for multiunit operations or chains. The use of these systems can improve the efficiency and productivity of a company or corporation because they enable data sharing throughout an organization. The corporate office, or enterprise, can receive information from all the units in a timely manner. This information can be broken out for each unit, or consolidated to provide totals for each area being monitored.

For example, suppose that Sheena's Substation is a 15-unit sandwich shop with locations throughout one state. Sheena is at the corporate office located in the state capital. Since Sheena installed an enterprise software system, she receives reporting from each of her 15 units. One report shows the sales figures of each unit. Another report gives the total sales of all of the units; the enterprise system can generate company-wide reports with data compiled from each individual operation. Therefore, Sheena can quickly access the total amount of sales for the company as a whole, as well as figures for each unit so she can gauge how each is performing.

In addition, an enterprise system is an efficient way to get information to all of the units with the click of a button. If Sheena wishes to add a new sandwich to the Sheena's Substation menu, she can create the recipe and send it out to all the units electronically. Then, she can update the order guide for the vendor with the needed ingredients. These items will be added to the inventory report, production sheets, and point-of-sale systems. She has added the sandwich to all 15 units without leaving her office.

An enterprise software system allows a company to efficiently monitor and update information at its corporate office. A key feature of the system is the use of virtual private networks. A **virtual private network (VPN)** uses public communications infrastructure, such as the Internet, to provide access to the enterprise's network remotely. The great advantage of VPN is that employees can access the company's data while they work remotely. Working from home or at the corporate office, a manager can update a menu and send it to the units within the restaurant chain.

An operator should ensure that its enterprise network and data are secure from public access on the Internet. This can be accomplished by encrypting the data at one end, and decrypting it at the other. Data that are not properly encrypted should be blocked from entering the connection.

High-Tech Foodservice Equipment

Besides the computerizing of foodservice operation processes, technology has been used to improve foodservice equipment. In general, the advantages to purchasing high-tech equipment include decreased production time, decreased labor costs, higher food quality, and increased efficiency, **12-3**.

Some equipment and computerized monitoring devices help ensure that food remains safe. Instruments in refrigerators and freezers can measure and record interior temperatures throughout the day. Instead of walking to each unit to check and record its temperature, the manager can pull up the temperatures of all the units on an office computer. The instruments can also alert the manager to problems, such as high or low temperatures, open doors, or unnecessary lighting.

Trend

Technology Use in Marketing

A growing number of foodservice operations are using technology to market themselves to customers. This trend is taking off as consumers become savvier in their use of technology and as inexpensive programs are more readily available. With the advent of technology, such as the mobile smartphone, businesses can reach and service consumers 24 hours a day, 7 days a week. For example, operations are

- texting discounts to customers that are redeemable during certain hours
- allowing customers to create personal order histories
- accepting orders sent by text by customers who have not yet arrived in the establishment
- providing access to menus, including nutrition and allergy information
- accepting payments by smartphone, enabling customers to bypassing servers and reduce the risk of credit card theft

Advantages of Using High-Tech Equipment		
Advantage of High-Tech Equipment	**How Advantage Assists in Foodservice**	**Example of High-Tech Foodservice Equipment**
Increases preparation speed	Decreases cooking time	Combination steamer
Decreases need for labor	Equipment self-operates	Automatic pot-scrubbing sink
Increases food quality	Retains moisture while cooking	Combi-oven
Increases kitchen efficiency	Recipes can be prepared in large quantities; retains quality and safe handling	Cook-chill equipment
Decreases utility costs	Saves water, electricity, and/or gas use and expense	Ventless steamer

Figure 12-3. Although high-tech foodservice equipment is often expensive, there are many advantages to their use. This chart lists some of them, along with examples of the types of equipment available.

Other applications of new technology are in the areas of security and loss prevention. Operations are installing security systems to ensure the safety of their guests and to deter theft. Managers can monitor their establishments by using security cameras that transmit images over the Internet. Recordings made by these cameras can be saved and viewed later, if needed.

Advantages and Disadvantages of Information Technology

Software and hardware products on the market are so numerous that the task of choosing products can be difficult. Before making a purchase, a manager should understand the operation's current and future needs and how a purchase can fulfill those needs. The manager should also keep the operation's budget constraints in mind. A list of questions to ask when purchasing information systems is given in **12-4.**

In summary, the use of information technology has advantages and disadvantages. They vary depending on the size of an operation, what it wishes to accomplish, and the need for data. For example, a large, corporate chain may benefit from a system that allows for a perpetual inventory. However, such a system would be of limited use in a small diner that offers only breakfast and lunch. Following is a list of advantages that information technology can offer and a discussion of some of the pitfalls.

Advantages

As discussed in this chapter, the use of information technology can save time, speed up processes, and provide a wealth of information. IT systems collect, store, and disseminate information efficiently. They can aid in the management functions of planning, control, and resource allocation. IT systems can also

- decrease paperwork and the time a manager needs for administrative activities. This leaves more time for other activities—strategic planning, staff training, marketing, and so forth.
- provide speed that manual functions cannot match. IT systems can help a fast-paced foodservice operation tighten control in a timely, cost-effective manner.

Questions to Ask in Assessing Information Systems
System Features and Functionality
• Is the operation looking for a financial return, improved customer service, or less paperwork? Does the system enable the operation to meet these goals? • What features or functionalities are available? • Are these provided in one program or in separate modules? • Can modules be purchased now, or later, depending on need? • Can the software support the growing needs of the operation? Is it scalable? • Is it stand-alone or can it be used for a chain or multisite application? • Can the modules or system be networked? What are the requirements? • At what speed does the software operate? Is this adequate? Will this become a problem as the operation grows? • How many workstations does the system support? • Can multiple users be in the system at the same time?
Cost
• What hardware components, including printers, PDAs, etc., are needed? How much do these cost? • What additional software must be purchased? How much will this cost? • How much will it cost to ensure data security? • If the modules or system can be networked, what are the costs? • What is the cost of training? • How many users are included in the licensing fee? • What other fees are incurred for maintenance and system updates? • Does the cost of the technology justify the investment? • What are the additional charges for extra support and additional training?
Training and Support
• How much training and support, on average, will be needed? • What training and support services are included? • Will the company provide training on-site? • What is the length of the training? • Does the operation have staff members who can perform the training, or will training be outsourced? • Will a user's manual be provided? • Does the company provide support 24/7? If not, when?
System Maintenance and Updates
• How many updates are expected each year? • How will new staff be trained once updates are made? • Are changes made in real time? • How does the information systems company adapt to industry updates? • How much data entry will be needed? How much time is required? What skills must employees have to do this?
System Security
• What is required to backup data? Is network-backup capability available? • How does the system prevent access to sensitive data on location and throughout a networked system? Is this adequate? • Is data security part of the service provided by the vendor? • How often is the system updated for new security threats? When will updates be performed?

Figure 12-4. Before purchasing technology, a manager needs to find answers to questions, such as the ones listed.

- deliver up-to-date information and a 24/7 picture of an operation. This aids in decision making and can help managers catch and resolve food-cost increases and other problems quickly.
- improve documentation and reports, which aids in compliance with sanitation, regulatory, and government requirements.
- control costs by decreasing guesswork on amounts to order and produce; provide consistent yields; decrease leftovers.
- decrease labor costs by scheduling labor based on forecasted need and by replacing labor with high-tech equipment.
- decrease utility costs through the use of resource-monitoring devices, high-tech equipment, and so forth.
- decrease an operation's use of paper and the cost of purchasing it.

Disadvantages

Having the latest technology does not replace the need for managers to know what is going on in their operations. Information technology can provide too much information, which can lead to "analysis paralysis," and a difficulty defining priorities. Also, the outputs are only as good as the inputs. The information and reports generated are only valuable if the data entered is accurate and timely.

There are dangers to transmitting information over the Internet or through integrated systems. Steps must be taken to ensure the security of sensitive financial information—such as customer credit card numbers, employee Social Security numbers, and the operation's own financial information. Operations need to develop a technology disaster plan in case records are lost due to fire, weather, and natural disaster. Electronic files should be backed up regularly, with copies stored off site. As an added precaution, some operations use online storage solutions.

In the end, managers need to determine the needs of their operations and which products and services best meet these needs. The functionality of IT products and services constantly changes. They have become more powerful and user friendly and less expensive, in some cases. Savvy foodservice managers stay informed about what vendors offer. They find new ways to incorporate technology into their operations to reduce costs, gain efficiencies, and simplify the management control process.

Key Terms

information technology (IT)

management information system

system integration

bar code

radio frequency identification device (RFID)

Global Trade Item Number (GTIN)

electronic funds transfer (EFT)

enterprise software systems

virtual private network (VPN)

Recap

- Most of the functions performed in a foodservice operation can be computerized.
- The application of information technologies can reduce an operation's costs due to significant labor savings, decreases in human error, and other advantages.
- The integration of purchasing, receiving, and inventory programs allows data to be shared across all three areas.
- Software solutions for the inventory process tells managers what to purchase and provides information about the value of the inventory, which is required for financial reporting.
- Production and forecasting can be automatically generated with the use of a recipe and menu software program.
- A point-of-sale (POS) system is a highly technical cash register.
- Financial management software solutions simplify the creation of balance sheets, income statements, and budgets.
- The purchase of high-tech foodservice equipment can result in cost savings.
- Enterprise systems improve the efficiency and productivity of a company.
- The use of information technology can have disadvantages.

Review Questions

1. List three advantages to computerizing the purchasing process. For each advantage, give an example of how costs can be saved.
2. Explain the difference between bar coding and RFID.
3. List three reasons why the use of an inventory software system can increase efficiencies and reduce costs.
4. Describe four advantages of using a recipe software program.
5. Describe how a POS system handles a customer's order—from the taking of the order by a server to the generation of the customer's bill.
6. Name three types of software programs used in the offices of foodservice operations. Give one example of how a manager would use each one.
7. Should a local restaurant use an enterprise software system? Why or why not?
8. Explain why an operation needs a technology disaster plan, and where the information should be stored.

Apply Your Knowledge

9. A customer orders salmon from the menu. Follow the product through the foodservice operation, starting with the POS, and discuss where and how technology may be used in the process.

10. Locate software companies online that specialize in POS systems. Select a vendor and describe the features it offers in its POS systems.

11. Interview a manager from a foodservice operation (cafeteria, hospital, or restaurant).
    A. Ask the manager to describe the most useful technology tool or system used by the operation. Ask why it is useful.
    B. Ask the manager what he or she wishes for in regards to technology, and how he or she believes it would benefit the operation.

12. Compare and contrast the use of technology in two operations of different sizes.
    A. Visit a small foodservice operation and observe the use of technology there. Write down your observations.
    B. Visit a larger operation, such as a chain restaurant or hospital operation, and observe the use of technology in that setting. Write down your observations.
    C. How does the use of technology differ between the two operations? What could each operation do to better control costs through the use of technology?

Course Project

13. Select one IT product to use in the operation you created for the Course Project. Determine which vendors sell this product and choose one of them. From the information provided on the vendor's website, answer any applicable questions that are listed in Figure 12-4. If the information is not available online, contact the vendor or the manufacturer for answers.

Appendix A
List of Equations Used

Chapter 1: Principles of Control in a Foodservice Operation

Relationship between cost, sales, and profit (or loss)

Profit = Sales − Cost

Cost = Sales − Profit

Ratios

$$X:Y = \frac{X}{Y} = X \text{ to } Y$$

Comparing Product Prices

Considering pack size

Number of Bags per Case × Weight per Bag = Weight per Case

$$\text{Price per Weight Measure (ex. pound)} = \frac{\text{Price per Case}}{\text{Weight per Case}}$$

Food Cost per Meal

$$\text{Food Cost per Meal} = \frac{\text{Cost of Food to Prepare Meals}}{\text{Number of Meals Served}}$$

Labor Cost per Meal

$$\text{Labor Cost per Meal} = \frac{\text{Labor Cost}}{\text{Meals Served}}$$

Variance Calculations

Budget – Actual = Variance

Variance as a percent difference

$$\frac{\text{Variance Amount}}{\text{Budgeted Amount}} \times 100 = \text{\% Difference}$$

Chapter 2: Menu Planning as a Control Tool

Menu-Pricing Methods

Food cost percentage method

$$\text{Selling Price} = \frac{\text{Food Cost}}{\text{Desired Food Cost \%}}$$

Factor system

$$\text{Pricing Factor} = \frac{100\%}{\text{Desired Food Cost \%}}$$

Selling Price = Food Cost × Pricing Factor

Contribution margin method

Selling Price – Variable Costs = Contribution Margin

Selling Price = Product Cost + Desired Contribution Margin

Prime cost method

Prime Cost = Food Cost + Wages + Employee Benefits and Payroll Taxes

$$\text{Selling Price} = \frac{\text{Prime Cost}}{\text{Prime Cost \%}}$$

Texas Restaurant Association (TRA) Markup Method

$$\text{Selling Price} = \frac{\text{Actual Food Cost}}{\text{Desired Food Cost \%}}$$

Chapter 3: Cost Control in Purchasing, Receiving, Storage, and Inventory Management

Buyer's Cost from Vendor's Cost and Markup %

Buyer's Cost = Vendor's Cost + (Markup % × Vendor's Cost)

Product Yield Percentage

$$\text{Product Yield \%} = \frac{\text{Edible Portion (EP) Weight}}{\text{As Purchased (AP) Weight}} \times 100$$

EP Cost

$$\text{EP Cost} = \frac{\text{AP Cost}}{\text{Product Yield \%}}$$

Estimating Storage Needs

Dry goods

Estimated Storage Space Needed = Number of Meals Served × 0.75 Sq. Ft.

Refrigerated or frozen goods

Estimated Storage Space Needed = Number of Meals Served × 1 (or 2) Cu. Ft.

Cost of Food Sold

Cost of Food Sold = (Beginning Inventory + Purchases) – Ending Inventory

Food Cost Percentage

$$\text{Food Cost \%} = \frac{\text{Cost of Food Sold}}{\text{Sales}} \times 100$$

Average Inventory Value

$$\text{Average Inventory Value} = \frac{\text{(Beginning Inventory Value + Ending Inventory Value)}}{2}$$

Inventory Turns

$$\text{Inventory Turns} = \frac{\text{Cost of Food Sold}}{\text{Average Inventory Value}}$$

Chapter 4: Cost Control from Production to Waste Management

Cost per Unit

$$\text{Cost per Unit} = \frac{\text{Purchase Unit Cost}}{\text{Number of Units}}$$

Cooking Loss

$$\text{Cost per Unit} = \frac{\text{Purchase Unit Cost}}{\text{Number of Units}}$$

$$\text{Product Yield \%*} = \frac{\text{EP Weight}}{\text{AP Weight}}$$

(*from Standard Yield Table)

Chapter 5: Labor Cost Control

Employee Turnover Rate

$$\text{Employee Turnover Rate} = \frac{\text{Employees Separated During Year}}{\text{Average No. of Employees on Staff During Year}} \times 100$$

Labor Cost Percentage

$$\text{Labor Cost \%} = \frac{\text{Labor Cost}}{\text{Sales}} \times 100$$

Covers per Labor Hour

$$\text{Covers per Labor Hour} = \frac{\text{Covers}}{\text{Labor Hours}}$$

Labor Cost per Cover

$$\text{Labor Cost per Cover} = \frac{\text{Labor Cost}}{\text{Covers}}$$

Labor Cost per Meal

$$\text{Labor Cost per Meal} = \frac{\text{Labor Cost}}{\text{Meals Served}}$$

Labor Cost per Labor Hour

$$\text{Labor Cost per Labor Hour} = \frac{\text{Labor Cost}}{\text{Labor Hours}}$$

Meals per Productive Labor Hour

$$\text{Meals per Productive Labor Hour} = \frac{\text{Meals Served}}{\text{Productive Labor Hours}}$$

Chapter 6: Beverage Cost Control

Cost of Beverages Sold

Cost of Beverages Sold = (Beginning Inventory + Purchases) – Ending Inventory

Beverage Cost Percentage

$$\text{Beverage Cost \%} = \frac{\text{Cost of Beverages Sold}}{\text{Beverage Sales}} \times 100$$

Pricing Methods

Beverage cost percentage method

$$\text{Selling Price} = \frac{\text{Beverage Cost}}{\text{Desired Beverage Cost \%}}$$

Factor system

$$\text{Pricing Factor} = \frac{100\%}{\text{Desired Beverage Cost \%}}$$

Selling Price = Beverage Cost × Pricing Factor

Contribution margin method

Contribution Margin = Selling Price – Variable Costs

Selling Price = Beverage Cost + Desired Contribution Margin

Prime cost method

Prime Cost = Beverage Cost + Wages + Employee Benefits and Payroll Taxes

$$\text{Selling Price} = \frac{\text{Prime Cost}}{\text{Prime Cost \%}}$$

Chapter 7: Facilities Management as a Cost Control Tool

Natural Gas Conversions

1 Therm of Natural Gas = Approx. 100 Cu. Ft. of Natural Gas = Approx. 100,000 BTUs of Heat Energy

Therms to kWh

1 Therm of Natural Gas = 29.3 kWh of Electricity

Chapter 8: Operating Budget and Performance Reports

Operating Budget (Also, see Chapter 11)

Prime cost

Prime Cost = Total Cost of Sales + Total Labor

Controllable income

Controllable Income = Total Sales – (Prime Cost + Total Other Controllable Expenses)

Operating income

Operating Income = Controllable Income – Total Noncontrollable Expenses

Performance Report

Variance $

Variance $ = Actual – Budget

Variance Percentage

$$\text{Variance \%} = \frac{\text{Variance \$}}{\text{Budget}} \times 100$$

Chapter 9: The Capital Budget

Depreciation (Straight Line)

$$\text{Annual Depreciation} = \frac{\text{Asset Cost – Salvage Value}}{\text{Anticipated Useful Life in Years}}$$

Comparison of Capital Purchase Options

Operating cost over life expectancy

Operating Cost over Life Expectancy = Annual Operating Cost × Life Expectancy in Years

Total cost

Total Cost = (Asset Cost + Operating Cost over Life Expectancy) – Salvage Value

Payback period

Annual Savings = Current Operating Cost – Operating Cost of New Equipment

$$\text{Payback Period} = \frac{\text{Asset Cost}}{\text{Annual Savings}}$$

Chapter 10: Revenue Control

Cashier Checkout Form

Cash owed for deposit

Cash Owed for Deposit = Cash Sales (from register) – Credit Card Tips Total

Total owed for deposit

Total Owed for Deposit = Cash Owed for Deposit + Checks Owed for Deposit

Actual cash for deposit

Actual Cash for Deposit = Total Cash Drawer – Credit Card Tips Total

Actual deposit

Actual Deposit = Actual Cash for Deposit + Actual Checks for Deposit

Chapter 11: Financial Management

Statement of Income (P&L)

Profit or loss

Revenue – Expenses = Profit (Loss)

Prime cost

Prime Cost = Total Cost of Sales + Total Labor

Controllable income

Controllable Income = Total Sales – (Prime Cost + Total Other Controllable Expenses)

Operating income

Operating Income = Controllable Income – Total Noncontrollable Expenses

Income before income taxes

Income before Income Taxes = Operating Income – [Corporate Overhead + Interest Expense + Other (Income)/Expense]

Net income

Net Income = Income before Income Taxes – Income Tax

Percent of total sales column

Cost of sales line items

$$\text{Percent Total Sales} = \frac{\text{Amount (In Dollars)}}{\text{Product Sales}} \times 100$$

All other line items

$$\text{Percent Total Sales} = \frac{\text{Amount (In Dollars)}}{\text{Total Sales}} \times 100$$

Balance Sheet

Assets

Assets = Liabilities + Equity

Comparative Analysis of Statements of Income

Difference %

$$\text{Difference \%} = \frac{\text{Difference \$}}{\text{Prior-Year Value}} \times 100$$

Percent Change

Percent Change = Current Period % − Prior Period %

Operating Ratios (Activity Ratios)

Average check ratio

$$\text{Average Check} = \frac{\text{Sales}}{\text{Customer Count}}$$

Profit margin ratio

$$\text{Profit Margin} = \frac{\text{Net Income}}{\text{Sales}} \times 100$$

Chapter 12: Controlling Costs through Technology

No formulas given.

Appendix B
Conversion Tables

Weight Measurements	
Unit of Weight	**Equivalent**
16 oz.	1 lb.
12 oz.	¾ lb.
8 oz.	½ lb.
4 oz.	¼ lb.

Volume Measurements	
Unit of Weight	**Equivalent**
1 Tbsp.	3 tsp.
¼ cup	2 fl. oz. = 4 Tbsp.
½ cup	4 fl. oz. = 8 Tbsp.
⅔ cup	5.3 fl. oz. = 10 Tbsp. + 2 tsp.
¾ cup	6 fl. oz. = 12 Tbsp.
1 cup	8 fl. oz. = 16 Tbsp.
½ pint	1 cup = 8 fl. oz.
1 pint	2 cups = 16 fl. oz.
1 quart	2 pints = 4 cups = 32 fl. oz.
½ gallon	2 quarts = 4 pints = 8 cups = 64 fl. oz.
1 gallon	4 quarts = 8 pints = 16 cups = 128 fl. oz.

Standard Foodservice Scoop Sizes

Scoop Number*	Cups	Ounces
4	1	8
5	¾	6
6	⅔	5⅓
8	½	4
10	⅖	3⅕
12	⅓	2⅔
16	¼	2
20	⅕	1⅗
24	2⅔ Tbsp.	1⅓
30	2⅖ Tbsp.	1⅕
40	1⅗ Tbsp.	⅘

*indicates the number of scoop serving sizes in a quart

Standard Foodservice Can Sizes

Can Size Number	Approximate Volume (Cups)	Approximate Weight (Ounces)
No. 1 picnic	1¼	10½
No. 300	1¾	14
No. 303	2	16
No. 2	2½	20
No. 2½	3½	27
No. 3	5¾	46
No. 10	12	6½ lbs.

Fraction-Decimal Equivalents

Fraction	Decimal
⅛	0.125
⅙	0.166
¼	0.250
⅓	0.333
⅜	0.375
½	0.500
⅝	0.625
⅔	0.666
¾	0.750
⅚	0.833
⅞	0.875

Pricing Factor

Product Cost Percentage	Factor
20	5.000
23	4.348
25	4.000
28	3.571
30	3.333
33⅓	3.000
35	2.857
38	2.632
40	2.500
43	2.326
45	2.222

	Depth (Inches)	Approx. Capacity (Quarts)	Serving Size	Ladle Size	Scoop Size	Approx. No. of Servings
Steam Table Pan Capacities (Full)						
Full Pan (12" × 20")	2½	8	1 cup	8 oz.	4	32
			½ cup	4 oz.	8	64
			¼ cup	2 oz.	16	128
	4	13	1 cup	8 oz.	4	52
			½ cup	4 oz.	8	104
			¼ cup	2 oz.	16	208
	6	20	1 cup	8 oz.	4	80
			½ cup	4 oz.	8	160
			¼ cup	2 oz.	16	320
½ Pan (12" × 10" or 20" × 6")	2½	3 ½	1 cup	8 oz.	4	28
			½ cup	4 oz.	8	56
			¼ cup	2 oz.	16	
	4	5 ½	1 cup	8 oz.	4	44
			½ cup	4 oz.	8	88
			¼ cup	2 oz.	16	
	6	8	1 cup	8 oz.	4	32
			½ cup	4 oz.	8	64
			¼ cup	2 oz.	16	128
⅙ Pan (7" × 6¼")	2½	1	1 cup	8 oz.	4	4
			½ cup	4 oz.	8	8
			¼ cup	2 oz.	16	16
	4	2	1 cup	8 oz.	4	8
			½ cup	4 oz.	8	16
			¼ cup	2oz.	16	32
	6	2 ½	1 cup	8 oz.	4	10
			½ cup	4 oz.	8	20
			¼ cup	2 oz.	16	40

Glossary

A

à la carte. French expression meaning "from the menu." A type of menu pricing in which each item is listed and assigned its own price. (2)

accounts payable. An operation's unpaid bills. (11)

accounts receivable. Invoices for which an operation is awaiting payment. (11)

Americans with Disabilities Act (ADA). Law that prohibits discrimination against qualified individuals with disabilities in the following areas of employment—job application, hiring, firing, advancement, and pay. (5)

as purchased (AP). Quantity that refers to the amount of a product—expressed in weight or count—that a vendor delivers to a foodservice operation. (3)

asset. Cash or anything that has monetary value. (9)

B

balance sheet. Financial statement that summarizes an operation's assets, liabilities, and shareholders' equity on the date it was issued. (11)

bar code. Code that contains information that can be read with a handheld device and stored electronically. They are used to label boxes, packages, and other objects. (12)

bar-code technology. Technology that uses bar codes. (12)

bar service. Type of beverage service in which beverages are ordered, prepared, and served from the bar. Also called *front service*. (6)

beginning inventory. Amount of inventory at the beginning of an accounting period. Usually the ending inventory figure from the previous month. (6)

benchmarking. Evaluation of the processes of an operation in relation to the operation's own experiences, industry best practices, or standards set by law. (5)

beverage cost percentage. Ratio of the cost of beverages sold to the total beverage sales. (6)

bid. Request for prices for supplies, services, or contracts. (3)

bid method. Purchasing method in which vendors submit bids for items a buyer wishes to purchase, and the buyer awards the business based on the results. (3)

bonding. Process in which employers purchase insurance to protect themselves from financial losses due to the actions of dishonest employees. (10)

bottom line. Income that remains after all expenses, including income taxes, are subtracted from sales. Also called *net income*. (8)

broad-line distributor. Type of distributor that has many clients which it supplies with a wide variety of goods. Also called a *broad-liner*. (3)

BTU (British thermal unit). Quantity of heat required to raise the temperature of one pound of water by 1°F. (7)

budget. Plan for the availability and use of funds to pay for the activities of an organization, a company, or an individual. (8)

bundling. A promotional pricing technique that allows customers to select items from three different menu categories for one set price. (2)

business crime insurance. Insurance that pays policy holders for losses due to crimes such as theft, embezzlement, arson, or forgery. (7)

business interruption insurance. Insurance that pays policy holders for losses that result when an operation is temporarily closed, or can only provide minimal service. (7)

business liability insurance. Insurance that covers claims against an operation that are generally filed as lawsuits. (7)

business property insurance. Insurance that pays policy holders for loss of or damage to assets, including buildings, inventory, and personal property. (7)

C

calibrate. To check, adjust, or compare a product against a standard. (7)

call brand. Spirit that a customer requests by its brand name. (6)

capital assets. Assets that have a useful life beyond one year, such as equipment, fixtures, buildings, and land. (9)

capital budgeting. Process of planning for the expenses of assets that are expected to last longer than one year. (9)

cash bar. Bar at which guests are asked to purchase their own drinks. (6)

cash budget. Budget that projects cash flow—how much money will come in and how much will go out— in the short term. (8)

cash drawer. Compartment underneath a cash register that holds the cash from transactions. (10)

cash outflow. Expenses over the course of the month. (8)

cash skimming. Theft of cash receipts before the receipts are recorded. (10)

cashier's bank. Cashier's own cash bag used with the cash drawer. (10)

collusion. Secret agreement or cooperation between people for purposes that are illegal or deceitful. (3)

combination menu. Menu that incorporates at least two of the other menu types, such as standard, cycle, or market menus. (2)

combination pricing. Type of menu pricing in which some menu items are priced à la carte, while others are priced with a few menu items included. (2)

commissary. Production system in which food is prepared in mass quantities and delivered to various locations for service, using either cook-serve or cook-chill. (4)

common-size analysis. Method of financial analysis in which each line on the financial statement is expressed as a percentage of either total assets or total sales, with the exception of cost of goods sold. (11)

comparative analysis. A method used in the analysis of financial statements to uncover emerging trends. It involves the item-by-item comparison of two or more like items. (11)

comparative balance sheet. A comparative analysis of balance sheets. (11)

comparative statement of income. A comparative analysis of statements of income. (11)

contribution margin. Dollar amount remaining after the variable costs are subtracted from the selling price. (2)

controllable expense. Expense over which a manager has direct influence. (6)

controllable income. Revenue that remains after all controllable expenses have been paid. (8)

controlling. Process of monitoring the performance of an operation against its plans, accomplished by setting measurable goals, measuring the results, and comparing those results against the goals. (1)

convenience item. A food that has been processed to some extent, which decreases preparation time. (3)

cook-chill system. Production system in which food is prepared on the premises, quickly cooled to a safe temperature, then packaged and refrigerated. (4)

cook-serve system. Production system in which food is prepared from the raw state and served with minimal delay or hold time between preparation and presentation. (4)

cost. Dollar amount spent to create the good or service being sold. Also called *expense*. (1)

cost control. Process an operation uses to ensure that its forecasted sales and expenses conform to its plans, goals, and objectives. (1)

cost of sales. Dollars that were spent for the food, beverages, and merchandise that were sold to customers. (8)

cost-plus price. Price that is the total of the product's cost to the vendor plus a certain markup. (3)

count sheet. Document a manager uses to keep track of inventory. (6)

cover. Industry term for a customer. (5)

covers per labor hour. Number of customers served per labor hour worked. (5)

current assets. A company's short-term assets, including cash, inventory on hand, accounts receivable, and any prepaid expenses. (11)

current liabilities. Debts that need to be paid within one year. (11)

cycle menu. Menu that repeats itself on a predetermined schedule. (2)

D

daypart. A specific meal period. (2)

decimal. Number representing a fraction based on the number 10. (1)

deposit in transit. Cash a company has received and reported on its balance sheet, but which has not yet appeared on a bank statement due to a normal processing lag. (10)

deposit lapping. Method of theft concealment in which the deposit from Day 1 is stolen and replaced with the deposit from Day 2, and so forth. (10)

depreciation. Accounting method that is used to distribute the cost of an asset—minus its salvage value—over its anticipated useful life. (9)

distributor. Entity that has agreements with one or more companies that allow it to offer and sell their products. (3)

dogs. Term used in menu engineering referring to menu items that are not popular or profitable. (2)

dramshop. Bar, tavern, or a similar operation where alcoholic beverages are sold. (6)

dramshop liability. Laws that establish the responsibilities of commercial establishments that serve alcoholic beverages. (6)

E

early-bird specials. A promotional pricing technique that encourages customers to arrive before the busier, traditional meal time. (2)

edible portion (EP). Quantity that refers to the actual yield from a particular meat or produce item after cooking and trimming. (3)

electronic funds transfer (EFT). Transfer of funds from one account to another, or from one financial institution to another, via an electronic or computer-based exchange. (12)

employee turnover rate. Speed with which employees leave an organization and are replaced. (5)

ending inventory. Amount of inventory at the end of an accounting period. (6)

ENERGY STAR. Government program that rates the energy efficiency of products and provides guidance in energy conservation practices. (7)

enterprise software systems. Business-oriented software systems designed for multiunit operations or chains. (12)

equipment justification. Process in which a manager recommends one equipment-purchasing option over another. Also called *project justification.* (9)

equity. A company's total assets minus its total liabilities. Also called *net worth.* (11)

even pricing. A pricing technique in which a menu item is assigned a price that ends in zero to create the illusion that it is of higher quality. (2)

expense. Dollar amount spent to create the good or service being sold. Also called *cost.* (1)

F

facilities management. Process of monitoring and controlling costs related to the building, equipment, and utilities. Also called *maintenance.* (7)

factor system. A menu-pricing method in which the selling price is based on the desired fraction of the price that the food cost represents. Also called the *food cost percentage method.* (2)

Federal Insurance Contributions Act (FICA). Payroll tax imposed by the federal government that is used to fund the Medicare and Social Security programs. (5)

financial analysis. Process of using financial data to monitor and evaluate an operation's performance, profitability, financing needs, and future growth. (11)

financial statements. Written reports that use quantitative data to provide insight into a company's financial health and describe changes in its performance. (11)

first in, first out (FIFO). Storage method in which inventory is rotated as it is put away to ensure that the oldest products are used first. (3)

fiscal year. A 12-month accounting period that may or may not coincide with the calendar year. (8)

fixed assets. Long-term assets that are not used up or sold during the normal course of business, including land, buildings, furniture, equipment, and any improvements made to an operation's building or grounds. (11)

fixed budget. Budget that bases the amounts of line items on a static level of business activity. (8)

fixed costs. Expenses that do not change in proportion to the activity of a business. (2)

fixed price. Price that remains the same for a stated period of time. (3)

flexible budget. Budget that bases the amounts of line items on a range of business activity levels. (8)

food cost percentage. The part or percentage of food sales spent on food expenses. (1)

food cost percentage method. A menu-pricing method in which the selling price is based on the desired fraction of the price that the food cost represents. Also called the *factor system*. (2)

food production. Process of converting purchased foods into finished menu items to serve to the customer. (4)

foodborne illness. Disease caused by consuming food contaminated with biological, chemical, or physical hazards. (4)

forecasting. Use of historical data to predict future trends, including future sales. (3)

fraction. Number that represents a part of a whole. Made up of a numerator (the top number) and a denominator (the bottom number). (1)

front service. Type of beverage service in which beverages are ordered, prepared, and served from the bar. Also called *bar service*. (6)

full-time equivalent (FTE). Ratio of the total number of paid hours in a given period divided by the total number of full-time hours worked. (12)

G

Global Trade Item Number (GTIN). Unique number assigned to a product or service that is used by all industries and information systems within a supply chain. (12)

grade. Quality level of a product. (3)

group purchasing organization (GPO). Company that leverages the purchasing power of a group of businesses to obtain discounts from vendors. (3)

guest service. Type of nonalcoholic beverage service in which guests dispense their own drinks at beverage stations. (6)

I

income statement. Financial statement that measures the financial performance of an operation over a specific period of time. Also called *statement of income* or *profit and loss (P&L) statement*. (11)

Information Technology (IT). Technology that involves the development, implementation, and support of computer-based information. (12)

ingredient room. Area in the kitchen where employees weigh and measure all of the ingredients for the recipes to be produced that day or the next. (4)

ingredient room system. Production system in which food is prepared in the ingredient room. (4)

insurance. Financial arrangement that protects individuals or businesses against financial loss. (7)

intentional revenue deviation. Theft or pilferage by an employee or a patron. Also called *intentional revenue loss*. (10)

intentional revenue loss. Theft or pilferage by an employee or a patron. Also called *intentional revenue deviation*. (10)

inventory turnover. Number of times an operation's inventory has been sold and replaced in a given period of time. Measures the effectiveness of inventory management. Also called *inventory turn*. (3)

J

job analysis. Process of conducting a detailed study of the responsibilities and requirements of a job in order to improve the performance of the operation and its workers. (5)

job description. Description that lists the requirements and essential functions of a position. (5)

job routine. Tasks an employee is to complete and the time at which each task should be started and completed. (5)

K

kitchenless system. Production system in which food is purchased in a prepared state from an outside source. (4)

L

labor cost analysis. Process of using a variety of ratios, or productivity indices, pertaining to labor, to determine how efficiently an operation is running. (5)

labor cost per cover. Total labor cost during a period of time divided by the number of covers for the same time period. (5)

labor cost per labor hour. Total labor cost divided by the total labor hours used. (5)

labor cost per meal. Total labor cost divided by the number of meals served during a given period of time. (5)

labor cost percentage. Percentage calculated by dividing the total labor cost by the total sales in a given time period. (5)

leading. Process of directing people to meet the goals and objectives set in the planning phase. The third function of management. (1)

leftover management. Processes an operation uses to minimize the amount of leftovers and to creatively utilize leftovers that remain. (4)

lessor. Owner of an asset who is paid a set rental rate over the life of the lease by the lessee. (9)

liability. Debt or obligation owed by an operation that is settled by the transfer of goods, services, or cash. (11)

limited liability corporation (LLC). Legal entity that limits a business owner's liability should the company fail or suffer a financial setback. (7)

long-term debt. Debt that is owed minus what was accounted for under current liabilities. Also called *noncurrent liabilities*. (11)

loss. Amount incurred when the expenses of an operation are greater than its sales. (1)

M

maintenance. Process of monitoring and controlling costs related to the building, equipment, and utilities. Also called *facilities management*. (7)

make-or-buy analysis. Analysis in which the cost of using a value-added product is compared with the cost of purchasing the ingredients and making it from scratch. (3)

management information system. Refers to the people, technology, and procedures used to solve business problems. (12)

market menu. Menu that may change routinely—even daily—to take advantage of what is seasonally available. (2)

market value. The amount a customer would be willing to pay for an item based on what other operations are charging. (2)

meals per productive labor hour. Number of meals served divided by the number of productive hours worked in a given period of time. (5)

menu engineering. Process used to grow sales and profits that separates menu items into four classes (stars, plow horses, puzzles, and dogs) based on their popularity and profitability. (2)

menu. List of the food and beverage items offered in an establishment. (2)

minimum wage. The lowest wage an employer can pay an employee. Set by federal and state governments. (5)

multivendor method. Purchasing method in which buyers purchase items from a variety of vendors, usually by product type. (3)

mystery shopper. Person hired to impersonate a shopper at a business or an operation. (10)

N

net income. Income that remains after all expenses, including income taxes, are subtracted from sales. Also called the *bottom line*. (8)

net worth. A company's total assets minus its total liabilities. Also called *equity*. (11)

noncontrollable expense. Expense outside the manager's sphere of influence. (6)

noncurrent liabilities. Debt that is owed minus what was accounted for under current liabilities. Also called *long-term debt*. (11)

O

odd pricing. A pricing technique in which a menu item is priced just below an even-dollar amount to create the illusion that it costs less. (2)

one-stop-shopping method. Purchasing method in which an operation negotiates and contracts with a broad-line supplier for the majority of the items it needs. Also called the *prime-vendor method*. (3)

operating budget. Financial plan that includes projections of sales, expenses, and profit for a period of time. (8)

operating ratios. Ratios that use data from the income statement to assess how well costs are controlled and how efficiently a business is run. (11)

organizational chart. Diagram that illustrates the structure of an organization in terms of the relationships and relative rank of its employees. (5)

organizing. Process of deciding what tasks need to be completed, who will perform those tasks, and how the tasks will be coordinated. The second function of management. (1)

P

par level. Level at which more of a product should be ordered. Also called *par stock.* (3)

par stock. Level at which more of a product should be ordered. Also called *par level.* (3)

payback period. Amount of time it will take to recover the cost of a capital purchase. (9)

payroll. Payments an operation makes to employees in exchange for their labor or services. (5)

per centum. Per hundred. (1)

percent. Number expressing a part of the whole. (1)

performance appraisal. Process by which a manager and employee review the employee's work performance to determine if it meets the requirements of the position. (5)

performance report. Statement of an operation's actual numbers or results compared with some standard, such as the budgeted numbers. (8)

perpetual inventory. Inventory process in which the inventory count is updated on a continuous basis. (3)

physical inventory. Inventory process in which employees go into the storage areas and count all items on hand. (3)

pilferage. Intentional stealing from a company by an employee or patron. Also called *theft.* (10)

planning. Process of determining what an operation will be; the first step in setting up a business. (1)

plow horses. Term used in menu engineering to refer to popular menu items that do not make as much money for the operation as some other items. (2)

point-of-sale (POS) system. A computerized system that can be used to take orders, generate bills, track revenue, create reports, manage inventory, facilitate communication between staff members, and other functions. (6)

portion control. Process of ensuring that the amount of food in a serving of a menu item is equivalent to the amount of food specified in the standardized recipe. (4)

position control sheet. Form that lists each position in a foodservice operation, the job classification of each position, the hours the employee holding the position works, and the total hours worked per pay period. (5)

premium liquor. Highest-quality product of a particular type of liquor that an operation stocks. Also called *top-shelf liquor* and *top-tier liquor.* (6)

presentation. Act of plating and serving menu items to the customer. (4)

preventive maintenance. Periodic inspections of equipment and building areas to ensure that they continue to operate efficiently. (7)

pricing program. Program that outlines what a vendor agrees to charge for various items over the course of the agreement. (3)

prime vendor. Supplier who negotiates with an operation in the prime-vendor method. (3)

prime-vendor method. Purchasing method in which an operation negotiates and contracts with a broad-line supplier for the majority of the items it needs. Also called the *one-stop-shopping method.* (3)

product cutting. Practice in which a vendor brings in the items per the buyer's specifications for evaluation. (3)

product maximization. Processes that enable an operation to gain the largest possible yield (edible portion) from a food item. (4)

product yield. Amount of a product that is usable after trimming, cooking, or other processing. (1)

product yield percentage. Percentage used by buyers to calculate the AP quantity that must be purchased to obtain the needed EP quantity. Also called *yield conversion* or a *yield factor.* (3)

production sheet. Form used to communicate to production staff that lists the types and amounts of food items to produce for each meal. (4)

production system. Type of operation that is used to produce the menu. (4)

profit. Dollar amount remaining after all expenses have been paid. (1)

profitability ratios. Ratios that are used to determine whether or not an operation is making a profit in comparison to its expenses. (11)

profit and loss (P&L) statement. Financial statement that measures the financial performance of an operation over a specific period of time. Also called *statement of income* or *income statement.* (11)

profit margin. Common ratio that measures how much a business earns out of every dollar it collects in sales. (11)

project justification. Process in which a manager recommends one equipment-purchasing option over another. Also called *equipment justification.* (9)

promotional pricing. Pricing technique that temporarily offers menu items at discounted prices. (2)

puzzles. A term used in menu engineering to refer to menu items that have a good profit margin, but are infrequently selected by customers. (2)

Q

quality measure. A means to rate the level of perceived value placed on the parameter being evaluated. (1)

R

radio frequency identification device (RFID). Device that reads information from a tag or a bar code and transmits it to a computer wirelessly and in real time. (12)

ratio. Expression showing how one number relates, or compares, to another. Usually in the form of *X:Y* or *X to Y*. (1)

ratio analysis. Method of financial analysis in which ratios are used to determine how well an operation is performing financially. (11)

recruiting. Process of locating applicants for a job opening. (5)

retention. Ability of an organization to keep its employees. (5)

revenue. The result from the exchange of goods or services for payment or promise to pay. Also called *sales*. (1)

revenue control. Management function of measuring whether expected revenue is equal to actual revenue, or the revenue an operation recorded it received. (10)

risk management. Process of analyzing exposure to risk and deciding how to best handle such exposure. (7)

routine-order method. Ordering method in which the buyer tends to buy the same items week after week from the same vendor(s). (3)

S

salary. Fixed payments that some employees, including managers, receive on a regular basis. (5)

sales. The result from the exchange of goods or services for payment or promise to pay. Also called *revenue*. (1)

sales mix. Purchasing decisions made by customers that determine the beverage cost percentage. (6)

scenario management. Type of financial management software that allows the manager to create and test various scenarios to see the impact a decision may have on an operation. (12)

scheduling. Process of assigning employees to specific working hours and workdays. (5)

screening interview. Interview conducted to determine if an applicant meets the basic qualifications for a position. (5)

semi-variable costs. Costs that have elements of both fixed and variable costs. (2)

separation of duties. Process in which different employees are given responsibility for different steps in the cash-handling process. (10)

server service. Type of beverage service in which drinks ordered by customers are prepared and served by the waitstaff. (6)

server's bank. Server's cash bag used with the cash drawer. (10)

special-purpose service. Type of beverage service used to supply beverages to guests during events, such as receptions and banquets. Often require a portable or temporary bar setup. (6)

specification. Written description of the requirements a product must have to be considered for purchase. (3)

spreadsheet method. Purchasing method in which buyers obtain quotes, or bids, from a variety of suppliers for every item to be purchased and enters them into spreadsheets. Also called the *weekly bid method*. (3)

standard menu. Menu that offers the same items every day. (2)

standardized recipe. Set of instructions to produce a consistent food product, including the amounts of the ingredients used and the preparation method necessary. (4)

stars. Term used in menu engineering to refer to menu items that are highly popular with customers and generate high profit margins. (2)

statement of cash flows (SCF). Financial statement that summarizes the actual or anticipated movement of cash into and out of an operation over a particular period of time. (11)

statement of income. Financial statement that measures the financial performance of an operation over a specific period of time. Also called *income statement* or *profit and loss (P&L) statement*. (11)

straight-line depreciation. A basic method used to depreciate an asset over its useful life. (9)

strategic planning process. Process an organization uses to assess where it is at, where it wants to go, and how it can determine its future direction. (9)

supplier. Entity that supplies goods or services to companies or consumers. Also called *vendor*. (3)

supply chain. Coordinated system that moves products or services from the source to the customer. (3)

system integration. Merging of various individual software programs used in an operation into a single system. (12)

T

table d'hôte. French expression meaning "host's table." A type of menu pricing that offers complete meals for a fixed price. (2)

theft. Act of taking property, such as food, that does not belong to the person taking it. Also called *pilferage*. (3)

therm. Unit of measurement for natural gas. (7)

tip. Form of income received by many foodservice workers, especially those who work in operations that provide table service. It is paid by customers. (5)

top-shelf liquor. Highest-quality product of a particular type of liquor that an operation stocks. Also called *premium liquor* and *top-tier liquor*. (6)

top-tier liquor. Highest-quality product of a particular type of liquor that an operation stocks. Also called *top-shelf liquor* and *premium liquor*. (6)

trend analysis. Analysis of various operating data and ratios to assess patterns over a period of time. (11)

Truth-in-Menu laws. Laws that require a menu description to accurately state the type, form, style, amount, method of preparation, and content of the menu item. (2)

2.5-times price spread. A pricing technique in which the most expensive item is not more than 2.5 times the cost of the least-expensive item. (2)

U

unintentional revenue deviation. Loss caused by an employee error, or by a malfunction of the cash register or POS system. Also called *unintentional revenue loss*. (10)

unintentional revenue loss. Loss caused by an employee error, or by a malfunction of the cash register or POS system. Also called *unintentional revenue deviation*. (10)

usage method. Approach to determining the amount of a product to order. (3)

utility cost control. Process of managing and controlling the costs related to utility usage. (6)

V

value analysis. Process that measures how well an item performs its job relative to its cost. (3)

value-added products. Convenience items that are used to save labor. (3)

variable costs. Expenses that increase or decrease as the activity of a business increases or decreases. (2)

variance. Difference between a budgeted amount and an actual amount. (1)

vendor. Entity that supplies goods or services to companies or consumers. Also called *supplier*. (3)

virtual private network (VPN). Network created by an operation that uses public communications infrastructure, such as the Internet, to provide access to the network remotely. (12)

W

wage. Payment for work that is usually computed on an hourly basis. (5)

waste management. Processes that enable an operation to minimize the amount of product left over. (4)

weekly bid method. Purchasing method in which buyers obtain quotes, or bids, from a variety of suppliers for every item to be purchased and enters them into spreadsheets. Also called the *spreadsheet method*. (3)

well brand. Lesser-quality brand of liquor. (6)

work simplification study. Process in which managers analyze how jobs are being done with the goal of finding easier ways to complete them. (5)

Y

yield conversion. Percentage used by buyers to calculate the AP quantity that must be purchased to obtain the needed EP quantity. Also called *product yield percentage* or *yield factor*. (3)

yield factor. Percentage used by buyers to calculate the AP quantity that must be purchased to obtain the needed EP quantity. Also called *product yield percentage* or *yield conversion*. (3)

Z

zero-based scheduling. The preparation of a unique schedule each week rather than using the same schedule from week to week. (5)

Bibliography

Chapter 1

Elan, Elissa. "Vermont recycling law could affect future sustainability laws," National Restaurant Association (blog). June 27, 2012.

First, Devra. "Cheapsteak." *The Boston Globe*, November 12, 2008.

Grossbauer, Sue. *The Master Track Series for Dietary Managers: Foodservice Math.* St. Charles, IL: Association of Nutrition & Foodservice Professionals, 2007.

Keiser, James, Frederick J. DeMicco, Cihan Cobanoglu, and Robert N. Grimes. *Analyzing and Controlling Foodservice Costs: A Managerial and Technological Approach,* 5th ed. Upper Saddle River, NJ: Prentice Hall, 2008.

Lewis, Pamela S., Stephen H. Goodman, Patricia M. Fandt, and Joseph F. Michlitsch. *Management: Challenges for Tomorrow's Leaders,* 5th ed. Mason, OH: Thompson/ South-Western, 2007.

Reynolds, Johnny Sue. *Hospitality Services: Food & Lodging,* 2nd ed. Tinley Park, IL: Goodheart-Willcox Publisher, 2010.

Sealed Air Corporation, "Sealed Air's Vision Enabled Training (VET) Solution Receives Kitchen Innovation Award from National Restaurant Association," press release, February 16, 2012.

U.S. Small Business Administration. http://www.sba.gov/

US Composting Council. "Mandatory Organics Recycling to Become Law in Vermont," July 7, 2012.

Chapter 2

"Appetizing Dining Program," *Food Management*, March 1, 2012.

County of Riverside Health Services Agency, Department of Environmental Health. "Storm Water Pollution: What You Should Know for the Food Service Industry."

Gregoire, Mary B. *Foodservice Organizations: A Managerial and Systems Approach,* 7th ed. Upper Saddle River, NJ: Prentice Hall, 2010.

Kotschevar, Lendal H., and Diane Withrow. *Management by Menu,* 4th ed. Hoboken, NJ: John Wiley & Sons, Inc., 2008.

National Restaurant Association Educational Foundation. *Controlling Foodservice Costs: Competency Guide.* Upper Saddle River, NJ: Prentice Hall, 2007.

The Food Allergy & Anaphylaxis Network. "Welcoming Guests with Food Allergies."

U.S. Food and Drug Administration. "New Menu and Vending Machines Labeling Requirements."

U.S. Food and Drug Administration. "Overview of FDA Proposed Labeling Requirements for Restaurants, Similar Retail Food Establishments and Vending Machines."

Chapter 3

Chefs Collaborative. "Five Tips for Managing Food Costs When Running a Sustainable Kitchen." October, 2009.

Gregoire, Mary B. *Foodservice Organizations: A Managerial and Systems Approach*, 7th ed. Upper Saddle River, NJ: Prentice Hall, 2010.

Holcomb, Rodney and Anh Vo, "Farm-To-School Templates: Tools for Participating Producers and Schools," Accessed April 23, 2012.

Keiser, James, Frederick J. DeMicco, Cihan Cobanoglu, and Robert N. Grimes. *Analyzing and Controlling Foodservice Costs: A Managerial and Technological Approach*, 5th ed. Upper Saddle River, NJ: Prentice Hall, 2008.

Kotschevar, Lendal H., and Richard Donnelly. *Quantity Food Purchasing*, 5th ed. Hoboken, NJ: Prentice Hall, 1999.

"National Restaurant Association member tells Congress of real impact of new health care law on business," National Restaurant Association (blog), March 30, 2011.

Schoenfeld, Bruce, "How the Farm-To-Table Movement Is Helping Grow the Economy," *Entrepreneur*, September 21, 2011.

Chapter 4

Centers for Disease Control and Prevention. "CDC Estimates of Foodborne Illness in the United States."

Garden-Robinson, Julie. "Food Safety Basics: A Reference Guide for Foodservice Operators," January, 2012.

Gregoire, Mary B. *Foodservice Organizations: A Managerial and Systems Approach*, 7th ed. Upper Saddle River, NJ: Prentice Hall, 2010.

Keiser, James, Frederick J. DeMicco, Cihan Cobanoglu, and Robert N. Grimes. *Analyzing and Controlling Foodservice Costs: A Managerial and Technological Approach*, 5th ed. Upper Saddle River, NJ: Prentice Hall, 2008.

Kotschevar, Lendal H., and Richard Donnelly. *Quantity Food Purchasing*. 5th ed. Hoboken, NJ: Prentice Hall, 1999.

U.S. Environmental Protection Agency. "Putting Surplus Food to Good Use," February 2012.

Weisberg, Karen, "Keep On Truckin'," *Food Management*, January 1, 2012.

Chapter 5

Berta, Dina, "Web-based Programs Take the Pain Out of Shift Scheduling," *Nation's Restaurant News*, July 20, 2008.

Collins, Jim. *Good To Great: Why Some Companies Make the Leap and Others Don't.* New York: HarperCollins Publishers Inc., 2001.

Dietetics in Health Care Communities. *Pocket Resource for Management.* Chicago: Academy of Nutrition and Dietetics, 2011.

Keiser, James, Frederick J. DeMicco, Cihan Cobanoglu, and Robert N. Grimes. *Analyzing and Controlling Foodservice Costs: A Managerial and Technological Approach*, 5th ed. Upper Saddle River, NJ: Prentice Hall, 2008.

Mills, Linda S. Eck, "Interviewing Prospective Employees," *Dietary Manager*, January 2007, 18-21.

Occupational Safety & Health Administration. "Youth Worker Safety in Restaurants eTool." http://www.osha.gov/SLTC/youth/restaurant/index.html/

Powers, Vicki, "Maximize Workforce Efficiency," *Hospitality Technology*, June 10, 2011.

Reynolds, Johnny Sue. *Hospitality Services: Food & Lodging*, 2nd ed. Tinley Park. IL: Goodheart-Willcox Publisher, 2010.

Ruggless, Ron, "People Report: Best Practices Winners Share HR Tips," *Nation's Restaurant News*, November 3, 2011.

U.S. Bureau of Labor Statistics. "Food Services and Drinking Places: NAICS 722." http://www.bls.gov/iag/tgs/iag722.htm/

Chapter 6

Bouckley, Ben, "New UK Wine Carton Can Win Over Fine Wine Producers, Tetra Pak," *Beverage Daily*, May 23, 2012.

Coleman, Tyler, "Box Wines That Can Be a Hit," *Forbes*, July 16, 2009.

Dittmer, Paul R. and Desmond J. Keefe. "Beverage Purchasing Control." Chapter 13 in *Principles of Food, Beverage, and Labor Cost Controls*, 9th ed. Hoboken, NJ: John Wiley & Sons, Inc., 2009.

Keiser, James, Frederick J. DeMicco, Cihan Cobanoglu, and Robert N. Grimes. *Analyzing and Controlling Foodservice Costs: A Managerial and Technological Approach*, 5th ed. Upper Saddle River, NJ: Prentice Hall, 2008.

Laube, J., and Barry K. Shuster, Eds. *The Uniform System of Accounts for Restaurants*, 8th ed. Washington, DC: National Restaurant Association, 2012.

Maran Graphics Development Group. *Wine*. Boston: Thompson Course Technology PTR, 2006.

Scotsman Industries, "Frank Announces Partnership with Scotsman Industries to Introduce Exciting New Ice Machine Sanitation Technology," news release, May 4, 2012.

ServSafe. "ServSafe Alcohol ® Training and Certification." http://www/servsafe/com/alcohol/training-and-certification/

Wolf, Barney, "From the Floor: Providers Seeing Green," *QSR*, May 8, 2012.

Chapter 7

Foodservice Technology Center. "Water Leaks." Accessed April 11, 2012. http://www.fishnick.com/saveenergy/energytips/waterleaks/

Keiser, James, Frederick J. DeMicco, Cihan Cobanoglu, and Robert N. Grimes. *Analyzing and Controlling Foodservice Costs: A Managerial and Technological Approach*, 5th ed. Upper Saddle River, NJ: Prentice Hall, 2008.

New York State Energy Research and Development Authority. http://www.nyserda.ny.gov/

Reynolds, Johnny Sue. *Hospitality Services: Food & Lodging*, 2nd ed. Tinley Park, IL: Goodheart-Willcox Publisher, 2010.

"Saving money: Focus on energy, water, waste," National Restaurant Association (blog), June 10, 2011.

Smart Energy Design Assistance Center. "Energy Smart Tips for Restaurants from the Illinois Smart Energy Design Assistance Center," May, 2011.

U.S. Department of Energy, "Database of State Incentives for Renewables & Efficiency." http://www.dsireusa.org/

U.S. Environmental Protection Agency. "ENERGY STAR Benchmarking Starter Kit," accessed April 11, 2012.

U.S. Environmental Protection Agency. "ENERGY STAR Guide for Restaurants Putting Energy into Profit," January 2012.

U.S. Environmental Protection Agency. "ENERGY STAR Rebate Finder." http://www.energystar.gov/index.cfm?fuseaction=rebate.rebate_locator/

U.S. Environmental Protection Agency. "How to Achieve the Most Efficient Use of Water in Commercial Food Service." http://www.energystar.gov/index.cm?c=heathcare.fisher_nickel_feb_2005/

U.S. Global Change Research Program. "Energy Supply and Use." http://globalchange.gov/images/cir/pdf/energy.pdf/

"Water Conservation Rebate Programs," accessed July 6, 2012. http://www.watersavinghero.com/rebate-program.html/

Wesler, Cathy A., Ed. *The Complete Cooking Light Cookbook*. Birmingham, AL: Oxmoor House, Inc., 2000.

Chapter 8

Keiser, James, Frederick J. DeMicco, Cihan Cobanoglu, and Robert N. Grimes. *Analyzing and Controlling Foodservice Costs: A Managerial and Technological Approach*, 5th ed. Upper Saddle River, NJ: Prentice Hall, 2008.

POS Nation. "Point of Sale Systems," Accessed June 12, 2012. http://posnation.com/articles/point-of-sale-systems-articles.php/

Richards, Lynn M. *Measure It, Manage It: Laying the Foundations for Benchmarking in Health Care Foodservice Operations*. Chicago: American Dietetic Association (now known as Academy of Nutrition and Dietetics), 1997.

The Federal Reserve. *Beige Book*. http://www.federalreserve.gov/monetarypolicy/beigebook/default.htm/

U.S. Environmental Protection Agency. "Food Waste Calculator." http://www.epa.gov/wastes/conserve/materials/organics/food/tools/

Chapter 9

Higgins, Michelle, "For Americans, Plastic Buys Less Abroad," *New York Times*, September 29, 2009.

Keiser, James, Frederick J. DeMicco, Cihan Cobanoglu, and Robert N. Grimes. *Analyzing and Controlling Foodservice Costs: A Managerial and Technological Approach*, 5th ed. Upper Saddle River, NJ: Prentice Hall, 2008.

Mastroberte, Tammy, "Smart Cards Usher in Future of Payment in the U.S.," *Hospitality Technology*, April, 5, 2012.

Peterson, Pamela P. and Frank J. Fabozzi. *Capital Budgeting: Theory and Practice*. New York: John Wiley & Sons, Inc., 2002.

US Department of Treasury Internal Revenue Service, Publication 946. Accessed June 6, 2012, http://www.irs.gov/publications/p946/index.html/

U.S. Green Building Council. "LEED 2009 for Retail: New Construction and Major Renovations."

Chapter 10

Collins, Michelle, "Bonding: Protect Yourself from Employee Theft," *CanadaOne*, January 2002.

Gillum, Blake, "4 Easy Ways Your POS System Can Go Green and Save You Green," DCR Profit Control Systems (blog).

Federal Trade Commission. "Protecting Personal Information: A Guide for Business." November, 2011. http://www.business.ftc.gov/sites/default/files/pdf/bus69-protecting-personal-information-guide-business_0.pdf/

Keiser, James, Frederick J. DeMicco, Cihan Cobanoglu, and Robert N. Grimes. *Analyzing and Controlling Foodservice Costs: A Managerial and Technological Approach*, 5th ed. Upper Saddle River, NJ: Prentice Hall, 2008.

"Trustwave 2012 Global Security Report," Accessed June 14, 2012.

"Intrusion Investigation," press release, May 14, 2008. http://www.secretservice.gov/press/GPA15-08_CyberIndictments_Final.pdf/

Chapter 11

"Food and Beverage Serving and Related Workers," *Occupational Outlook Handbook*, March 29, 2012.

Keiser, James, Frederick J. DeMicco, Cihan Cobanoglu, and Robert N. Grimes. *Analyzing and Controlling Foodservice Costs: A Managerial and Technological Approach*, 5th ed. Upper Saddle River, NJ: Prentice Hall, 2008.

Laube, J., and Barry K. Shuster, Eds. *The Uniform System of Accounts for Restaurants*, 8th ed. Washington, DC: National Restaurant Association, 2012.

National Restaurant Association, "New Research Helps Restauranteurs Optimize Operational Performance, "news release, June 22, 2010. http://www.restaurant.org/pressroom/pressrelease/?id=1971/

Richards, Lynn M. *Measure It, Manage It: Laying the Foundations for Benchmarking in Health Care Foodservice Operations*. Chicago: American Dietetic Association (now known as Academy of Nutrition and Dietetics), 1997.

Stennson, Annika, "Restaurant Industry Outlook Remains Positive as Restaurant Performance Index Stood above 100 for 6th Consecutive Month," news release, May 31, 2012.

The Foodservice Technology Center. http://www.fishnick.com/

U.S. Bureau of Labor Statistics. "Food Services and Drinking Places: NAICS 722." http://www.bls.gov/iag/tgs/iag722.htm/

Chapter 12

Dietetics in Health Care Communities. *Pocket Resource for Management*. Chicago: Academy of Nutrition and Dietetics, 2011.

Keiser, James, Frederick J. DeMicco, Cihan Cobanoglu, and Robert N. Grimes. *Analyzing and Controlling Foodservice Costs: A Managerial and Technological Approach*, 5th ed. Upper Saddle River, NJ: Prentice Hall, 2008.

Melnick, Jordan, "How to Take Advantage of the Cloud," *QSR Magazine*, May 8, 2012.

Peregrin, Tony. "Business Plan 2.0: Putting Technology to Work." *Journal of the American Dietetic Association* (now known as the Journal of the Academy of Nutrition and Dietetics) 108, no. 2 (2008): 212-214.

Pierce, Kathleen, "Technology's Place at the Table," *The Boston Globe*, February 16, 2011.

"The Lean Path Tracker." http://leanpath.com/tracker.shtml/

Weaver Hartman, Ellen, "Today's Technology Rules Restaurant Marketing," November 30, 2011. http://www.restaurantinformer.com/2011/11/todays-technology-rules-restaurant-marketing/

Index

A

à la carte, 22
accounts payable, 218
Affordable Care Act of 2010, 17
alcoholic beverages, 116–130. *See also* beverages
Americans with Disabilities Act (ADA), 89
as purchased (AP), 45
asset, 172
atmosphere, as menu consideration, 16
auditing, 142–143, 202
    random, 202
    utility cost control, 142–143

B

balance sheet, 217–219
    assets, 218
    definition, 217
    equity, 219
    liabilities, 218
banquets and catered events, 205
bar code, 237
bar service, 116
beer, 117–130
benchmarking, 110–111, 143
    definition, 110–111
    beverage cost, 124
    energy usage, 143
    financial ratios, 166
beverage cost percentage, 124–126
beverage cost percentage method, 126
beverages, 116–130
    calculating cost of sold items, 124–126
    classification, 117–118
    inventory, 121–124
    issuing, 121
    pricing, 126–128
        beverage cost percentage method, 126
        contribution margin method, 127
        prime cost method, 127–128

purchasing, 118–120
receiving, 120
serving, 128–130
    dispensing systems, 129
    guest checks, 129
    point-of-sale (POS) systems, 128–129
    responsibilities, 129–130
    standardized glassware, 129
    standardized recipes, 128
storage, 120
types, 116–117
bid, 40
bid method, 40, 42
    advantages and disadvantages, 40
    definition, 42
bonding, 194
brand or message, as menu consideration, 16
British thermal unit (BTU), 137
broad-line distributor, 39
budget
    capital, 172–187
    cash, 160–162
    definition, 151
    fixed and flexible, 162–163
    operating, 151–163 (*see also* operating budget)
    process, 158–160
budgeting process, 158–160
    consider goals, 158
    determine level of costs, 159–160
    establish a time line, 158
    gather data, 158–159
    submit for approval, 160
bundling, 28
business crime insurance, 147
business interruption insurance, 148
business liability insurance, 147
business proprietary insurance, 147

C

calibrate, 140
call brand, 119
capital asset form, 184
capital assets, 172–187
capital budget, 172–187
    assets, 172–173
    definition, 172
    determining need, 173–176
    investigation, 176–181
    justifying the request, 181–184
    pre-planning, 173
    prioritizing requests, 184–185
    purchasing or leasing, 185–187
capital investigation, 176–181
    buying new versus used, 178–180
    calculating depreciation, 180
    requirements, 176–178
    soliciting bids, 180–181
    sources of information, 177–178
careers. *See* labor
cash bar, 117
cash budget, 160–162
cash drawer, 195. *See also* cash handling policies and procedures
cash handling policies and procedures, 194–204
    cash-drawer practices, 195–196
    cashier job duties, 196–199
    deposit practices, 199–200
    monitoring, 202–204
        direct, 202–203
        indirect, 203
    separation of duties, 194
    using a safe, 200
cashier checkout form, 197–199
cashier's bank, 195
cash outflow, 162
cash skimming, 194–195
    definition, 194
    techniques, 195
catered events and banquets, 205
chip-and-PIN technology, 177
climate control, storage, 57–58
collusion, 54
combination menu, 19
combination pricing, 22

commissary, 65–67
    advantages and disadvantages, 67
    definition, 65
common-size analysis, 223
comparative analysis, 220
comparative balance sheet, 220
comparative statement of income, 220
computerized foodservice operations, 234–245
    inventory, 237–239
    labor management, 243
    menu planning and production, 239–242
    office systems and financial
        management, 243–245
    point of sale, 242–243
    purchasing, 235–237
    receiving, 237
contribution margin, 24
contribution margin method, 24, 127
    beverages, 127
    menu planning, 24
controllable expense, 155
controllable income, 156, 214
    definition, 156
    statement of income, 214
controlling, 2
convenience item, 44
cook-chill system, 65–67
    advantages and disadvantages, 67
    definition, 65
cook-serve system, 65–67
    advantages and disadvantages, 67
    definition, 65
corrective-action process, 204
cost, 3
cost analysis for labor, 86–87, 106–110. *See also* financial analysis; labor
cost control
    beverages, 116–130
    calculations as a function, 3–4
    capital budget, 172–187
    definition, 2
    facilities management, 136–148
    financial management, 209–227
    food safety and sanitation, 79
    inventory, 58–60
    labor, 85–111

menu planning, 14–34
operating budget, 151–163
other costs, 80–82
performance report, 164–166
portion control, 72–74
presentation and service, 75–77
production, 65–72
purchasing, 38–51
receiving, 52–55
revenue, 191–205
storage, 55–58
technology, 234–249
waste management, 77–79
cost of sales, 152, 210–212
    definition, 152 (under operating budget)
    statement of income, 210–212
cost-plus price, 42
count sheet, 122–123
cover, 108
covers per labor hour, 108
current assets, 218
current liability, 218
cycle menu, 18

D

Database of State Incentives for Renewables &
    Efficiency (DSIRE), 141
daypart, 19
decimal, 5
deposit in transit, 200
deposit lapping, 200
deposit practices, 199–200, 202
depreciation, 157, 180–181
    definition, 180
    operating budget, 157
    calculating, 180
    IRS, 181
    straight-line, 180
dispensing systems, beverages, 129
distributor, 39
dogs, 33–34
dramshop, 130
dramshop liability, 130

E

early-bird special, 29
edible portion (EP), 45
electronic funds transfer (EFT), 245
employee. *See* employment; labor
employee benefits, 87
employee turnover rate, 95–96
employment. *See also* labor
    analyzing and benchmarking results, 110–111
    bonding, 194
    calculating labor requirement of a position, 101
    cost analysis, 106–110
    determining needs, 86, 96–101
    factors affecting, 97
    interviewing, 90–91
    job analysis, 96
    job application, 89–90
    job description, 88–89
    job routines, 96–98
    limits of labor analysis, 111
    organizational chart, 100
    orientation and training, 91–93
    payroll, benefits, and taxes, 86–87
    performance appraisal, 94
    position control sheets, 100–101
    recruiting, 89
    retention, 94–96
    scheduling, 101–106
    selecting and retaining staff, 88–96
    supervision, 94
    theft, 193–194
    work simplification study, 98–100
EMV, 177
ENERGY STAR, 122, 138–142
energy types, 137–138
enterprise software systems, 245–246
Environmental Protection Agency (EPA), 78
equipment. *See also* capital budget
    as menu consideration, 15
    receiving, 52
    technology, 246–247
    utility cost control, 139–140
equipment justification, 181
equity, 219
even pricing, 28

expenses, 155–157, 163
   controllable, 155–156
   fixed, 163
   interest, 157
   noncontrollable, 156–157
   other, 157
   semi-variable, 163
   types, 163
   variable, 163

F

FAAN, 31
facilities management, 136–148
   definition, 136
   preventive maintenance programs, 143–145
   risk management, 145–148
      avoidance, 147
      loss control, 147
      minimizing risk exposure, 146
      retention, 147
      steps, 145–146
      transfer, 147–148
   utility cost control, 136–143
      energy types, 137–138
      equipment, 139–140
      food production methods, 140
      heating, venting, and air conditioning (HVAC), 142
      hoods and vents, 140–141
      lighting, 141
      refrigeration, 140
      water usage, 141–142
factor system, 22–23, 126
Fair Labor Standards Act (FLSA), 87
Federal Insurance Contributions Act (FICA), 87
Federal Trade Commission (FTC), 203
FICA, 87
FIFO, 56
financial analysis, 220–227
   comparative, 220–223
   definition, 220
   profitability, 226–227
   ratio, 223–227

financial management, 207–227
   analysis, 220–227
   computerized, 244
   statements, 209–216
   trend analysis, 227
financial ratios, 166
financial statements, 209–219. *See also* forms
   balance sheet, 217–219
   definition, 209
   income, 209–216
   statement of cash flows (SCF), 219–220
first in, first out (FIFO), 56
fiscal year, 152
fixed assets, 218
fixed budget, 162–163
fixed costs, 24
fixed price, 42
flexible budget, 162–163
FLSA, 87
food allergies, 31
Food Allergy & Anaphylaxis Network (FAAN), 31
Food and Drug Administration (FDA), 17
foodborne illness, 79
food cost percentage method, 22–23
food production, 65–72, 140. *See also* production
   as utility cost control, 140
   definition, 65
food safety, as cost control measure, 79
foodservice applications, 5–11
   comparing product prices, 6–8
   food or labor cost per meal served, 8
   quality measures, 10–11
   ratios, 6
   selling price, 6
   variance calculations, 9
forecasting, 47
forms, 51, 184, 197–199. *See also* financial statements
   capital asset 184
   cashier checkout, 197–199
   requisition, 51
fractions, 4
fraud, 201
front service, 116
full-time equivalent (FTE), 243

G

glassware, 129
Global Standards One (GS1), 237
Global Trade Item Number® (GTIN®), 237
grade, 44
group purchasing organization (GPO), 43
guest checks, 129, 201
    beverages, 129
    fraud, 201
guest service, 117

H

hackers, 193
heating, venting, and air conditioning (HVAC), 142
hire purchase, 186
hiring staff, 88–96. *See also* employment; labor
hoods and vents, 140–141

I

income, 156–158, 209–216
    before taxes, 158
    controllable, 156
    operating, 157
    other, 157
    statement, 209–216
information technology (IT), 234
ingredient room, 66–67
    advantages and disadvantages, 67
    definition, 66
insurance, 147–148, 194
    bonding, 194
    business crime, 148
    business interruption, 148
    business liability, 147
    business proprietary, 147
    definition, 147
intentional revenue, 191
interviewing, 90–91
inventory control, 58–60, 121–124
    beverages, 121–124
    calculating cost of food sold, 59–60
    perpetual, 59
    physical, 58
    turnover, 60

inventory technology, 237–239
inventory turnover, 60
issuing, beverages, 121
IT, 234

J

job analysis, 96
job application, 89–90
job description, 88–89
job routines, 96–98
jobs. *See* employment; labor

K

kitchen layout, as menu consideration, 15
kitchenless system, 66–67
    advantages and disadvantages, 67
    definition, 66

L

labeling, storage, 56
labor, 85–111
    analysis limits, 111
    analyzing and benchmarking results, 110–111
    bonding, 194
    cost analysis, 106–110
        covers per labor hour, 108
        labor cost per cover, 108
        labor cost per labor hour, 109
        labor cost per meal, 108–109
        labor cost percentage, 107
        meals per productive labor hour, 109–110
    determining needs, 86, 96–101
        calculating labor requirement of a position, 101
        factors affecting, 97
        job analysis, 96
        job routines, 96–98
        organizational chart, 100
        position control sheets, 100–101
        work simplification study, 98–100
    menu planning, 15
    operating budget, 154
    payroll, benefits, and taxes, 86–87

P

par levels, 47, 120
par stock, 47
payback period, 183
payroll, 86–87
    definition, 86
    taxes, 87
percent total sales, statement of income, 216
performance appraisal, 94
performance report, 164–166
perpetual inventory, 59. *See also* inventory control
pest control, 58
physical inventory, 58. *See also* inventory control
pilferage, 191
planning, 2
plow horses, 33–34
PO, 51
point of sale, computerized, 242–243
point-of-sale system (POS), 117, 128–129, 154
    beverages, 128–129
    definition, 117
    tools, 154
portion control, 72–74
    definition, 72
    implementing, 74
    size, 73–74
position control sheet, 100–101
POS system, 117, 128–129, 154
    beverages, 128–129
    definition, 117
    tools, 154
premium liquor, 119
presentation and service, 75–77
preventive maintenance, 143–145
    contracting, 145
    definition, 143
pricing, 6–8, 22–27, 126–128
    beverages, 126–128
        contribution margin method, 127
        cost percentage method, 126
        prime cost method, 127–128
    comparison, 6–8
        pack size, 7
        product yield, 7–8

menu planning methods, 22–27
    contribution margin, 24
    food cost percentage, 22–23
    prime cost, 24–26
    summary, 27
    Texas Restaurant Association (TRA)
    markup, 26
pricing program, 42
prime cost, 155, 210–212
    operating budget, 155
    statement of income, 210–212
prime-cost method, 24–26, 127–128
    menu pricing, 24–26
    beverages, 127–128
prime vendor, 42
prime-vendor method, 40, 42–43
    advantages and disadvantages, 40
    definition, 42
product cutting, 50
product grade, 49
production, 65–72
    areas, 67–68
    controls, 68–72
        forecasting, 71
        ingredient amounts, 69–71
        production sheets, 72
        standardized recipes, 68–69
    systems, 65–67
        commissary, 65
        cook-chill, 65
        cook-serve, 65
        ingredient room, 66
        kitchenless, 66–67
production sheet, 72
production system, 65–67
    definition, 65
    commissary, 65
    cook-chill, 65
    cook-serve, 65
    ingredient room, 66
    kitchenless, 66–67
product maximization, 77–78
product quality, 44, 49
product yield, 7
product yield percentage, 45
profit, 3

profitability ratio, 226
profit margin, 226–227
project justification, 181
promotional pricing, 28–29
purchase orders (PO), 51
purchasing, 38–51
    beverages, 118–120
    capital assets, 172–187 (*see also* capital budget)
        borrowing cash, 186
        hire purchase, 186
        outright, 186
    capital pre-planning, 173
    distributor selection, 50
    methods, 39–43
        bid, 42
        multiple sources of supply, 40–41
        prime vendor, 42–43
        routine order, 43
    noncommercial, 43
    quantities, 46–48
        forecasting, 47
        usage method, 47–48
    requisitions and purchase orders, 51
    specifications, 43–45
        amount per container, 45
        federal grade, brand, or quality
          designation, 44
        product condition, 45
        product package, 45
    technology, 235–237
    value analysis, 48–50
        pack size, 49
        private label versus national brand, 49
        product grade, 49
        quality review, 50
        value-added products, 49–50
    yield percentage as consideration, 45–46
puzzles, 33–34

Q

quality measure, 10

R

radio frequency identification device (RFID), 237
ratio analysis, 223–227
    definition, 223
    operating, 223–225
    profitability, 226–227
ratios, 5–6
    as foodservice application, 6
    definition, 5
receiving, 52–55, 120, 237
    beverages, 120
    equipment, 52
    policies and procedures, 52–55
    staff, 52
    technology, 237
recruiting, 89
reference pricing, 29
refrigeration, 140
requisition form, 51
Restaurant Performance Index (RPI), 210
retention, 94–96
    definition, 94
    employee turnover rate, 95–96
revenue control, 191–205
    cash handling policies and
      procedures, 194–200
    corrective-action process, 204
    definition, 191
    employee selection and screening, 193–194
    fraud using guest checks, 200
    implementing a control procedure, 192
    loss, 191–193
    monitoring cash handling, 202–204
    patron theft, 204–205
revenue loss, 191–193
RFID, 237
risk management, 145–148
    avoidance, 147
    definition, 145
    loss control, 147
    minimizing risk exposure, 146
    retention, 147
    steps, 145–146
    transfer, 147–148
routine order method, 40, 43
    advantages and disadvantages, 40
    definition, 43

S

safety, as capital requirement, 176
salary, 87
sales, 3, 31–32, 152
    definition, 3
    how menu layout affects, 31–32
    operating budget, 152
sales mix, 125
sanitation, 79, 177
    capital requirement, 177
    cost control measure, 79
SBA, 3
scenario management, 244
scheduling labor, 101–106
    definition, 101
    factors affecting, 102–106
    staffing fluctuations over time, 104–106
    zero-based, 106
screening interview, 90
security, 54–55, 203
selling price as foodservice application, 6
semi-variable costs, 24
separation of duties, 194
server's bank, 195
server service, 117
service, 75–77
    beverages, 128–130
        dispensing systems, 129
        guest checks, 129
        point-of-sale systems, 128–129
        responsibilities, 129–130
        standardized glassware, 129
        standardized recipes, 128
    buffet, 76
    cafeteria, 76
    drive-through and take-out, 77
    full, 77
    over-the-counter, 75
    presentation, 75–77
Small Business Administration (SBA), 3
special-purpose service, 117
specification, 44
spirits, 117–130
spreadsheet method, 40
standardized recipe, 44, 68–69
    definition, 68–69
    beverages, 128

standard menu, 18
stars, 32–34
statement of cash flows (SCF), 219–220
statement of income, 209
storage, 15, 55–58, 120, 140
    as menu consideration, 15
    beverages, 120
    guidelines, 56–58
    location, 55
    refrigeration, 140
    size, 55–56
straight-line depreciation, 180
strategic planning process, 173
supervision, 94
supplier, 39
supply chain, 39
system integration, 235

T

table d'hôte, 22
taxes, payroll, 87
technology, 234–249
    advantages and disadvantages, 247–249
    assessing information systems, 248
    computerized foodservice operations, 234–245
        inventory, 237–239
        labor management, 243
        menu planning and production, 239–242
        office systems and financial management, 243–245
        point of sale, 242–243
        purchasing, 235–237
        receiving, 237
    enterprise software systems, 245–246
    foodservice equipment, 246–247
    marketing, 246
Texas Restaurant Association (TRA) markup method, 26
theft, 54, 191, 194, 204–205
    bonding, 194
    definition, 54
    employee, 191
    patron, 204–205
tips, 87
top-shelf liquor, 119

TRA markup method, 26
training and orientation, 91–93
trend analysis, 227
Truth-in-Menu laws, 30

U

Uniform System of Accounts for Restaurants, 110
unintentional revenue deviation, 191
usage method, 47–48
U.S. Department of Agriculture (USDA), 44
utility cost control, 136–143
    audit, 142–143
    definition, 137
    energy types, 137–138
    equipment, 139–140
    expense, 155
    food production methods, 140
    heating, venting, and air conditioning
      (HVAC), 142
    hoods and vents, 140–141
    lighting, 141
    refrigeration, 140
    water usage, 141–142

V

value-added products, 49–50
value analysis, 48–50
    definition, 48
    pack size, 49
    private label versus national brand, 49
    product grade, 49
    quality review, 50
    steps, 48
    value-added products, 49–50
variable costs, 24
variance, 9
vendor, 39
ventilation, storage, 57–58
vents and hoods, 140–141
virtual private network (VPN), 246

W

wage, 87
waste management, 77–79
    definition, 77
    leftover management, 79
    product maximization, 77–78
    technology, 239
water usage, 141–142
weekly bid method, 40
well brand, 119
wine, 117–130
work simplification study, 98–100

Y

yield conversion, 45
yield factor, 45
yield percentage as purchasing
    consideration, 45–46

Z

zero-based scheduling, 106